LOST VICTORIES

ALSO BY BEVIN ALEXANDER

The Strange Connection: U.S. Interference in China, 1944–72

Korea: The First War We Lost

LOST VICTORIES

THE MILITARY GENIUS OF STONEWALL JACKSON

BEVIN ALEXANDER

A JOHN MACRAE BOOK

HENRY HOLT AND COMPANY ★ NEW YORK

Published by Henry Holt and Company, Inc.,
115 West 18th Street, New York, New York 10011.
Published in Canada by Fitzhenry & Whiteside Limited,
91 Granton Drive, Richmond Hill, Ontario L4B 2N5.

Library of Congress Cataloging-in-Publication Data
Alexander, Bevin.
Lost victories : the military genius of Stonewall Jackson /
Bevin Alexander.—1st ed.
p. cm.
Includes bibliographical references and index.
1. Jackson, Stonewall, 1824–1863. 2. Virginia—History—Civil War, 1861–1865—Campaigns. 3. United States—History—Civil War, 1861–1865—Campaigns. I. Title.
E467.1.J15A42 1992
973.7′3′092—dc20 92-8699
CIP

ISBN 0-8050-1830-1 (alk. paper)

First Edition—1992

DESIGNED BY LUCY ALBANESE

Printed in the United States of America
Recognizing the importance of preserving the written word,
Henry Holt and Company, Inc., by policy, prints all of its
first editions on acid-free paper.∞

1 3 5 7 9 10 8 6 4 2

To my sons
Bevin, Jr., Troy, and David,
whose great great-uncles
were at Appomattox

CONTENTS

PREFACE

★ ★ ★ There is nothing inevitable about military victory, even for forces of apparently overwhelming strength. The Greeks at Marathon, Alexander against the Persian empire, the success of the American colonists against the British in the American Revolution, Napoleon over the Austrians in the 1796–97 Italian campaign, all offer dramatic evidence to the contrary.

In the absence of inspired military leadership, wars are usually won by attrition: the more powerful side wears down the weaker. Germany lost World War I in this fashion. Yet victory is only partially dependent upon the numbers of troops and material factors of war. For example, the German general Erwin Rommel recovered nearly all of Libya from a far larger British army early in 1941 by employing an audacious strategy based on surprise and speed.

Since shortly after the end of the Civil War, there has been little critical analysis of Robert E. Lee's abilities to take advantage of his strategic military opportunities. Few historians have questioned the general assumption that Lee was a brilliant general who achieved all that was possible against superior forces.

This book examines that assumption by taking a fresh look at primary sources and battlefield conditions. The evidence suggests that, on the Confederate side, Stonewall Jackson, not Lee, possessed the strategic vision necessary to win key battles and, possibly, entire campaigns. Instead Robert E. Lee blocked the more daring and opportunistic Jackson, while pursuing a destructive strategy that permitted the North to wear down the South. Though Lee's course guaranteed a Union triumph, Northern victory was by no means preordained.

The South desperately needed a mythic hero to justify its immense wartime losses. This is a major reason why there has been little critical examination of Lee's military leadership by Southern historians and other writers.

Out of this need for moral justification grew other myths, including those suggesting that Southern soldiers had exhibited greater valor and their commanders more inspired leadership than their enemies; in short, that the Confederacy had succumbed, inevitably, to overwhelming force. Many soldiers on both sides did display valor (some did not), but Confederates were neither braver nor more effective than their opponents and there were few inspired generals, North or South.

Recovery came slowly to the South in the decades after the war and its need to idealize the carnage caused its people, especially Virginians, to elevate Lee to something resembling sainthood: a hero without fault, personifying bravery and an absolute dedication to his men and to the Cause. By 1915 Lee's apotheosis was complete, as a reading of the papers in the Southern Historical Society makes clear. Two decades later a fellow Virginian, Douglas Southall Freeman, published a respectful biography of Lee, followed by his classic study of Lee's lieutenants. Freeman's dedication, scholarship, and crusading zeal caused these works to become the standard, virtually unquestioned sources: the authority. Thereafter writers rarely looked farther. They seldom disputed Freeman's judgment or sought evidence in primary sources and official documents to question Lee's military sagacity. As a consequence, Freeman's largely uncritical look at Lee and frequently mistaken view of Jackson were reflected in much of the literature that has followed.

This book leads the reader back to the Virginia and Maryland battlefields of 1861–63, to Jackson's lost victories and to strategies and command decisions that could have been otherwise if the military genius of General Stonewall Jackson had been honored by Confederate President Jefferson Davis and Robert E. Lee.

—Bevin Alexander
July 1992

LOST VICTORIES

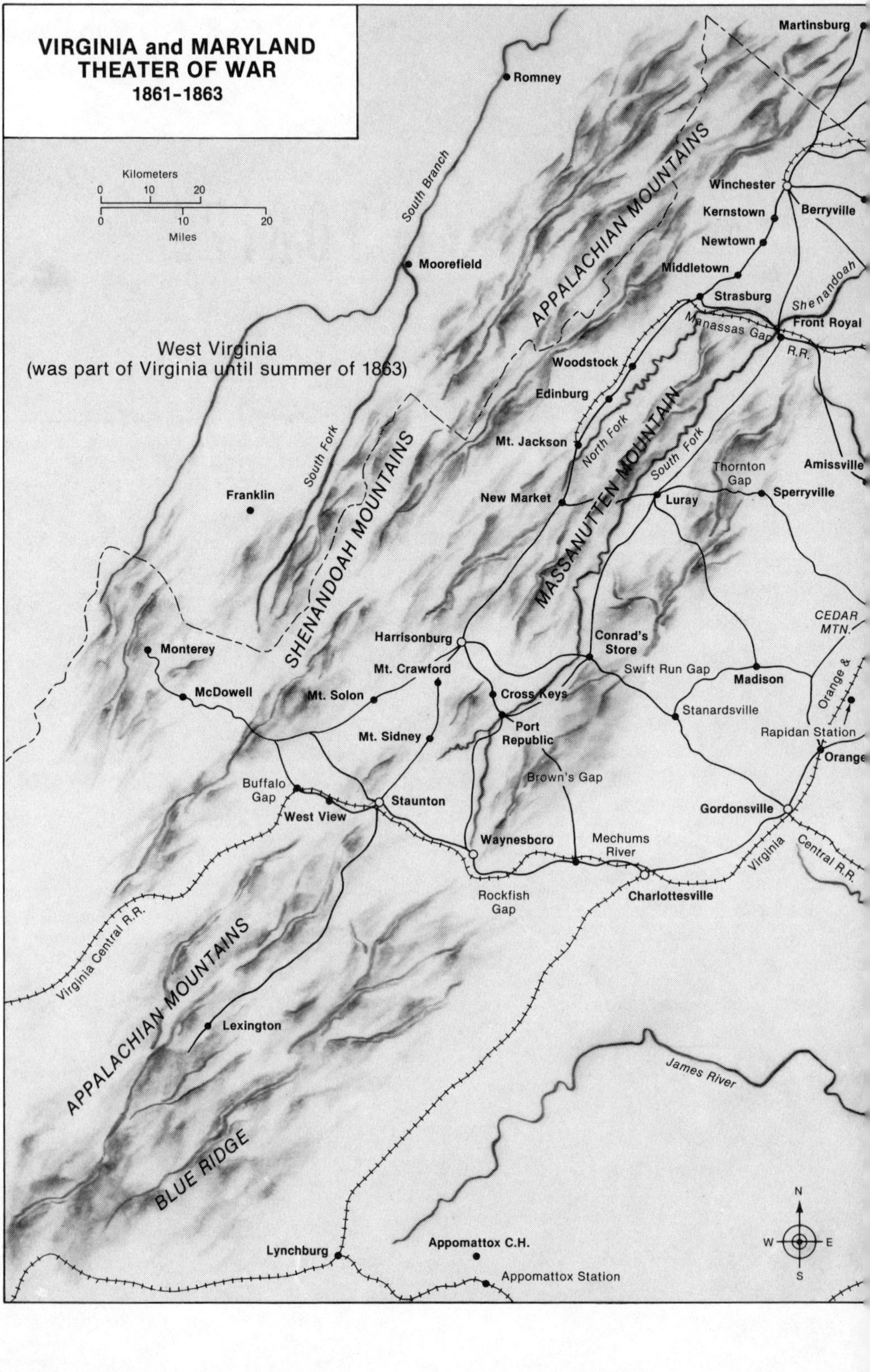

VIRGINIA and MARYLAND
THEATER OF WAR
1861–1863
Kilometers
0
10
20
0
10
20
Miles
West Virginia
(was part of Virginia until summer of 1863)
APPALACHIAN MOUNTAINS
SHENANDOAH MOUNTAINS
MASSANUTTEN MOUNTAIN
BLUE RIDGE
South Branch
South Fork
North Fork
Shenandoah
James River
Manassas Gap R.R.
Virginia Central R.R.
Orange &
Martinsburg
Romney
Winchester
Kernstown
Berryville
Newtown
Moorefield
Middletown
Strasburg
Front Royal
Woodstock
Edinburg
Mt. Jackson
Amissville
Thornton Gap
Franklin
New Market
Luray
Sperryville
CEDAR MTN.
Harrisonburg
Conrad's Store
Monterey
Mt. Crawford
Swift Run Gap
Madison
McDowell
Mt. Solon
Cross Keys
Port Republic
Stanardsville
Mt. Sidney
Rapidan Station
Orange
Brown's Gap
Buffalo Gap
West View
Staunton
Gordonsville
Waynesboro
Mechums River
Rockfish Gap
Charlottesville
Lexington
Lynchburg
Appomattox C.H.
Appomattox Station
N
W
E
S

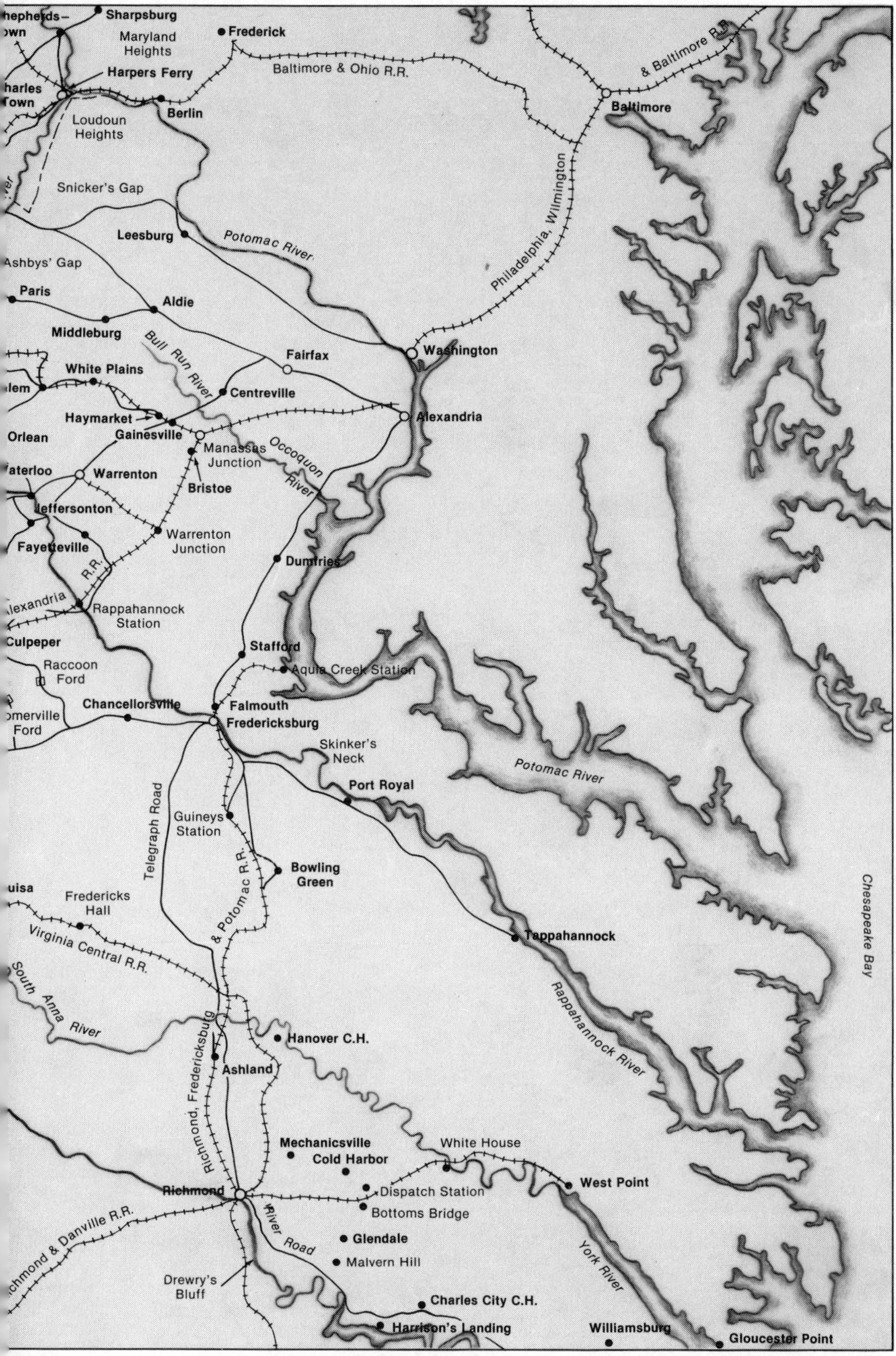

Sharpsburg
Maryland Heights
Frederick
Harpers Ferry
Baltimore & Ohio R.R.
& Baltimore R.R.
Baltimore
Berlin
Loudoun Heights
Snicker's Gap
Philadelphia, Wilmington
Leesburg
Potomac River
Ashbys' Gap
Paris
Aldie
Middleburg
Bull Run River
Fairfax
Washington
White Plains
Centreville
Haymarket
Alexandria
Gainesville
Orlean
Manassas Junction
Occoquon River
Warrenton
Bristoe
Jeffersonton
Warrenton Junction
Fayetteville
R.R.
Dumfries
Rappahannock Station
Culpeper
Stafford
Raccoon Ford
Aquia Creek Station
Chancellorsville
Falmouth
Fredericksburg
Ford
Skinker's Neck
Potomac River
Port Royal
Telegraph Road
Guineys Station
Bowling Green
& Potomac R.R.
Fredericks Hall
Chesapeake Bay
Virginia Central R.R.
Tappahannock
South Anna River
Rappahannock River
Hanover C.H.
Richmond, Fredericksburg
Ashland
Mechanicsville
White House
Cold Harbor
Richmond
West Point
Dispatch Station
Bottoms Bridge
Richmond & Danville R.R.
River Road
Glendale
York River
Malvern Hill
Drewry's Bluff
Charles City C.H.
Harrison's Landing
Williamsburg
Gloucester Point

1

FIRST MANASSAS

A New Kind of War

★ ★ ★ The opening drama of the Civil War seemed on the surface like something out of a boys' storybook—massed bodies of soldiers marching resolutely on the enemy, banners unfurling dramatically, officers leading heroically on beautiful steeds, raised sabers pointing the way for the faithful soldiery to go.

Although early in the war such scenes did occur and *Harper's Weekly* and other journals printed representations of them, this romantic vision bore little relationship to the real challenges the men faced. Far more gruesome than anyone had foreseen, the Civil War introduced the most intense and deadly fire in the history of warfare, fire no one could prepare for or counter.

Quickly consigned to memory were the gaily dressed and garlanded women waiting at stops on the railways to ply Confederate troops heading to the battlefield with drinks and dainties and to sing rousing patriotic songs like "Dixie" and "The Bonnie Blue Flag." Likewise, it was a mark of the end of innocence to remember the crowds of well-dressed civilians who followed the Union army out of Washington in expensive carriages, determined to see this first and last battle to restore the Union.

Though commanders were less naive on the morrow of the battle of First Manassas, or Bull Run, on July 21, 1861, they did not yet comprehend the profound change in war that had been demonstrated in the Crimean War. Technology had transformed the tools of war since the Napoleonic era, which ended in 1815, but the implications of this change had not penetrated deeply. In Napoleon's time the principal infantry weapon was the single-shot, muzzle-loaded smoothbore musket shotted with a loose-fitting metal ball fired by gunpowder ignited with a flintlock. This weapon had an effective range of less than a hundred yards.[1] By the Mexican War of 1846–48 the only change in the musket was a more reliable detonator, a tiny copper percussion cap containing fulminate of mercury, for the flintlock.

Between the Mexican War and the Civil War, however, came a revolution in firearms: the rifle became a practical military weapon, dooming the smoothbore to oblivion.

Gunsmiths had known for centuries that bullets could be fitted tightly against spiral rifling in a barrel. The close fit prevented exploding gases from escaping around the projectile, greatly increasing range, while the rifling caused the bullet to spin, greatly increasing accuracy. However, gunpowder fouled the grooves after only a few rounds, requiring painstaking cleaning. This prevented the rifle from being used as the main military weapon; infantry had to be able to fire repeated volleys, which the smoothbore musket could do, despite fouling.

In 1849, however, a French army officer named Claude-Étienne Minié solved the problem of rifle fouling by inventing a self-cleaning cylindrical bullet with a hollow base. When fired, the base expanded to fit snugly against the rifling grooves, scouring the fouling of the previous shot from the grooves. A Minié-ball rifle could fire many rounds before the barrel had to be cleaned.

The conical Minié bullet (usually called a ball), fired with a percussion cap and loaded into the muzzle of a single-shot rifle, radically altered the conditions of battle. It had four times the effective range of the musket—four hundred yards. It was highly accurate at two hundred yards and somewhat controllable and lethal up to one thousand yards.

Traditional tactics with the smoothbore musket were to march bodies of men in tight lines, usually two men deep, within one hundred to thirty paces of the enemy and there unleash volleys of fire. In theory this was supposed to disrupt the enemy line to such an extent that the attackers could then rush forward and settle the issue with the bayonet. In fact, the defenders often gave as fierce volleys as they got. And even when an attack did disrupt a line, the men seldom employed the bayonet, for disordered troops usually surrendered or ran instead of crossing blades with the enemy.

With the short-range smoothbore these tactics made sense, because a commander rarely could effect a decision otherwise. But the rifle, with quadruple the effective killing range of the musket, required entirely new tactics. Initially no general recognized this fact and none developed an assault formation to counter it.[2]

This was because there was no antidote in the Civil War to the ruinous defensive power of the rifle. The solution had to wait for the decades after the war, when technology provided artillery superior to the rifle. This came when artillery shells acquired better fuses, chemists developed more-powerful explosives than gunpowder, and experts devised a method for cannons to fire accurately while out of sight of the target.

In the Civil War the Minié ball tended to dominate artillery, reversing the traditional order on the battlefield. When Napoleon prepared for a breakthrough, he wheeled out smoothbore fieldpieces well in *front* of his infantry and opened fire with case or canister shot, which riddled a wide swath of enemy with deadly metal balls and fragments. This was designed to break a hole in the opposing line and permit Napoleon's infantry and cavalry to burst through and scatter the enemy. Although some of Napoleon's cannons could fire canister at 580 yards, they were decisive only at closer range. Rolling up cannons within a couple hundred yards of opposing infantry presented little danger, since defenders—armed only with the smoothbore musket—could do nothing about it.

However, the effective range of the new rifle was actually *greater* than the effective range of smoothbore cannons firing canister. Observers in the Crimean War of 1854–56 discovered that gunners and horses could be picked off by sharpshooters before they could move far enough forward for canister to break enemy lines. With artillery in danger of being chased from the battlefield, gun designers began a frenzied effort to develop long-range rifled artillery that could be withdrawn to a safe distance. When the Civil War opened, there were a number of effective rifled cannons, the most popular being the Parrott gun.[3]

Rifled cannons, however, were not as effective in destroying infantry as canister-firing smoothbores. Rifled cannons tended to spin out the balls and pellets of canister into a doughnut pattern, with nothing in the center. Seldom could solid shot strike enough infantry to make its use effective. Explosive shells were not efficient against infantry because the gunpowder charges inside were too weak to shatter the shells into enough pieces. Shrapnel, containing just enough gunpowder to scatter a container of metal projectiles, depended for its effectiveness on the shell's exploding directly on enemy infantry. This was difficult, because often the time fuses required to fire the gunpowder were inaccurate.

Probably the most effective use of rifled cannon was in counterbattery fire. The Federal army was able to take advantage of the fact that it had far more such pieces than the South. At the battle of Antietam in September 1862, and on other occasions, Union artillery damaged or neutralized Confederate batteries by long-range fire, while being safe from counterfire.

The limitations of rifled artillery meant that generals could not dispense with the firepower of canister and continued to move smoothbores up close to the infantry, despite heavy losses. In a preliminary engagement on Bull Run on July 18, 1861, one not authorized by the Federal commander, Irvin McDowell, Union brigadier general Daniel Tyler ordered two fieldpieces almost up to the banks of the stream at Blackburn's Ford to blast Confederate positions. Promptly subjected to Rebel rifle fire, the battery lost half of its horses and several of its men and had to withdraw before it could inflict damage.[4]

As the war progressed, commanders modified this destructive policy by displacing batteries to the rear when opposing infantry got within ordinary volley range of about two hundred yards. This reduced the guns' effectiveness and, since commanders also could do little about long-range snipers, artillery played a lesser role than it had in the Napoleonic wars.[5]

The Minié ball also revolutionized cavalry. In Napoleon's time and in the Mexican War, cavalry was often the arm of decision; its mobility permitted it to reach around and behind an enemy and the shock effect of charging horses could shatter an opposing infantry line. The infantry would form a tight square, sometimes protected by cannons, as the principal defense against cavalry charges. On occasion cavalry still broke these squares with devastating effect. With the Minié ball, however, the cavalry lost its place in the assault, because an infantry line usually could empty the saddles of charging cavalry long before the horses got close enough to break the line with shock. Cavalry's use instantly fell to screening army advances and retreats, protecting flanks, exploiting routs, reconnaissance, and hit-and-run raids on the enemy's rear. These were important roles, but hardly the decisive ones that had given the arm such élan and dash in previous wars.

Since no one developed a defense against the Minié ball, the attack became many times more dangerous than in the Mexican War and a successful assault became many times less likely. And late in 1862, when soldiers began systematically to throw up defensive fortifications in the field, the assault became more difficult still, so difficult as to become unprofitable. In the Civil War as a whole, more than seven out of eight assaults failed.[6] Despite this, frontal attacks continued right up to the war's end, and this is the major reason for the high casualties on Civil War battlefields.

Col. G. F. R. Henderson points out that "in 1861–65 the side that stood on the defensive, unless hopelessly outnumbered, was almost invariably successful."[7] This seems to argue for a Southern defensive strategy—allowing the North to attack and finally winning when the North grew weary of losing. However, the great Confederate leaders—Robert E. Lee and Stonewall Jackson—realized that a wholly defensive battle strategy was an illusion.[8]

In the Atlanta campaign of 1864, when Confederate general Joseph E. Johnston adopted this policy, Federal general William T. Sherman avoided battle—and defeat—simply by moving *around* Johnston's positions, displacing them and slowly driving Johnston back on Atlanta. When General Lee, his offensive power vanished, was reduced to fighting a wholly defensive campaign in Virginia in 1864, Ulysses S. Grant did not act as wisely as Sherman and pounded repeatedly against Lee's fronts. But each time, after losing the battle and many men, he slipped off to Lee's flank and advanced. Like Sherman, he could have achieved the same result in most cases without battle and without vast expenditure of blood.

To be successful, therefore, a defensive strategy had to include offensive operations that could defeat the enemy and force him to withdraw from seized territory. Without this a defensive strategy guaranteed ultimate defeat.

By First Manassas the South had developed an unrealistic policy to pursue the war. It rested on two premises: (1) Confederate armies would block every incursion into the South, wherever it occurred, by head-on battle until (2) Britain and France, dependent on cotton for their huge textile industries, finally recognized the cotton-growing Confederacy and forced a peace.

British and French mills had large stocks of cotton on hand, and limited alternative sources of the fiber developed—Egypt, for example. Though many textile workers soon lost their jobs, London and Paris saw no compelling reason to intervene in the American Civil War. Robert E. Lee recognized this fact by Christmas Day, 1861, when he wrote his wife: "We must make up our minds to fight our battles and earn our independence alone. No one will help us."[9]

The principal reason the Confederate states adopted the policy of defending every point exposed to attack, by land or sea, was that they feared slave uprisings and consequent chaos and anarchy if Federal forces penetrated into the interior. A lesser but important reason was that each state considered itself more or less sovereign and looked first to keeping its own territory unoccupied and only secondarily to pursuing a strategy aimed at preserving the Confederacy as a whole. For this reason states maintained substantial forces within their borders, resulting in a wide dispersal of troops throughout the South and the inability of the Confederate government to concentrate manpower in a few strategic locations.[10]

As a consequence the South never seriously considered what is called a Fabian strategy, probably its best chance of gaining independence.[11] A Fabian policy would have denied the Union armies head-on battles. Instead the Northern armies would have been enticed deep into the South's vast interior; once they were overextended, the South could have severed their supply lines, inflicting a thousand cuts in small engagements and, though winning no great victories, imposing a steady drain on Federal manpower, supplies, and morale. This would have drawn out the war to an indefinite length, forcing enormous burdens on both sides but no inordinate strain on Southern manpower—the single greatest Confederate weakness.

The South was well suited to pursue such a policy. Its dearth of roads, slender railway system, impenetrable swamps, mountains, deep forests, and rivers would have slowed invading armies and offered, with every advancing mile, opportunities to cut off the enemy's lines of supply and communication.

The great Confederate raider Nathan Bedford Forrest stopped Union armies from advancing on several occasions by blows on their rear, yet he possessed only small forces. If the South had devoted its major strength to a semiguerrilla war designed to draw Northern armies deep into the interior, it might have brought about a stalemate and ultimate Northern weariness with the war.

Denied this strategy for fear of slave uprisings and due to the self-interests of the states, the South had only one other means of attaining independence: striking at a vulnerable point or points in the North and threatening enough damage that the Northern people would allow the South to go in peace. Some believed that the South could achieve this objective by destroying the main Union field army; another view favored a movement around the army and a quick strike into the North before the Federal army could move to stop it. Jackson proposed the latter repeatedly, as we will see; when his efforts failed, he attempted the former.

With a navy capable of blockading the South, and with many times more industry and more than twice as many troops, the North was certain to win a war of attrition.[12] Destruction of the Union field army would be most unlikely, given the immensely larger and better-equipped military force the North could put into the field. The alternative strategy of striking into the North was frequently available because a large part of Northern military power was tied up in protecting Washington—close by the Virginia border. To thrust *behind* the forces guarding the symbol of the Union and to attack other Northern cities and vital supply routes, the railway lines, would have caused panic and might have forced the government to evacuate Washington.

The main Union field army could not always prevent a march behind Washington, because Abraham Lincoln was extremely sensitive to the protection of the capital and devoted a large part of the North's total military strength to guarding it. He also hobbled the mobility of his field army by requiring large portions of it to remain as a shield between the Confederate field army and Washington.[13]

★ ★ ★

On July 17, 1861, the Union army of thirty-five thousand men, under Brigadier General McDowell, gave unmistakable proof to Rebel spies that it was marching out of the Washington defenses to challenge the Confederate army of about twenty thousand men under Brig. Gen. Pierre G. T. Beauregard. The Rebels were lined up some twenty-five miles southwest of the capital on the south side of Bull Run, a large and, in places, deep stream about three miles north of Manassas Junction.[14]

McDowell, forty-two years old, was a humorless Ohio West Pointer (class of 1838) who had served with distinction in the Mexican War but since had been satisfied with a staff appointment to Lt. Gen. Winfield Scott, seventy-five years old, chief of the army. Beauregard, from Louisiana, had been part of the same military academy class as McDowell and likewise had distinguished himself in the Mexican War. He was briefly superintendent of West Point in 1861 before his Southern sympathies caused his removal.

Beauregard failed to organize his six brigades and several unattached regiments into divisions, a formation whose effectiveness had been demonstrated by Napoleon's time. As a result Beauregard's command was far too cumbersome; many of his orders were either misunderstood or never received.

Beauregard's plan to defeat McDowell depended on McDowell's attack at Mitchell's Ford, south of Centreville and due north of Manassas. Since this was the most obvious point to attack, it was the one McDowell was least likely to choose. The Confederate position was poor; north of Bull Run the ground was higher and afforded the Federals the opportunity to approach closely under excellent cover, whereas south of the stream the ground was lower, rising gently to the rear and giving no cover except for scattered woods. Robert E. Lee, not Beauregard, had selected the Rebel position behind Bull Run.[15]

However, Beauregard had assembled most of his force on the east, leaving long, fordable stretches of Bull Run west of Mitchell's Ford either undefended or protected only by small bodies of troops. Therefore, McDowell could have broken through at a number of places by a direct assault.[16]

Fortunately for the Confederates, McDowell did not see the possibilities of a direct attack and planned to move on the extreme right, or east, of the Confederate line northeast of Manassas. But on July 18 he had to change his plan, because he found the country in this direction to be too wooded, broken, and deficient in roads for operations.[17] Furthermore, he was convinced that the unauthorized assault General Tyler had launched July 18 against Blackburn's Ford, only a mile east of Mitchell's Ford, had drawn most of Beauregard's forces to this sector, making the main effort at this point dangerous.

Meanwhile, in response to Beauregard's pleadings, every spare Confederate unit within reach was hurrying to Manassas, especially the eleven thousand men of Gen. Joseph E. Johnston, who had been guarding the Shenandoah Valley at Winchester to the west of Manassas. Four of Johnston's five brigades arrived by train—the first strategic use of railroads in the history of war—between July 19 and 21.[18]

These reinforcements raised Beauregard's strength to about thirty-three thousand men and caused a command problem for Beauregard: Johnston, a Virginian and a West Pointer who had achieved the rank of brigadier general in the U.S. Army, was a full Confederate general and outranked him. However, Johnston, not knowing the terrain or the situation at Manassas, deferred to Beauregard and approved his dispositions and plan of battle.[19]

Johnston had been able to slip away from the valley because of the timidity of the Union commander there, Maj. Gen. Robert Patterson, who refused to march on Winchester with his fifteen thousand troops, believing—on no good evidence—that Johnston greatly outnumbered him. This failure cost Patterson his career, for Scott ousted him a week later. But the damage he had done was incalculable.

Johnston's First Virginia Brigade was commanded by Thomas Jonathan Jackson, a thirty-seven-year-old West Pointer from western Virginia who also had distinguished himself in Mexico but who had resigned from the army in 1851 to become professor of artillery tactics, optics, mechanics, and astronomy at Virginia Military Institute (VMI). Jackson had been promoted to brigadier general only the month before and was, like most of the other generals on both sides, an unknown quantity in regard to the upcoming battle.[20]

At VMI Jackson was not thought of as a good teacher and was considered to be distinctly odd, having been dubbed "Tom Fool Jackson" by the cadets. Yet some of his students saw a spark of genius in his eccentricity and one described him as "systematic as a multiplication table and as full of military as an arsenal."[21] He was tall, slender, extremely reticent to express his views, stiff and unbending with most people, and possessed of an intense Presbyterian religious faith; he suffered from dyspepsia and other, less specific, physical ailments, which led him to undertake treatments at various spas and to suck on lemons with regularity.

Jackson had a profound capacity to concentrate his mind on a subject and held commitment to duty as his single guiding principle. When one of his officers applied for leave to visit his dying wife, Jackson refused, saying, "Man, man, do you love your wife more than your country?" Yet when a mother standing by a road asked him whether her son would be passing with the column, he found her son and allowed him to stay with her until the next morning.[22]

Jackson had acted briskly and efficiently in April 1861 when General Lee,[23] then commanding Virginia's forces, had sent him to guard the arsenal at Harpers Ferry, where the U.S. government operated a rifle factory. Jackson had quickly organized the various Virginia militia units there into effective bodies, and from them and other sources he had built the First Brigade.

To reach the railway and get to Manassas, Jackson's brigade had crossed the Blue Ridge in an exhausting march of more than twenty miles on July 18. The First Brigade had already collapsed at the little village of Paris when an officer reminded Jackson that not enough pickets had been posted. Jackson's reply: "Let the poor fellows sleep. I will guard the camp myself."[24] And Jackson, through the summer night, stood sentry over his sleeping men.

NOTES

Concerning notes: citations by last name or short title in this and subsequent chapters refer to authors or works that are listed fully in the bibliography. The first citation in a note is the source of any direct quotation in the preceding text.
General sources: Dabney, 177–209; Cooke, 9–63; Johnson and Buel, vol. 1, 111–25; Henderson, 86–101; Chambers, vol. 1, 309–63; Freeman, *Lee's Lieutenants,* vol. 1, 38–50; Sanger, 21–27; and Vandiver, 133–54.

1. The Prussian army at the close of the eighteenth century set up a canvas target one hundred feet long by six feet high, simulating an enemy unit. At 225 yards, 25 percent of a unit's bullets hit the target; at 150 yards, 40 percent; at 75 yards, 60 percent. But if fire was held to fifty yards, horrific casualties resulted, often 50 percent or more. See David G. Chandler, *The Campaigns of Napoleon* (New York: Macmillan Publishing Company, 1966), 342. Porter Alexander says the Confederate "caliber 69" smoothbore musket, used in the first two years of the war, had an effective range of only two hundred yards. However, it was *accurate* at far less a range, certainly not over one hundred yards. See Alexander, *Military Memoirs,* 202.

2. Ibid., 202; Alexander, *Fighting for the Confederacy,* 122. The Federals got more rifles sooner. Even as late as the battle of Antietam in September 1862 many Confederates still were equipped with the musket, and it was only by Gettysburg in July 1863 that all of the Rebels were armed with rifles. Porter Alexander has contradictory estimates, saying in one place that half of the Southerners were armed with smoothbores in the Antietam campaign and in another that 30 percent were so armed (Alexander, *Military Memoirs,* 223 and 245). Since twenty thousand stand of Federal arms were picked up on the battlefield of Second Manassas shortly before, probably more than 70 percent of the Confederates were armed with the rifle at Antietam. Edward Hagerman maintains that the rifle was not introduced in sufficient numbers to make a significant impact until late 1862 (Edward Hagerman, "From Jomini to Dennis Hart Mahan: The Evolution of Trench Warfare," in *Battles Lost & Won: Essays From Civil War History,* ed. John T. Hubbell [Westport, Conn.: Greenwood Press, 1975], 47). However, commanders and soldiers from First Manassas onward recognized the rifle's power, range, and effect. It immediately altered the nature of battle, since some troops on both sides were certain

to be armed with the rifle and a given unit had to maneuver in the expectation that it would meet rifle fire. Federal forces received the rifle in quantity early in the war and its acquisition was a matter of great urgency to the South. This accounts in part for the careful numbering by Confederate commanders of Union weapons picked up on the battlefield. For a meticulous analysis of the influence of the infantry rifle and rifled cannon, see Grady McWhiney and Perry D. Jamieson, *Attack and Die: Civil War Military Tactics and the Southern Heritage* (University: University of Alabama Press, 1983). The North experimented with even more advanced breech-loaded repeating rifles with brass cartridges, but these did not become standard weapons in the war.

3. Alexander, *Military Memoirs,* 14; and Ian V. Hogg, *The Illustrated Encyclopedia of Artillery* (Secaucus, N.J.: Chartwell Books, 1987), 19, 21, and 199. Several European rifled cannons were invented in the 1840s, but William Armstrong, an English engineer, developed the first production model in 1855, followed by French and Prussian types. Capt. Robert P. Parrott manufactured rifled cannons in Cold Spring, New York. The new pieces were mostly high-velocity guns used for direct fire. Confederate brigadier general John D. Imboden complained that they tended to bury projectiles in sloping ground and seemed little improvement over the older smoothbore cannon. See Johnson and Buel, vol. 1, 233–34 n. This was primarily because fuses were not always accurate and shells buried before bursting. Rifled guns for the first time in war caused serious casualties among troops far in the rear of the front. Also, rifled cannons sometimes caused losses at long range among soldiers attacking in the open in the massed two-man-deep lines of battle that characterized the Civil War.

4. *Official Records,* vol. 2, 440 ff.; Alfred Roman, *The Military Operations of General Beauregard* (New York: Harper and Brothers, 1884), vol. 1, 92 ff.; Longstreet, 33 ff.; and Freeman, *Lee's Lieutenants,* vol. 1, 45.

5. Confederate major John Pelham won fame by dashing his guns ahead of infantry support, firing, then withdrawing swiftly but with many halts on good ground to delay pursuit. Some observers thought his methods might keep artillery well forward. However, they required extreme dash, audacity, and mobility on the part of gunners and depended on catching enemy infantry unawares. Pelham's methods never became accepted tactics. Pelham was cavalry general J. E. B. Stuart's artillery chief and was killed at Kelly's Ford, Virginia, on March 17, 1863. See Freeman, *Lee's Lieutenants,* vol. 2, 452; and *Southern Historical Society Papers,* vol. 38, 381. Porter Alexander (*Fighting for the Confederacy,* 248–49) describes graphi-

cally the difficulties of advancing artillery to assist attacking infantry, pointing out the need for both infantry and artillery to have fields of fire unobstructed or unencumbered by the other and the high visibility and vulnerability of cannons to enemy counterbattery and rifle fire.

6. Hagerman points out in Hubbell (50–53) that orthodox military doctrine early in the war advocated entrenchments for defense but did not allow for troops to entrench while engaged in offensive operations. The fear was that the mostly nonprofessional soldiers, if they had entrenchments, would not leave them to attack the enemy. Ulysses S. Grant did not entrench at Shiloh on April 6–7, 1862, but Henry Halleck afterward used one entrenched line after another to advance from Shiloh to Corinth, Mississippi. Hagerman says: "Robert E. Lee was one of the last commanders to accept the superiority of the entrenched defensive over the frontal assault under the changed conditions of warfare." Though he built fixed entrenched lines to defend Richmond, Lee did not construct fortifications in the open field until the battle of Fredericksburg in December 1862. Gunners emplaced some cannons behind revetments for this battle, but the principal infantry protection was the existing stone wall of the "sunken road," which proved the tremendous defensive advantage of field fortifications. Thereafter Lee used them consistently and it became a standing order on both sides to entrench whenever halted. See also Fuller, 268–72.

7. Henderson, 600.

8. "Strategy," as used in this book, is that as defined by Basil H. Liddell Hart: "The art of distributing and applying military means to fulfill the ends of policy." Strategy is concerned with the effect of forces, with how to achieve the purpose that brought a nation into war in the first place. When the use of military force merges into actual fighting, the disposition and use of forces are termed "tactics." The purpose of strategy is to diminish the possibility of resistance, and it seeks to achieve this by movement and surprise. Perfect strategy would be to achieve a nation's aims without battle, a goal practically unattainable by human beings, who are ruled by passions. See B. H. Liddell Hart, *Strategy* (New York: Frederick A. Praeger, 1954), 333–37. The Prussian theorist Carl von Clausewitz focuses on battle, which is only one *means* to achieving the *end* of policy. He defines strategy as "the theory of the use of combats for the object of the war" and tactics as "the use of military forces in combat." See Clausewitz, *On War*, bk. 2, chap. 1 (Harmondsworth, England: Penguin Books, 1968), 173 (reprinted in New York by Dorset Press in 1991).

9. Maurice, 89.

10. Charles Marshall, an aide of Robert E. Lee and great-nephew of Supreme Court Justice John Marshall, gives an astute analysis in Marshall (63–71) of the Confederacy's Achilles' heel, its slave population and the fear that it could be enticed into revolt by the North. Although revolt did not occur, many slaves did escape to Union lines at the first opportunity. Thus, incursions of Federal troops into regions with slaves disrupted the system because even loyal slaves departed when presented with a realistic chance for freedom. See William J. Cooper, Jr., and Thomas E. Terrill, *The American South: A History* (New York: Alfred A. Knopf, 1990), 379–81. Given the extreme states' rights position that brought about secession in the first place, Confederate politicians, especially President Davis, were unwilling to demand sacrifices from states or the people to save the Confederacy as a whole. The Confederacy more resembled an alliance of sovereign states than a nation. Davis felt he could request and coax the states only to operate in the common interest. In this he probably underestimated the willingness of the Southern people to make sacrifices, but the policy persisted.

11. Fabian strategy was named after Quintus Fabius Maximus Verrucosus (died 203 B.C.), the Roman general and statesman who avoided the Carthaginian Hannibal on the plains in Italy in the Second Punic War because Hannibal's cavalry was superior. Fabius hovered in the hills, where the cavalry could not be decisive, and fought a guerrilla-type war. He won no victories, but Hannibal also could not defeat him. The policy raised the morale of the Romans and depressed the Carthaginians.

12. The 1860 census shows that the North had 22 million people and the eleven states of the Confederacy had 9.5 million, of which 3.5 million were slaves. The North possessed 92 percent of the nation's manufacturing capacity and two and a half times as many miles of railroad as the Confederacy. The South expected to import its needs, since it held a virtual monopoly on the world's supply of cotton. However, it had almost no warships and could do little against a naval blockade. See John D. Hicks, *The Federal Union* (Boston: Houghton Mifflin Company, 1937), 620.

13. Carl von Clausewitz holds that in a country involved in an insurrection or torn by internal dissension, the capital, the chief leader, and public opinion constitute the "center of gravity," where collapse has the greatest chance of occurring. Following this theory, the Confederacy's greatest opportunity lay not in attacking the Northern field army, but in isolating or capturing Washington, evicting Lincoln and his government, and, by

inflicting damage on Northern industry and railroads, influencing public opinion. See Clausewitz, 389–90; and Raymond Aron, *Clausewitz, Philosopher of War* (Englewood Cliffs, N.J.: Prentice-Hall, 1985), 108–9, 158–59, and 213.

There were several proposals for, and one attempt by, the South to advance through Kentucky and into the Ohio River Valley and beyond, rather than around Washington and along the East Coast. Although strategic control of the Ohio River would have given the Confederacy a hold on the Middle West, nothing could have damaged the Union war effort like seizure of eastern cities, such as the rail hub of Baltimore or the metropolis of Philadelphia, with nearly six hundred thousand people—the second-largest city in the country (after New York). The bulk of the North's industry was concentrated from northeastern Maryland to southern New Hampshire. Severing rail service to these areas could have resulted in the loss of Washington and the inability of Union forces to invade Virginia and capture Richmond. Also, a Confederate strike into this region of heavy population would have damaged Northern morale far more than a drive into the Midwest.

14. P. G. T. Beauregard, *Commentary on the Campaign and Battle of Manassas* (New York: Harper and Brothers, 1884), 30.

15. Alexander, *Military Memoirs,* 22.

16. *Official Records,* vol. 51, pt. 1, 25 ff.

17. Alexander, *Military Memoirs,* 25.

18. *Official Records,* vol. 2, 473, 478.

19. Ibid., 473–74; Johnston, 40–41.

20. Freeman, *Lee's Lieutenants,* vol. 1, 41.

21. Douglas, 233.

22. Ibid., 236–37.

23. Robert E. Lee, born in 1807 into a famous Virginia family, graduated from West Point in 1829 and distinguished himself while serving on the staff of Gen. Winfield Scott in the Mexican War. He was superintendent of West Point from 1852 to 1855 and resigned from U.S. service only when offered command of an army to fight secession.

24. Jackson, 176.

2

"THERE STANDS JACKSON LIKE A STONE WALL"

★ ★ ★ The plans McDowell and Beauregard developed for First Manassas were almost mirror images of each other. Though each was faulty, McDowell's was superior. Beauregard had assembled most of his and Johnston's forces on his eastern flank, with eight brigades around Mitchell's and Blackburn's fords and two brigades a mile east, where the railroad crossed Bull Run. He was still convinced that McDowell would attack Mitchell's Ford, and his plan called for two Confederate brigades to counterattack: one, a South Carolina force under Milledge L. Bonham, defending the ford; the other, a Virginia outfit commanded by Philip St. George Cocke, stretched along Bull Run for more than two miles to the west.

Beauregard expected these two brigades to hold and perhaps advance against McDowell's army while five other brigades on his right crossed Bull Run and executed a wide end movement around the Union eastern flank to cut off the Union army by seizing Centreville and Fairfax Court House, eight miles east of

Centreville.[1] Although Beauregard committed an inadequate force to holding the Union army along Bull Run, his plan would not have been wrong except for three factors: he did not give the five brigades on the east clear instructions, he did not appoint an overall commander, and his entire left flank was protected only by a "demibrigade" of the First Louisiana and Fourth South Carolina with two field guns.

This half brigade of thirteen hundred men had the additional job of guarding the Stone Bridge over Bull Run on the Warrenton-Alexandria turnpike (present-day U.S. Route 29) about three miles west of Mitchell's Ford—a point, because of its easy access, that was likely to be assaulted. This force was under Col. Nathan G. (Shanks) Evans, thirty-seven years old, a hard-drinking, hard-fighting West Pointer and Indian fighter from South Carolina.

McDowell's plan was to send three brigades under Daniel Tyler straight down the Warrenton pike to assault the Stone Bridge while a brigade under Col. Israel B. Richardson made a demonstration toward Mitchell's and Blackburn's fords. With the Confederate army absorbed in repulsing these attacks, McDowell planned for two of his divisions, thirteen thousand men, to make a wide circuit around the Confederate left to undefended Sudley Springs Ford, two air miles northwest of the Stone Bridge. From there the divisions—the lead one under Brig. Gen. David Hunter, followed by Brig. Gen. Samuel Peter Heintzelman's force—would attack eastward on the south side of Bull Run, uncover the Stone Bridge, and, with Tyler now joining, roll up all Rebel forces from the flank and rear.

The great fault of McDowell's plan was that he did not order a powerful, determined assault along Bull Run to keep the Confederates occupied while the flank attack developed.

He committed Tyler's division against Shanks Evans but told him not to press his attack and to stay on the north side of Bull Run until Hunter's flank movement had cleared the south bank. Against Mitchell's and Blackburn's fords McDowell sent at the outset only Richardson's brigade to demonstrate, not assault. Although he designated his reserve division to help Richardson,

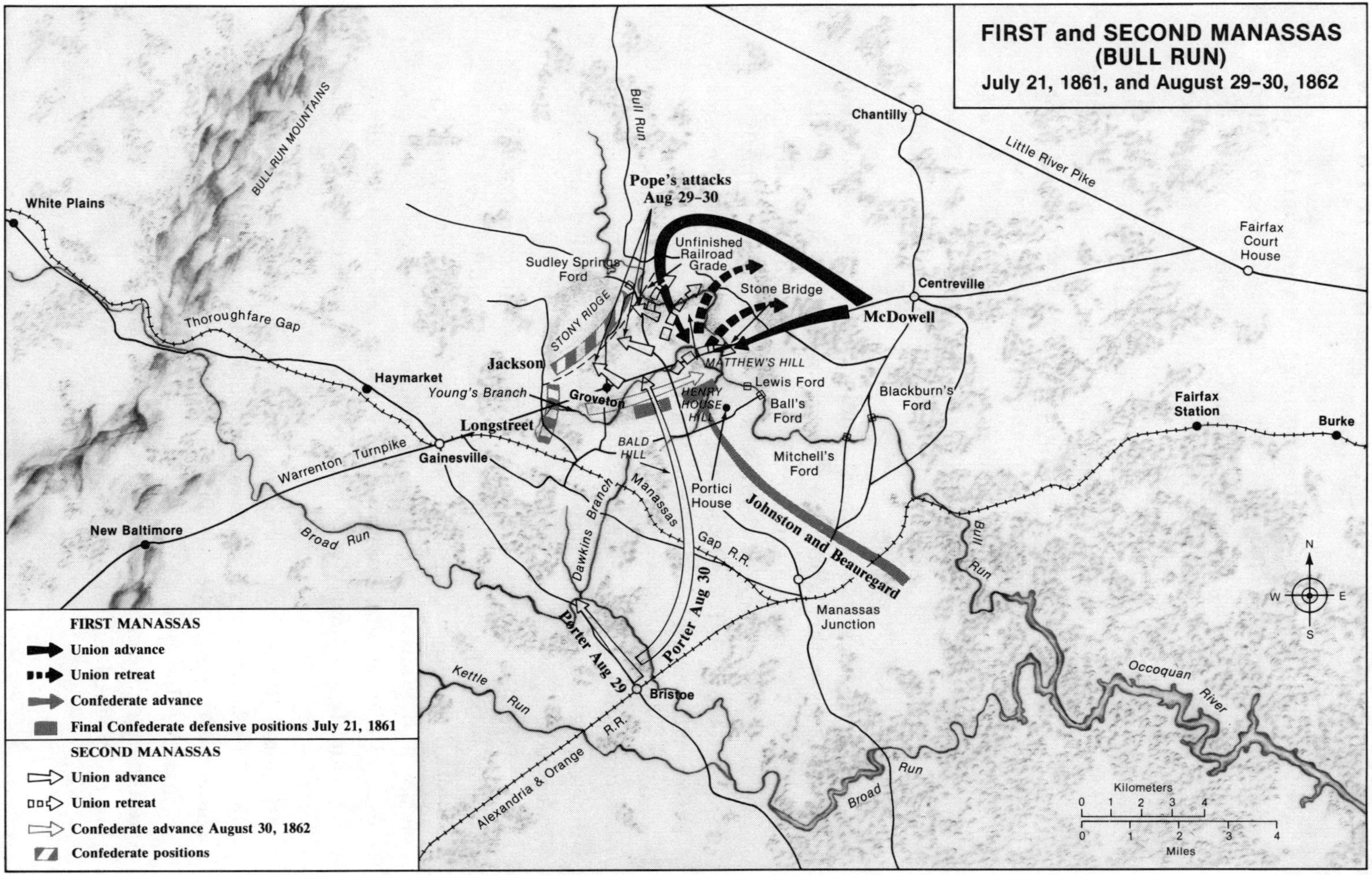
FIRST and SECOND MANASSAS
(BULL RUN)
July 21, 1861, and August 29–30, 1862
Chantilly
Little River Pike
Fairfax Court House
Centreville
McDowell
Bull Run
Pope's attacks Aug 29–30
Unfinished Railroad Grade
Stone Bridge
Sudley Springs Ford
STONY RIDGE
MATTHEW'S HILL
Lewis Ford
Ball's Ford
Blackburn's Ford
Mitchell's Ford
HENRY HOUSE HILL
BALD HILL
Portici House
Johnston and Beauregard
Manassas Junction
Manassas Gap R.R.
Jackson
Groveton
Young's Branch
Longstreet
Haymarket
Gainesville
Warrenton Turnpike
White Plains
BULL RUN MOUNTAINS
Thoroughfare Gap
New Baltimore
Broad Run
Dawkins Branch
Porter Aug 29
Porter Aug 30
Bristoe
Kettle Run
Alexandria & Orange R.R.
Fairfax Station
Burke
Occoquan River
Broad Run
N
W
E
S
Kilometers
0 1 2 3 4
0 1 2 3 4
Miles
FIRST MANASSAS
Union advance
Union retreat
Confederate advance
Final Confederate defensive positions July 21, 1861
SECOND MANASSAS
Union advance
Union retreat
Confederate advance August 30, 1862
Confederate positions

this force also was only to demonstrate. This division had the added disadvantages of being badly led by Col. Dixon S. Miles, who was drunk during the battle, and of getting no movement priority. Miles arrived with only a fraction of his force hours after the battle had started and made no impression. McDowell relieved Miles, but the command failure was McDowell's.

It is axiomatic that a "holding" attack must convince the enemy of the attackers' resolution and be in such strength as figuratively to grasp the enemy by the throat and hold him in place. Otherwise a move on the enemy's flank or rear is likely to collapse, because the enemy can detach forces to meet this threat. McDowell was about to destroy his own plan by just such a failure to hold the Rebels in place.

Inexperience in moving large numbers of men accounted for another error: the tardy deployment of McDowell's army. He ordered Tyler's brigades and both Howard's and Heintzelman's divisions to march out of Centreville on a single road—the Warrenton turnpike. Tyler brought along a heavy, thirty-pounder Parrott rifle, which moved at a snail's pace. It took Tyler three hours to travel the four miles to the bridge. His delay slowed the two divisions coming behind, as did the trees the Rebels had cut down across the roads through the heavily wooded area they traversed.

At around 6:30 A.M. on July 21, Tyler fired three rounds from his Parrott, signaling that the battle had begun.[2] Federal guns pounded the ground around the Stone Bridge.[3] But Shanks Evans, who had already hidden his command under cover, did not respond except with a company of skirmishers spread out along the bank, thus concealing from the Federals the small size of his force.[4]

Colonel Richardson's brigade had arrived at around 5 A.M. at Mitchell's Ford, exactly as Beauregard had predicted, and was content with long-range artillery and rifle fire, making no effort to attack. The arrival of Tyler at the Stone Bridge, however, stunned Beauregard and proved that McDowell was not following the script Beauregard had written for him.

Nevertheless, while telling Bonham and Cocke to defend the Bull Run line, he persisted in his plan to envelop McDowell's eastern flank, sending confusing orders to Brig. Gen. Richard S. Ewell on the extreme east to be ready to move his brigade on Centreville along with the brigades of brigadier generals Theophilus H. Holmes and David R. Jones. But he neglected to inform Holmes; nor did he communicate with Brig. Gen. James Longstreet at Blackburn's Ford, who also had orders to advance on Centreville. Beauregard then changed his mind and decided to order all of his eastern brigades to attack Centreville, but Ewell, whose movement was supposed to set all other brigades in motion, never got the order.

While it now appeared that McDowell was trying to seize the Stone Bridge, Beauregard directed two brigades from Johnston's army, Bernard E. Bee's and Francis S. Bartow's, to rush to Evans's assistance, while sending Jackson's brigade to cover the largely undefended ground along Bull Run between Cocke and Bonham.

Thus, although McDowell still had not yet committed himself to a major attack, Beauregard had already dispatched his reserves to points where he *expected* McDowell to strike.

Evans quickly surmised that Tyler was not going to assault the Stone Bridge, but a real danger materialized. One of his pickets brought word that a Federal column was moving toward Sudley Springs Ford, and at the same time Evans got warning by means of a technological innovation—a semaphore flag system inaugurated by a young Georgian and 1857 West Point graduate, E. Porter Alexander. From his central signal tower three miles southeast of Mitchell's Ford, Alexander spotted through his telescope the glint of Federal bayonets and brass cannons near the Sudley Ford. The column was more than half a mile long and thus was a division or more. Alexander informed Beauregard and quickly semaphored Evans: "Look out for your left; you are turned."[5]

Beauregard's proposed attack on the eastern Union flank instantly vanished, but he forgot entirely to cancel it, although he sent a courier to order Jackson and Wade Hampton's six hundred–man legion, just arrived from Richmond, to go to the aid of Evans.

A more timorous officer than Evans would have withdrawn in the face of such overwhelming strength. But he was fearless. Informing Cocke on his right and leaving about two hundred men to guard the Stone Bridge, Evans rushed the remainder of his demibrigade with his two fieldpieces onto Matthew's Hill to his immediate northwest and just north of the Warrenton pike. There, a little more than a mile from Sudley Ford, spread out in a deceptively long line to give the impression of strength, Evans's men awaited the enemy.[6] They were partially protected by a grove of trees with a clear field ahead over which the Federals would have to march. It was 9 A.M.

At 9:15 A.M., after having marched for seven hours, Hunter's lead brigade, commanded by Col. Ambrose E. Burnside, climbed onto the slopes of Matthew's Hill and emerged from thick woods into the open field. There the advance First Rhode Island Regiment met fierce fire from Evans's entire line.

Burnside ordered the Second Rhode Island and its battery to attack, and the New Englanders rushed forward with shouts but immediately were checked by Confederate volleys. Before trying to assault again, Hunter brought up other brigades to form into a long and more powerful line. While this was happening, Confederate fire was so intense that the Rhode Island battery was badly pressed and Hunter himself suffered a severe neck wound.

Colonel Andrew Porter took command. But in the confusion surrounding Hunter's wounding, Evans sent the First Louisiana "Tigers" in an assault directly on the center of the Federal line. The charge from such a small force had no chance of routing the Union division but its ferocity delayed the advance, giving more time for Rebel reinforcements to arrive. The Tigers' commander, Major Roberdeau Wheat, suffered a bullet wound in his chest that surgeons pronounced fatal. Wheat replied that he didn't feel like dying, and he did not.

Evans delayed the much vaster Union force for over an hour,

partly a measure of Rebel determination but mostly due to Federal error. Porter sent in one regiment after another, individually, to the attack. Had he formed two brigades in a double line he could have enveloped both flanks of Evans's small force and crushed it inside of ten minutes.[7] Evans, consequently, was able to hold until Bee's brigade of Alabamians and Mississippians arrived, having marched at double time to the sound of the guns.

The brigade moved up beside Evans. There, hearing the eerie hiss of Minié balls, Bee ordered his men to drop to the ground. The men rose to fire, then fell to the ground again to reload.

Soon thereafter, Bartow's brigade of Georgians arrived and went into the line to the right of Bee, the men also lying down to escape the Minié balls and artillery rounds.

Total Confederate strength along this critical line was fewer than forty-five hundred men, not half the size of the Federal brigades arrayed against them. Even so, the entire Confederate line rose up to charge the two strong Union artillery batteries emplaced beside a grove of trees. The Federal cannons had found the range and outgunned the few Rebel fieldpieces.

Only Bartow's Eighth Georgia and Bee's Fourth Alabama got very far. The "bold and fearful movement," as a Georgian described it afterward, "was made through a perfect storm" of Minié balls and shells. "The balls just poured on us, struck our muskets and hats and bodies," before the men reached the grove, "the place of slaughter." From the grove the Rebels opened fire on the gunners and a body of Federal infantry guarding them, while several Union regiments moved toward them. The Georgians silenced the guns, but they faced "a whirlwind of bullets," as one soldier would describe it later. "Our men fell constantly. The deadly missiles rained like hail among the boughs and trees."[8]

The Georgians remained in the grove and the Alabamians in the open for fifteen minutes, suffering fearsome casualties. But they stopped the Federals.

Now, however, Heintzelman's division finally reached the field and formed up on Porter's right, threatening to envelop the Confederate left. Heintzelman's arrival was opportune. Burnside's and Porter's brigades had been handled badly by the Rebels, some parts becoming disorganized and some men running out of the fight to Sudley Ford. Some of Heintzelman's regiments also could not stand under Confederate fire and became disorganized.

Meanwhile, Col. William Tecumseh Sherman's thirty-four-hundred-man brigade from Tyler's division had marched upstream for about a mile, crossed Bull Run at a ford Sherman had discovered, and advanced on the Rebel rear.[9] Sherman's unexpected approach settled the issue on Matthew's Hill, for it unnerved the Rebels, making them afraid of being cut off and surrounded.

The Confederates retreated in increasing panic, crossed the Warrenton turnpike and, at around 11:30 A.M., climbed the lower slope of Henry House Hill immediately to the south. Tyler meanwhile rushed the brigade of Col. Erasmus D. Keyes across Bull Run, while twenty Union cannons, including eleven long-range rifled guns, moved up in support.

As Beauregard and Johnston arrived on Henry House Hill to help hold the retreating Confederates in line across the lower slope near the Warrenton pike, General McDowell rode along the Federal line descending Matthew's Hill shouting, "Victory! Victory! The day is ours."[10] The situation was indeed desperate for the Confederates. The Federal army was spreading out to envelop the Rebel left wing and it seemed only a small task for the Federals to sweep up and over Henry House Hill.

If the undulating, open high ground of Henry House Hill were lost, there was no rallying point to the east and the Confederate army would collapse in chaos. This was all the more likely because McDowell had concentrated more than half of his army on the Rebel left flank, while Beauregard had managed to get less than a third of his forces there.

While Evans, Bee, and Bartow were streaming off Matthew's Hill, the first Confederate reinforcements reached the field—the legion of Wade Hampton, the South's richest planter, who had personally outfitted and equipped his force of South Carolinians. Though losing a fifth of his men, Hampton covered the retreat from the lower Henry House Hill and formed a line farther up the slope.

However, the situation was saved by General Jackson and his twenty-five-hundred-man First Virginia Brigade. Originally guarding Bull Run some two and a half miles east of Henry House Hill, Jackson had moved off immediately and without waiting for orders as soon as he heard the sound of battle on the left flank, notifying Bee by courier that he was coming.

While the Federal troops were driving the Rebels off Matthew's Hill, Jackson had moved onto Henry House and ordered his artillery battery and that of Capt. John D. Imboden, already on Henry House, to take position in the center of the hill crest. Soon two other batteries arrived and began firing. The horses and men of these exposed batteries suffered greatly from Union rifle and cannon fire thereafter.

Jackson directed his infantry to lie down to the rear of the artillery in a shallow depression on the reverse slope. There, protected from Union fire, they could still sweep the crest of the hill if Union troops reached it and silhouetted themselves against the sky.

As the disorganized Rebels of Evans's, Bee's, and Bartow's units straggled up Henry House Hill, only Hampton's and Jackson's units still were cohesive. When General Bee rode up, Jackson suggested that he regroup his men behind the First Brigade. Bee quickly rode into the mass of retreating Southerners and urged them to rally behind the Virginians. "There stands Jackson like a stone wall!" Bee cried.[11] Bee's men eagerly rallied and other refugees assembled around Jackson's brigade—forever after known as the Stonewall Brigade—and, somewhat haphazardly, began to recover their organization and coherence.

When General Johnston arrived he found the Fourth Alabama in line with ordered arms about two hundred yards behind the new line. The regiment had lost all of its field officers and did not know what to do. Johnston found the color-bearer. "Sergeant," he said, "hand me your flag." "General," the sergeant replied, "I cannot give up my flag but I will put it wherever you command." With the sergeant at his side, Johnston led him and the rest of the regiment to the right of Jackson's brigade and assigned S. R. Gist, a member of Bee's staff, as commander.[12] Thereafter it performed splendidly.

This action encouraged the remaining Rebel fragments, and they rallied on either side of Jackson. At the same time, Confederate regiments from the right were rushing frantically forward to get into the fight—two Virginia outfits from Cocke's brigade, the Sixth North Carolina, and the cavalry of Col. J. E. B. Stuart. The North Carolina regiment moved to the extreme left to protect against envelopment. Beauregard, who remained on the field, and Johnston, who retired to direct the whole army from Portici House, about a mile away, got fourteen cannons and an estimated sixty-five hundred men in place against about nine thousand effective Federals. The odds were still formidable against the Rebels but the battle could be saved if Beauregard held long enough for the arrival of other Confederate forces rushing forward from the east.

McDowell assisted Beauregard with three decisive errors: (1) his reluctance to attack gave the Rebels time to establish a new defensive line around Jackson; (2) he failed to get four brigades into the final battle; and (3) he did not take advantage of an opportunity to turn the Confederate flank near the Stone Bridge. Instead he focused on a frontal attack directly against the Confederate line on Henry House Hill.

The four unused brigades would have approximately doubled McDowell's strength. One was Burnside's force, which he allowed to move back to rest. Another was Oliver O. Howard's brigade of Heintzelman's division, which he kept in reserve. Although he finally sent for it, Howard's brigade arrived too late.

The other two brigades were Keyes's and Robert C. Schenck's of Tyler's division. Keyes was on the south side of Bull Run near the Stone Bridge and Schenck just to the north. Both could have moved around Henry House Hill on the Confederate right flank and rear—and there was little to stop them. McDowell called on neither brigade.[13]

For the next two hours the Union and Confederate artillery rained projectiles on enemy positions, doing little damage and firing mostly at the other's smoke. Meanwhile, McDowell ordered charge after charge against the Confederate line. The Union forces formed in sheltered spots along Young's Branch, a small stream between Matthew's and Henry House hills, then marched forward. When the regiments came into view of the Confederate line, Federal artillery accelerated its fire on the Southerners and the Union infantry fired a volley or two. Enduring heavy return fire from the Confederates, the regiments then ran back down the hill for cover. Some of the commands tried several times, but none ever made a lodgment.[14] The Union commanders made the invariable mistake of sending in one regiment at a time instead of brigades or groups of brigades. The Rebels were able to concentrate their fire on the single exposed regiment and achieve terrible effect.

Sherman, who also sent in his regiments singly, was appalled at the intensity of the fire. Days later he wrote: "First one regiment and then another and another were forced back, not by the bayonet but by a musketry and rifle fire, which it seemed impossible to push our men through." His brigade was on the verge of demoralization. "I do think it was impossible to stand long in that fire," he wrote.[15]

As their assaults failed, many Union regiments fell back in confusion. Sometimes soldiers singly or in small groups fled down the hill without orders. Other regiments withdrew in order at first but then broke in near panic. The overriding thought in all cases was to get out of the enemy fire. Part of their fear was caused by the Confederate shelling. But the greater damage came from the bullets of the unseen Rebel riflemen.

The wonder is not that the green and scarcely trained Union regiments fell into disorder. The real wonder is how any of them, ordered to charge into the hail of fire, kept their integrity at all. They were being subjected to fire of an intensity and accuracy unprecedented in history, fire for which none of the men had been prepared and against which they possessed only two defenses: falling to the ground or running away.

Although the Confederates were holding their line and their regiments did not break, the effect of the fire on individual units and soldiers was similar. The Eighteenth Virginia of Cocke's brigade arrived on the field but at first did not enter the fight because its colonel was hiding. As the Second South Carolina of Bonham's brigade moved toward the battlefield, one member observed: "We saw hundreds of our men retiring, crying that we were ruined, that the battle was lost and that nothing could save us from being cut up."[16] Other observers commented on the large numbers of Southern skulkers and stragglers who had abandoned their positions and fled to the rear.

Confederate regiments from the eastern fords were rushing toward the sound of the battle and several got into the line, adding to Rebel strength as the extremely hot afternoon wore on. The regiments folded in at whatever points they could, sometimes relieving heavily pressed regiments, like the Sixth North Carolina, which had stood bravely much of the afternoon on the extreme left flank and had been badly battered, losing its colonel, C. F. Fisher, and many men. General Bee and Colonel Bartow also were killed.

Since his infantry was failing to advance, McDowell decided at around 3 P.M. to order forward two Regular Army batteries of eleven guns, soon joined by two more pieces, to within a thousand feet of the Confederate line, far in advance of the Union infantry and within canister range of the Rebels. It was Napoleonic tactics aimed at breaking a hole in the Rebel line—with complete disregard for the Minié ball. Capt. Charles Griffin, who'd seen what rifle fire could do, protested. He commanded a battery that had been posted at West Point. McDowell's artillery chief told Griffin that he should go ahead anyway and that two New York regiments would move up to protect the battery.

The New Yorkers stood only the first volley from Jackson's brigade. They retreated and then faced an unexpected charge by

150 of Jeb Stuart's cavalry. The New Yorkers got off a volley that shot down nine of Stuart's men and eighteen horses, but the charge went through the New Yorkers, already shaken by Jackson, and they fled.

The Thirty-third Virginia now charged the guns. They were loaded with canister, but a Union officer insisted that the regiment was Federal, allowing it to get within seventy paces. There it fired a volley, which killed or wounded forty gunners and seventy-five horses. The surviving gunners were able to pull three cannons back to safety, but the others remained where they were. They became the object of charges on both sides and changed hands three times. After the battle Porter Alexander mourned the losses—he and his classmates had ridden the horses at West Point and had known the gunners.[17]

The most dramatic reinforcement was E. Kirby Smith's brigade, the last of Johnston's men from the valley. Smith's train arrived at Manassas Junction at about 12:30 P.M. after a long, tiresome ride. The brigade, minus Col. A. P. Hill's regiment, which was left behind to guard Manassas, immediately departed for the left flank, six miles away. Smith found the road clogged with dust and stragglers but pushed doggedly forward, eager to get into the battle. The column met General Johnston at Portici House. He told Smith to move his sixteen hundred men to the left flank, which was in danger of being driven back.

While reconnoitering, Smith was struck by a bullet in the left breast, seriously but not fatally wounding him. Command devolved on Col. Arnold Elzey, who placed the brigade on the extreme left opposite Howard, who finally had come up into position. Shortly after 4 P.M. Elzey ordered his men to charge, driving Howard's dispirited men before them. This sudden, surprise move turned the Federal flank and caused the entire right wing of McDowell's army to give way.

Only an hour before, Beauregard had received word from Porter Alexander that, from the main semaphore tower he had seen a large column approaching from the southwest. Beauregard feared it might be Union general Patterson coming from the

Shenandoah Valley. If so, the battle was lost for the South. Soon, a mile away, Beauregard could make out a flag, but it was drooping in the heat and he could not tell whether it was the Stars and Stripes or the Confederate flag. Although anxious, Beauregard determined to wait a bit before ordering a retreat. At last a gust of wind caught the flag and he saw that it was a banner of Jubal A. Early's brigade. Early was marching to the battle, having come six miles from the eastern fords.

The arrival of Early made the Union position untenable. Learning from Stuart that the Federal right flank was about to break, Early thrust his brigade to the left of Elzey's force and ordered it to charge. Howard wrote afterward: "It was evident that a panic had seized all the troops in sight."[18] The Federals, some of them screaming that the enemy was upon them, rushed backward, offering practically no resistance. By the time Early reached the crest of Bald Hill, just to the west of Henry House Hill, he could see thousands of Federal troops on the Warrenton turnpike heading toward the Stone Bridge and Sudley Ford in full retreat.

Beauregard now realized that the battle was won. He ordered a general charge from the line centered around the Stonewall Brigade. As the Rebels surged forward, the Union soldiers withdrew rapidly, retreating toward Bull Run, increasingly losing order and cohesion. Union colonel Keyes saw the retreat close up. He wrote later: "As we emerged from the woods [near the Stone Bridge] one glance told the tale; a tale of defeat, and a confused, disorderly and disgraceful retreat. The road was filled with wagons, artillery, retreating cavalry and infantry in one confused mass, each seemingly bent on looking out for number one and letting the rest do the same."[19]

The retreat soon became a rout. General Johnston had no readily available Rebel force to order in immediate pursuit. However, he was able to send part of the Thirtieth Virginia Cavalry across Bull Run in an attempt to cut off the retreat between the Stone Bridge and Centreville. Colonel Keyes saw what happened: "A scene of confusion ensued which beggars description. Cavalry horses without riders, artillery horses disengaged from the guns with traces flying, wrecked baggage wagons and pieces of artillery drawn by six horses without drivers, flying at their utmost speed and whacking against other vehicles." Keyes saw men throw down their rifles "as if they were snakes."[20] Even so, some Federals repulsed the Thirtieth Virginia's charge while most of the Union soldiers continued to flee.

Meantime, Col. Joseph B. Kershaw of South Carolina got some Rebels across the Stone Bridge, along with Capt. Delaware Kemper's battery. A lucky cannon shot overturned a wagon on the wooden bridge over Cub Run, two miles from Centreville, effectively blocking passage. Drivers still south of the bridge abandoned their wagons and artillery and the soldiers rushed away on foot back to Centreville and continued on, heading for Washington.

Confederate president Jefferson Davis had arrived shortly after the battle ended and he and generals Johnston and Beauregard decided not to dispatch a pursuit force that night but to send Bonham forward the next morning. Davis later remembered that Bonham was to pursue the Federals on July 22, but Beauregard understood that he was to make only a reconnaissance, and this is what was done.

It was an irretrievable error. The two generals and the Confederate president, by their timidity, lost the opportunity that might have achieved Southern independence at a stroke.

Stonewall Jackson, whose finger had been broken by a Minié ball during the battle, shouted as Davis passed by while the surgeon was treating his wound: "We have whipped them! They ran like sheep! Give me 5,000 fresh men and I will be in Washington city tomorrow morning."[21] There were, of course, no fresh troops in Jackson's immediate vicinity, but there were more than five thousand men on the eastern fords who had seen little action, and they could have been ordered forward quickly.

Porter Alexander, who was present, is extremely critical of President Davis and generals Johnston and Beauregard, who spent the two hours between victory and sunset riding over the battlefield. Instead, Alexander says, Beauregard should have pushed up the pike with every soldier he could find while Johnston gathered up the three Rebel brigades on the eastern fords, which had not been engaged, and led them personally on Centreville. "No hard fighting would have been needed," Alexander writes. "A threat upon either flank would doubtless have been sufficient; and, when once a retreat from Centreville was started, even blank volleys fired behind it would have soon converted it into a panic." He points out that although both generals sent orders urging advances, "neither went in person to supervise and urge forward the execution of the orders, though time was of the essence."[22]

The reason for the failure to pursue comes down to the lack of resolve of the high command. Jackson, like all great captains, had this resolve. But neither Johnston, Beauregard, nor Davis did; nor did they grasp the full meaning of the opportunity that had been gained. The fruits of all great victories by a weaker nation must be picked quickly, before a stronger force regains its balance, composure, and strength.

The disheartened and disorganized Federal detachments would have yielded at a touch if the Confederates had pressed diligently forward on the night of July 21. The history of war is replete with examples of this. In the great chase across the north German plain after Napoleon's victory at Jena in 1806, strong Prussian units and even intact fortresses surrendered at the mere appearance of French cavalry.

Rain fell heavily on July 22, raising creek levels and turning roads soggy. For Beauregard, Johnston, and Davis, the weather provided an excuse for not advancing on Washington. But it was only an excuse.

George B. McClellan, who was to succeed Scott and McDowell, arrived in Washington on July 26, five days after the battle, and rode around the city. He observed:

> I found no preparations whatever for defense, not even to the extent of putting the troops in military position. . . . A

> determined attack would doubtless have carried Arlington Heights [opposite the capital] and placed the city at the mercy of a battery of rifled guns. If the Secessionists attached any value to the possession of Washington, they committed their greatest error in not following up the victory of Bull Run.[23]

Stonewall Jackson knew this, even if Beauregard, Johnston, and Davis did not. He put his brigade on alert with three days' cooked rations in their haversacks, impatiently awaiting the order to advance. None came.

Casualties at First Manassas were remarkably modest, considering the bullets and shot that inundated the field. Union casualties were 2,706, including 1,460 prisoners. Confederate losses were 1,981, mostly killed and wounded. The relatively low cost can be attributed to three primary reasons: many men were still armed with smoothbore muskets, soldiers were not as accurate or disciplined in their firing as they were to become later, and the green regiments on both sides simply could not stand up long to heavy fire. The Federal regiments, required to attack, buckled quicker than the defending, and therefore less tested, Rebels. In later battles, more disciplined and trained soldiers, armed almost wholly with rifles, unleashed merciless fire—and imposed horrendous casualties.

Even so, the battle foreshadowed what was to come. The Thirty-third Virginia, which assaulted the guns on Henry House Hill, suffered 30-percent losses, Hampton's legion 20 percent, while the Stonewall Brigade and Bee's and Bartow's brigades lost around 16 percent.

The Confederate victory was won by McDowell's mistakes combined with quick Southern reaction. Little credit could be accorded Beauregard, who allowed his left flank to be all but bare. If Shanks Evans had not reacted the moment he learned from Porter Alexander that his flank was turned, the South almost certainly would have sustained a devastating, and perhaps irrecoverable, defeat. If Bee, Bartow, and Jackson had not marched immediately to the sound of the guns, there would have been insufficient Confederate strength to stop Hunter and Heintzelman.

As it was, Beauregard ultimately got only about seventeen thousand Confederates into the battle on Henry House Hill—more than McDowell, but the Rebel units filtered in one by one, sometimes just barely in time to avert disaster.

The South did not learn how narrow the dividing line was between its victory and its utter defeat. Too long Southerners believed that their fighting prowess, their tactical superiority, and of course their superior valor, had been proved at First Manassas, not, as was the case, that McDowell's errors represented the only real distinction between the two armies. The battle was more beneficial to the North. The belief in a single victory vanished. Leaders girded themselves for a long and bitter war.

The aftermath of First Manassas demonstrated not only Southern apathy but the inability of President Davis to see that an early offensive was necessary before Northern strength grew beyond anything the Confederacy could match. In October Beauregard and Johnston, along with a new division commander, Maj. Gen. Gustavus W. Smith, met with Davis at Fairfax Court House and urged a strike before new armies being trained by General McClellan could take the field.

Davis refused. He did not possess the strength of will to face down the political storm that would have come if he had stripped troops from other points in the South to attack the northeast. Robert E. Lee was not present to advise. Shortly after First Manassas Davis had sent Lee to recover West Virginia, which McClellan had gained with an easy victory over a small Rebel force. Lee's campaign failed utterly because he refused to impose his will on Confederate commanders who competed more with one another than against the enemy. Faced with public criticism, Davis relieved Lee in November and sent him to build defenses along the south Atlantic coast.

Johnston and Beauregard deferred to Davis regarding an offensive. The president of the Confederacy, as of the Union, was the constitutional commander in chief. As a West Point graduate himself, a former chairman of the Military Affairs Committee of the U.S. Senate, and secretary of war in President Franklin Pierce's cabinet, Davis considered himself a military expert, though in fact his strategic vision was extremely limited. Johnston and Beauregard, as his senior generals charged with prosecution of the war, had the duty to press Davis for the military course they believed to be best. Yet both let the matter slide. Only Stonewall Jackson, still only a brigade commander, made an independent proposal for a Northern offensive. Four times rebuffed, Jackson's proposal from its first appearance exhibited brilliant strategic vision that showed he understood better than any other general in Confederate service that the way to victory was to strike not primarily at the Federal army, but at the will of the Northern people to wage war.

Jackson was promoted to major general in October and named commander in the Shenandoah Valley. But, following military channels, he presented his plan shortly before leaving for the valley on November 4, 1861, to General Smith, his division commander, and asked him to press it on Johnston and Beauregard and, through them, Davis.

Jackson told Smith that McClellan's "army of recruits" would attempt nothing in the autumn. But by spring of 1862 McClellan would have an army vastly superior to the South's. The time for the Confederacy to strike with its veterans was now.

The Rebel army should cross the upper Potomac above the falls and sweep around behind Washington and occupy Baltimore, Jackson advised. "Taking possession of Maryland, we could cut off the communications of Washington, force the Federal government to abandon the capital, beat McClellan's army if it came out against us in the open country," occupy Philadelphia and other large cities, and destroy important parts of Northern industry and commerce. This course of "making unrelenting war" amid the homes of the Northern people, Jackson said, would force them "to understand what it will cost them to hold the South in the Union at the bayonet's point."[24]

Jackson was certain such a campaign would lead to victory. Especially the loss of Washington, symbol of national unity, would have far-reaching psychological effects, depressing the Northern people, discrediting Lincoln's administration, and giving strength to elements in Britain and France pressing for recognition of the Confederacy.

Jackson's proposal demonstrated that he had a solid grasp of the strategic situation. He believed that "the Scipio Africanus policy was the best," referring to the Roman general in the Second Punic War who carried the war to Carthage in north Africa. This drew the Carthaginian general, Hannibal, out of Italy and led to his defeat at Zama in 202 B.C. Jackson realized that the South had to go for the Northern jugular vein. It could not win by peripheral blows. Its best chance was to strike, like Scipio, at the resources and morale of the enemy.

General Smith, however, had seen that President Davis was not a man of imagination who could be stirred by great ventures. He told Jackson of the conference with Davis some days before and said he could do nothing to change the president's position. Jackson replied, "I am sorry, very sorry," and rode sadly away. Smith forwarded Jackson's proposal, but, as predicted, it received scant attention.[25] Jackson's biographer, Col. G. F. R. Henderson, says that Jackson never forgave Davis "for his want of wisdom after Manassas."[26] Though Jackson always avoided any criticism of the president, he was convinced that Davis had allowed great opportunities to slip away that might never come again. Nevertheless, he hoped for a Federal misstep that would give the South a second chance. And he never gave up the conviction that his plan offered the best chance for the South.

NOTES

General sources: Dabney, 210–51; Cooke, 63–86; Johnson and Buel, vol. 1, 167–261; Henderson, 102–34; Alexander, *Military Memoirs,* 13–51; Freeman,

Lee's Lieutenants, vol. 1, 50–110; Sanger, 28–37; Alexander, *Fighting for the Confederacy,* 37–72; Davis; Chambers, vol. 1, 364–406; and Vandiver, 155–64.

1. Freeman, *Lee's Lieutenants,* vol. 1, 50, n. 18, and 51–52; P. G. T. Beauregard, *Commentary on the Campaign and Battle of Manassas* (New York: Harper and Brothers, 1884), 52–53 and 61–62; *Official Records,* vol. 2, 473–78; Johnson and Buel, vol. 1, 246 (Johnston's comments); and Johnston, 41.

2. Evans, in *Official Records,* vol. 2, 558, says the firing began at 5:15 A.M. British major general Sir Frederick Maurice (Marshall, 57 n.) points out that Confederate generals, especially in the early part of the war, tended to make the sound of firing by one body of troops the signal for the advance of other bodies. "As an expedient," Maurice writes, "it almost always failed."

3. *Official Records,* vol. 2, 474; and Freeman, *Lee's Lieutenants,* vol. 1, 53.

4. At the start of the war companies usually had about fifty men. Regiments usually had ten companies and thus possessed about five hundred men. Brigades contained at least two but usually more regiments. Casualties and sickness reduced company, regimental, and brigade sizes drastically as the war went on, especially in the Confederate army. The Federal army tended to put newly recruited men into new regiments.

5. Alexander, *Military Memoirs,* 30; and Maury Klein, *Edward Porter Alexander* (Athens: University of Georgia Press, 1971), 34.

6. Here and throughout the war the customary tactical formation was the line of battle, two men deep. In First Manassas and other battles commanders lined up individual regiments in line of battle and attacked. At other times they formed entire brigades in line of battle, with another brigade or brigades behind as a "column of brigades." Customarily skirmishers preceded the line of battle when it attacked, to distract the enemy and prepare the way. Such "Indian fighting" had been practiced by Americans in the French and Indian War and the American Revolution and by some continental armies of the eighteenth century. It became common in the wars of the French Revolution in the 1790s. See J. F. C. Fuller, *The Conduct of War, 1789–1961* (New Brunswick, N.J.: Rutgers University Press, 1961), 36; Hans Delbrück, *History of the Art of War,* trans. Walter J. Renfroe, Jr. (Westport, Conn.: Greenwood Press, 1985; reprint, Lincoln: University of Nebraska Press, 1990), 401 and 403–6.

7. Alexander, *Military Memoirs,* 33.

8. Davis, 178–79.

9. B. H. Liddell Hart, *Sherman: Soldier, Realist, American* (New York: Dodd, Mead and Company, 1929), 87–88. (A different edition of this book was published as *Sherman: The Genius of the Civil War* [London: Ernest Benn, 1930].)

10. Davis, 187.

11. Freeman, *Lee's Lieutenants,* vol. 1, 81–83 and 733–34; and Davis, 197–78.

12. Freeman, *Lee's Lieutenants,* vol. 1, 65; Davis, 198–99; Johnston, 48; and J. A. Chapman, "The 4th Alabama Regiment," *Confederate Veteran* vol. XXX (May 1922): 197.

13. Alexander, *Military Memoirs,* 37–38.

14. Ibid., 38.

15. Davis, 218–9.

16. Ibid., 224.

17. Alexander, *Fighting for the Confederacy,* 53.

18. Davis, 232.

19. Ibid., 234–36. See also Erasmus D. Keyes, *Fifty Years' Observation of Men and Events* (New York: 1884), 434–35.

20. Davis, 237.

21. Alexander, *Military Memoirs,* 42. Henderson doubles the number, saying that Jackson said: "Give me 10,000 fresh troops and I would be in Washington tomorrow" (117).

22. Alexander, *Military Memoirs,* 43.

23. George B. McClellan, *McClellan's Own Story* (New York: Charles L. Webster and Company, 1887), 66–67. See also Henderson, 118.

24. Henderson, 131–32.

25. Henderson, 131–33. Henderson's source for Jackson's proposal was a letter from Gen. G. W. Smith to Henderson. John Esten Cooke (Cooke, 86–88) cites the reference to Scipio Africanus. Jackson also called for a Scipio strategy nearly a year later, after the Seven Days, demonstrating that he understood thoroughly the necessity of striking at the center of the Northern will to resist. See Cooke, 247.

26. Henderson, 159.

3

THE VALLEY

Keeping McClellan Out of Richmond

★ ★ ★ In the spring of 1862 the chief of the Union army, Maj. Gen. George B. McClellan, turned the Civil War in a strange and unexpected direction that presented Jackson with the opportunity he was seeking to pit Southern strength against Northern weakness.

Three other Confederate generals saw the chance, including the top commander, General Johnston, but Jackson alone pressed the South to follow it. The top military leadership, President Jefferson Davis and Gen. Robert E. Lee, pursued virtually an opposite approach, attempting to confront Northern power head to head and to defeat it.[1] For the South, with less than half the North's population and only a fraction of its industry, this was an impossible task.

General McClellan reveled in the title of the "Young Napoleon" bestowed on him by the Northern public after he had cleared West Virginia of Confederates and issued bombastic manifestos in the process. Because of his success, Lincoln named

McClellan chief of the Union army in November 1861, with the duty of destroying the Confederacy.

Actually, there was nothing Napoleonic about George McClellan. Though he had been painstakingly training an army three times larger than the South's, he did not know how to exploit his power, he was extremely slow in moving, and he always exaggerated enemy strength.

McClellan decided to take advantage of the Union's control of the sea and began massive preparations in early spring 1862 to transfer the bulk of the Union army by ship through the Chesapeake Bay to Fort Monroe, an old army post the North had retained at the tip of the peninsula between the York and James rivers southeast of Richmond. McClellan's plan was to concentrate forces there and move up the peninsula for a direct assault on the Confederate capital.

Strategically this idea would have had much to say in its favor if McClellan had coupled it with an offensive to hold in place the main Confederate army, still positioned around Manassas. A flank attack up the peninsula would have required the Confederacy to divide its inadequate forces. Richmond was symbolically important as the Confederate capital and militarily important because it was Virginia's railway hub and the South's major munitions-manufacturing center.

An even more effective Union move would have been to attack, not toward Richmond, but across to the south side of the tidal James River to Petersburg and beyond, severing railway lines and cutting off troops and supplies from states to the south. This would have forced the evacuation of Richmond without a fight.

McClellan, however, did not see the advantages of moving to the south of Richmond and also did not understand the need to immobilize the main Confederate army in northern Virginia. Instead he conceived a campaign that would strike at only a single target, Richmond. The Southern leadership, therefore, could concentrate its forces to meet this sole threat.

Before McClellan embarked for the peninsula, he pushed the

main Confederate army out of Manassas with threatening movements in early March 1862. General Johnston drew back to the more defensible line of the Rapidan and Rappahannock rivers, about halfway to Richmond.

Johnston's withdrawal also required the retreat of Stonewall Jackson, who, in Winchester, had been watching the lower (northern) end of the wide Shenandoah Valley with only forty-six hundred men, including a few hundred horsemen under a reckless and daring northern Virginia farmer and consummate cavalry commander named Turner Ashby.

Johnston told Jackson to defend the valley as best he could with the troops he had, to use his own judgment, and, if possible, to keep his pursuer, Maj. Gen. Nathaniel P. Banks, with twenty-three thousand troops, from detaching any large number of men to reinforce McClellan.

During the past winter Jackson had shown both strengths and weaknesses as a field commander in a campaign to recover parts of northwestern Virginia beyond the Allegheny Mountains. In this campaign, beginning on January 1, 1862, Jackson foiled a projected offensive by Union major general William S. Rosecrans to seize Winchester and threaten the left of the main Confederate position at Manassas. Jackson drove his small army relentlessly through snow and rain and along atrocious roads, leaving supply wagons far behind; attacking Federal garrisons, he temporarily broke the Baltimore and Ohio Railroad along the Potomac River and seized Romney, thirty-five air miles northwest of Winchester. This highly successful campaign threatened Federal rail communications with the Midwest and regained a large part of western Virginia at little cost.

Officers and men of Jackson's chief subordinate, Brig. Gen. W. W. Loring, became angry with the conditions they faced, and Loring apparently supported them. Jackson preferred charges against Loring, although authorities in Richmond did not pursue them. Loring's force, left to hold Romney, felt isolated and exposed, although it was in no danger. Eleven officers complained through channels to the Confederate secretary of war, Judah P.

Benjamin. Without investigating, Benjamin ordered Jackson to bring the Romney garrison back to Winchester immediately. Jackson complied but sent in his resignation at once. "With such interference in my command I cannot expect to be of much service in the field," he wrote.[2]

This abrupt response shook General Johnston, who recognized Jackson's ability. By his pleadings and the influence of Virginia governor John Letcher, Jackson withdrew his letter—and no secretary of war tried to second-guess Jackson again. The War Department transferred Loring and part of his troops elsewhere.[3]

★ ★ ★

At Winchester in March 1862 Banks found out how small Jackson's force was and decided it was a mere corps of observation. But the Virginians who made up his army knew better. They were calling Jackson "Old Blue Light" on account of his Presbyterian fanaticism, the strange look in his blue eyes, and the suspicion that he considered himself an Old Testament prophet reincarnated to smite the enemies of God.

By this time Southern poverty and Jackson's belief in long, fast marches were creating the "foot cavalry" for which his army became famous. Uniforms were not standard, ranging from light blue to the "real" Confederate color, butternut brown, produced by dye from the white walnut. Overcoats had disappeared, brogans had superseded boots, the slouch hat was more common than the kepi. Knapsacks had been replaced by the shoulder-hung haversack. There were few tents; instead the men slept in pairs, in blankets and rubber sheets. These they rolled up and carried over their shoulders, along with frying pans or skillets. Compared to the Federal soldiers in their neat blue uniforms, Confederates looked decidedly "unmilitary." But they were lean and hard and they knew how to use the devastating firepower of the Minié ball.[4]

Turner Ashby and his cavalry, country boys who had spent much of their lives on horses, provided Jackson with a shield against surprise, rear and flank protection, and a means of reconnaissance without peer. Jackson expected his cavalry to penetrate enemy camps, count the men in enemy columns, and determine with exactitude what the enemy was doing or planning to do. They rarely failed him. Said one young horseman: "We thought no more of riding through the enemy's bivouacs than of riding round our fathers' farms."[5] The cavalry's one fault: lack of discipline.

Banks's infantry was a match for the Rebel foot soldiers. The Union troops were also country fellows, largely from Midwestern farms, and they were as familiar with rifles and axes as the Virginians. Though they were not as good horsemen, their artillery, counting more rifled guns, was superior. Both sides possessed human material of comparable skill, endurance, and determination. The single significant difference between them was the quality of their commanders.

From the moment he retreated from Winchester on March 11, Jackson tried to draw Banks into a battle. He calculated that only by fighting could he prevent most of the Union army from abandoning the valley. He called a council of his top officers and proposed an attack before dawn on the Union camp about four miles north of town, figuring that such an assault would confuse and disorder the inexperienced Federal soldiers. Realizing how outnumbered their force was, the officers protested, but Jackson insisted. Something went wrong with communications, and instead of stopping the brigades at the outskirts of Winchester, the officers moved them about six miles south. This meant a ten-mile march to reach the enemy, too far to be sure of surprise. Jackson, frustrated and angry, abandoned the attack and vowed never to hold a council of war again.

By nature a man who kept his thoughts and plans to himself, Jackson allowed the experience to wrap him even deeper into his cloak of secretiveness. To achieve victory it is vital to deceive one's enemy. But Jackson, afraid to divulge anything for fear it would be misconstrued, also had a policy of deceiving his own officers. He said later: "If I can deceive my own friends I can make certain of deceiving the enemy."[6]

There was nothing to do now but retreat. Leaving Ashby with a cavalry screen, Jackson fell back fifteen miles south up the macademized valley pike (now U.S. Route 11) to Strasburg and then to Mount Jackson, twenty-one miles farther south, hoping to pull the Federal army after him.[7] But Banks, former governor of Massachusetts for three terms and speaker of the U.S. House of Representatives, wanted glory, and he saw no point in chasing a small Rebel force up the valley. He wanted to get in on the big operations shaping up under McClellan. Consequently, Banks left nine thousand men in the valley under Brig. Gen. James Shields and began to move his remaining troops east toward Manassas.[8]

Ashby reported to Jackson on March 21 that all but four of Shields's regiments had departed. Jackson acted instantly, marching his men so fast the thirty-two miles down the valley pike that only three thousand of them were still in ranks at 2 P.M. Sunday, March 23, when he came upon Ashby in an artillery skirmish with Federals at Kernstown, four miles south of Winchester. Ashby assured Jackson that the force facing them, visible on open ground to the east of the pike, was only a rear guard.

Between him and the visible Federals was open grassland. To send his men across it would have invited heavy enemy fire. Instead, telling Ashby to demonstrate with his artillery, Jackson moved the bulk of his troops and guns three miles to his left up a long, low wooded hill called Sandy Ridge. In this way Jackson hoped to get on the flank and rear of the Union forces. Ashby's information turned out to be incorrect. Shields's entire division was hidden in woods and behind a hill north of Kernstown. Under Col. Nathan Kimball's temporary command, following a wound Shields received in cavalry action, the Federals dispatched a brigade onto Sandy Ridge to stop Jackson. The Rebels contested the hill bitterly until Kimball sent parts of two more brigades. Now greatly outnumbering the Confederates, the Federals pressed forward. Jackson realized that he was fighting a much larger force than Ashby had indicated and ordered his last three reserve regiments to come onto the ridge, but before these reinforcements could arrive, the Stonewall Brigade commander, Richard B. Garnett, feared that the thinned Confederate line was about to crack and ordered withdrawal. Jackson, incensed that Garnett had not held until aid arrived, tried to stem the frenzied retreat. He failed, and—as is generally the case when a force withdraws under pressure before an advancing, resolute enemy—it quickly turned into a rout.

Jackson still had much to learn about tactics. Had he pressed a real attack against the Federal front, Union troops might have been held in place long enough for him to make the turning movement over Sandy Ridge. Instead Kimball, knowing that he faced no danger to the front, was able to block him on the ridge with vastly superior forces.

Jackson relieved Brigadier General Garnett of his command and preferred charges against him because he had retreated without orders. His officers and men felt that the charges were unjust, but Jackson believed that if Garnett had held a little longer, he could have brought up the reserves and stemmed the Union advance. Although the army did not pursue a court-martial, every officer under Jackson thereafter knew never to order a retreat.[9] The new commander of the Stonewall Brigade was a Marylander, Brig. Gen. Charles S. Winder, an 1850 graduate of West Point and former Indian fighter in the Pacific Northwest.

After nightfall, shielded by the Rebel cavalry, the foot soldiers retreated four miles south of Kernstown to lick their wounds. The fight cost Jackson 718 casualties to the Federals' 590. Nearly one-fourth of Jackson's infantry had been killed, wounded, or captured.

It was not a promising premiere of Jackson as an independent field commander. Yet Kernstown illustrates a significant fact about war: a battle does not always have to be a tactical success to result in a strategic victory.

General Shields was stunned by the unexpected Confederate attack and surmised that Jackson never would have attempted it unless he was being greatly reinforced. Suddenly fearing for the safety of the valley, he recalled one of Banks's divisions, and on March 24 President Lincoln sent Banks and his whole corps back to the valley. To strengthen Maj. Gen. John C. Frémont, who was to the west of Jackson in the Alleghenies, Lincoln transferred to his command the seven thousand–man division led by a German soldier of fortune named Louis Blenker.[10]

McClellan had expected to use the thirty thousand–man corps of Maj. Gen. Irvin McDowell in his attack up the peninsula, but on April 3 Lincoln ordered McDowell to stay put near Washington. Lincoln assured McClellan that this force could march overland to Richmond as soon as any threat to the capital disappeared. By withholding troops from McClellan, Lincoln caused him to become even more deliberate and hesitant than he already had proved to be.[11]

Jackson had lost a battle, but he had forced a major change in Northern strategy. Seldom in the history of warfare has so small a military force achieved so enormous a strategic gain.

McClellan complained that holding McDowell to protect Washington imperiled his entire campaign. Meanwhile, the main Confederate army of fifty-seven thousand men, bivouacked on the Rapidan and Rappahannock rivers, moved back to defend Richmond and the peninsula.

The Confederate situation remained precarious. Union forces were threatening from the northwest, north, and east, with the main threat being McClellan's army of 128,000 men forming on the lower peninsula. The only barrier McClellan faced was a weak defensive line between Yorktown and the James River, commanded by Maj. Gen. John B. Magruder.

On April 14 Johnston came back to Richmond from a visit to Magruder's line. He was not happy. Federal artillery and naval ordnance could outrange the old Confederate smoothbores at Yorktown and across the York River at Gloucester Point. Once these Rebel guns were knocked out, Union transports could move up the York River and land beyond the entrenchments or even steam up the Pamunkey close to Richmond. On the opposite, broad, James side only the ironclad *Virginia* (formerly the *Merrimac*) was available to keep Union gunboats from passing the Rebel flank, and this warship's usefulness was in doubt because the Union ironclad *Monitor* had fought it to a draw on March 9 and might do so again.[12] Magruder's position was indefensible, Johnston told President Davis. Something had to be done.

Davis convened a meeting with Johnston; George W. Randolph, the new secretary of war, a grandson of Thomas Jefferson; Robert E. Lee, whom President Davis had returned to Richmond on March 13 as his chief of staff; and, at Johnston's request, two of his division commanders, major generals Gustavus Smith and James Longstreet. Both were West Pointers. Smith, thirty-nine years old, was the former street commissioner of New York City; at forty-one, Longstreet, from Georgia, was morose after the deaths of all three of his children from scarlet fever in January. Johnston told the group that McClellan could turn the Yorktown line by sending gunboats up the James and York rivers, that this line and the port of Norfolk had to be abandoned and another plan had to be devised. To lose Norfolk would mean to lose the unseaworthy and deep-drafted *Virginia,* the only hope of contesting Chesapeake Bay. Secretary Randolph, an old navy man, fought against this idea. General Smith, with Johnston's approval, proposed that after the Yorktown line was abandoned and Norfolk evacuated, forces should be concentrated at Richmond and reinforced by all troops that could be drawn from the Carolinas and Georgia. Then the Confederate army should either attack McClellan or march on Washington and Baltimore and perhaps beyond, shielding Richmond with a small garrison.

McClellan had locked up the bulk of Union military strength on the peninsula, where it was useful only for an offensive against Richmond. He would be unable to extricate his army in time to stop the main Confederate army if it marched northward. If Richmond could be shielded, even temporarily, it might be saved, especially since McClellan was known to be a procrastinator and slow acting.

Longstreet had intended to propose a plan along similar lines —Magruder to detain McClellan temporarily at Yorktown and the main army to march on Washington by way of the Shenandoah Valley, "as proposed by Jackson a few days before," indicating that Stonewall may have renewed the recommendation he had made after First Manassas.[13] This, Longstreet believed, would force McClellan to withdraw to protect the capital.

President Davis, as he had demonstrated in October, was incapable of such dramatic thinking. Like Randolph, he placed great value in the *Virginia,* even though its usefulness had been severely compromised by the Union ironclad. Davis's mind was fixed on the immediate problem on the peninsula. Davis admonished Longstreet not to underrate McClellan's initiative and, since Lee gave neither Longstreet nor Smith any support, the idea of an attack into the North remained stillborn.

The discussion now focused on Smith's other proposal—to evacuate the lower peninsula and concentrate forces at Richmond for a blow against McClellan. The argument on this issue raged all evening and into the next morning. President Davis announced at the end that Johnston's army would be united with Magruder's on the lower peninsula and Norfolk would be held. Johnston, rebuffed, believed that events soon would compel the Confederate government to adopt his view of fighting in front of Richmond.

McClellan sniffed out the defenses of the Yorktown line and, though Johnston called its engineering atrocious, the Union commander hesitated to attack, while building massive siege emplacements for his troops and guns.

★ ★ ★

The concentration of Confederate forces against McClellan left only Jackson in the position to make a strategic move. Johnston and Lee saw this. However, they conceived Jackson's opportunity in terms of distracting Lincoln and inducing him to retain excessive forces to defend Washington. Jackson saw it more broadly.

The origin of Jackson's valley plan was an order from General Johnston in early April 1862 after it became clear that the main Confederate army would have to withdraw from the Rapidan and Rappahannock to meet McClellan's threat.

Johnston wanted to keep Banks and his now nineteen thousand–man force from reinforcing McClellan, but he also wanted to preserve the rich Shenandoah and save the valley town of Staunton from capture. On the Virginia Central Railroad, running from Richmond to a point near Covington, Staunton was being threatened not only by Banks coming south up the valley but by Frémont marching east over the Alleghenies with more than fifteen thousand men.

The Confederacy had only modest resources to deny the valley to the Federals. By recruiting after the battle of Kernstown, Jackson had increased his little "Army of the Shenandoah" to six thousand men. Facing Frémont at Buffalo Gap, about nine air miles west of Staunton, was a force of twenty-eight hundred men under Brig. Gen. Edward Johnson. Maj. Gen. Richard S. Ewell's eight thousand–man division, resting close by on the eastern slopes of the Blue Ridge Mountains near Gordonsville, was ready when Stonewall called for it. A West Pointer (class of 1840) who turned his head sideways when he talked, Ewell was dyspepsic, bald, bug-eyed, eccentric; he was also a superb horseman, a former Indian fighter, and a capable field general. He, like Jackson, believed in speed and traveling light. "The road to glory," he told a subordinate, "cannot be followed with much baggage."[14] Total Rebel troops were about seventeen thousand, fewer than half the Union forces arrayed against them.

Johnston asked only to save the valley and the main east-west Virginia railroad connection. But Jackson conceived a much more ambitious campaign to defeat Frémont and Banks, prevent their juncture, and drive Banks out of the valley.

After Kernstown, Banks came after Jackson up the valley, but his pace was slow. On April 17, however, he seized New Market, forcing Jackson back through Harrisonburg, twenty-five miles north of Staunton. Jackson now stood between Banks and Frémont, whose advance units under Brig. Gen. Robert H. Milroy were in the vicinity of Monterey, thirty-five miles west of Staunton.

Jackson knew he could not stay on the valley pike. Banks might turn his western flank and so threaten Edward Johnson at Buffalo Gap that Johnson would have to withdraw for fear of being assailed on the front by Frémont and the rear by Banks.[15] If Johnson had to withdraw east or south of Staunton, he would be separated from Jackson, while Frémont could pass the Allegheny barrier without opposition and unite with Banks. This would put Jackson's army in jeopardy, even if Ewell came up to help.

On April 19 Jackson moved his army out of direct danger by marching fifteen miles due east of Harrisonburg to Conrad's Store (present-day Elkton) at the base of Massanutten Mountain, an enormous block over three thousand feet high isolated in the midst of the Shenandoah Valley.

Massanutten runs forty-five miles northeast with Harrisonburg and Conrad's Store at its southern anchor and Strasburg and Front Royal at its northern end. Only one road crossed this great massif: about halfway between the northern and southern ends, a twelve-mile stretch ran from New Market on the valley pike to Luray. To the west of Massanutten, the rich, mostly open main valley spread out ten to fifteen miles wide before reaching the steep slopes of the Alleghenies. To the east ran the narrow, deeply wooded Luray Valley, in a few places five or six miles wide but mostly squeezed to a width of a couple of miles or less between Massanutten and the sharply rising Blue Ridge to the east. Down the main Shenandoah Valley runs the North Fork of the Shenandoah River, while down the Luray Valley courses the bolder South Fork, fordable at only a few places. The two forks unite at Front Royal.

At Conrad's Store Jackson was protected defensively because he was east of the strong-flowing South Fork and, if attacked, could escape through Swift Run Gap in the Blue Ridge immediately to the east. Banks, meanwhile, seized Harrisonburg. If he marched on Staunton Jackson could assail his left flank. But his position was no protection for Edward Johnson at Buffalo Gap facing Milroy's advance.

The situation in eastern Virginia now worsened dramatically. Lee wrote Jackson on April 21 that McDowell's corps was about to move toward Fredericksburg. This proved that Lincoln believed Banks could keep Jackson in the valley and McDowell now could march on Richmond. "If you can use General Ewell's division in an attack on Banks," Lee wrote, "it will prove a great relief to the pressure on Fredericksburg."[16]

Jackson already had made plans for a counter in a wholly unexpected direction, using his and Ewell's forces. He told only General Lee in a letter of April 29 and General Ewell when Ewell arrived on April 30 with his division at Conrad's Store in response to Jackson's summons.[17] Even to Lee and Ewell, however, Jackson sketched only the barest outline of his thinking.

Jackson had reason for secrecy. The plan was a stunning strategic concept designed to neutralize three separate Union armies, all far larger than his, and jeopardize McClellan's advance up the peninsula. The plan also offered conclusive evidence that great strategic gains can be achieved without bloodshed.

Jackson himself and his six thousand men were marching away as Ewell arrived and occupied the campsite. Jackson instructed Ewell merely to remain at Conrad's Store to watch Banks and attack him if he moved on Staunton. All Jackson told his cavalry commander, Turner Ashby, was to "feel out" the Federals toward Harrisonburg.

Ewell was not happy about being left in the dark and without a clear mission. When Col. James A. Walker of the Thirteenth Virginia Regiment arrived at his headquarters, Ewell asked abruptly: "Colonel Walker, did it ever occur to you that General Jackson is crazy?" Walker had been one of Jackson's cadets, and he answered: "I don't know, General. We used to call him 'Tom Fool Jackson' at the Virginia Military Institute but I do not suppose that he is really crazy."

Ewell stormed: "I tell you, sir, he is crazy as a March hare. He has gone away, I don't know where, and left me here with instructions to stay until he returns. But Banks's whole army is advancing on me and I have not the most remote idea where to communicate with General Jackson. I tell you, sir, he is crazy."[18]

It was perhaps fortunate for their future relationship that Ewell at this time didn't know how ingrained Jackson's resistance was to telling plans to his subordinates.

Ashby, likewise, did not realize that his was a screening move to keep Banks from learning of Jackson's departure soon enough to contest it. Neither he nor Ewell knew that Jackson was marching his army to Port Republic, twelve miles south of Conrad's Store, and then *east* over the Blue Ridge through Brown's Gap, on a steep road made extremely difficult by recent rains.

Jackson's method of operation was to "mystify, mislead and surprise," and his march east of the Blue Ridge did all of this—while also frightening the enemy and bewildering his own men besides.[19] Jackson and his army emerged at Mechums River station on the Virginia Central Railroad about nine miles west of Charlottesville. But after his men had climbed aboard cars waiting for them there, the train moved not east toward Richmond, as the men were expecting, but west, back into the valley and Staunton! For Jackson's target was General Milroy and his force advancing across the Alleghenies.

Few marches have had such consequences as Jackson's roundabout journey from Conrad's Store to Staunton.

Many observers at first thought Jackson was going to Richmond to fight McClellan, a conclusion he deliberately fostered by his march to the railway at Mechums River. This deception avoided a direct move to the aid of Edward Johnson, which would have given Milroy warning and a chance to bring up substantial reinforcements. The march, therefore, left Milroy isolated and made his defeat all but certain. Far more important for the defense of the Confederacy, the move *also* held McDowell at Fredericksburg. Union secretary of war Edwin M. Stanton, fearing that Jackson might be heading to attack him by way of Gordonsville, told McDowell that his first job was to defend Washington and not to move until Jackson's intentions were better known.

Jackson's march prevented any possibility that three currently separated Federal armies could combine into a force of more than seventy thousand men, far greater than anything the Confederacy could bring against it. A combined army could have defended Washington and still marched against Richmond to aid McClellan. If this had happened, Richmond could not have been saved and the Confederate army would have been shattered if it had attempted to fight. These separated armies were Frémont's beyond the Alleghenies, Banks's in the valley, and McDowell's at Fredericksburg. Union generals Shields and Rosecrans had proposed such a concentration and Banks and Frémont were already moving toward a junction.

But Jackson's march east and then back west to Staunton held McDowell in doubt and motionless, interposed Jackson's army between Frémont and Banks, and gave him an opportunity to defeat each detached army separately.

The march had the wholly unanticipated additional effect of making Jackson's task against Banks only *half* as difficult, because it caused Stanton and Lincoln to divide Banks's army in two and send half to McDowell at Fredericksburg—to reinforce him if Jackson attacked and to help in the march to Richmond if he did not. This dramatic reduction of the Union army opened dazzling new opportunities for Jackson in the Shenandoah.

For losing half of his army, Banks himself was partly to blame. When Jackson marched off from Conrad's Store, Banks was sitting at Harrisonburg, but he was lusting for a share in the fame he was certain was coming to Union arms east of the Blue Ridge. Banks wanted out of the valley and therefore found it easy to play down both the appearance of Ewell at Conrad's Store and Jackson's mystifying departure from it. On April 28 he had telegraphed the War Department that he was "entirely secure" at Harrisonburg. When Jackson crossed the Blue Ridge he reported Jackson "bound for Richmond" and suggested that his corps be sent to McDowell or McClellan.[20]

After talking with President Lincoln, Secretary Stanton took Banks at his word. But instead of following Banks's suggestion, he ordered him to *send* Shields's division to General McDowell at Fredericksburg. Banks himself, with his remaining ten thousand men, was to remain in the valley.

Neither Stanton nor Lincoln demonstrated any real understanding of military strategy and therefore overlooked precisely what Banks had overlooked—that cutting the Union army in the

Shenandoah in half presented an irresistible opportunity to Jackson—if he by chance returned to the valley—to defeat this detached fragment and drive to the Potomac River. If this happened, it would terrify Lincoln, anxious as he was for the safety of Washington. But Lincoln and Stanton, convinced that Jackson was moving either east to Richmond or northeast against General McDowell, accepted Banks's word that there was no danger in the valley, and Shields's division moved toward Fredericksburg.

★ ★ ★

The people of Staunton, believing they had been abandoned, were delighted when the trains arrived at the station on May 4 containing Stonewall Jackson's little army. In gratitude some of the ladies produced a properly fitted Confederate uniform for him in the regulation gray. He had been wearing an old VMI cap and the unstylish coat he'd had as a professor at the institute.

Jackson arrived in Staunton the day after Johnston pulled out of the Yorktown line on the lower peninsula, thereby forestalling McClellan's long-delayed bombardment, scheduled for May 6. The Rebels fought a fierce rear-guard action the next day at Williamsburg and another May 7 at Barhamsville on the York River side, and then they slowly retreated to the outskirts of Richmond. Meanwhile, Maj. Gen. Benjamin Huger abandoned Norfolk and retreated with his ten thousand men to Petersburg, where he could assist Johnston. The crew of the *Virginia,* with no home for their ship, ran her ashore and set her afire.

Jackson joined his forces with Edward Johnson's and, with the two hundred cadets of Virginia Military Institute as a reserve, they marched into the Alleghenies against Frémont's advance force. Jackson was fortunate in the enemy he faced in these mountains. Frémont had his fifteen thousand troops spread out in four major packets stretching from McDowell, twenty-seven miles west of Staunton, to Romney, eighty air miles northeast down the valley of the South Fork of the Potomac. Frémont had reasons why this was so, bad roads and difficult supply being the main ones. But these adverse conditions were not insurmountable; Frémont, by his failure to concentrate his forces in the face of the enemy, exhibited a cardinal military blunder that permitted Jackson to defeat him strategically, although Jackson lost the battle.

Waiting for Jackson May 8 in a strong defensive position at the little village of McDowell were brigadier generals Schenck and Milroy with four thousand men. Schenck arrived at midday on the eighth from Franklin and assumed command by seniority. The Union position rested just west of the rain-swollen Bullpasture River and Federal guns commanded the steep road running down to the river bridge. Jackson occupied the high Sitlington's Hill opposite the river and far above the village. The hill was too steep to haul artillery up it and Jackson did not want to endure the casualties that would have resulted had he attacked the Union position directly from the hill. Instead he began to maneuver his main force around McDowell to the north, then onto the Union rear in hopes of blocking the main Federal line of retreat.

Milroy, however, feared that the Confederates were mounting cannons on Sitlington's Hill and received Schenck's approval to attack, although he could not elevate his artillery pieces enough to hit the hill. Milroy sent twenty-five hundred of his West Virginia and Ohio soldiers up two sides of the hill and they demonstrated the effectiveness of rifles loaded with Minié balls. Some of the Rebel soldiers who had never faced small-arms fire before were unprepared for its penetrating power. This applied especially to the Twelfth Georgia Regiment, holding the center of Jackson's line. The valorous but incautious Georgians advanced to the crest to get better sight of the attackers, thereby silhouetting themselves against the sky and offering an excellent target. They refused to move back; as one Georgian said, "We did not come all this way to Virginia to run before Yankees."[21] Jackson got about 5,000 men on Sitlington's Hill and repulsed the Union attacks, but the Confederates lost 498 men (175 in the Twelfth Georgia) to Milroy's 256.

Schenck and Milroy, however, knew their force was no match

for Jackson's and, during the night, slipped quietly away toward Franklin, gaining a march on Jackson's army. Jackson pressed after them, but the Federals delayed him by setting the woods afire and creating a heavy smokescreen. The retreating Union force reached Franklin and, picking up the rest of Schenck's brigade, continued on north.

Jackson captured the Federal wagon train but pursued only to Franklin and turned back. Destroying Milroy's force was not his purpose. His aim was to drive Frémont's army far back into the mountains so it could not join Banks or capture Staunton behind his back, thereby eliminating it as a factor in the second part of the strategic plan. To make doubly sure that Frémont remained bottled up, Jackson dispatched his topographical engineer, Capt. Jedediah Hotchkiss, with a few cavalry to block all of the passes to the north through the Alleghenies by means of felled trees and burned bridges.

NOTES

General sources: Allan, *Campaign of Gen. T. J. (Stonewall) Jackson,* 2–82; Dabney, 252–355; Cooke, 88–137; Henderson, 134–231; Selby, 48–74; Chambers, vol. 1, 407–514; Freeman, *Lee's Lieutenants,* vol. 1, 111–224 and 303–61; Sanger, 38–49; Johnson and Buel, vol. 2, 112–22, 160–288, and 298–313; Freeman, *R. E. Lee,* vol. 2, 30–40 and 50–52; Long, 145–60; Vandiver, 165–234; and Robert G. Tanner, *Stonewall in the Valley* (Garden City, N.Y.: Doubleday and Company, 1976), 8–180.

1. The principal policymaker for the Confederacy was Davis, who jealously retained his constitutional power as commander in chief. See Freeman, *R. E. Lee,* vol. 1, 6–7, and vol. 3, 534–35. Lee exerted strong influence on Davis and was his principal adviser on military affairs. However, since the two leaders shared similar views on how the war should be conducted, there was little examination of alternative strategic approaches.

2. Henderson, 152.

3. Allan, *Campaign of Gen. T. J. (Stonewall) Jackson,* 19–33. Jackson's January 31, 1862, letter to Governor Letcher closed with this: "I desire to say

nothing against the secretary of war. I take it for granted that he has done what he believed to be best, but I regard such a policy [of interfering with a field commander's dispositions] as ruinous" (31). See also Freeman, *Lee's Lieutenants,* vol. 1, 303–4; and Henderson, 151–56.

4. Henderson, 168–69.

5. Ibid., 170.

6. Ibid., 333.

7. The terrain of the Shenandoah Valley rises to the south. Thus the Shenandoah River drains northward and one moving south in the valley goes up, not down.

8. McClellan ordered Banks's main body toward Manassas to shield Washington and the line of the Potomac while the main Union army was moving to the peninsula. Banks's other tasks were to seize Warrenton, advance as far as the Rappahannock, if possible, and reopen the Manassas Gap Railroad running from Manassas to Strasburg to ensure supplies to forces guarding the lower (northern) valley, including a brigade ordered to entrench at Strasburg. See Allan, *Campaign of Gen. T. J. (Stonewall) Jackson,* 43 and 45.

9. Garnett later became commander of a brigade in George E. Pickett's division and died leading it in Pickett's charge at Gettysburg, July 3, 1863. See ibid., 54 n.

10. Blenker's division left Alexandria ten thousand men strong on about April 1, 1862, but took until May 11 to join Frémont at Petersburg, Grant County, West Virginia, some 170 miles away. Although the country was well settled for most of the route, the division lost its way on one occasion and Gen. W. S. Rosecrans found it with a search party. By the time it got to Frémont the number of men fit for duty was below seven thousand. See ibid., 83 n.

11. Lincoln also created new military departments commanded by Banks and McDowell, removing both commanders from McClellan's control. Secretary of War Edwin Stanton instructed McDowell on April 11, 1862: "You will consider the national capital as especially under your protection and make no movement throwing your force out of position for the discharge of this primary duty." See ibid., 57 n. and 85.

12. For a full analysis of the *Monitor* and the *Merrimac,* see Johnson and Buel, vol. 1, 692–750.

13. Longstreet, 66; Sanger, 42. Longstreet's memoirs are the only authority for the idea that Jackson proposed an attack behind Washington in early April, 1862. Jackson had urged such a course in the fall of 1861 through G. W. Smith but it is likely that Longstreet confuses the sequence and that, in this instance, he refers to Jackson's proposal in late May, 1862 (see chapter 5).

14. *Official Records,* vol. 12, pt. 3, 890.

15. On April 20, 1862, Johnson fell back even farther, to West View, only seven miles west of Staunton. See Allan, *Campaign of Gen. T. J. (Stonewall) Jackson,* 66.

16. *Official Records,* vol. 12, pt. 3, 859; Freeman, *R. E. Lee,* vol. 2, 36–37; Johnston, 109; and Allan, *Campaign of Gen. T. J. (Stonewall) Jackson,* 62–63.

17. Jackson's letter to Lee is printed in *Official Records* (vol. 12, pt. 3, 372) and in Allan, *Campaign of Gen. T. J. (Stonewall) Jackson* 68 n. In it he recommended as his first choice reinforcing Johnson, stopping Frémont, then turning on Banks. However, he also gave Lee another choice, which provides a dazzling glimpse into the depth and scope of his strategic thinking. He could, Jackson wrote, move north down the South Fork of the Shenandoah and cross over to Sperryville east of the Blue Ridge. From Sperryville he could move either on Front Royal and Winchester or on Warrenton, only twenty-five miles from Centreville and Manassas and the main Federal defensive positions protecting Washington. In this letter Jackson sketched a complete "plan with branches" that would, by the movement of his forces along a single line, immobilize the Washington garrison, keep McDowell's corps from marching to aid McClellan, and force Banks into retreat. At Harrisonburg Banks's army would have been in danger of destruction by Jackson's closing off its communications, since Jackson could have severed Banks's two supply lines, one by way of the Manassas Gap Railroad, which passed through Front Royal, and the other by Winchester, served by a railway from Harpers Ferry. Jackson could have ensured this triple strategic result entirely by marching on Sperryville, expending no lives in the process. The only flaw in his plan, which Jackson saw instantly and which led him to reject it as his primary choice, was that it did not eliminate the danger of Frémont, who, if Jackson marched beyond the Blue Ridge, could move on and capture Staunton. If Jackson could have received five thousand reinforcements, which he had requested, it is likely that he would have used them to assist Edward Johnson in driving back Frémont's advance detachment at McDowell and would have marched to Sperryville with the

remainder of his troops. However, he expected no additional men, and Lee on the next day (April 30) wrote him that the threat of McDowell at Fredericksburg and McClellan on the peninsula prevented his sending Jackson any more troops (see Lee's letter, in *Official Records,* vol. 12, pt. 3, 875; Walter H. Taylor, 38; Allan, *Campaign of T. J. (Stonewall) Jackson,* 65). Nevertheless, no other general in the Civil War, with the exception of the Union commander William Tecumseh Sherman, exhibited such spectacular strategic thinking as Jackson did in this single proposal.

18. *Southern Historical Society Papers,* vol. 9, 364. See also Freeman, *Lee's Lieutenants,* vol. 1, 350–51.

19. The full statement on Jackson's battle philosophy comes from Brig. Gen. John D. Imboden, who quotes Jackson as saying there are two things never to lose sight of by a commander: "Always mystify, mislead and surprise the enemy, if possible; and when you strike and overcome him, never let up in the pursuit so long as your men have strength to follow; for an army routed, if hotly pursued, becomes panic-stricken and can then be destroyed by half their number. The other rule is, never fight against heavy odds, if by any possible maneuvering you can hurl your own force on only a part, and that the weakest part, of your enemy and crush it. Such tactics will win every time and a small army may thus destroy a large one in detail and repeated victory will make it invincible." See Johnson and Buel, vol. 2, 297. Field Marshal Viscount Wolseley described these maxims in 1889 as "golden sentences which comprise some of the most essential of all principles of war." See Wolseley's *The American Civil War: An English View,* edited by James A. Rawley (Charlottesville: University Press of Virginia, 1964), xxiii. G. F. R. Henderson writes that Jackson learned the truth of the famous Napoleonic maxim that in war the moral is to the physical (that is, to armament and numbers) as three to one. "He learned, in a word, that war is a struggle between two intellects rather than the conflict of masses and it was by reason of this knowledge that he played on the hearts of his enemies with such extraordinary skill" (Henderson, 638–39).

20. Henderson, 219.

21. Ibid., 228.

4

THE SWEEP TO THE POTOMAC

★ ★ ★ Stonewall Jackson's repulse of Frémont's advance guard at McDowell had dramatically altered the situation in the Shenandoah Valley. With no chance now of joining Frémont, Banks was in positive danger at Harrisonburg. Shields's division was moving to join McDowell and Banks was left with only ten thousand men. Meantime, Jackson was marching toward him with nine thousand men after absorbing Edward Johnson's force, while Ewell, with eight thousand, could advance at any moment from Conrad's Store.

Suddenly feeling his isolation, Banks withdrew fifty miles north to Strasburg. Here the Manassas Gap Railroad brought him supplies from Washington and he was only about fourteen miles south of his rear base at Winchester. At Strasburg, Banks posted seventy-four hundred of his men and started building strong entrenchments facing the valley pike to the south, down which he now feared Ewell or Jackson—or both—might attack. Banks placed fifteen hundred men at Winchester and one thousand at Front Royal, ten miles east, where the Manassas Gap Railroad crossed the Blue Ridge.

On May 14 Jackson ordered Ewell to follow Banks down the valley. Jackson added significantly: "[Banks] will be liable to be attacked as soon as he shall have sufficiently weakened his forces on this side of the Shenandoah."[1]

Ewell was eager to oblige, but he had received a contradictory order dated May 13 from General Johnston: if Banks moved out of the valley to join McDowell, Ewell and Jackson should march to the assistance of the small Confederate force in a blocking position at Fredericksburg or join the main army at Richmond.[2]

Jackson immediately wired the Confederate commander that Banks was fortifying at Strasburg and he was moving down the valley to attack him. He would continue on this course, he said, unless Johnston directed otherwise.[3]

Johnston responded that it would be too hazardous to attack in such a situation and that Banks should be left "in his works." Ewell, Johnston said, should come eastward while Jackson remained to observe Banks.[4]

This was not in the least what Jackson had in mind, for the plan he had devised would dispose of Banks and his works, but he needed Ewell's division to carry it out. Anyway, he believed that he had received the necessary support in a May 16 letter from General Lee: "Whatever movement you make against Banks do it speedily and if successful drive him back toward the Potomac and create the impression, as far as practicable, that you design threatening that line."[5]

Jackson countermanded Ewell's instructions and appealed to Lee: "I am of opinion that an attempt should be made to defeat Banks but under instructions just received from General Johnston I do not feel at liberty to make an attack. Please answer by telegraph at once."[6] Lee responded authorizing Ewell to remain.[7]

Jackson now explained to Ewell the dramatic and mystifying strategy that he had conceived. Ewell, no longer believing Jackson to be crazy, became an enthusiastic lieutenant and together they set to work to put it into operation.

While Jackson's force moved onto the valley pike and marched north to New Market, Ewell—to deceive Banks—sent his Louisiana brigade from Conrad's Store around the base of Massanutten Mountain to New Market. The brigade was commanded by Brig. Gen. Richard Taylor, the only son of President Zachary Taylor, educated at West Point, Harvard, and Yale and, before the war, a successful sugar planter in Louisiana.

When Taylor arrived with his Louisianians, many of them French-speaking Cajuns, one of his Creole bands struck up a gay waltz while several of the men, shockingly, danced with one another. The unmusical, Presbyterian Jackson, sitting on a rail fence, stopped sucking on a lemon, watched, then said to Taylor, "Thoughtless fellows for serious work," and returned to his lemon.[8] Jackson was soon to realize that his judgment of the Louisianians was greatly in error and he manfully made it up to Taylor.

The army at New Market had no idea where it was going. Jackson said nothing, telling Taylor merely that his brigade would lead the march the next morning, May 21, and that it was heading north. Jackson instructed Turner Ashby to place a cavalry screen in front of Strasburg while other horsemen cut all communication between the Federal and the Confederate lines to prevent any scouts or spies getting through. On May 22 the cavalry was to follow the route of the army.

The army moved north on the valley pike, Jackson riding with Taylor in the van, the men confidently expecting that they were marching direct on Strasburg. When they got into the village of New Market, Jackson quietly turned the head of the column to the right—up the long, sloping road leading over Massanutten Mountain to Luray! While Banks was waiting at Strasburg for the Confederates to come straight down the pike, the Rebel army had turned completely away and was marching eastward over the one road crossing Massanutten. Taylor, as mystified as any of the men in the army, decided that Jackson was an unconscious poet who wanted the army to enjoy the beauties of the Shenandoah Valley.

Jackson's strategy became much clearer to the soldiers when, hours later, the army filed into the Luray Valley and found Ewell's soldiers waiting. In one swift maneuver Jackson had concentrated all of the Confederate troops in his command.

When the combined army then turned north from Luray toward Front Royal, the soldiers realized that the unified force of seventeen thousand men was going to fall on the Union flank and rear—though Banks and the leaders in Washington had not the slightest inkling. Secretary Stanton had been encouraged by Jackson's withdrawal from in front of Frémont and, suspecting nothing, had authorized McDowell, reinforced by Shields, to move south of Fredericksburg on May 26 on Richmond to the aid of McClellan.[9]

Front Royal was indefensible and Banks had made a great mistake in stationing a thousand Union troops there under Col. J. R. Kenly with not a single cavalryman to scout for hostile advances. Front Royal lies in a depression with high ground overlooking it everywhere but to the northeast. The South Fork of the Shenandoah borders the town on the west, with only side-by-side road and railway bridges crossing it just before it joins the North Fork north of town. The only route of retreat was across these bridges and then across the pike bridge over the North Fork only a couple of hundred yards beyond. The garrison easily could be surprised and overwhelmed by a Rebel army now seventeen times its size.

Kenly's only strengths were two ten-pounder Parrott guns, muzzle-loaded three-inch rifles that were extremely accurate up to nineteen hundred yards.

On the morning of May 23 Jackson—showing far better tactical dispositions than he had demonstrated at Kernstown—sent cavalry on the west side of the South Fork to cut the rail and telegraph lines and prevent retreat to or reinforcement from Strasburg. He moved infantry around to flank the Federals and seize the Parrotts from the east while other infantry assailed them from the south.

The Federals were thrown into a panic and only the effective fire of the Parrotts north of town permitted most of them to rush over the bridges and get beyond the North Fork. The Federals tried to burn the pike bridge but only damaged it, and 250 Confederate cavalry got across the river by a ford and charged the shaky Union infantry when it made a stand at Cedarville, three miles north. Never, Jackson said, had he seen such a magnificent charge of cavalry. The Federals dispersed through woods and orchards with the Rebel horsemen right behind. They brought in six hundred Union prisoners. Total Federal casualties were 904, Confederate, 26. In the fighting, Taylor's Louisianians distinguished themselves. Jackson made no comment, but Taylor writes that he "looked at me kindly."[10]

By massing his forces at Strasburg and leaving a weak garrison at Front Royal, Banks set himself up for defeat even if he had kept his entire force of nineteen thousand. Jackson had distracted his opponent by adopting a strategy similar to that which Napoleon had followed when he unexpectedly moved around the flanks of Austrian armies in the Marengo campaign of 1800 and the opening act of the Austerlitz campaign of 1805. Jackson had entirely deceived Banks as to his movements and objective. His cavalry at Strasburg gave the impression that this was the target, while his move of Taylor's Louisiana brigade around from Conrad's Store led Banks to believe that Jackson was concentrating his army preparatory to a strike down the pike. Instead he marched in a different direction, swiftly united his army, and struck an exposed and now-indefensible fragment of Banks's force.

Jackson had learned, as Col. G. F. R. Henderson writes, "that war is a struggle between two intellects rather than a conflict of masses."[11] He realized that an indirect approach was far more likely to ensure his opponent's unreadiness to meet it. Like Hannibal, who advanced through the supposedly impassable Arnus marshes of Tuscany to get at the rear of the Roman army in 217 B.C., Jackson chose a long and difficult roundabout march rather than hazard a direct attack. He knew what to expect on his march. But he could not predict, nor can any commander predict, the effects of a frontal assault against a prepared and resolute enemy, such as Banks was at Strasburg. All physical obstacles are inherently less formidable than the hazards of battle. Human resistance is the one great incalculable in warfare. No general can predict human response, and therefore, great generals avoid battle whenever they can.

There can, perhaps, be no more powerful example of the contrast between commanders than the response of Jackson and Johnston to the entrenchments of Strasburg. Johnston, a solidly conventional soldier, assumed that any attack on Banks would be frontal and thus dismissed it as too hazardous. He decided that Banks must be left "in his works." Jackson did not consider making a perilous direct assault but he also knew that Banks would achieve a victory if left in possession of Strasburg, since McDowell, with no threat to Washington to worry about, could march on Richmond. Jackson resolved this dilemma with a strategic turning movement to force Banks out of his strong position and throw him into precipitate retreat without a single Rebel soldier being launched against the Strasburg fortifications.

In approaching Front Royal, Jackson had taken the line Banks least expected and for which he had prepared the least defense. Banks waited in vain at Strasburg. In one brilliant and unanticipated stroke Jackson not only avoided such a bloody confrontation but achieved complete surprise at the selected point of attack. At the same time, he severed Banks's direct rail link with Washington, sealed off Banks's retreat route to the east, placed himself on Banks's flank, and was as close to Winchester, his main rear base, as Banks himself.

It's possible that Banks was so insensitive that he did not immediately appreciate the significance of the blow Jackson had struck. This may explain why he refused, until the morning of May 24, to move from Strasburg. More likely, however, Jackson had affected Banks's ability to make decisions and he responded with stunned immobility and denial. Evidence of this is that Col. George H. Gordon believed that Banks was "afraid of being thought afraid," and this accounts for his outburst when Gordon pleaded with him to move back: "By God, sir, I will not retreat!

We have more to fear, sir, from the opinions of our friends than the bayonets of our enemies!"[12]

When Banks at last acknowledged his jeopardy at around 10 A.M., May 24, he realized that his eastern exit was closed and retreat westward over the Alleghenies impossible because of bad roads and inadequate supply routes. He therefore ordered an immediate withdrawal to Winchester, abandoning a mountain of supplies. Once ordered, the retreat went fast.[13]

Jackson sent Ewell's main force straight down the direct road from Front Royal toward Winchester, but he struck toward the valley pike at Middletown, five miles north of Strasburg, in hopes of blocking Banks. He failed. Gordon had prudently sent out a Pennsylvania cavalry regiment east of Middletown to keep the pike open till the army was through. It delayed Turner Ashby's horsemen and the Louisiana brigade long enough for Banks's main force to get north of the village. Ewell's cavalry under George H. Steuart struck at Newtown, five miles farther north, caused wagons to overturn, and gave hungry Rebels a few minutes to plunder. But Federal infantry from Middletown drove the riders away and Steuart returned to Ewell.

The biggest engagement of the day was at Middletown, where Ashby and the Louisiana brigade encountered the rear guard of two thousand Union cavalry with a battery and a small group of infantry. There was a fierce firefight at close quarters before the Federal survivors escaped, mostly by smaller roads to the west.

Jackson's infantry then moved north on the pike after the fleeing Federals, but the foot cavalrymen were tired after days of hard marching and the pace was slow. Jackson feared he would not catch Banks's infantry but he was confident that his cavalry at least would block Banks's wagon train. By the time Jackson got to Newtown, however, he found that Ashby's cavalry advance had melted away. Nearly all of the horsemen had stopped to pillage halted wagons and, especially, to seize horses. Many led captured animals back to their homes, taking one or two days to make the journeys and abandoning the army for this period. The Rebels had to supply their own horses and this, to some extent, explains what happened. Nevertheless, this breakdown in discipline largely nullified the usefulness of Ashby's cavalry.

Encouraged by the failure of pursuit, Banks sent back an infantry force to Newtown. This slowed the Confederates until nightfall, when Banks's army reached Winchester. Though his men were dropping in the road from exhaustion, Jackson was determined to prevent Banks from organizing a strong defense or to flee too far toward the Potomac to be caught.

Most of all Jackson wanted to seize a commanding hill southwest of Winchester to prevent the Federals from occupying it in force and with artillery. He drove his soldiers onward deep into the night. At about 1 A.M. on May 25, the chief of the Third Brigade of Jackson's division, Col. Samuel V. Fulkerson, suggested that the men be allowed to rest for an hour or two.

"Colonel," Jackson replied, "I yield to no man in sympathy for the gallant men under my command; but I am obliged to sweat them tonight that I may save their blood tomorrow." The army, he said, had to be in position below the Winchester hills by daylight. "You shall, however," Jackson added, "have two hours' rest."[14]

The column halted. Thousands of Rebel soldiers slumped in their tracks and fell asleep in the road.

At 4 A.M. on Sunday, May 25, Jackson, who'd kept watch as his men slept, passed the word down the column for the men to arise. They quickly got under arms and were on their way. Jackson had not heard from Ewell but had sent a message to him at about 2:30 A.M. to be on his right and in order of battle at Winchester at daybreak.

When the vanguard Stonewall Brigade reached Abrams Creek in front of the hill and began to deploy in the dawn's light, it was clear that the Federals held a skirmish line on the hill but nothing else. Banks's army was standing along another broken ridge lined in places with drystone walls some eight hundred yards north and just outside the town. The failure of Banks to mount his artillery and his main line of defense on the first crucial elevation with the creek in front is an indication of his distraction. The battle would have been closer and more bloody for the South if Banks had done so.

Though Banks's dispositions were otherwise good, his situation was desperate. He had lost the Front Royal garrison and about fifteen hundred of his rear guard, scattered at Middletown. He had no more than seventy-five hundred men and they had been discouraged by the retreat, whereas Jackson had concentrated about sixteen thousand men invigorated by success.

Union colonel Gordon's brigade held the turnpike and the hills to the west while Col. Dudley Donnelly's brigade faced Ewell to the east of the pike, protected by Abrams Creek.

Jackson's plan of attack was excellent, demonstrating that he had absorbed the mistakes of Kernstown and had matured into a first-rate tactician. Two brigades were to attack Gordon, while Ewell was to fall directly on Donnelly, holding both Union brigades in place. Once the Union army had been committed to defending its line, Jackson planned to send a heavy column around Gordon's right, or west, flank to sweep onto the Federal rear.

Jackson ordered the Stonewall Brigade and Col. John A. Campbell's Second Brigade to climb the hill beyond Abrams Creek and drive in the Union pickets. Meantime, the Twenty-first North Carolina in Isaac R. Trimble's brigade of Ewell's division attacked on the east through early morning fog along the creek. The Federals resisted stoutly behind stone walls and drove the Tar Heels back with several score casualties. A little later, when the mist lifted somewhat, Ewell opened up with artillery and moved around the Federal left flank. His was not an extremely vigorous attack, but it kept Donnelly's brigade in place, and that was all he was supposed to do.

On the west, Jackson rode up the hill just behind the Stonewall Brigade and discovered that, on a ridge four hundred yards in his front—about halfway to the Federal line—Union gunners had mounted eight rifled guns protected by an infantry regiment. These swept the hill the Rebels were on with shells and heavy rifle fire. Jackson ignored the fire, which wounded Colonel Campbell but missed him.

Jackson ordered up two more batteries to assist the single battery already there. These batteries suffered heavily from the Federal artillery and rifle fire from sharpshooters. It took more than an hour to drive the Federal guns away; though the Confederate cannons helped, it was rifles that did the major job.[15]

Because of the distances involved, the Stonewall Brigade and Campbell's brigade did not closely engage the Union infantry to their front. Rather, they engaged in the artillery duel and exchanged long-range rifle fire. Against a stronger and more enterprising enemy the two brigades' failure to hold the enemy in a tight battle embrace could have caused Jackson's flank attack to go awry, as it had at Kernstown. Indeed, Gordon, anticipating such a move, sent two regiments and a battery to his western flank.

Jackson decided to launch the flank movement at once, calling up Taylor's and Fulkerson's brigades, with W. C. Scott's in reserve.

The two brigades formed in a long line and climbed the hill. Taylor himself rode in front. His men marched forward in perfect order and without firing a shot, ignoring the Union fire from a stone wall that hit some of them. Halfway up the hill and within hearing of the Federal soldiers, Taylor gave the order to charge, and the entire line broke into a run and rushed forward. Gordon's regiments and the single battery could not stand before this relentless assault, and the men tumbled down the hill.

Gordon, seeing his line beginning to crumble, ordered a charge with his cavalry. As the Union horsemen rode bravely forward, the Confederate line halted and fired rolling volleys that emptied many saddles and sent the remaining cavalry flying away. Here, for all to see, was evidence that the day of the cavalry charge was ended.

Seeing the Union soldiers reeling from the flank attack, the Rebel brigades on the hill rose up and charged. As the men rushed forward, ten thousand men bearing down on the Union lines from two directions, they joined in the wild "Rebel yell" that became the harbinger of the charge—encouraging the Rebels, unnerving the Federals.

The greatly outnumbered Union troops were unable to hold before this massive onslaught and they gave way, many of them fleeing in panic, pulling Donnelly's brigade on the east after them in their flight. The Rebels pressed directly behind and both sides rushed into the streets of Winchester and out again northward, the Union order quickly disintegrating.

Near the outskirts of town, Jackson met Taylor. Without a word, he reached over from his saddle, silently wrung Taylor's hand, and hurried on. In this way he apologized for his assertion that the Louisianians were "thoughtless fellows for serious work."

Union soldiers, in increasing chaos, rushed toward the Potomac, twenty-five miles away.

Jackson did not want a repetition of the battle of Manassas. He wanted to exploit this victory and looked around for his cavalry to pursue and round up the fleeing Federals. But he found none at hand. Ashby had only a few men present for duty this day and these had gone east at daybreak to Berryville, expecting that the enemy might try to escape through Snicker's Gap in the Blue Ridge. Ashby had not been heard from since. Ewell's cavalry commander, General Steuart, had two cavalry regiments on the right, but no one knew where he was.

"Never," cried Jackson, "was there such a chance for cavalry! Oh, that my cavalry were in place!"[16]

With no horsemen, Jackson had no alternative but to advance the artillery horses and have the infantry follow. But this was a gesture of despair. The artillery horses were exhausted and the infantry scarcely less so.

Jackson was oblivious to the fatigue. "Order every battery and brigade forward to the Potomac," he cried, and pressed forward himself.[17] But few men, and no cavalry, followed. He sent one of his staff, Lt. Alexander S. Pendleton, to find Steuart and bring him up to pursue the fleeing enemy. Steuart was about two and a half miles east of Winchester, his six hundred men dismounted and the horses grazing. When Pendleton delivered Jackson's order Steuart replied stiffly that he was under Ewell's command and would not move until Ewell said so. Young Pendleton rushed to find Ewell, who authorized Steuart's immediate departure.

It took Steuart two hours to get his cavalry under way, and this was enough for the Federals to rush out of range of effective pursuit. When Ashby came up even later, he had no satisfactory answer why he had not returned sooner.

Against four hundred Confederate casualties, Jackson's army caused three thousand Federal losses, mostly prisoners of war, and gained ninety-three hundred rifles, two field guns, many wagons, and rich commissary supplies, especially medicines and bandages, which the South desperately needed. Impressive as these figures were, Jackson was unable to destroy Banks's entire army.

The failure had to be laid at the feet of Stonewall Jackson. He had been remiss in allowing his cavalry virtually a free hand. Part of the reason for this was respect for Turner Ashby and recognition that his men idolized him for his bravery and audacity. But Ashby was no disciplinarian and his failure to control his men left Jackson virtually without cavalry at critical moments on May 24 and 25, 1862.

Jackson's broader failure rested on his excessive fear of divulging his plans. This permitted him to conceive plans that led to stunning victories but inhibited him from giving his commanders explicit instructions in advance on how to exploit his successes. He knew precisely what he wanted to do in attacking Banks on the road from Strasburg to Winchester on May 24, and he anticipated a victory and a chance for a great cavalry roundup between Winchester and the Potomac after the battle. If he had confided in advance in his cavalry commanders, Ashby almost certainly would have made extraordinary efforts to carry out his wishes, and Steuart, though a stiff-necked pedant, might have performed properly had he known what was expected of him.

Most of Banks's survivors found sanctuary at Williamsport,

thirty-six miles away on the Potomac, though some got to Harpers Ferry, twenty-five miles from Winchester. There was now manifestly no Union force that could interpose itself between Jackson and either a drive into Maryland and Pennsylvania or a swing around behind Washington to seize Baltimore.

The spectacular rout of Banks had an immediate effect. Abraham Lincoln wired McClellan that he thought Jackson's movement "is a general and concerted one, such as could not be if he was acting upon the purpose of a very desperate defense of Richmond. I think the time is near when you must either attack Richmond or give up the job and come to the defense of Washington."[18] Secretary Stanton, in a panic, telegraphed the governors of the Northern states to prepare all of their armed forces for a sudden call. Lincoln, once again fearful for the capital, halted McDowell's corps marching south from Fredericksburg and ordered it, in conjunction with Frémont, to cut Stonewall Jackson off and destroy his army.

McDowell protested, and rightly so. He was seventy air miles from Strasburg and on the other side of the Blue Ridge, whereas Jackson was on the hard valley pike, which could carry him to safety well before McDowell arrived.

"It is impossible," McDowell wired Lincoln, "that Jackson can have been largely reinforced. He is merely creating a diversion and the surest way to bring him from the lower valley is for me to move rapidly on Richmond."[19]

Lincoln did not listen, and as Jackson now pushed on toward the Potomac, Lincoln and Stanton believed that they had a great chance to cut Jackson off from his rear. But in stopping McDowell for the third time, Jackson had already done his damage. Rarely in history has a commander been able to achieve such far-reaching, decisive results by such indirect methods and with the expenditure of so few resources.

To men without Jackson's strategic vision, Lincoln and Stanton, for example, Jackson's position far in the north appeared to offer him danger, not opportunity. Banks at Williamsport and Rufus Saxton at Harpers Ferry had about fifteen thousand men with instructions to move south. Frémont was at Franklin with fifteen thousand men, his army at last largely concentrated. From there Lincoln directed him to drive immediately against Harrisonburg, thirty miles over the Alleghenies and eighty miles south of Jackson. Meanwhile, Gen. James Shields, with ten thousand troops from McDowell's corps, moved quickly west toward the valley, with ten thousand more Federals behind him under E. O. C. Ord (shortly superseded by James B. Ricketts). Shields's goal was to get behind Jackson or attack him in flank. Federal forces totaling fifty thousand men were converging on Jackson from three directions.

If Frémont had moved east to Harrisonburg, as Lincoln had ordered, he might have blocked Jackson's retreat up the valley. He actually started in this direction, but Jackson sent a message to Col. John D. Imboden, recruiting at Staunton, to send every man he could find to block the passes leading eastward. Imboden wrote: "I knew that within four miles of Franklin, on the main road leading to Harrisonburg, there was a narrow defile hemmed in on both sides by nearly perpendicular cliffs over five hundred feet high. I sent about fifty men, well armed with long-range guns, to occupy these cliffs and defend the passage to the last extremity."[20] The small body of Confederates allowed the head of Frémont's leading cavalry column to get well into the gorge on May 25 and then poured a deadly volley into the closely packed force. The column halted. The Confederates fired another volley and let out a loud Rebel yell. Frémont was hunting for a reason to avoid marching on Jackson's rear and immediately turned back, taking the road to Moorefield, nearly forty miles north along the South Branch of the Potomac, thus placing himself on the west side of the Shenandoah Mountains about forty miles from Strasburg! His reasons, he explained to Lincoln, were the "impossible" road leading to Harrisonburg and the need to get food for his troops. But his real reason was excessive fear of being cut off from his supplies.[21]

Frémont marched on Strasburg. This now became the point where the Federal pincers were supposed to come together, for

Shields was rapidly approaching Front Royal, only ten miles east.

Jackson, meanwhile, was making menacing moves toward the Potomac, implying that he was about to invade Maryland and exhibiting not the least fear of being cut off.

It was soon to become clear that Stonewall Jackson possessed plans for a far more decisive and dramatic campaign than he had conducted so far. But he already had accomplished the tasks he had set out to do—he had driven Banks from the valley and, far more important, he had saved the Confederacy from fighting a two-front war to preserve Richmond. Now Johnston and Lee had to look only at McClellan. Their rear was secure. And forty thousand Federal troops that might have helped McClellan were either chasing Jackson or guarding Washington's portals against him.

NOTES

General sources: Allan, *Campaign of Gen. T. J. (Stonewall) Jackson,* 87–129; Dabney, 355–86; Cooke, 137–57; Henderson, 232–65; Alexander, *Military Memoirs,* 94–101; Freeman, *Lee's Lieutenants,* vol. 1, 362–410; Douglas, 50–76; Selby, 74–84; Chambers, vol. 1, 515–52; Johnson and Buel, vol. 2, 287–91; R. Taylor, 37 and 38; Freeman, *R. E. Lee,* vol. 2, 50–57; Vandiver, 235–60; and Robert G. Tanner, *Stonewall in the Valley* (Garden City, N.Y.: Doubleday and Company, 1976), 181–259.

1. *Official Records,* vol. 12, pt. 3, 889–90.

2. Ibid., 888; and Freeman, *R. E. Lee,* vol. 2, 52–55.

3. *Official Records,* vol. 12, pt. 3, 894–95.

4. Ibid., 896–97.

5. Ibid., 892–93; Freeman, *R. E. Lee,* vol. 2, 54; Henderson, 233; and Allan, *Campaign of Gen. T. J. (Stonewall) Jackson,* 88.

6. *Official Records,* vol. 12, pt. 3, 898.

7. There is no record of Lee's response, but he probably got President Davis's approval, for Ewell remained under Jackson's command. See Freeman, *R. E. Lee,* vol. 2, 57; Henderson, 235; and Allan, *Campaign of Gen. T. J. (Stonewall) Jackson,* 89.

8. R. Taylor, 49–50.

9. Stanton's authorization, sent to McDowell on May 17, 1862, contained this caveat: "You will hold yourself always in such a position as to cover the capital of the nation against a sudden dash by any large body of Rebel forces" (Allan, *Campaign of Gen. T. J. [Stonewall] Jackson,* 87). Lincoln's instructions to McClellan, sent the same day, are similar: "McDowell has been ordered to march upon that city [Richmond] by the shortest route. He is ordered—keeping himself always in a position to cover the capital from all possible attack—so to operate as to put his left wing in communication with your right. . . . The specific task assigned to his command has been to provide against any danger to the capital of the nation" (Cooke, 138).

10. R. Taylor, 54.

11. Henderson, 638.

12. George H. Gordon, *From Brook Farm to Cedar Mountain* (Boston: James R. Osgood and Company, 1883), 191–93; and Henderson, 247. An indication that Jackson's move had affected General Banks's capacity to make rational judgments is given by Colonel Gordon (citation above), who says that Banks, in response to his repeated requests to order a retreat, refused and kept repeating, "I must develop the force of the enemy." He says that Banks seemed brooding, spiritless, and dejected.

13. Allan, *Campaign of Gen. T. J. (Stonewall) Jackson,* 100–101; and Gordon, 194–98.

14. Freeman, *Lee's Lieutenants,* vol. 1, 393–94; and Douglas, 57.

15. Allan, *Campaign of Gen. T. J. (Stonewall) Jackson,* 113; and Cooke, 150–51.

16. Dabney, 381; *Official Records,* vol. 12, pt. 1, 706 (Jackson's report); and Alexander, *Military Memoirs,* 99–100.

17. Dabney, 381.

18. *Official Records,* vol. 11, pt. 1, 31; and Allan, *Campaign of Gen. T. J. (Stonewall) Jackson,* 120.

19. *Official Records,* vol. 12, pt. 3, 220; Alexander, *Military Memoirs,* 102; and Cooke, 139.

20. Johnson and Buel, vol. 2, 290–91.

21. Allan, *Campaign of Gen. T. J. (Stonewall) Jackson,* 127–28.

5

CARRYING THE WAR TO THE SUSQUEHANNA

★ ★ ★ On the morning of May 30, 1862, Stonewall Jackson's advance troops were making much sound and fury around Harpers Ferry. But it was all a sham. Ever since the battle of Winchester, Jackson had been pressing his quartermasters to get into wagons the mountain of supplies and arms that had fallen to the Confederacy, since there was no railway between Winchester and Strasburg. Today the long wagon train, along with twenty-three hundred Federal prisoners, started south up the valley pike. Behind them most of the army was forming up and moving south as well, to spend the night at Winchester. Only the old reliable Stonewall Brigade remained around Harpers Ferry, veiling the retreat.

Jackson went to Harpers Ferry to watch an artillery duel and some lively skirmishing. It began to rain and Jackson got under a tree for shelter and fell asleep. When he awoke, his old friend and former congressman Col. A. R. Boteler was sketching the general. Jackson looked at the sketch, remarked how poorly he'd done in drawing at West Point, and said: "Colonel, I have some harder work than this for you to do."

While Boteler listened, Jackson began: "I want you to go to Richmond for me. I must have reinforcements. You can explain to them down there what the situation is here. Get as many men as can be spared and I'd like you, if you please, to go as soon as you can."

Jackson then disclosed his plan: if his command were raised to forty thousand men, he would cross into Maryland, "raise the siege of Richmond and transfer this campaign from the banks of the Potomac to those of the Susquehanna."[1]

Here, like the similar plan Jackson had proposed the previous October, was a strategic concept with war-winning possibilities. Even if Jackson retreated far up the valley he could still rush back and strike behind Washington before any Northern army could stop him. Although there were more than sixty thousand Union troops arrayed against Jackson, they were scattered—Banks at Williamsport, Rufus Saxton at Harpers Ferry, McDowell between Fredericksburg and the valley, and Frémont approaching from the Alleghenies. They could not concentrate against him, for McDowell had to shield Washington and the other forces in the valley. Jackson could slip between them and burst across the Potomac.

Jackson's greatest advantage, however, was that McClellan had isolated by far the largest Union army on the peninsula. His was the only force that could defeat Jackson. Even if Lincoln ordered McClellan to move at once, it would take at least a week and probably much longer to assemble a superior army in Maryland. Only ten thousand men at a time could be carried by transports up Chesapeake Bay, necessitating numerous trips to and from Fort Monroe.

In a week or two Jackson could transform the military situation—possibly cutting off Washington's rail communications and food supply, seizing Baltimore and perhaps other cities, and spreading panic. If Washington were isolated, there would be intense pressure to evacuate the government for fear that its members would be captured. A government that could not secure the capital would raise grave doubts among the Northern people as to its capability and would indicate to Britain and France that it was on the verge of defeat. This might lead to their recognition of the Confederacy and a forced end of the war.

The dangers to the Confederacy were much less. McClellan would be unlikely to attack the strong entrenchments in front of Richmond, not only because he had shown himself to be extremely hesitant, but because Lincoln was almost certain to order him to come to Washington's defense the moment he felt it threatened.[2]

Therefore, a move by Jackson into the North at the very least would end the siege of Richmond without a single Southern soldier being sacrificed and would throw the North on the strategic defensive. It might win the war.[3]

However, Lee and President Davis were soon to demonstrate that neither understood the strategic opportunity McClellan had given the South by placing his army where it could not block the North from invasion. They were obsessed with defeating the North's main *army* directly in front of them. They were unwilling to look seriously at Jackson's wholly different strategy: saving Southern lives by striking at the North's *will* to win.

The difference between Lee and Jackson as generals can be seen most cogently in this context. Jackson wanted to move *away* from the Union armies and win indirectly and with little bloodshed by deception, surprise, and distraction. Lee sought to destroy McClellan's army *in place* by frontal attack, main force, and direct blows into the heart of Union strength.

★ ★ ★

As Jackson and Boteler were riding toward Winchester they learned that Shields had driven the Twelfth Georgia Regiment out of Front Royal, while Frémont had arrived only a few miles west of Strasburg. The noose seemed to be tightening, but Jackson was unperturbed. He knew that one of the most difficult tasks in war is to concentrate two separated armies against an enemy, especially, as was true of both detachments, if they cannot communicate with each other and they possess irresolute commanders.

At Winchester, Jackson calmly prepared papers for Boteler, then saw him off to Richmond. The only caution he exhibited was to tell Jed Hotchkiss in the early hours of May 31 to go back and bring the two thousand–man Stonewall Brigade from near Harpers Ferry. If the enemy blocked the brigade, Jackson said, Hotchkiss would have to bring it around through the mountains.

On May 31 the main Army of the Shenandoah filed out of Winchester for Strasburg. Frémont was still six miles west of town, making noises and little else. Shields had remained immobile at Front Royal all of May 30, and on May 31 seemed to be more frightened that Jackson would attack him than resolved to advance himself.[4]

Jackson's victories had caused the Union commanders to credit him with double his actual strength. Neither Shields nor Frémont was willing to confront him alone, and he knew it. Jackson was certain they could never pull off a juncture. Thus the popular image of Jackson's snatching his army at the last moment from the Federal snare is erroneous. It never was in danger.

While Jackson was moving south, Gen. Joseph E. Johnston was sending his army into an attack on McClellan immediately east of Richmond. The two-day battle, May 31 to June 1, known as Seven Pines in the South and Fair Oaks in the North, was mismanaged and confused. Johnston had planned an intricate double-envelopment of the Federal line, but poor staff work turned the battle into a series of piecemeal frontal attacks against well-emplaced Union troops. It cost the Confederacy more than six thousand casualties to the North's five thousand and the services of General Johnston, who sustained a severe wound. Davis placed Robert E. Lee in command of the Rebel forces, which he now began to style the Army of Northern Virginia.

In the Shenandoah now commenced one of the most remarkable running battles in the history of warfare. It lasted a week and extended from Strasburg up the valley some seventy miles to the south. The Federals had orders to seek out and destroy Jackson's army. Frémont and Shields, with James B. Ricketts coming behind, could muster over thirty-five thousand men, more than twice the size of Jackson's whole army. But Jackson knew that he would remain superior to any single Union force so long as he kept the two parts separated. This became his principal objective. And, far from running for his life, Jackson hatched plans to concentrate against each Federal wing and defeat it.

Jackson had one other vital task: he had to get his army to a position where it would be safe from attack and from where it could move to Richmond if Lee called for it—or toward the Potomac if he and Davis authorized an attack into the North.

Jackson had just such a position in mind: the little village of Port Republic, twelve miles southeast of Harrisonburg, where the North and South rivers come together to form the South Fork of the Shenandoah. A bridge spanned North River there and fords gave passage across South River. From the village Jackson could reach an unassailable defensive position at Brown's Gap in the Blue Ridge just to the east, or he could march to the Mechums River railroad station or toward the Potomac.[5]

As his main force moved south up the pike in the main valley, Jackson sent Ewell out to confront Frémont on the morning of June 1, to ensure that the Stonewall Brigade, now slightly north of Strasburg and marching hard for it, could get safely through. Ewell was eager for a fight, but Frémont, though he had moved fast to get within striking distance, now exhibited extreme hesitation at coming to blows. Even Ewell's skirmish line stopped him. Since the Stonewall Brigade soon pushed through Strasburg and on south, Jackson called Ewell back onto the valley pike.

As a Federal juncture at Strasburg had failed, the Union commanders now embarked on the obvious alternative strategy—Frémont moved onto the pike to chase Jackson's tail, hoping to delay his retreat, while Shields turned south from Front Royal up the Luray Valley, with the aim of maneuvering around the east side of Massanutten Mountain and closing on Jackson's rear—hopefully by crossing the only road over Massanutten from Luray to

New Market. Failing this, Shields had two other chances to sweep behind Jackson: by going around the southern base of Massanutten from Conrad's Store or by marching twelve miles farther south and seizing Port Republic.[6]

Jackson saw these possibilities as quickly as the Union generals, and he calculated a way to counter them. The South Fork was a bold stream, made turbulent by heavy rains that now swept the valley, and there were only four bridges that spanned it: two near Luray, one at Conrad's Store, and one at Port Republic.

Jackson immediately resolved to burn the Luray and Conrad's Store bridges. But he took a calculated risk and left intact the Port Republic bridge, in hopes that Shields would be unable to beat him to it. If Jackson lost this span he might be isolated west of the South Fork and cut off from the Blue Ridge.

While Frémont now began to strike hard at Jackson's rear guard, a race began by both sides to get to the crucial South Fork bridges. Shields ordered his cavalry to make straight for the Conrad's Store bridge. He believed that his infantry could reach the Luray bridges before Jackson could save them. Shields was wrong; Turner Ashby's native cavalrymen, who knew every path and byway in the valley, moved faster. When Shields arrived at Luray on June 2 he found the bridges gone. Although he could plainly hear the sound of cannons on the other side of Massanutten, he was unable to go to Frémont's aid, since he had no pontoon bridge. And when his cavalry reached Conrad's Store on June 4 the link was burned and the river in spate there as well.

Shields thought he might still beat Jackson to Port Republic and he ordered his vanguard commander, Col. Samuel S. Carroll, to press forward. Jackson had sent a small cavalry detachment to hold the Port Republic bridge, but it would stand little chance against Carroll's regiments.

Although the valley pike was hard and little affected by the heavy rains, Jackson was slowed by the long wagon train, by the column of Union prisoners, and by Frémont, who exhibited much more energy in pursuit than he had evidenced in battle.

On June 2 near Woodstock the Federal cavalry forced Ashby and Steuart to pull back. Some of Steuart's men broke in panic and fled. The Twenty-seventh Virginia thought they were Federals and fired, causing a stampede. Ashby ended the rout by forming up some infantry stragglers and stopping the charging Federals with rifle volleys. Steuart's officers felt that he had mismanaged the affair and Jackson placed Ashby in command of all the cavalry.

To slow Frémont and allow time for the goods train and prisoner column to get well away, Jackson ordered Ashby on June 4 to destroy the only bridge, at Mount Jackson, over the now-raging North Fork. Frémont was carrying pontoons and actually got them across the stream, but the river rose again and, to avoid losing his floating bridge, he had to cut it loose from the south bank, holding up his army for a full day.

Jackson now made at all speed for Port Republic, with Ashby's horsemen ably shielding the army. Jackson sent his sick and wounded across the North River by ferry at Mount Crawford, moving them to Staunton and sparing them a longer trek. Time after time during the retreat Ashby had exposed himself to protect the army. Near Harrisonburg, after his horse had been shot from under him, he led his supporting infantry on foot in a charge that stopped a Federal rush. In the fight a bullet struck him in the heart and he died. The whole South, and Jackson especially, mourned the loss.

Shortly before reaching Port Republic, Jackson got a bare message from President Davis regretting that he could send Jackson no additional reinforcements for his proposed offensive to the banks of the Susquehanna. Colonel Boteler's mission had failed. Jackson took the news stoically but did not give up.

Jackson's advance force arrived at Port Republic on June 7. The bridge was still in Confederate hands. Jackson had won the race by a single day. Swollen streams prevented Carroll from reaching Port Republic until the next morning.[7]

Jackson could keep Shields from joining Frémont so long as he held this remaining bridge. However, east of the river Shields still could block Jackson's escape route to Brown's Gap, capture the wagon train, which was still only a short distance below Port Republic, and press on to Waynesboro and cut the railway.[8]

Nevertheless, Jackson had ably maneuvered his army into the "central position," as Napoleon described a location between two enemy armies that permitted him to attack one before having to deal with the other. Jackson resolved to strike Shields's division and send it reeling northward. He hoped then to turn on Frémont and drive him back as well.

Jackson left Ewell's division near Cross Keys, five miles northwest of Port Republic, to block Frémont and assembled the remaining troops to deal with Shields, who had allowed his force to become badly stretched out along the Luray Valley, with only two small brigades south of Conrad's Store. Unfortunately, the Federal advance party under Colonel Carroll rushed up to Port Republic on the morning of June 8, scattered Jackson's cavalry vedettes, crossed the South River by a ford, captured part of Jackson's staff and nearly captured Jackson, and threatened the army ammunition train parked just south of the village. Jackson barely escaped over the bridge to the hill above North River where he had posted his artillery. A few Rebel skirmishers and a battery contested the Union cavalry in the village and a hastily organized infantry assault across the bridge drove the Federals back over the South River and liberated the Confederate prisoners.

The same morning Frémont, showing unexpected zeal, came up on Ewell where he was occupying a strong position on wooded hills a mile and a half southeast of Cross Keys. This forced Jackson to deal with him before challenging Shields.

Between Ewell and the village were open fields, across which Frémont's men would have to march. Although Frémont had twice the force of Ewell, his courage vanished when he saw that the Confederates were awaiting him. He had twenty-four regiments but used only five of Louis Blenker's division of Germans and other foreign immigrants under Brig. Gen. Julius Stahel. These Frémont directed on the Confederate right where Brig.

Gen. Isaac R. Trimble's Deep South troops were hidden among oak trees on a flat ridge. Trimble's men lay down and allowed the Union troops to advance within sixty paces in solid, tight lines. Then the Rebels rose abruptly and released a sheet of flame at the surprised and unsuspecting enemy. Stahel's men staggered, attempted to rally, received another blistering volley, and retired.

Trimble moved a regiment through a sheltered ravine on Blenker's left to threaten a flank attack, surprising the "Dutchmen," as the Rebels called them, and forcing them back a mile as Trimble's whole line, aided by two Virginia regiments, pressed forward.

That was about all there was to the battle of Cross Keys. General Milroy engaged in artillery fire with the Confederate center but made no attack. General Schenck made a modest advance on Ewell's left, but Frémont, alarmed by Trimble's advance, ordered him back. Of the total Federal losses of 684 (versus 288 Confederate), Trimble's riflemen accounted for 500 and one regiment, the Eighth New York, was nearly annihilated.

Once more Ewell had mastered Frémont, who cowered on the defensive. Jackson left two brigades to guard Frémont and gathered the rest of his force at Port Republic to dispose of Shields's advance guard, whom scouts had reported were only a short distance north. He hoped to accomplish this quickly and then move back and shatter Frémont.

Early on June 9 Jackson crossed the South River and advanced to meet the waiting Federals a couple of miles north in a mile-wide, mostly cleared valley between the river and the thickly vegetated slopes of the Blue Ridge. He moved up with the Stonewall Brigade and two batteries under General Winder in the lead and Taylor's Louisiana brigade behind. Jackson believed that the rest of his troops would follow quickly. But they had difficulty getting across an improvised bridge of boards laid over wagons pulled into the stream. Although it was rickety, the officers directing the crossing did nothing and the soldiers would cross only one at a time.

As a result, Jackson did not concentrate his forces until late in the day against the small Federal force of three thousand men from Pennsylvania, Ohio, West Virginia, and Indiana, most of whom had fought at Kernstown. They were excellently led by Brig. Gen. Erastus B. Tyler.

The Union general had posted his men well behind a sunken road and small stream running to the river. On the Federal left was an open "coal hearth" where charcoal was prepared on a high terrace, or hill, overlooking the valley, just below the slopes of the Blue Ridge. Here Tyler had posted seven guns that commanded the field. Jackson sent two Stonewall Brigade regiments and a battery to assault the guns from the Blue Ridge flank. But mountain laurel slowed the men, and the Union gunners and guarding infantry, hearing them approach, drove them back with rifle and canister fire.

The guns from the coal hearth enfiladed the rest of the Stonewall Brigade and one Louisiana regiment that Jackson sent against the stream and sunken road. Heavy fire began to cut up the Confederates and they retreated, causing the Union line to advance exultantly. Winder threw in a just-arrived regiment and a single cannon to form his line again, but the Fifth Ohio charged the piece, shot down gunners and horses, and seized it. Two of Ewell's regiments, hurrying forward, drove in the Union flank briefly, but the Federals pushed it off and were on the verge of buckling the Confederate line.

Meanwhile, Jackson had ordered the main body of the Louisiana brigade to assault the guns at the coal hearth. Just as the Confederate left was about to disintegrate, Taylor's Louisianians, arriving undetected by way of a forest path, crashed through the undergrowth onto the guns. Union gunners swung their trails around and fired canister but the Louisianians seized the battery. Federal infantry rushed forward and drove off Taylor's brigade, but some Louisianians, aided by the two regiments under Ewell that had turned toward the coal hearth, stormed the guns once more, this time carrying them.

Tyler saw he must retake the battery or withdraw, because the guns, in Southern hands, would dominate his position. He sent his reserves forward. But he was too late. Ewell's main force had reached the field and a brigade moved toward the hearth. As the Federal soldiers advanced they saw their own cannons turned against them—with Ewell himself serving as a gunner.

The Northerners broke for the rear, pursued by Jackson's cavalry—not absent today as they had been at Winchester. The Ohio regiments checked the cavalry but the horsemen pursued Tyler's force for nine miles north to where Shields, marching desperately toward the sound of the battle, had formed a line.

Jackson had won the field against a much-inferior Federal force, but the cost was the heaviest of the valley campaign: 804 men. Tyler lost one thousand, more than half of them captured.

Before the battle had ended Jackson realized he had no chance to turn back and defeat Frémont. He ordered the small force guarding Frémont to retreat to Port Republic, burn the bridge, and join the army on the east bank. The Rebel guard accomplished this with speed.

Jackson, fearing that Frémont might try to join Shields, called off the pursuit of Tyler and marched the whole army to safety onto the lower cove of Brown's Gap.

Frémont tried to bridge South River but changed his mind. The next day, influenced by his repulse and the fact that Shields, meantime, had withdrawn, Frémont also retreated. Shields blamed his retreat on supposed orders to march with McDowell's corps on Richmond. But McDowell was going nowhere and had authorized Shields to remain if he had a reasonable chance of defeating Jackson.[9] Shields withdrew to Luray, while Frémont, followed by Confederate cavalry, retreated hastily to Harrisonburg and by June 24 had moved all the way to Middletown, ten miles south of Winchester, where Banks and Franz Sigel, who had replaced Saxton, had stopped after advancing from the Potomac.

It was a strange, anticlimactic end to the fighting, the abrupt departure of both pursuing Federal armies. Jackson came down from the Blue Ridge on June 12, pitched camp just below Port Republic, and gave his men a much-needed five-day rest.

Jackson's performance in the battle of Port Republic had not been exemplary. He had failed to work out a speedy method of crossing the ford and had allowed subordinates to oversee the passage. This delayed much of the army and nearly caused the Confederate line to break. Only when Ewell's division at last came on the scene was the situation transformed.

Jackson, however, operated under extreme difficulties. Because Frémont was threatening, he had to defeat Shields's advance force speedily. This forced him to attack Tyler in his excellent, narrow defensive position anchored and unturnable against the South Fork and extremely difficult to flank against the Blue Ridge.

Tyler's superb performance eliminated any chance Jackson might have had to defeat Frémont. Thus Jackson could achieve a decisive victory against neither foe.

But a tactical victory was not necessary for Jackson to attain his strategic aims. Indeed, he *already* had gained everything that could be expected by drawing most of McDowell's corps so far from Fredericksburg that it could not be a factor in the upcoming battle in front of Richmond.[10] Yet his own army was at the Blue Ridge, poised, he hoped, to execute a strategic move against Washington. Failing that, he still could march to Richmond.[11]

Jackson's hopes for a counteroffensive into the North had received scant attention, despite the efforts of Colonel Boteler. The threat of McClellan, the unsatisfactory outcome of the battle of Seven Pines, and the change in command made necessary after Johnston was wounded had distracted the leadership. But there was a greater factor, a fixed belief on the part of Lee and Davis that the most important task before the Confederacy was the defense of Richmond and that nothing else could be allowed to interfere.

Lee exemplified this attitude on June 5 when he wrote President Davis that if Jackson could be reinforced, "it would change the character of the war." But, he wrote, this could be done only by convincing the Carolinas and Georgia to dispatch troops, not by sending any men from Richmond. Davis was not prepared to press these states for troops, and the matter lapsed.[12]

Lee also demonstrated his feelings after hearing of Jackson's victories at Cross Keys and Port Republic. He sent Jackson eight thousand reinforcements under brigadier generals W. H. C. Whiting and Alexander R. Lawton, seeking to make Lincoln and Stanton believe that Jackson was planning another offensive. But Lee simultaneously directed Jackson to make secret preparations to move his whole army, including reinforcements, to Ashland, just north of Richmond, to assist in the counterstroke he was preparing against McClellan.[13]

To keep up the pretense that another valley campaign was being threatened, Lee allowed the reinforcements to leave Richmond openly by train and Union captives about to be paroled to witness the departure and learn their destination. Meanwhile, Jackson's cavalry commander, now Col. Thomas T. Munford, pressed Frémont back down the valley pike, convincing the Federal commanders that Jackson's infantry was just behind. Stanton and Lincoln kept Banks and Sigel at Middletown, Shields at Luray, and Ricketts's division at Front Royal. Jackson's infantry, far from pursuing the Federals, continued to rest only a few miles south of Port Republic and close to the Virginia Central Railroad.

While Jackson prepared to move to Richmond he did not give up hope for an offensive beyond Washington. He called in Colonel Boteler on June 13 and asked him to take a letter to the capital to explain his plan and to solicit troops. "By that means," he told Boteler, "Richmond can be relieved and the campaign transferred to Pennsylvania."[14]

Jackson told Boteler to inform Lee that if he could get forty thousand soldiers, he would cross east of the Blue Ridge and proceed northward until he found a gap that would put him on the rear of General Banks's army. Once he had disposed of Banks, Jackson would invade western Maryland and Pennsylvania.

Jackson never outlined a precise battle plan. But by divulging that he would march east of the Blue Ridge he demonstrated that he had already thought out a strategy that would lock all opposing enemy forces in place.[15] The forces protecting Washington could not move for fear that he might directly strike the capital. The forces in the valley had to remain in place for fear that he would seize the Shenandoah. By alternately threatening Washington and the valley Jackson could prevent the juncture of Union forces. And he could defeat any single detachment that might venture against him.

After Jackson had defeated or bypassed the forces guarding the valley and Washington, he could then cross the Potomac, beyond which there were no substantial Union field forces.[16]

Boteler rushed off to Richmond to see Lee. When he arrived, Lee said: "Colonel, don't you think General Jackson had better come down here first and help me to drive these troublesome people away from before Richmond?"[17]

Though Boteler loyally supported Jackson, Lee on June 16 wrote an endorsement on Jackson's June 13 letter, which Boteler brought back. There was no mention of Jackson's plans for an offensive. Boteler was left to state verbally Lee's decision: the pressure on Richmond prevented the detachment of enough troops for an offensive. But Lee's opposition was clear. When he sent Jackson's letter to President Davis, his endorsement said: "I think the sooner Jackson can move this way [toward Richmond] the better—The first object now is to defeat McClellan." Davis endorsed the letter back to Lee, saying: "Views concurred in."[18]

Jackson's proposal never received more than a passing nod from Lee or Davis. Instead Lee was planning to relieve Richmond by a method opposite from that advocated by Jackson—an assault into the teeth of McClellan's awesome military power. Lee's battle plan offered little possibility of destroying this army. The effects of the frontal attack Lee was planning had already been seen in gruesome detail at Seven Pines and at Shiloh in Tennessee on April 6–7, 1862. The cost in blood would be enormous and, to the manpower-weak South, irreplaceable.

When Jackson got the news he made no comment but, leaving his cavalry to guard the valley, secretly set his army in motion for Richmond.

NOTES

General sources: Allan, *Campaign of Gen. T. J. (Stonewall) Jackson,* 130–71; Dabney, 387–434; Cooke, 158–204; Henderson, 265–300; R. Taylor, 26–90; Selby, 84–100; Freeman, *Lee's Lieutenants,* vol. 1, 225–302 and 411–488; Douglas, 68–94; Chambers, vol. 1, 553–97; Johnson and Buel, vol. 2, 291–301; Jackson, 283–84; Alexander, *Military Memoirs,* 101–8; Freeman, *R. E. Lee,* vol. 2, 83–84, 95–96, and 102–4; Vandiver, 261–83; and Robert G. Tanner, *Stonewall in the Valley* (Garden City, N.Y.: Doubleday and Company, 1976), 263–325.

1. A. R. Boteler, *Southern Historical Society Papers,* vol. 40, 165. See also Dabney, 431; Cooke, 158–59; Freeman, *Lee's Lieutenants,* vol. 1, 414 n; and Freeman, *R. E. Lee,* vol. 2, 83–84.

2. Lincoln warned McClellan by telegram on May 25 that he might have to return. See *Official Records,* vol. 11, pt. 1, 32; and Allan, *Campaign of Gen. T. J. (Stonewall) Jackson,* 120.

3. Alexander (*Military Memoirs,* 94) downplays the possibilities of capturing Washington by referring to the forts that McClellan had built around the capital during the winter of 1861–62. Union officials, he says, "might have laughed at any idea of real danger from such an invasion," because "no invasion could maintain itself long enough to carry on a siege, or to do more than fight one great battle." However, Jackson did not need to besiege Washington. He could have isolated it by severing the railways from the north, thereby cutting off supplies. He also needed only to fight "one great battle." If he were victorious, the issue would have been settled.

4. Allan, *Campaign of Gen. T. J. (Stonewall) Jackson,* 133.

5. Dabney (403–4) gives an eloquent description of the fortresslike character of Brown's Gap, with mountains twenty-six hundred feet high dominating it.

6. Allan, *Campaign of Gen. T. J. (Stonewall) Jackson,* 134–35; and U.S. Senate, *Report of the Committee on the Conduct of the War,* Report No. 108 (Washington, D.C.: Government Printing Office, 1863), vol. 1, 265.

7. Allan, *Campaign of Gen. T. J. (Stonewall) Jackson,* 147–48.

8. Jackson sent his twenty-three hundred Federal prisoners ahead to Waynesboro, where they were loaded on trains and sent to Richmond. See ibid., 146.

9. Ibid., 164.

10. On June 1, 1862, Lincoln and Secretary Stanton ordered the nine thousand–man division under Brig. Gen. George A. McCall in McDowell's corps to move by water from Fredericksburg to reinforce McClellan. It arrived on June 12–13. But Jackson's victory at Port Republic paralyzed the remainder of McDowell's forces and resulted, finally, in the withdrawal of Ricketts's and Shields's divisions toward Manassas, beginning June 17, and retention of Rufus King's division at Fredericksburg. On June 20 McClellan had 105,000 men before Richmond, while Federal forces in the valley and around Washington totaled about 60,000. With the eight thousand men sent under W. H. C. Whiting and A. R. Lawton to Jackson, Lee retained only sixty-four thousand men at Richmond and Petersburg. Even so, McClellan had so exaggerated Lee's numbers that he hesitated to strike. See Allan, *Army of Northern Virginia,* 60–61, 67–69; Allan, *Campaign of Gen. T. J. (Stonewall) Jackson,* 170; and *Official Records,* vol. 11, pt. 2, 490.

11. Garnet Wolseley (Field Marshal Viscount Wolseley), commander in chief of the British army, wrote in the *North American Review* of August 1889 (vol. 149, 165–66) that Jackson's actions at Cross Keys and Port Republic constituted "an operation which stamped him as a military genius of a very high order." Reprinted in Field Marshal Viscount Wolseley, *The American Civil War: An English View,* ed. James A. Rawley (Charlottesville: University Press of Virginia, 1964), 129.

12. Freeman, *R. E. Lee,* vol. 2, 84; and Lee, 5–10.

13. *Official Records,* vol. 12, pt. 3, 910; and Freeman, *R. E. Lee,* vol. 2., 95–96. In a June 8, 1862, letter Lee alerted Jackson that he was likely to be called to Richmond. On June 11, while informing Jackson that he was sending the brigades of Lawton and Whiting, Lee also directed him to move to Ashland, north of Richmond. On June 16 Lee wrote Jackson: "The sooner you unite with this army [at Richmond] the better. . . . In moving your troops you could let it be understood that it was to pursue the enemy in your front. Dispose those to hold the Valley so as to deceive the enemy." See Allan, *Campaign of Gen. T. J. (Stonewall) Jackson,* 165 and 169.

14. *Southern Historical Society Papers,* vol. 40, 172–73; and Cooke, 201.

15. This is not conjecture. Jackson wrote Lee on April 29, 1862, prior to the battle of McDowell, outlining a strategic plan of similar scope. This letter proves that Jackson already had worked out the strategic ramifications of a march east of the Blue Ridge. See *Official Records,* vol. 12, pt. 3, 872; and Allan, *Campaign of Gen. T. J. (Stonewall) Jackson,* 68 n.

16. There was a large Union garrison guarding Washington, but it was not a mobile force.

17. Freeman, *R. E. Lee,* vol. 2, 102; and *Southern Historical Society Papers,* vol. 40, 173–74.

18. MS. in *The Centennial Exhibit of the Duke University Library* (Durham, N.C.: Duke University, 1939), 15–16. Lee and Davis failed to appreciate that the strategic offensive proposed by Jackson presented a chance to win the war. This indicates that Lee's and Davis's horizons were too narrow to envision the sweeping concepts that opened up so clearly in Jackson's mind. Since Davis and Lee thought along much the same lines, the president consistently supported Lee as senior commander throughout the war and seldom challenged Lee's strategic views. On the other hand, Lee bowed to Davis as commander in chief, even when his military decisions were wrong.

6

THE FIRST TWO OF THE SEVEN DAYS

★ ★ ★ Robert E. Lee believed that George McClellan had given him a chance to defeat his army by inadvertently uncovering his supply base. McClellan's supplies came by boat to the small river port of White House, twenty-three miles northeast of Richmond, on the Pamunkey, a York River tributary. From there the Richmond and York River Railroad carried them to stations behind McClellan's front just east of Richmond.

White House and the railway would have been safely shielded if McClellan's original plan had been carried out and McDowell's corps had marched down from Fredericksburg. Now that McDowell was not coming, Lee believed that the Confederates could attack around McClellan's shallow northern flank and drive on the railway. Lee calculated that the Federals would come out of their redoubtable entrenchments to protect this vital railway, as well as White House, and might be defeated in open battle.

McClellan had chosen White House because the Confederate ironclad *Virginia* had blocked access to the broader and deeper

James River, the southern boundary of the peninsula. However, the deep-drafted *Virginia* had lost her berth when the Confederates abandoned Norfolk and now lay scuttled at the bottom of the James.

On June 23, 1862, as Jackson's eighteen thousand men were marching toward Ashland, Jackson arrived on the Virginia Central Railroad at Fredericks Hall, a few miles west, and there mounted his horse and rode fifty-two miles to Lee's headquarters at the Dabb House on the Nine Mile Road east of the capital. Here Lee convened a council of war. Besides Jackson it included James Longstreet, the Virginian A. P. Hill, and the North Carolinian D. H. Hill, an old friend who had married the sister of Jackson's second wife, Mary Anna Morrison, of Lincoln County, North Carolina.

Lee's attention focused on the thirty thousand–man Union corps of Maj. Gen. Fitz-John Porter, which occupied a salient north of the Chickahominy River, immediately northeast of Richmond at Mechanicsville. McClellan had placed Porter here to protect White House and the railroad and to reach out toward McDowell's corps.

Now Porter was exposed. His corps lay about four miles northwest of the main Federal force, located on the south side of the Chickahominy. There McClellan had seventy-five thousand men emplaced in a strong line of defensive entrenchments running from Golding's farm at the river over three miles south to Fair Oaks and Seven Pines.

Porter's salient was doubly vulnerable because the Chickahominy constituted a formidable barrier. It had muddy banks and a soft bottom, meaning that wagons and artillery could not cross without bridges and even infantry might have a hard time fording it.[1]

Lee's plan was to concentrate fifty-two thousand men, including cavalry, drive down the high ground north of the Chickahominy, and turn the flank of Porter's strong defensive position along Beaver Dam Creek about a mile east of Mechanicsville. This would force Porter to abandon his entrenchments without a battle. The Confederate army would continue on to sever the Richmond and York River Railroad at Dispatch Station, about eleven miles southeast of Mechanicsville.

The only risk was that McClellan might take advantage of Lee's move and attack Richmond directly, since the Confederate entrenchments shielding the city would be left with only twenty-eight thousand troops.[2] However, Lee had strengthened these earthworks and was confident that he could recross the Chickahominy behind the Federal army and get "on McClellan's tail" if he attacked toward Richmond.[3]

In theory, Lee's plan was foolproof. On June 11 he had dispatched his cavalry chief, Jeb Stuart, to reconnoiter the right flank of Porter's corps to find how far north it extended, though he easily could have gained this information by sending out scouts. The flamboyant Stuart, with twelve hundred men, quickly discovered that Porter's line did not extend any distance above the Chickahominy. This proved that Lee could get *around* Porter's corps and drive east to the railroad.

In fact, Lee's plan rested on a false premise. It depended on the Federals' reacting instantly to protect White House and the railway. But with *Virginia* gone, McClellan had been thinking about moving his base to the more accessible James. Stuart's raid convinced McClellan to do so at once.

Stuart, deciding that his force could not return the way it had come and relishing the fame he would garner, rode entirely around McClellan's army, arriving back in Richmond on June 15 by way of the New Market, or River, Road (now Virginia Route 5), running just north of the James. This demonstrated the ease by which the railway and White House could be approached, and McClellan immediately arranged for loaded transports to move up the James.[4]

White House and the Richmond and York River Railroad thus had become expendable and, although he did not know it, Lee's entire strategy had been nullified.

Lee expected to threaten the Richmond and York River Railroad by placing Stonewall Jackson's eighteen thousand–man force on Porter's northern rear. This would make Porter's Beaver Dam Creek position untenable.

However, Lee's method of concentrating Jackson's troops with the thirty-two thousand men he had assembled was complex in the extreme. Jackson was to depart from Merry Oaks Church, about six miles southeast of Ashland, at 3 A.M. on Thursday, June 26, and move to northeast of Mechanicsville and thus to the north of and behind Porter.

Although Lee made no arrangements to ensure coordination, Jackson's advance was to set in motion, in a sort of clockwork fashion, three further movements of troops poised just south of the Chickahominy—Lawrence O'B. Branch's North Carolina brigade of A. P. Hill's division a little west of Meadow Bridge, the remainder of A. P. Hill's division at Meadow Bridge, and the divisions of D. H. Hill and Longstreet on the Mechanicsville turnpike.

A. P. Hill was to unite with Jackson northeast of Mechanicsville, D. H. Hill to move to support Jackson, and Longstreet to support A. P. Hill.[5] Thereafter Jackson, "bearing well to his left," or northeast, was to drive toward Old Cold Harbor, six miles east of Mechanicsville. Then, with the other three divisions in echelon to the west and south of Jackson, the Confederates were to sweep down the Chickahominy, link up with Rebel forces south of the river at New Bridge, three miles downstream, and press forward to the Richmond and York River Railroad.[6]

Lee anticipated no major action near Mechanicsville. Indeed, the movement on Porter's rear was intended to force Porter to retreat without battle. However, because of rain, high water, and exhaustion of his men, Jackson's army got only to Ashland on the night of June 25. He informed Lee of this by courier early the next morning and was six hours late in reaching Merry Oaks on June 26.

Lee realized that his timetable had been thrown off. But a delay of six hours should make no difference, since Lee was not planning to drive Porter out by main strength and Jackson's arrival on Porter's right rear would force him to withdraw the next morning. Though critics later berated Jackson for tardiness, Lee made no complaint and referred only to Jackson's "unavoidable delays" in reaching Ashland.[7]

A great error occurred, but it was Lee and A. P. Hill who made it, not Jackson. At the Dabb House conference Hill, a nervous thirty-seven-year-old West Pointer, somehow did not grasp what Lee was trying to accomplish. This was not apparent to the other generals, because none quite knew A. P. Hill. He had been named a major general only a month previously and neither Lee nor the other generals were aware of his impatience, impetuosity, and extreme aggressiveness.

The problem might have been alleviated if Lee had informed the generals south of the Chickahominy that Jackson had been delayed and would arrive later than expected. Apparently he did not. Also, Lee made no arrangements for communication between the two separate wings. Lee could have detailed some of Stuart's cavalry to keep the two wings in touch. Instead he sent Stuart's entire force to the east to guard against attack, though Stuart's recent raid had showed that there was little danger in that direction. As a result, both wings operated largely in the dark.[8]

The Seven Days were to demonstrate the style of command of Lee, which was utterly unlike Jackson's. Whereas Jackson expected his commands to be obeyed without question and provided subordinates only the information necessary to carry out such commands, Lee was extremely sensitive to the feelings of others and frequently allowed his subordinates a voice in battle plans as they developed. In addition, he had been taught by Winfield Scott in the Mexican War that the commanding general's job was to devise the strategy, bring troops on the field at the proper time and place, and leave tactics to the division commanders.[9]

Although military historians generally consider Jackson a poor communicator, it was Lee who left many key details unsettled and too many options in the hands of inexperienced division commanders whose capabilities, industry, and drive varied widely. It is ironic that Jackson, who obeyed Lee's orders pre-

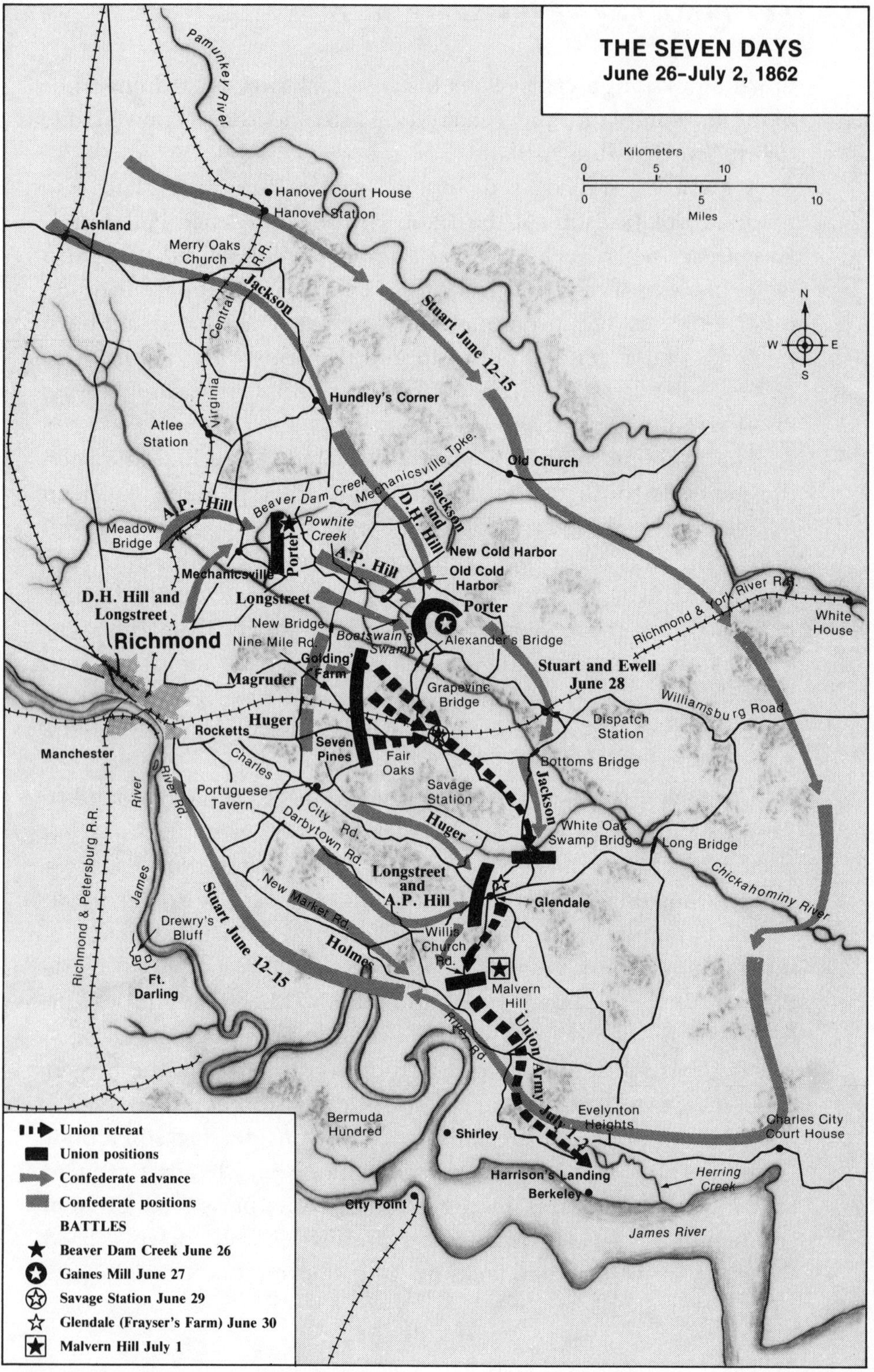
THE SEVEN DAYS
June 26–July 2, 1862
Kilometers
0 5 10
0 5 10
Miles
N
W
E
S
Pamunkey River
Hanover Court House
Hanover Station
Ashland
Merry Oaks Church
Virginia Central R.R.
Jackson
Stuart June 12–15
Hundley's Corner
Atlee Station
Old Church
Mechanicsville Tpke.
Beaver Dam Creek
A.P. Hill
Meadow Bridge
Porter
Powhite Creek
Jackson and D.H. Hill
New Cold Harbor
Old Cold Harbor
Mechanicsville
D.H. Hill and Longstreet
Longstreet
Porter
Richmond
New Bridge
Nine Mile Rd.
Boatswain's Swamp
Alexander's Bridge
Golding's Farm
Magruder
Grapevine Bridge
Stuart and Ewell June 28
Richmond & York River R.R.
White House
Williamsburg Road
Dispatch Station
Huger
Rocketts
Seven Pines
Fair Oaks
Manchester
Charles City Rd.
Savage Station
Bottoms Bridge
Jackson
Portuguese Tavern
Darbytown Rd.
Huger
White Oak Swamp Bridge
Long Bridge
River Rd.
River
James
Richmond & Petersburg R.R.
Longstreet and A.P. Hill
Glendale
Chickahominy River
New Market Rd.
Stuart June 12–15
Drewry's Bluff
Holmes
Willis Church Rd.
Malvern Hill
Ft. Darling
River Rd.
Union Army July 1–3
Bermuda Hundred
Shirley
Evelynton Heights
Charles City Court House
Harrison's Landing
Berkeley
Herring Creek
City Point
James River
Union retreat
Union positions
Confederate advance
Confederate positions
BATTLES
Beaver Dam Creek June 26
Gaines Mill June 27
Savage Station June 29
Glendale (Frayser's Farm) June 30
Malvern Hill July 1

cisely (as he expected his subordinates to obey his), found Lee's method of command constricting. Jackson, the subordinate, did not exercise the independent judgment in the Seven Days that Jackson, the commander, demonstrated in the valley.

When Jackson got to Merry Oaks he sent a courier to Branch, as arranged. Branch marched out but soon got into a nasty, time-consuming fight with a small Union force around Atlee Station, about four miles north of Mechanicsville.[10]

A. P. Hill probably knew of Branch's movement but not of Jackson's delay. Hill's uncertainty regarding Jackson's whereabouts worked on his anxieties and increased his impatience. By 3 P.M. he could stand the wait no longer and sent a brigade across Meadow Bridge, driving back the Federal pickets and marching on Mechanicsville. Hill sent only a single battery in support, and more than thirty Union field guns promptly disabled six of its eight cannons and killed or wounded half of its horses and gunners.

The Union troops facing A. P. Hill withdrew to their formidable positions on Beaver Dam Creek east of the village. Despite heavy Federal fire, A. P. Hill moved up his whole division with the intention of assaulting the position. This, of course, was entirely contrary to plan.

Lee, D. H. Hill, and Longstreet, seeing A. P. Hill drive into Mechanicsville, assumed that Hill and Jackson had made contact and they crossed the Mechanicsville pike bridge with their troops. When Lee got into the village (President Davis, several cabinet members, and politicians had eagerly rushed in ahead) he realized that Hill had moved on his own volition and that Jackson had not been seen.

At about 5 P.M., unbeknownst to Lee, Jackson did arrive at Hundley's Corner, four miles northeast of Mechanicsville, thereby flanking Porter's entire position. Though he was late, Jackson had reached the point where Lee had said that A. P. Hill would be on his right and D. H. Hill in support. Neither was there, though he could hear cannon fire toward Mechanicsville. Jackson assumed that Confederate forces were crossing the

Chickahominy and Lee had come to the same conclusion as he—the movement should be called off for the day and a fresh start taken on the morrow. Accordingly, he bivouacked for the night.

Lee now exhibited for the first time as commander a tendency to revert to direct assault when indirect methods seemed not to be working. Throwing aside his carefully planned strategy of a turning movement to dislodge Porter without a battle, he approved A. P. Hill's plan to assail the very position that he had planned to avoid and ordered D. H. Hill to send a brigade to assist![11] Yet the turning movement had not failed. As soon as Porter learned of Jackson's position, he would have to evacuate.

At around 6 P.M. A. P. Hill sent three brigades to the north of Mechanicsville, in Jackson's direction. But instead of marching around the Beaver Dam Creek position, probing for a rendezvous with Jackson, Hill sent the brigades directly against the Federal line, using only one of his eight artillery batteries in support. Federal cannons had an easy time of it. Shotted with canister, they ripped great holes in the Confederate lines. Hill's men doggedly came on, only to be staggered with sheets of Minié balls and driven back into the creek's swamps and thickets. Once more the Rebels tried, getting within a hundred yards of the Union lines but unable to weather the withering fire.

Just at twilight, Hill tried again, this time on the southern reaches of the creek at Ellerson's Mill. He sent in W. Dorsey Pender's North Carolina brigade and the brigade of Roswell Ripley of D. H. Hill's division. Pender's brigade fell apart from heavy artillery fire and only the Thirty-eighth North Carolina made the attack, crossing the creek and reaching the final summit of the hill. There the Tar Heels charged the Federal cannons lined up to the rear of entrenched infantry with abatis of pine trees in front of them. However brave, the Carolinians had no chance. They withdrew, leaving 142 of the regiment's 420 men on the field. Ripley got only the Forty-fourth Georgia into the Union position and it also charged into the mouths of the guns. The guns unleashed canister at seventy yards and killed or wounded 335 out of the 514 men.

A. P. Hill's attack was one of the most terrible and useless slaughters of the Civil War: 1,400 men fell, whereas Porter lost only 360 men all day, most of them guards retreating from Meadow Bridge and Mechanicsville.

Jackson's move had been designed specifically to avoid a battle, and it had succeeded—his position on Porter's flank and rear rendered the line of Beaver Dam Creek untenable. The battle had been unnecessary. McClellan ordered Porter to withdraw a few hours after reports of Jackson's position reached him.[12]

Lee did not know that the railroad and White House were being abandoned and assumed that Porter would try to prevent Confederate passage toward Dispatch Station. Instead, on McClellan's orders, Porter took on an entirely different mission—holding the bridges over the Chickahominy and protecting the flank of the main Union army from attack.[13]

Lee fought an entire battle the next day basing his dispositions on the erroneous conception that Porter was still trying to protect the railroad.

Porter pulled out most of his men and guns during the night, abandoning the New Bridge over the Chickahominy but leaving a strong rear guard to shield his corps while it took up another position about three miles downriver behind a low, underbrush-covered stream known as Boatswain's Swamp.

Porter's position was at an entirely different location than Lee had calculated. Lee thought he would build his line on Powhite Creek, three-quarters of a mile west of Boatswain's, and align his defense facing west, to protect Dispatch Station. In fact, Porter aligned it facing north to protect his retreat route directly south across the Grapevine, Alexander's, and two other bridges over the Chickahominy.

Lee, on the morning of June 27, was not aware of the existence of Boatswain's Swamp. His map did not show it. As Richard Taylor, commander of the Louisiana brigade, later wrote, "The Confederate commanders knew no more about the topography of the country than they did about central Africa."[14]

Lee found Jackson and directed him to turn the Powhite line

by getting east of its northern flank at Old Cold Harbor, only six miles from Dispatch Station. Lee believed that the Federals, as soon as they learned of Jackson's presence, would try to block the Confederates from the station and could be trapped en route by Jackson. This effort, Lee figured, would weaken the Powhite position, making it easier to assault.[15]

Jackson moved as ordered, while D. H. Hill's division, now attached, marched to assist him by way of the Mechanicsville turnpike. Jackson posted D. H. Hill in an ambush position and kept most of the rest of his command on the road leading to Old Cold Harbor, ready to move as needed.

Meanwhile, A. P. Hill's troops probed from the west, searching for the main Union line on Powhite Creek. Lee got his first sign that something was amiss at 1:30 P.M. at Gaines Mill, where the Cold Harbor road crossed Powhite Creek. Here Maxcy Gregg's South Carolina brigade clashed with Federal infantry, unsupported by artillery, and quickly drove them away. It was too easy. The reason soon became clear—heavy cannon and rifle fire erupted some distance to the east and part of Gregg's brigade recoiled in panic.

Lee had found the Federal position along Boatswain's Swamp. Nevertheless, he assumed that Porter was still facing west, blocking passage to Dispatch Station. Not waiting to send in small probes to determine if Porter's line actually was oriented in the direction he thought, Lee ordered A. P. Hill to assault as soon as possible in maximum force.[16] He expected Hill to dislodge the Federals and drive them back into the mouths of Jackson's cannons.[17]

Lee's order demonstrates how dangerous it is to make decisions without checking out the enemy's dispositions in advance. If he had done so he would have learned that McClellan had eliminated the basis for Lee's strategy by abandoning White House and the Richmond and York River Railroad.

The evidence could have been readily ascertained in the manner that Porter had established his line. He had turned it ninety degrees to protect his retreat route south across the bridges, not to block Rebel passage to the railroad. This way was now entirely open. McClellan, in his anxiety to protect his main army's flank along the Chickahominy, had forgotten to close the back door to his army!

If Lee had probed Porter's whole position instead of ordering A. P. Hill to attack without checking, he would have discovered Porter's orientation. This would have revealed that Jackson was already past Porter and had a clear path to Dispatch Station.[18] Jackson could have seized Dispatch Station and Bottoms Bridge, a mile below, without opposition and placed his force on the rear of the entire Federal army![19] No attack was necessary against Boatswain's Swamp. Porter would have had to withdraw across the Chickahominy for safety the moment Jackson moved on Dispatch Station.

Porter saw the danger at once. He had no idea that Jackson was waiting in ambush, assuming instead that Jackson was aiming at the railroad and Bottoms Bridge. Porter considered striking Jackson, but scouts reported that his force was larger than any Porter could bring against him, while Porter had to deal directly with Rebels forming to attack. "This compelled me to keep my troops united and under cover," he would write.[20]

By crossing the Chickahominy on the railroad trestle and Bottoms Bridge and moving west, Jackson could have closed off any retreat down the peninsula and McClellan's only feasible route of withdrawal to the James River by way of the north-south Willis Church, or Quaker, Road. This would have forced McClellan to turn about part of his army to face Jackson advancing from the east while defending against the Rebels advancing from the entrenchments on the west. Pinned between the two, McClellan's army could have been destroyed.

Lee, convinced that the Federals were determined to defend White House and the railroad, sent A. P. Hill into a bloody frontal assault directly into Porter's guns.

Porter held a bastion of great strength. His line followed the course of the swamp, which described nearly a half circle and rested on a long hill behind the swamp, with steep grades in front. The swamp lay in a deep, boggy, almost ravinelike depression. Porter had augmented the natural barrier with three defense lines—one low, sheltered by the creek; a second farther up, shielded by abatis of felled trees; and a third on the crest of the hill with eighty rifled guns massed behind.

Hill lined up his division in woods edging the south side of the Cold Harbor road and ordered it forward at 2:30 P.M. On the west the approach was mostly over an open field; on the center and east cleared land gave way to woods as the men approached the swamp. As soon as the Rebels moved into the open, a hail of shrapnel from the eighty Union guns fell on them. Hill had pulled up only three batteries and only one was positioned to strike at the Federal guns. Many men fell, but the lines swept downward to the swamp, getting entangled in thick underbrush. There an overwhelming blast of artillery and rifle fire struck the division. General Porter wrote afterward that "brigade after brigade seemed almost to melt away before the concentrated fire of our artillery and infantry."[21]

Hill's division staggered and halted. Many survivors bolted for the rear. Some units withdrew. Confederate officers pushed the remaining men forward, sometimes two and three times, but it was impossible to penetrate the sheets of bullets and shell fire.

Although Lee saw that Hill's assault had failed, he waited nearly an hour and a half while Hill's division was being broken to pieces before devising a new plan. Meantime, he sent messages to Jackson to move up and attack and to Longstreet, nearer the Chickahominy, to make a demonstration. Longstreet tried, but opposition was so powerful he called off his effort.

Richard S. Ewell's division went in to support the left half of A. P. Hill's division. Ewell's men passed points where Hill's men were clinging, but they had no more success than Hill's division. Rob Wheat, commanding the Louisiana Tigers, fell of a mortal wound and the Louisiana brigade broke for the first time. But other gallant units held on.

Jackson ordered D. H. Hill, posted in ambush, to change front and advance against the Federal line. D. H. Hill was unable to make headway against Federal artillery and fire of the Regular Army division of George Sykes, a close friend and classmate of Hill at West Point.

Jackson sent a staff officer, Maj. John A. Harman, back to bring up the divisions of W. H. C. Whiting and Charles S. Winder and the Georgia brigade of Alexander R. Lawton waiting on the road to Old Cold Harbor. They were to go into the line between Ewell and D. H. Hill.

General Whiting, a proud Mississippian who had graduated number one in the class of 1845 at West Point, was jealous of Jackson and angry because his advice had been ignored. He elected to conclude from Harman that he was to await further instructions. Since Whiting's division was first in line, Winder and Lawton could not advance, either.

Because of Whiting's obstinacy, a large Confederate force stood immobile for some time while D. H. Hill was advancing and Ewell was wearing away his strength. Fortunately, Jackson's aide, Maj. R. L. Dabney, had heard Jackson's order and he rode back to Whiting and set him straight. Whiting now moved fast, led by the Texas brigade of John Bell Hood, with Winder and Lawton coming behind.

The battle was now moving toward a climax and Jackson's excitement rose. He sent officers to all of his division commanders with orders to "tell them that this affair must hang in suspense no longer; sweep the field with the bayonet!"[22]

It was now after 5 P.M. Jackson, dusty, sucking on a lemon, rode down the road toward New Cold Harbor and found Lee to ascertain his plan. "Ah, General," Lee said, "I am very glad to see you. I had hoped to be with you before." Jackson nodded a brief reply. "The fire is very heavy," Lee continued. "Do you think your men can stand it?" Jackson listened for a moment, then replied: "They can stand almost anything! They can stand that."[23]

Lee explained that he had decided on a general assault of all troops and arranged with Jackson the method of attack and distribution of those not yet in line. Jackson returned to his command post and the Confederates moved into position.

The Rebels all across the front now advanced at a trot in a vast wave in lines two men deep, trailing arms and ordered not to fire a shot, for fear of hitting other Rebel soldiers huddled in clusters ahead of them. It was this speed of advance that made the charge irresistible. E. M. Law, commanding one of Whiting's brigades, said: "No troops could have stood long under the withering storm of lead and iron that beat in their faces as they became fully exposed to view from the Federal line."[24]

As the line pushed on without flinching, the weird, shrill, terrifying Rebel yell rose from thousands of throats, the surviving soldiers disregarding the men dropping all around them from Minié balls and shell fire. The Union fire increased to a deadly roar, more than a thousand Rebels fell, but the lines kept on, scarcely a rifle fired, and the men rushed through the swamp and onto the first Federal emplacements. The apparition of the Confederates, unfazed by the terrible fire right in front of them so terrified the Union defenders that they vacated the works, many throwing away their arms. The Rebels made for the second line. A great volley of Rebel fire, delivered at close range, shattered several points and the Confederates rushed through the breaches.

The Union line was disintegrating, but the Federal cannons remained as rallying points and the Rebels made for these death-dealing guns. They assaulted and captured fourteen of them, despite gallant defense by the gunners. One wounded Union cannoneer dragged himself up by the spokes of a wheel and fired the cannon into the faces of charging Confederates. Another battery discharged a round of double canister into the attacking line and managed to escape in the confusion. Three squadrons of the Fifth U.S. Cavalry made a brave but useless charge, losing six out of seven officers and many men.

Although small groups of Union soldiers courageously held their ground and fought the onrushing Rebels, most withdrew rapidly and many, including two full regiments, gave themselves up. The remaining Union troops made for the bridges over the Chickahominy, protected by nightfall, fierce rear guards, and heavy woods along the stream. The exhausted Confederates did not pursue them.

Lee had won, but by the narrowest of margins. Had Porter not already committed every one of his reserves the battle might have had a vastly different ending. A Union counterstroke earlier by fresh troops would have imperiled Lee's army. A single Federal division committed when the Confederates made their general assault probably would have maintained Porter's line unbroken. But McClellan, changing his base to the James, allowed Porter to be overwhelmed. Though McClellan had reinforced Porter with one division before the battle started, he sent over just two brigades later, and those only to cover the retreat.[25]

Lee had not destroyed Porter's corps, and McClellan's main army remained intact. Yet for this partial victory Lee had lost more than eight thousand killed and wounded, one in six of the men engaged. There could scarcely be more graphic proof that Lee's policy of frontal attacks was going to bleed the Confederate army white. Some individual regiments endured appalling casualties. The First Texas lost 600 of its 800 men; the Fourth Texas 250 men and all of its field-grade officers; the Third Alabama 200; the Twentieth North Carolina 270; the Twelfth North Carolina 212; the Thirty-first and Thirty-eighth Georgia each 170. The slaughter of officers especially was staggering, pointing to grave deficiencies ahead in the quality of leadership.

Porter's corps lost about 4,000 dead or wounded and 2,380 captured or missing. Therefore the total real casualties for the Union army were half those of the Confederate.

NOTES

General sources: Dabney, 432–57; Cooke, 205–27; Allan, *Army of Northern Virginia,* 27–94; Wise, 199–205; Freeman, *R. E. Lee,* 108–58 and 566–72; Henderson, 339–70; Maurice, 92–122; Marshall, 63–103; Alexander, *Military*

Memoirs, 109–32; Freeman, *Lee's Lieutenants,* vol. 1, 489–537; Alexander, *Fighting for the Confederacy,* 94–104; Robertson, *Stonewall Brigade,* 114–20; Chambers, vol. 2, 3–53; Bridges, 58–75; R. Taylor, 37–56; Sanger, 62–68; Johnson and Buel, vol. 2, 313–65; Long, 161–74; Robertson, *A. P. Hill,* 59–86; and Vandiver, 284–309.

1. This point is essential to understanding why the Chickahominy played such a major role. It was made by British Lt. Col. Garnet Wolseley, later Field Marshal Viscount Wolseley and commander in chief of the British army, after he visited the battlefields in September 1862. See Garnet Wolseley, *The American Civil War: An English View,* edited by James A. Rawley (Charlottesville: University Press of Virginia, 1964), 21 (reprinted from *Blackwood's Edinburgh Magazine,* January 1863).

2. This figure and that of Lee's force north of the Chickahominy are only approximate. Lee had assembled about eighty thousand men before Richmond, as follows: Jackson (including Ewell, Whiting and Lawton), about eighteen thousand; Longstreet, nine thousand; D. H. Hill, ten thousand; A. P. Hill, thirteen thousand; Magruder, thirteen thousand; Holmes, sixty-five hundred; Huger, nine thousand; cavalry, twenty-five hundred; artillery reserve, fifteen hundred. See Allan, *Army of Northern Virginia,* 77; Jubal A. Early, in *Southern Historical Society Papers,* vol. 1, 415–16; and W. H. Taylor, 53.

3. Marshall, 90. In Lee's report on the battle he says: "It was therefore determined to construct defensive lines so as to enable a part of the army to defend the city and leave the other part to cross the Chickahominy and operate on the north bank. By sweeping down the river on that side and threatening communications with the York River, it was thought that the enemy would be compelled to retreat or to give battle out of his entrenchments" (*Official Records,* vol. 11, pt. 1, 1039).

4. Johnson and Buel, vol. 2, 178; and Freeman, *R. E. Lee,* vol. 2, 236.

5. Freeman, *R. E. Lee,* vol. 2, 111–12; and Freeman, *Lee's Lieutenants,* vol. 1, 499–500. Jackson had a memorandum, apparently prepared during the June 23 meeting, that specified that A. P. Hill and Jackson would unite on the Mechanicsville turnpike "in rear of Mechanicsville," or to the northeast, since the turnpike (now U.S. Route 360) ran in this direction from the village. When Jackson started from Merry Oaks Church he was to communicate with Branch, posted about eight miles southwest of Merry Oaks at Halfsink on the Chickahominy. Branch then was to march on Mechanicsville. Lee's order did not require Branch to inform A. P. Hill and specified only that "as soon as the movements of these columns

are discovered," Hill was to cross the Meadow Bridge and descend on Mechanicsville, two miles to the east. A. P. Hill's movement, in turn, was to open up passage of the divisions of Longstreet and D. H. Hill over the Mechanicsville turnpike bridge immediately south of the village. See *Official Records,* vol. 11, pt. 2, 489–99; Alexander, *Military Memoirs,* 113; and Henderson, 347–49.

6. Marshall, 88–89; Freeman, *R. E. Lee,* vol. 2, 111 and 566–72; and Robertson, *A. P. Hill,* 67. Lee's report on the battle says: "Jackson . . . was to advance at 3 A.M. on the 26th to turn Beaver Dam." See *Official Records,* vol. 11, pt. 2, 490–91 (Lee's report), and vol. 11, pt. 2, 553 (Jackson's report).

7. *Official Records,* vol. 11, pt. 2, 491 and 552–53.

8. Lee's essential mistake was his failure to establish a mechanism to inform the commanders south of the Chickahominy when Jackson in fact arrived at his flanking position northeast of Mechanicsville. Lee set up no method by which Jackson's movement could be "discovered" across the several miles of enemy-occupied, wooded terrain that intervened between the point Jackson was to reach and A. P. Hill's position at Meadow Bridge. There is no evidence that couriers operated between the two wings throughout the movement. Jackson expected A. P. Hill to be in touch when he reached his assigned position, while Hill expected some overt sign to show him that Jackson was moving there before he marched to join him.

9. Freeman, *R. E. Lee,* vol. 2, 239–40.

10. Freeman, *Lee's Lieutenants,* vol. 1, 509; *Official Records,* vol. 11, pt. 2, 886; and Henderson, 352–53.

11. Johnson and Buel, vol. 2, 361; Robert E. Lee, Jr., *Recollections and Letters of General Robert E. Lee* (New York: 1904), 415; Marshall, 94; Robertson, *A. P. Hill,* 71; Bridges, 66–67; Freeman, *Lee's Lieutenants,* vol. 1, 514; Henderson, 350; *Official Records,* vol. 11, pt. 2, 834–40 (A. P. Hill's report); and Freeman, *R. E. Lee,* vol. 2, 133–35. Freeman remarks that "a turning movement upstream [on Beaver Dam Creek] had been regarded as the sine qua non because the strength of Porter's position was so well known." Thus Lee knew that a frontal attack at Beaver Dam would be disastrous. Roswell S. Ripley reports (*Official Records,* vol. 11, pt. 2, 648) that Lee and D. H. Hill ordered him to attack.

12. McClellan realized shortly after the Beaver Dam Creek battle "that Jackson's corps had taken little or no part in this attack and that his blow

would fall farther to the rear." It was this knowledge—not A. P. Hill's attack—that caused McClellan to order Porter's corps to withdraw. See Johnson and Buel, vol. 2, 180.

13. This change in Porter's responsibility is clearly seen in ibid., in which McClellan writes that he ordered Porter "to fall back and take position nearer the bridges, where the flanks [of the Union army] would be more secure" (180). Porter reports that McClellan ordered him to withdraw to the Boatswain's Swamp position, "where I could protect the bridges across the Chickahominy, over which I must retire if compelled to leave the left bank" (ibid., 331). McClellan made no attempt to counter Lee's assault on Porter by moving directly against Richmond south of the river. McClellan believed the figures of his Secret Service Corps, which put Lee's army at between 180,000 and 200,000 men. In his dispatch to Washington on the evening of June 25, 1862, McClellan said he feared that his army might be "destroyed by overwhelming numbers," in which case McClellan said he would "die with it and share its fate." See *Official Records,* vol. 11, pt. 1, 51.

14. R. Taylor, 107–8.

15. Lee's orders were verbal, but Freeman, in *R. E. Lee* (vol. 2, 141), asserts that Jackson understood that he was to move to Old Cold Harbor and wait for A. P. Hill and Longstreet to drive the enemy past and not to attack immediately himself. See also Henderson, 360. This is all the more reasonable because Lee sent D. H. Hill to Old Cold Harbor and he believed that Porter was nearly a mile farther west, at Powhite Creek, not along Boatswain's Swamp. Porter Alexander (*Military Memoirs,* 125 ff.) criticizes Jackson for failing to attack at once. But Porter, along Boatswain's Swamp, was facing north. Jackson could not have made a flank attack, only a frontal assault. Besides, Lee had given him an entirely different assignment—to wait for Porter's troops to move *past* to protect Dispatch Station, and attack them as they moved.

16. Freeman, *R. E. Lee,* vol. 2, 146–47.

17. Ibid., 142; and Longstreet, 125. Confederate troop dispositions are shown in *Official Records,* vol. 11, pt. 1, 492; and Freeman, *R. E. Lee,* vol. 2, 116–17. Lee's misunderstanding of where the Federal line was gave rise to naming the battle that followed Gaines Mill, after a mill on Powhite Creek, instead of after Boatswain's Swamp, where the battle actually took place.

18. Porter specifically identified Jackson's position as being on his "right front," not on his flank. See Johnson and Buel, vol. 2, 336. Since Jackson

had been placed in an ambush position and was awaiting a movement of some of Porter's corps past him to shield Dispatch Station, he did not realize that there was an unobstructed passage to the railway.

19. Even if McClellan had decided to move troops from south of the Chickahominy to the bridges, they scarcely could have reached them before Jackson. Also, such a move would have been extremely dangerous and unlikely, for it would have required McClellan to denude a part of his main defensive line facing Magruder and Huger.

20. Johnson and Buel, vol. 2, 336–37.

21. Ibid., 337.

22. Dabney, 455.

23. John Esten Cooke, *The Life of Stonewall Jackson, by a Virginian* (New York: Charles B. Richardson, 1863), 200.

24. Johnson and Buel, vol. 2, 363; and Henderson, p. 366.

25. *Official Records,* vol. 11, pt. 2, 492; and Freeman, *R. E. Lee,* vol. 2, 146.

7

FRAYSER'S FARM AND MALVERN HILL

★ ★ ★ General Lee had failed to see that Porter's dispositions at Boatswain's Swamp, protecting only the Chickahominy bridges, had signaled that McClellan was abandoning the Richmond and York River Railroad and White House. He assumed that Porter would maintain a bridgehead north of the river and defend the supply line to the Pamunkey.

Lee was astonished, therefore, the next morning, Saturday, June 28, 1862, when couriers rushed up with the news that all Federal forces had moved across the river, burned the bridges opposite Boatswain's Swamp, and mounted numerous cannons on the south bank, making impossible any bridge repair or reconnoitering beyond the stream.

Although McClellan had turned the Chickahominy into a fortress line, giving clear evidence that he had abandoned everything north of it, Lee refused to be swayed.

To gird for the fight for the railroad he expected, Lee ordered Jeb Stuart to take his cavalry immediately down to seize Dispatch

Station and sever McClellan's connections with White House. He sent Dick Ewell's division behind in support.

During the morning there was much evidence of Federal activity south of the river. An officer climbed a tall tree and saw the Federals marching. Magazines exploded, sending sulphurous smoke into the air. Great clouds of dust rose, showing that an immense movement of men and animals was under way. But the Federal frenzy could prove either a shift of forces to defend the railroad or the beginnings of a withdrawal. If it were a pullout, McClellan could be retreating down the peninsula to Fort Monroe or across to the James River.

However, unequivocal information reached Lee before noon—Stuart sent back the news from Dispatch Station that the small Federal force guarding the station had *burned* the railroad trestle over the Chickahominy before withdrawing. Before long he also reported immense clouds of smoke from White House.[1]

Burning the railroad trestle was final proof that McClellan was abandoning his supply base on the Pamunkey. And since Federal forces were not guarding Bottoms Bridge, a mile below Dispatch Station and on the main road to Fort Monroe, Lee knew by noon or shortly thereafter on June 28 that McClellan had only one probable destination: the James River. Nevertheless, he was unwilling to discount a Union retreat down the peninsula and held his army idle all afternoon and all evening.[2] As a precaution he ordered Ewell down to Bottoms Bridge and Stuart to send parties to the lower bridges. They found no evidence of Federal activity.[3]

Lee should have gotten his army on the march *immediately* after learning that the railway trestle had been burned. The bulk of his army was north of the Chickahominy and had to move a number of miles farther than McClellan if it was going to beat him to the James. Time was of the essence. Napoleon said he might lose a battle, but never a minute. Yet Lee did not start his army until the morning of Sunday, June 29, eighteen or twenty hours after he learned of the trestle burning!

Lee could have countered what little chance remained of Mc-

Clellan's striking for Fort Monroe by burning the Chickahominy bridges and leaving Ewell and part of Stuart's cavalry to guard them. He then could have marched Jackson, Longstreet, and the two Hills around by the Confederate rear to the New Market, or River, Road along the James, picking up the ninety cannons and fifteen hundred men of the army artillery reserve and absorbing Gen. Theophilus H. Holmes's six thousand men coming over a pontoon bridge from south of the river. The concentrated army of about forty-seven thousand men then could have marched directly across McClellan's path at or near Malvern Hill.

This hill was on the main north-south Willis Church Road McClellan was bound to take and just northwest of Harrison's Landing at Berkeley and Westover plantations. The landing was fourteen miles southeast of McClellan's main positions around Seven Pines and Fair Oaks and was the closest point at which McClellan's transports could tie up. Farther upriver the James narrowed and transports could be shelled from the south side.

If a Confederate army had beaten the Federals to Malvern Hill, McClellan would have been forced to attack under desperate conditions. Boatswain's Swamp had demonstrated how powerful defensive positions could be erected in hours—positions that McClellan might have crashed against in vain. If, in addition, the twenty-one thousand men of Benjamin Huger and John Magruder had pressed on McClellan's rear from Seven Pines and Fair Oaks, the Federal army might have been destroyed.[4]

Opportunities must be seized. Once lost, they can lead to lost wars. The day before, Lee had failed to see an opportunity to descend on McClellan's rear by way of Dispatch Station. Now he had a second chance. But the only way Lee could get around McClellan was by quick, hard marching. This he did not do, and this was his second crucial mistake. By failing to move south on the twenty-eighth Lee forfeited any possibility of intercepting and destroying McClellan's army.

The plan Lee actually adopted was of great complexity. He divided his army into five disconnected columns, each moving along separate routes. Only one had any prospect of getting across McClellan's path—Holmes moved east down the River Road. But his six thousand–man force was too small to block McClellan even if he had marched fast, which he did not do. The other columns moved behind the Federals along more direct, shorter routes and accordingly failed. As Porter Alexander writes, "on the shortest roads will be found the enemy's most formidable rear guards and obstructions."[5]

In summary, Lee called only for striking the Federals on the march—that is, glancing blows on the flank and rear. The Union army could be destroyed only by blocking its passage and attacking it front and rear.

Lee further limited his army's opportunities by forcing it to blunder forward blindly. He left Stuart's entire cavalry force to idle along the Chickahominy, even after it was certain that McClellan was heading toward the James. Had Lee recalled even a third of the cavalry, he might have anticipated positions McClellan would take and developed more effective measures.[6]

McClellan had announced plans to withdraw on the night of June 27. Maj. Gen. Erasmus D. Keyes's corps was to cross White Oak Swamp on the twenty-eighth and there block any Confederate move on the flank. White Oak was a boggy, smaller-scale version of the Chickahominy about five miles south. Fitz-John Porter's corps was to follow and move south. The other three Federal corps, commanded by major generals William B. Franklin, E. V. Sumner, and Samuel P. Heintzelman, were to hold the rear in the vicinity of Savage Station, some three miles east of Fair Oaks, and then withdraw on the evening of June 29. Heintzelman, in fact, found so many Union troops around Savage Station that he crossed White Oak on the afternoon of June 29.[7]

Lee realized he could not get around White Oak in time to block the Federals and elected only to press their rear on June 29 and to strike the next day, June 30, while the Union army was marching from White Oak to the James.[8]

Lee's orders for pursuit of the Federals on June 29 were as follows: Magruder, with 11,500 men, was to follow the Federal rear down the Williamsburg road from Fair Oaks and engage it before it reached White Oak Swamp. Huger, with nine thousand men, was to move south of the swamp, then east on the Charles City Road and take the Federals in flank the following day around Glendale, where the Charles City and Darbytown roads joined Long Bridge Road from the north and where Willis Church Road led south to the James. Longstreet, with A. P. Hill under his command and about eighteen thousand men, was to cross the Chickahominy on the New Bridge and march down to Darbytown Road, a couple of miles south of the Charles City Road. He also was to assail McClellan around Glendale on the thirtieth.[9] Meanwhile, General Holmes, after crossing the James, was to march eastward down River Road.[10]

Lee's orders to Jackson for June 29 were for him to rebuild Grapevine Bridge, march eastward down the Chickahominy to protect against any move McClellan might make down the peninsula, and then get onto the Northern rear.[11] However, it took nearly all of June 29 to rebuild Grapevine Bridge and Jackson did not get his men across until after midnight.[12]

Had Magruder held the Federal rear guard in place by assailing Savage Station with every man in his command and had Huger been able to march undisturbed on Glendale, there is an outside chance that part of McClellan's rear guard might have been trapped. But Magruder delayed excessively and accomplished little. Lee allowed Magruder to hold up Huger's advance for most of the day because of Magruder's fear of a Federal attack, even though Lee realized that none was likely.[13] Huger, not too aggressive to begin with, got only six miles along the Charles City Road on the twenty-ninth and came nowhere close to blocking the rear guard's retreat.

Magruder finally attacked at Savage Station in the afternoon. But it took him two hours and a loss of 441 men, and the Federals stopped him with a single brigade. The Union rear then retreated under cover of darkness, taking all remaining trains but leaving behind twenty-five hundred Federal sick and wounded.[14]

Longstreet, with A. P. Hill, meanwhile, got within seven miles of Glendale by nightfall. Holmes proceeded only a short distance down River Road.[15]

Without Stuart to reconnoiter, Lee did not know where McClellan was. He found some small groups of cavalry, however, and ordered them up Willis Church Road. The Rebel horsemen suffered a bloody repulse, proving that at least portions of the Federal army were well south of Glendale. The chance for heading off McClellan's main army was lost, but Lee still hoped to strike his rear.

Lee's plan for Monday, June 30, was for the Confederates to close from three directions on the Federal rear guard in the vicinity of Glendale. However, the Federals were well ahead of the Rebels and almost certain to be firmly in position there.

Lee ordered Longstreet to continue down Darbytown Road and Huger down Charles City Road toward Glendale. Jackson was to march to the main White Oak Swamp bridge about three miles northeast of Glendale, cross it, and—while continuing to guard the Federal right flank against any move north or east—drive the Union rear guard toward Huger and Longstreet.

For Lee's plan to succeed, Longstreet had to block Willis Church Road leading toward Harrison's Landing. Otherwise the Federal rear guard could avoid destruction by moving south if Huger or Jackson pressed them from the flank or rear.

Since Magruder's position at Savage Station now was redundant, Lee directed him to swing around to Darbytown Road and advance behind Longstreet as the general reserve, while Holmes was to continue down River Road toward Malvern Hill.

Longstreet's division formed in line of battle and advanced, with A. P. Hill's division in immediate reserve. Near Glendale at Frayser's Farm the Confederates came up on Federal skirmishers, alert and waiting.

Lee, who had joined Longstreet, expected Huger to arrive momentarily at Glendale by way of the Charles City Road. Huger, however, reported that his progress was obstructed.[16] He had delayed for fear that Federals still might be north of White Oak Swamp, then was held up by trees felled by Federal axemen across the road. Instead of leaving his cannons and sending his men around he cut a new road through the woods. When at last Huger approached Glendale he found it so strong (H. W. Slocum's division was blocking him) that he made no assault.

Lee got no word on Jackson's progress and sought none. At about 3 P.M., however, Lee learned from Holmes that the Federals were moving over Malvern Hill, proof that the main Federal army was escaping.

Lee rode down to Holmes's position just west of Malvern Hill, saw Federal columns on the hill, and told Holmes to open up with his artillery. Holmes quickly found, however, that Union guns on Malvern and Federal gunboats on the James nearby were of much more danger to him than he was to them. Porter, in command on Malvern, was mounting the entire artillery reserve of a hundred guns. Some of Holmes's units broke badly and he made no progress.

Longstreet, meanwhile, ordered Magruder to march to the support of Holmes, his purpose being to cover his own right flank.[17] But Magruder could be of no help and retraced his steps to reinforce Longstreet, returning long after the time for his use had passed, having marched the whole day to no avail.

Jackson, joined by Ewell, who had come from Bottoms Bridge, reached the bridge over White Oak Swamp around noon with his twenty thousand men. There he found the structure destroyed and a strong Union force lined up on the south bank, contesting his passage. This force, under General Franklin, consisted of twenty thousand men and a number of long-range rifled Parrott guns. When Jackson pulled up thirty-one cannons, Franklin switched his Parrotts back beyond reach of Jackson's smoothbores and began pounding the Confederate positions.[18] Discouraged, Jackson remained on the north side of the swamp.

Gen. Wade Hampton built an infantry footbridge over an unguarded point a short distance east of the broken bridge. But Jackson, able to advance only his foot soldiers, feared that the Union cannons would cut his infantry to pieces without artillery support.

Longstreet later criticized Jackson for not marching west to the head of White Oak Swamp and down the Charles City Road. Lee, however, had ordered Jackson to protect the Confederate left flank, and Jackson felt that he had no authority to change his approach without Lee's order. Jackson knew, moreover, that—although Fisher's Ford, three miles west, was unguarded—he could not approach by the Charles City Road because it was jammed with Huger's division, as he learned through a messenger sent to Huger by D. H. Hill.[19] A march to Glendale, therefore, would have necessitated a long, roundabout approach by way of Darbytown Road.[20]

Lee rode from Holmes's position back to Longstreet at Frayser's Farm and found Confederate and Union artillery blazing away. It was now late afternoon. Without Magruder and having heard nothing from Huger or Jackson, Lee had available only the eighteen thousand men of Longstreet's and A. P. Hill's divisions.

Neither Longstreet nor Lee appeared to have felt the need for reinforcements. Longstreet had sent Magruder away, and Huger's men, two miles away, could easily have been summoned through the woods.[21] Lee decided, in the time remaining before dark, to launch an unsupported attack with only the divisions of Longstreet and A. P. Hill.

Yet Lee knew that the Union forces around Glendale were rear guards and that even a successful attack would leave his strategic position unchanged. He was unlikely, in the daylight remaining, to cut off the rear guard's retreat. With neither Huger nor Jackson pressing behind, he had little chance of destroying the guard. At worst, since the Federals were in strength, he would be defeated; at best he would impel the Federals toward the main army at a faster pace. And, battle or not, the rear guard was certain to close up with the main army before daylight the next day.

Lee's decision demonstrates, perhaps more clearly than at any other point in the war, his lust for a trial by battle and his inability to see a strategic alternative that would have had a better chance of success and caused fewer casualties.

The Federal position on Malvern Hill proved that McClellan's most logical stopping place was Harrison's Landing, just to the southeast. Even if this were not his destination, the course of the River Road would force him to pass the landing to get farther downriver.

The solution, therefore, was not to attack the strong Federal rear guard at Glendale or to press after McClellan directly, but to march toward Harrison's Landing, sending only a small force in direct pursuit.

Harrison's Landing was badly sited for the Federals. It was on a peninsula of low ground three miles long, defined by the James to the south and the wide tidal Herring Creek to the north, while slightly farther north, beyond the creek and River Road that ran alongside it, was Evelynton heights. These heights dominated both the road and the landing. Lee should have occupied these heights, brought up every fieldpiece available, and pounded the Federals as they appeared below. This would have forced McClellan to abandon Malvern Hill without a fight and for the Federals to attack Evelynton heights, an enterprise of extreme difficulty if occupied by Lee's main force, because Herring Creek left only a narrow front exposed to attack.

Against so intractable a position the cost to the Union army could have been horrendous, very likely leading to failure and possibly to surrender or forced evacuation at great cost.[22]

There were many men in Lee's army who knew the neighborhood intimately. Lee himself was well acquainted with it, for his mother's childhood home was at Shirley plantation, five miles due west of the Berkeley plantation, and he had visited frequently.

There is no evidence that Lee even considered striking toward Evelynton heights and avoiding further head-on battles with the Federal army. In this Lee ignored the salient example of Napoleon. The French emperor never made a frontal attack when he could do otherwise, and he always attempted to block the enemy's retreat. Napoleon counted on the menace of a move on the rear—even if it failed—to shake the enemy's morale and to cause him to make a mistake, which might give Napoleon a chance to strike.[23]

Lee reasoned instead that he must attack at Frayser's Farm. As he had done at Beaver Dam Creek, Lee, with only a fragment of his strength, resorted to a frontal assault on an enemy in position and in unknown strength because his earlier strategic plans had miscarried. In fact, McClellan had more men than Longstreet and A. P. Hill at Frayser's Farm.

Longstreet's division went into an assault at around 5 P.M. straight at the Federal positions just west of the Glendale crossroads. The Confederates swept forward with incredible valor but were met with equal valor. In this battle occurred the most hand-to-hand fighting in the war. The Rebels made some gains but were stopped by heavy rifle and cannon fire from the powerful Union lines.

Longstreet now committed A. P. Hill's division, except for a single brigade held in reserve, but the division could not advance against the tremendous sheets of fire; Union brigades began to move ominously on the Confederate line. As night was falling, Hill ordered forward his last brigade, J. R. Anderson's, and told it to march to within seventy paces of the Federal line without firing, receive the fire of the enemy, then charge with every man raising the Rebel yell. This ploy, though costing the brigade dearly, deceived the Federals into thinking that the Confederates had been heavily reinforced, and they fell back to their emplacements. With this charge, the battle ended.

Frayser's Farm was a tragic defeat. About thirty-three hundred Confederates fell. Federal losses were about two thousand. The Union wagons continued unmolested toward the James. Like Beaver Dam Creek, it was a battle that should not have been fought.

The next morning, Tuesday, July 1, the enemy was gone from Glendale and from before the White Oak Swamp bridge and had massed atop Malvern Hill, rising some 150 feet above the surrounding country three miles down Willis Church Road. Malvern was a high plateau a mile and a half long and half a mile wide, sloping gradually in all directions except south and southwest, where it terminated in bluffs almost overlooking the James. To the southeast was a large millpond. On Malvern Hill the Union infantry stood behind hastily constructed earthworks, while more than a hundred fieldpieces, many of them long-range rifled cannons as well as heavy siege guns, were massed tier upon tier to sweep the ground below. In addition, gunboats positioned in the James could fire on any Rebel advance.

Malvern was easily approachable only from the River Road on the west and Willis Church Road on the north. These approaches McClellan had fortified most heavily.[24] It was a position of great strength, protected on the west and northeast by streams and marshy ground, while to the north beyond the hill and a large, open field were thick woods, through which Rebel artillery could be brought only with difficulty. "In all directions for several hundred yards," writes General Porter, in immediate charge, "the land over which the attacking force must advance was almost entirely cleared."[25]

D. H. Hill had discussed Malvern Hill with the Reverend L. W. Allen, who had been reared in the neighborhood and knew it well. Allen spoke of its commanding height and difficulties of approach, satisfying Hill that "attack upon the concentrated Federal army so splendidly posted, and with such vast superiority in artillery, could only be fatal to us." When he was discussing Malvern Hill with Lee and Longstreet on the morning of July 1, Hill said: "If General McClellan is there in force, we had better let him alone." Longstreet laughed and said, "Don't be scared, now that we have got him whipped." According to Hill, Lee was so convinced that the Federal army was demoralized that he decided to risk the attack.[26]

When the Confederate army arrived at about noon, Jackson's force deployed on the left, or east, D. H. Hill in the center, and Magruder and Huger to the west. The divisions of Longstreet and A. P. Hill remained in reserve behind Magruder. Holmes stayed on the River Road but took no action all day.[27]

Lee and Jackson rode forward to reconnoiter while Lee directed Longstreet to examine the Federal west flank to determine if an attack was feasible. The enormous strength of the Federal artillery positions was readily apparent, as were great blue masses of infantry (two full corps).

Jackson opposed a direct attack and preferred to turn the Federal right, or east, flank. But Longstreet thought there was space on Jackson's front for a hundred or more guns, while a hill to the west of Malvern could support forty or more cannons. From these two positions, Longstreet said, Rebel cannons could cross fire and enfilade the Union guns and throw them into disorder. If this occurred, a concerted charge of infantry from several directions at the same time might seize the hill. Lee rejected Jackson's proposal for a flank movement and ordered Longstreet's plan to be carried into effect.[28]

The entire success of the Confederate assault rested, in Lee's judgment, on getting large numbers of Rebel cannons forward and into position and for these guns to win a duel with the Federal cannons.

The Confederate gunners found it difficult to bring up fieldpieces through the swamps and thickets, and Lee did not arrange for adequate protected avenues to be cut to get the batteries on the two fields quickly and in large numbers. Instead, one battery at a time moved into the open, only to be met by devastating massed fire from the Federal guns as soon as it appeared.

Also, Lee had made no arrangements for the artillery reserve, with most of the army's rifled guns, to come up, and he did not do so now. The army artillery commander, Brig. Gen. William N. Pendleton, had failed to deploy his guns so far in the Seven Days, and on July 1, by his own report, he spent the day "seeking" but not finding Lee and making no attempt to bring up his twenty batteries.[29] There is no evidence that Pendleton came anywhere near the battlefield, where he easily could have found Lee. Pendleton was derelict in his duty, but the greater failure was Lee's—in ordering a concentration of artillery and making no effort to find where his reserve guns were or to bring them forward, or even to concentrate the divisional artillery already on the field.[30]

Confederate guns assigned to divisions were still operating as separate batteries, generally in support of brigades (instead of being employed as consolidated battalions), and could be overpowered if brought out, one by one, against so powerful a concentration as that on Malvern Hill.[31] In addition, many batteries were short of ammunition because of the battles already fought. D. H. Hill's ammunition was entirely depleted and he sent to the rear to replenish it.

Lee distributed an order to each division commander: "Batteries have been established to rake the enemy's line. If it is broken, as is probable, [Brig. Gen. Lewis A.] Armistead, who can witness the effect of the fire, has been ordered to charge with a yell. Do the same."[32]

Armistead's brigade of Huger's division was on the right front of Lee's line.

But Lee was far too optimistic. Since the Confederate artillery had not been concentrated, the individual batteries taking position were crushed in a short while. General Armistead said the batteries of captains William J. Pegram and C. F. Grimes, the only ones behind him, faced forty Federal batteries. "They worked their guns after their men were cut down and only retired when entirely disabled."[33] Jackson got eighteen cannons into operation, more than most commanders. Though Union cannons disabled several, the majority continued to fire, but they were unable to subdue the hostile guns.

At around 3 P.M. Lee concluded that the Confederate batteries would fail to break the Federal front and rode out with Longstreet beyond Jackson's extreme left to see if he could turn the Union right from the east. This was much too late.

Even so, Lee decided to move Longstreet's and A. P. Hill's divisions (in reserve) to the left for a turning movement. Meantime, two events occurred that changed Lee's mind. Shortly after returning from the left flank Lee learned that Armistead had advanced half of his brigade to the base of Malvern Hill to counter Federal skirmishers. Lee also got a report at around 4 P.M. that Union troops were withdrawing from Malvern, although all that had happened was that Union general Sumner was moving his corps under the crest of Malvern Hill nearest the James to protect against the Rebel artillery fire still coming in.

If Sumner's move had been a ruse, it could not have worked better. Lee now seized on the belief that the Federal army was retreating and—entirely disregarding his earlier conclusion that no attack could succeed until the Federal cannons had been neutralized—he hastily sent a verbal order to General Magruder, whose division was coming up, to "press forward your whole line and follow up Armistead's success." Similar orders went to other commanders.[34]

Lee organized no combined assault. Instead he allowed uncoordinated, separate charges by individual brigades at various times all across the front. Magruder was, rashly, first off the mark, sending piecemeal, and unsupported by artillery, nine brigades from his and other commands against the northwest and west slopes of Malvern, beginning at around 4:45 P.M. and continuing until twilight. The individually committed brigades drew almost all of the Federal cannon and rifle fire, and the Confederates endured great casualties but were unable to reach the enemy guns.

"I never saw anything more grandly heroic" than the advance of the brigades, writes D. H. Hill, who witnessed the assaults. "Unfortunately they did not move together and were beaten in detail. As each brigade emerged from the woods, from fifty to one hundred guns opened upon it, tearing great gaps in its ranks; but the heroes reeled on and were shot down by the reserves at the guns, which a few squads reached. Most of them had an open field half a mile wide to cross, under the fire of field artillery in front and the fire of heavy ordnance of the gunboats in their rear. It was not war—it was murder."[35]

Now D. H. Hill's division of five brigades advanced and promptly attracted the fire of practically every Federal battery. Though hundreds fell and others ran to the rear, most of Hill's men pressed forward into the hail of canister and grapeshot. When they got close to the Union lines, the bluecoat infantry stood up and poured volley after volley into them. D. H. Hill's assault stopped, the men fell to the ground, endured more artillery fire, lost a bitter rifle duel with the Federals, and withdrew. Jackson, meanwhile, had sent forward four brigades to support D. H. Hill, but they arrived only after Hill's division had been beaten back, so they contributed little. Huger's division and the remainder of Magruder's division moved to support D. H. Hill, but they, too, made little progress and retired.

The Rebel assault appeared to Union general Porter "as if moved by a reckless disregard of life" as the uncoordinated brigades moved across the mostly open ground, giving clear targets, one after the other, to the Union gunners.[36]

John Esten Cooke writes that "Malvern Hill was less a battle, scientifically disputed, than a bloody combat in which masses of men rushed forward and were swept away by the terrible fire of artillery concentrated in their front."[37]

At nightfall the Confederate attack finally died out, never having seriously threatened the Union position. McClellan already had left the field. If, instead, he had stayed and ordered a Federal attack he might have defeated the Confederate army. But, intent on retreat, he took advantage of the victory to withdraw his army during the night to the landing.

The cost to the Confederacy was staggering—nearly fifty-six hundred men killed or wounded, compared to about two thousand Federal casualties. The next morning, Wednesday, July 2, over the field of battle the wounded and the dead were still lying. A third were corpses, a Federal officer who was there said, "but enough were alive and moving to give the field a singular crawling effect."[38] The Army of Northern Virginia had been exceedingly demoralized and thrown into disorder by the terrible damage it had suffered. In the Northern army as well spirits were low, and the exhausted men, when they reached Harrison's Landing, collapsed and made no effort to prepare a defensive position.

In the informal truce that set in on Malvern Hill, thousands of hungry Rebel survivors emerged from the woods to look for missing comrades and food in dropped haversacks. Never had the gruesomeness of war been more real.

Lee made little progress toward Harrison's Landing this day, heavy rain adding to the misery. But early on Thursday, July 3, Jeb Stuart, with a few of his cavalrymen, ran off a small Federal outpost on Evelynton heights, hauled up a single howitzer, and began shelling the Union camps below them at Harrison's Landing. This caused consternation and McClellan dispatched a division, which seized the heights during the afternoon.

Had Stuart not exhibited such zeal, the Federals probably would not have realized the strategic significance of Evelynton heights and Lee might have occupied them with little opposition when he came up with his infantry on July 4. Although Longstreet wanted to assault the heights even so, Jackson protested, saying that the troops, after the fearful bloodletting of the Seven Days, were in no condition for another frontal assault. Lee, when he arrived, sided with Jackson.

Thus the Seven Days ended. Lee had driven McClellan from the gates of Richmond but he remained in great strength on the James and in a position to resume the offensive once his army had recovered. Although Southerners felt they had been delivered, the actual power balance had tilted against the South. Total Confederate losses, overwhelmingly in killed and wounded, were 20,168, one man in four of the Rebel forces engaged. Total Federal killed and wounded were less than half that of the South—9,796—although the Confederates took 6,000 prisoners (plus nearly 4,000 wounded Federals left behind).[39] With the direct-assault kind of war Robert E. Lee unveiled in the Seven Days, the South might win battles, but it would bleed to death long before it could achieve victory.

Nevertheless, Lee learned something important: he abandoned the sweeping strategy of envelopment by several uncoordinated columns converging from different directions, which had failed so signally. These methods required a commander in full control of his forces, which Lee was not, and were difficult even for the most experienced subordinates. For Lee's still-green division and corps commanders, they had proved impossible. Lee now moved to flank attacks and marches on a narrower compass on the enemy's rear.[40] As was to be shown, this strategy could produce great results, provided that it did not end with costly and unnecessary frontal battles into the teeth of enemy emplacements.

NOTES

General sources: Allan, *Army of Northern Virginia,* 65–150; Dabney, 457–85; Cooke, 227–47; Sanger, 68–76; Henderson, 371–95; Alexander, *Military Memoirs,* 133–74; Freeman, *R. E. Lee,* vol. 2, 159–250; Freeman, *Lee's Lieutenants,* vol. 1, 538–669; Alexander, *Fighting for the Confederacy,* 105–20; Robertson, *Stonewall Brigade,* 120–24; Wise, 213–40; Bridges, 75–83; Chambers, vol. 2, 54–88; Robertson, *A. P. Hill,* 86–98; Johnson and Buel, vol. 2, 366–438; Long, 175–81; and Vandiver, 309–22.

1. Alexander, *Military Memoirs,* 133; *Official Records,* vol. 11, pt. 2, 493; Freeman, *Lee's Lieutenants,* vol. 1, 638, n. 19; Cooke, 230; and Allan, *Army of Northern Virginia,* 97.

2. In his report Lee explains in detail his reasons for hesitating. See *Official Records,* vol. 11, pt. 2, 493.

3. Stuart's horsemen guarded Long Bridge, five miles below Bottoms Bridge, and Forge Bridge, seven miles below Long Bridge. Below Forge Bridge there was no adequate crossing, for all lower roads led into a cul-de-sac where the Chickahominy turned south, about eight miles west of Williamsburg, and became a wide tidal barrier.

4. Porter Alexander thought Lee should have adopted this plan. See Alexander, *Military Memoirs,* 134–35.

5. Ibid.

6. Freeman, *R. E. Lee,* vol. 2, 237–38. The British military writer Gen. J. F. C. Fuller considered Lee's misuse of Stuart an egregious error (Fuller, 161). Likewise, Lee made no plans for employment of the twenty batteries of the reserve artillery. These guns, one-fourth of the army's entire stock, were not used in mass and only occasional batteries went into action at all. Thus Lee made inadequate provisions to counter the Federals' greatest strength, their field and siege guns. See *Official Records,* vol. 11, pt. 2, 489 and 533–37; Freeman, *R. E. Lee,* vol. 2, 115 and 239; Wise, 199–206; and Freeman, *Lee's Lieutenants,* vol. 2, 615–19.

7. *Official Records,* vol. 11, pt. 1, 59–60 and 62, and pt. 2, 99 and 192; Freeman, *Lee's Lieutenants,* vol. 1, 539; and Allan, *Army of Northern Virginia,* 96–97.

8. Freeman, *Lee's Lieutenants,* vol. 1, 540–41; and Freeman, *R. E. Lee,* vol. 2, 167.

9. Freeman, *R. E. Lee,* vol. 2, 168–69; and Freeman, *Lee's Lieutenants,* vol. 1, 541. Federal dispositions for June 29 were for Brig. Gen. H. W. Slocum's division to cross White Oak Swamp during the morning and relieve Keyes's corps, which was to move to the James River and occupy defensive positions around Malvern Hill. Porter's corps was to follow Keyes and prolong the Federal line to the right. The trains were to be pushed to the James in rear of these corps and placed under protection of Federal gunboats. See *Official Records,* vol. 11, pt. 1, 62–63.

10. Freeman, *R. E. Lee,* vol. 2, 172.

11. Ibid., 169; Freeman, *Lee's Lieutenants,* vol. 1, 541 and 560–63; *Official Records,* vol. 11, pt. 2, 680, and 687; and Henderson, 373. In a note to Magruder on June 29 Lee said Jackson was to support Magruder and to push the pursuit of the enemy. This did not invalidate Jackson's responsibility to protect the Confederate flank.

12. Porter Alexander criticizes Jackson for not crossing by New Bridge, less than three miles upriver, and going to the assistance of Magruder. However, Jackson's orders were to operate on the Federal northern flank and he had no authority to change his instructions or route of approach. See Alexander, *Military Memoirs,* 136.

13. *Official Records,* vol. 11, pt. 2, 662, 680, and 789; Freeman, *R. E. Lee,* vol. 2, 170–71; and Freeman, *Lee's Lieutenants,* vol. 1, 550–51.

14. *Official Records,* vol. 11, pt. 2, 687; Freeman, *R. E. Lee,* vol. 2, 174; and Freeman, *Lee's Lieutenants,* vol. 1, 554.

15. Lee's staff organization was defective. He had made no arrangements for continuing communication with the separate Confederate columns, while the column commanders, likewise, did not see the need to keep Lee constantly informed. The result was that Lee lost all grip of the battle and each commander operated too independently and without coordination. See Freeman, *R. E. Lee,* vol. 2, 233–37.

16. There were forty thousand Federal soldiers in the vicinity of Glendale, consisting of half of Sumner's and Franklin's and all of Heintzelman's corps. See Allan, *Army of Northern Virginia,* 107.

17. Longstreet, 139; and Freeman, *Lee's Lieutenants,* vol. 1, 585–86. Longstreet's narrative does not make clear whether he or Lee was responsible for sending Magruder to Holmes.

18. *Official Records,* vol. 11, pt. 2, 556–57, 566, and 627; and Allan, *Army of Northern Virginia,* 109–11.

19. Johnson and Buel, vol. 2, 388; Freeman, *R. E. Lee,* vol. 2, 574–75; Longstreet, 150; and Henderson, 382–83. Jackson felt that it was Lee's responsibility to change his route of approach. Nearly two weeks later, when Jackson walked in while members of his staff were discussing whether Jackson should have moved to Longstreet's aid, Jackson said curtly: "If General Lee had wanted me he could have sent for me." An incident that reflects Jackson's concept of obedience to orders is recounted by John Esten Cooke (Cooke, 17). At the Virginia Military Institute in 1858 some cadets teased Jackson because he had refused to pull his battery out of a heavily shelled position during the Mexican War. "Why didn't you run, major?" one cadet asked. "I was not ordered to do so," Jackson replied. "If I had been ordered to run, I would have done so; but I was directed to hold my position and I had no right to abandon it."

20. Since the Civil War it has become customary by Jackson's critics to attribute all sorts of reasons for Jackson's so-called failures of command during the Seven Days, ranging from fatigue and sickness to an alleged inability of Jackson to operate well while under Lee's direct command. Since Jackson later operated in spectacular fashion as Lee's lieutenant in several campaigns, the last charge appears to be spurious. As regards the other charges, Jackson no doubt was weary from his long march from the valley and there is some evidence that he was suffering from a fever. However, close examination of the "failures" reveals that they were not failures at all. The major criticisms have been directed at his alleged lateness in arriving northeast of Mechanicsville on June 26 and inactivity afterward, his failure on the twenty-ninth to find some other way to cross the Chickahominy when the Grapevine Bridge proved so difficult to rebuild, and his failure on the thirtieth to cross the White Oak Swamp at a ford upstream when he found the main bridge broken and a strong Federal force in front. In regard to Mechanicsville, Jackson abided by his orders when some of the other commanders did not. Lee knew that Jackson had been delayed on the twenty-sixth and therefore his "lateness" was not a real factor. Lee knew that the Federal position at Beaver Dam Creek was formidable and had conceived the entire approach to the Federal right, or northern, flank to turn this line and avoid a fight. Jackson *did* arrive where he was supposed to—the right flank and rear of the Federal position. This guaranteed that the Federals would abandon the Beaver Dam position as soon as they learned of his presence. Once arrived, Jackson did not have to do anything. That was the whole point

of the maneuver—to *avoid* a battle. Yet Lee allowed A. P. Hill to attack and be severely repulsed along Beaver Dam Creek, a completely unnecessary engagement, since shortly Porter's position there was to be abandoned. In regard to Grapevine Bridge, Jackson remained along this line because Lee had instructed him to protect the Chickahominy in the remote case that McClellan decided to retreat, after all, down the peninsula. A crossing by Jackson to the west of Grapevine Bridge would have uncovered the eastern line of the river and been a violation of Jackson's instructions. Lee had not directed Jackson to assist Magruder in his attack. In regard to crossing White Oak Swamp, Jackson had similar orders from Lee to operate on the Federal flank and rear, and any move to the west would have uncovered the Federal right flank. The only fair criticism of Jackson's conduct is that made by Col. G. F. R. Henderson: "[Jackson] should have informed Lee of his inability to force the passage across the swamp and have held three divisions in readiness to march to Glendale" (Henderson, 383).

21. Freeman, *R. E. Lee,* vol. 2, 198–99 and 572–82; and Henderson, 375–83.

22. Porter Alexander, G. F. R. Henderson, and Walter H. Taylor, Lee's aide, thought that occupation of Evelynton heights was by far the best strategy, even four days later, after much Confederate bloodshed. See Alexander, *Military Memoirs,* 167–71; Henderson, 393–94; and R. Taylor, 41–44.

23. Commandant J. Colin, *The Transformations of War* (London: Hugh Rees, 1912), 279–89.

24. Allan, *Army of Northern Virginia,* 125.

25. Johnson and Buel, vol. 2, 409.

26. Ibid., 391.

27. *Official Records,* vol. 11, pt. 2, 907–8 (Holmes's report).

28. Col. G. F. R. Henderson writes: "If Jackson had been in charge of operations, the disastrous battle of Malvern Hill would never have been fought" (Henderson, 384 and 707).

29. Susan P. Lee, *Memoirs of William Nelson Pendleton* (Philadelphia: 1893), 194.

30. Jennings Cropper Wise, a historian of Lee's artillery, defends Pendleton (Wise, 226–29), saying that Lee and Longstreet decided on the artillery duel "without the slightest consultation with the chief of artillery of the army." This is disingenuous, since Pendleton was nowhere to be found.

However, Wise says that Pendleton's batteries were readily available, "literally blocking the few roads that existed in rear of the army." Therefore, any staff officer of Lee could have "brought them galloping to the front," even if Pendleton was absent.

31. Alexander, *Fighting for the Confederacy,* 104–5.

32. *Official Records,* vol. 11, pt. 2, 496, 628, 669, and 677; Johnson and Buel, vol. 2, 392; Freeman, *R. E. Lee,* vol. 2, 207; Freeman, *Lee's Lieutenants,* vol. 1, 595; and Alexander, *Military Memoirs,* 157.

33. Alexander, *Military Memoirs,* 160; Freeman, *Lee's Lieutenants,* vol. 1, 596.

34. *Official Records,* vol. 11, p, 2, 677–78; Alexander, *Military Memoirs,* 162; Freeman, *Lee's Lieutenants,* vol. 1, 599; Freeman, *R. E. Lee,* vol. 2, 211; and Henderson, 387.

35. Johnson and Buel, vol. 2, 394.

36. Ibid., 417; and Freeman, *R. E. Lee,* vol. 2, 211–15.

37. Cooke, 234.

38. Gen. William W. Averell, in Johnson and Buel, vol. 2, 432. See also Freeman, *R. E. Lee,* vol. 2, 220.

39. Allan, *Army of Northern Virginia,* 143–44; Johnson and Buel, vol. 2, 404; *Southern Historical Society Papers,* vol. 1, 421; *Official Records,* vol. 11, pt. 2, 498 and 502–10; Freeman, *R. E. Lee,* vol. 2, 230–31; and Alexander, *Military Memoirs,* 171 and 174.

40. Freeman, *R. E. Lee,* vol. 2, 249.

8

JACKSON MOVES NORTH

★ ★ ★ Shortly after the Seven Days, Stonewall Jackson altered his strategy for achieving Southern independence. Although there is no direct documentation of this change, his actions show that he followed a radically different policy after he failed for the fourth time to convince the Confederate military leaders, Robert E. Lee and Jefferson Davis, to mount an invasion of the North and to challenge the will of the Northern people to wage war.

On July 7 Jackson made his last recorded try to get his old strategy accepted, once more calling in his political friend Col. A. R. Boteler and asking him to approach President Davis to urge an immediate invasion of the North. The South, Jackson pleaded, was losing valuable time watching McClellan at Harrison's Landing. It was repeating the blunder of idleness made after the battle of Manassas, allowing the weakened enemy time to recover. McClellan was beaten, Jackson emphasized. He would have to reorganize and reinforce his army before it would be capable of taking the offensive again. This alone assured Richmond's safety.

The Confederacy should seize the advantage and strike into the North. With sixty thousand men the South could march into Maryland and threaten Washington. Jackson persuaded Boteler to see Davis directly because Jackson already had approached Lee without success.[1]

Boteler failed. President Davis could focus only on the obvious dangers facing the Confederacy, not the opportunities Jackson saw so clearly. He thought up a litany of reasons why Jackson's proposal could not be attempted: McClellan might be reinforced by a corps under Ambrose E. Burnside being withdrawn by sea from New Bern, on the North Carolina coast; McClellan might cut the railways supplying Richmond from the south and flank the line of fortifications defending the capital; the losses of the Seven Days were so great that the Army of Northern Virginia could not undertake so dangerous an expedition.[2]

In consequence of this failure, Jackson turned to the only remaining method of achieving Southern independence: destruction of the Union field army, or a major part of it, in battle. This army shielded the North; without it, the Union was defenseless.[3]

In all of the engagements he fought, of course, Jackson tried to defeat the enemy utterly. However, he understood that battle is only a single, and extremely uncertain, method of imposing a nation's will on the enemy. And he realized how difficult and costly it would be for the South, palpably weak in manpower and weapons, to shatter the Northern army. That is why he had sought repeatedly to win victory at less cost by avoiding the enemy's military strength and striking at human nature—the willingness of most people to accept peace if faced with demolition of their wealth and property.

But he recognized at last that neither Davis nor Lee would accept his concept. From this point on, Jackson concentrated on plans to overwhelm the Northern field army, or parts of it, in decisive battles or campaigns, and he attempted to convince General Lee to adopt them.

Lee, however, was fighting the war in a fundamentally different way. In the Seven Days he had focused on limited objectives

—to break the enemy's railway supply line, defeat Porter's isolated corps, and descend upon McClellan's rear guard. He had not shown an ability to make sweeping strategic moves aimed at the defeat of the entire enemy army, such as could have occurred if he had struck for Evelynton heights rather than pursued the tail of McClellan's army. He also had demonstrated a dangerous tendency to be deflected from his original objectives and drawn into frontal battles that had little or no hope of success.

Lee's limited horizon greatly constricted Stonewall Jackson's opportunities to destroy at least parts of the Union army. As was to be seen, Jackson led Lee four times to within sight of this goal, and each time, Lee backed off. Only on the fifth occasion was he able to convince Lee to dare all, and this turned into the fateful climax of his career.

★ ★ ★

Jackson recognized that quick action was demanded because the Confederacy was in peril—it was in a worse strategic position immediately after the Seven Days than it had been in before. Abraham Lincoln was at last consolidating Union military command under Maj. Gen. Henry Wager Halleck, promising an end to the chaotic system of separate, uncoordinated armies that had hobbled the war effort so far. A new Federal "Army of Virginia" of more than seventy thousand men was forming under a recently appointed commander, Maj. Gen. John Pope, and he was energetically preparing to assist McClellan by marching on Richmond or its communications.[4]

Because of disastrous Confederate losses in the Seven Days, either Federal army, McClellan's or Pope's, was stronger than the Army of Northern Virginia. If Pope attacked and McClellan resumed his advance, Lee's army was almost bound to be defeated. In the midst of the gloom, Jackson saw a flash of light: if the Confederates could strike Pope before he could consolidate his forces, they might destroy his army before McClellan could come to his assistance. Robert E. Lee, however, like President Davis, continued to be mesmerized by McClellan's ninety thousand men at Harrison's Landing, despite the fact that it was a dispirited army because McClellan labored under the delusion that he had been defeated by more than twice his numbers. Lee, fearing that McClellan might move, refused to commit large forces against Pope.

Lee did at last send Jackson north—not to break up Pope's army, but to block his advance toward a strategic point too important to ignore: on July 12, 1862, some of Pope's cavalry occupied Culpeper Court House, only twenty-seven miles north of Gordonsville. This move exposed the "Gordonsville loop" of the Virginia Central Railroad, the only rail line between Richmond and the Shenandoah Valley. The next day, July 13, Lee ordered Jackson with the Stonewall Division under Brig. Gen. Charles S. Winder and Dick Ewell's division—twelve thousand men in all—to move to Gordonsville.[5]

Jackson immediately set about developing a strategy to trap parts of Pope's army and shatter them one at a time. However, Lee had no large strategic plan in mind and shaped his actions in response to Federal moves. His aim from first to last in the campaign about to unfold was to relieve northern Virginia of Union troops, not to fight a general battle or to reach a decision in the war.[6]

It took Jackson until July 16 to get his leading brigades into Gordonsville. Pope had time to beat him to that critical point, and on July 14 Pope ordered Brig. Gen. John P. Hatch to seize the town with cavalry. Cautious Hatch waited to assemble infantry, artillery, and a wagon train with more cavalry before attacking and was still some distance from his objective when Jackson arrived and sealed off Gordonsville from anything short of a major assault.[7]

McClellan's proper response to the news of Jackson's departure would have been to strike at once for Richmond or Petersburg against the weakened Rebel army. McClellan saw this, but Jackson had read his character accurately—McClellan did not lack men, he lacked will. He was not going to move on his own volition, and Halleck would not order him to take the offensive.[8]

On July 24, 1862, the day after arriving in Washington from his previous assignment in the West, General Halleck took ship to visit McClellan on the peninsula. McClellan made a strong case for a strike south of the James and seizure of Petersburg by a coup de main, but not until his army was strengthened. He claimed that the Confederates had 200,000 soldiers.[9]

With ninety thousand troops and control of the James, McClellan had the resources necessary to seize Petersburg. This would have forced the evacuation of Richmond, as it did in 1865. However, Halleck did not recognize the superlative strategic position McClellan occupied. He wrote McClellan after their meeting that it was unsafe to permit Lee to remain between two divided Union armies that could not support each other.

Halleck had made up his mind to evacuate Harrison's Landing by July 27, but he did not tell McClellan until August 3.[10]

Halleck's decision meant the abandonment of the only position from which he could have forced the evacuation of Richmond in a reasonable time. As Porter Alexander writes, the Federals "were only to find it again after two years' fighting and the loss of over 100,000 men; and they would find it then only by being defeated upon every other possible line of advance."[11]

★ ★ ★

John Pope was the most ridiculed and vilified of the Union generals who faced the Army of Northern Virginia. His reputation was scarcely better in the Federal army. Pope made the mistake of issuing a bombastic order to his troops on July 14, 1862, from his "headquarters in the saddle." In it he said: "I come to you from the West where we have always seen the backs of our enemies; from an army whose business it has been to seek the adversary and beat him when he was found; whose policy has been attack and not defense. . . . I presume I have been called here to pursue the same system and to lead you against the enemy. . . . Meantime, I desire to dismiss from your minds certain phrases, which I am sorry to find so much in vogue amongst you. I heard constantly of 'taking strong positions and holding them'; of 'lines of retreat' and of 'bases of supplies.' Let us discard such ideas. . . . Let us study the probable lines of retreat of our opponents and leave our own to take care of themselves. . . . Success and glory are in the advance. Disaster and shame lurk in the rear."[12]

This pronunciamento angered Union soldiers of the eastern army as much as it entertained Confederates. More serious was a set of orders that, for the first time, authorized Federal soldiers to subsist on the country, leading to pillage and insults to females. Pope also held the local populace responsible for damage by guerrillas and was not careful in distinguishing between guerrillas and regular Confederate cavalry. He authorized reimbursement for requisitions only to persons who took the oath of allegiance to the United States and the evacuation to Confederate lines of anyone who refused. If any such person returned or if any citizen communicated with the enemy, he or she was subject to death. A mother who wrote her soldier son could be treated as a spy. One of Pope's subordinates, Brig. Gen. Adolph von Steinwehr, arrested five Luray citizens and said that if a guerrilla killed one of his soldiers, one of the hostages would be shot.

The Confederate government protested these total-war ordinances and said it would be compelled to retaliate if they were enforced. Halleck modified Pope's "pillage order" materially on August 15 and rebuked Steinwehr.[13]

Pope's draconian approach symbolized a severe hardening of attitudes in the North. In light of the horrible casualties at Shiloh and in the Seven Days, a new mood spread that the South could be subdued only by brute force. No longer were the Southern states thought of as "erring sisters"; now they were considered intractable enemies.

Abraham Lincoln and others had resisted Northern abolitionists' efforts to free the slaves. But in the face of the incredible sacrifices required, many Northerners were finding less resolve to pursue the original purpose of keeping the nation intact. Even moderate Northerners now saw that slaves were contributing immensely to the rebellion—raising food and forage, building entrenchments, producing cotton that blockade runners exchanged for European weapons, and much more.

On July 22 Lincoln proposed an emancipation proclamation to his cabinet. It would leave slavery intact in the border states, Delaware, Maryland, Kentucky, and Missouri, that had not seceded, but declare slavery ended on January 1, 1863, in the Confederate states. Its immediate purpose was less to free slaves, since few would be affected, than to transform the war into a crusade. Lincoln's cabinet convinced him to hold off while the war was going so badly for the North. As Secretary of State William H. Seward said, it "may be viewed as the last measure of an exhausted government . . . our last shriek on the retreat." Lincoln agreed. He waited for a successful Northern battle to announce his revolutionary move.[14]

Nevertheless, signs that the North was moving toward a radical transmutation of the war into another form were clear to astute observers, such as the South Carolinian Mary Chesnut, who wrote on July 8: "This war was undertaken by us to shake off the yoke of foreign invaders, so we consider our cause righteous. The Yankees, since the war has begun, have discovered it is to free the slaves they are fighting, so their cause is noble."[15]

★ ★ ★

Lee wrote twice that Pope must be "suppressed." He reviled the general and said of his own nephew, Col. Louis Marshall, who served on the staff of Union general Nathaniel P. Banks: "I could forgive [his] fighting against us but not his joining Pope."[16]

Pope was to demonstrate that he was no match for Lee or Jackson. But he was not a contemptible enemy. He used his cavalry more effectively than other Federal commanders, his defensive dispositions on the whole were adequate, and on two occasions, when he discovered that his army was in danger, he moved it back rapidly.

When Stonewall Jackson arrived at Gordonsville he was eager to undertake aggressive operations. But his force of twelve thousand was inadequate and he appealed to Lee for more troops.

Lee hesitated, because McClellan still occupied Harrison's Landing. However, with Pope's menace growing, he ordered A. P. Hill's division, now with twelve thousand men, to go to Jackson's support on July 27.[17] Hill arrived on the twenty-ninth.

Meanwhile, Halleck instructed Pope to make demonstrations toward Gordonsville to occupy Jackson and prevent interference with McClellan's withdrawal from the peninsula. In response Pope's cavalry moved to the Robinson River, a tributary to the Rapidan, south of Culpeper Court House, only about sixteen air miles north of Gordonsville.[18]

On August 5 Federal forces at Harrison's Landing reoccupied Malvern Hill and made menacing gestures. But Lee was certain it was a bluff and on August 7 Confederates found them gone. Federal troops began boarding transports for Aquia Creek near Fredericksburg and Alexandria to join Pope.[19]

The war was taking a new direction. Although abandoning the peninsula forfeited a powerful strategic advantage, uniting Federal forces would mean that no Confederate army could stand against them. Though Lee hesitated in sending Jackson additional troops, he did authorize him to advance.[20]

This left Jackson in a difficult spot. His twenty-four thousand men were just half the force Pope was assembling. Nevertheless, hoping to lure Pope forward with a fraction of his command, Jackson withdrew south of Gordonsville. Halleck warned Pope that it was probably a ruse, but Pope telegraphed back: "Within ten days, unless the enemy is heavily reinforced from Richmond, I shall be in possession of Gordonsville and Charlottesville."[21]

Pope planned to demonstrate toward Charlottesville, believing that this would force Jackson to protect the town or give battle under adverse circumstances. Halleck urged Pope to be cautious, but Pope impetuously ordered his closest forces to converge on Culpeper.

Culpeper was important because several roads met there, three of which the Federals were using in their advance. However, only a small portion of Pope's army arrived at Culpeper; Jackson, informed by spies, saw a chance to trap this vanguard. If successful he might prevent the junction of Pope's forces and then turn on one or two of the others, isolating and defeating them, before they could be reinforced.[22]

Jackson set his army in motion, sending his cavalry under Brig. Gen. Beverly H. Robertson to drive Federal horsemen across the Rapidan and to join up with his infantry at Orange the night of August 7. The next day he intended to press on to Culpeper, nineteen miles north. Through a series of mixups he got only eight miles up the road.[23]

Pope had posted twelve hundred of his cavalry along the Robinson River, about seven miles north of Orange. Despite Halleck's instructions to be cautious, Pope sent about eighty-seven hundred men of Banks's corps to join them. The corps formed up north of Cedar Run, dangerously exposed, about five miles north of the Robinson River.

Pope's orders, delivered on the morning of August 9 by Lee's nephew, Colonel Marshall, were vague enough to give the impetuous Banks, still smarting under the defeats Jackson had handed him in the valley, the leverage to attack in hopes of redeeming his reputation. Jackson, who had learned that he was facing Banks again, commented: "He is always ready to fight and he generally gets whipped."[24]

Meanwhile, Pope pressed James B. Ricketts's division of ninety-two hundred infantrymen behind Banks on the Culpeper Road. Rufus King's division was marching from Fredericksburg, while Frémont's corps (now commanded by Franz Sigel, upon Frémont's resignation) was hastening from Sperryville.[25] None could get on the field, however, to help Banks on August 9.[26]

★ ★ ★

The battle of Cedar Run (or Cedar Mountain) was the last fully directed by Stonewall Jackson as an independent commander. It also was a model of the way the Civil War was fought in the summer of 1862, demonstrating the continuing stand-up nature of infantry assaults, the failure of defenders to emplace, a residual effort by cavalry to turn the scales of battle, the increasingly sophisticated positioning of artillery, and the necessity of troops forced to approach the battlefield on a single road to be fed into combat unit by unit.

Jackson still believed as he approached the Robinson River that no more than advance detachments of Pope's army had reached Culpeper, and he expected to press on to that town. Although he had twenty-four thousand men, he was anxious about the active Federal cavalry under Brig. Gen. George D. Bayard and detailed two brigades totaling four thousand men to guard his twelve hundred wagons, left just south of the river.[27]

About midmorning, preceded by cavalry, Jackson's advance guard, Jubal A. Early's brigade of Ewell's division, crossed the Robinson River on the Orange-Culpeper road (now U.S. Route 15) and advanced up a small valley bounded a mile on the right, or east, by the rounded, forested ridge of Cedar (or Slaughter) Mountain, more or less parallel to the road. The land between road and mountain was mostly open meadow or fields planted in Indian corn. On the left, or west, the land rose to a forested upland, except for a rectangular field cut out of these woods, with one side fronting the road. This field of about forty acres had recently been harvested and shocks of wheat still stood on it. Known thereafter as the Wheatfield, it became the critical arena of the battle.[28]

Ewell rode up, and he and Early, observing Union horsemen ahead, decided that the Federals might be in strength. Ewell directed Early to move to the right across the open fields between the road and the mountain. Early pressed forward, drove back the Federal cavalry, reached the crest of a ridge, and came into sight of Union infantry and artillery emplaced twelve hundred yards beyond on a plateau rising above the north fork of Cedar Run. Early stationed his infantry on the reverse slope of the ridge and posted eight guns nearby around a clump of cedars.[29]

When Jackson arrived soon after, he and Ewell conceived a double envelopment of the Federal position—Ewell moving to the right around Cedar Mountain and Winder and Hill around the left, or west of the Orange-Culpeper road, while Early held the enemy's attention in the center.

In preparation Jackson ordered artillery placed just east of the road and west of Early's position near the gate of a lane leading eastward to a farmhouse. This point became known as the Gate. Winder called up every rifled gun he could locate and opened fire.

Meantime, Jackson sent Ewell with his other two brigades to the northwest slope of Cedar Mountain. There Ewell set up six guns on a promontory a couple hundred feet above the valley, facing north, and hid his infantry in the deep woods of the mountain. Commander of the guns was an eighteen-year-old captain fresh from the Virginia Military Institute, Joseph W. Latimer, who soon became Ewell's acting artillery chief and died at Gettysburg.[30]

Seizing Cedar Mountain was the master stroke of the day. Jackson had seen that the high promontory commanded a large part of the terrain. By grabbing it, his cannons, elevated above the fields, could dominate Banks's entire left flank and prevent any Federal move in this direction wholly by artillery fire. In conjunction with the guns at the Gate and around Early, the batteries could also provide converging fire to shield a Confederate advance or protect against any assault on the center of the Confederate line.[31] Jackson had secured his right wing.

Meanwhile, as the Stonewall Brigade came up the Orange-Culpeper road, Jackson sent William B. Taliaferro's Third Brigade east of the road between the Gate and Early and the seventeen hundred–man Second Brigade under Lt. Col. Thomas S. Garnett into the woods west of the road facing the Wheatfield. To help protect the guns near the Gate, Garnett placed his Twenty-first Virginia and half of the Forty-eighth Virginia along the western edge of the road, curving his line nearly ninety degrees to accomplish it.[32] Winder ordered the Stonewall Brigade under Col. Charles A. Ronald into immediate reserve directly behind the guns.[33]

A. P. Hill, when he arrived, was to envelop the Federal right, or west. However, the Confederate column occupied more than seven miles of road and it would take two hours to deploy. It was a little after 3 P.M. when the Rebels formed their lines and turned their guns on the Federal batteries. For the next two hours artillery duels thundered across the valley. The Confederate fire was especially accurate. One shell killed six of Banks's bodyguards. Though Federal fire was less damaging, it also extracted casualties. At around 4:45 P.M. a Federal shell mortally wounded Winder. Command of the Stonewall Division devolved on Brigadier General Taliaferro.[34]

Shortly after Jackson got the news of Winder's fall, he heard from Early that Federal troops were forming on the northern side of the Wheatfield and might be preparing to assault his left flank. Jackson sent a message to Garnett, warning him to watch his left, and soon thereafter rode up to Garnett's position himself. Garnett reported that Jackson told him "to look well to my left flank and to report at once to General Taliaferro for reinforcements." Garnett sent an officer and orderly to reconnoiter the woods to his left and two officers to go back and secure more support.

While on the way to see Garnett or immediately after, Jackson ordered forward the Stonewall Brigade to form on Garnett's left in line of battle. Unfortunately, due to its inept commander, Colonel Ronald, the brigade emerged 450 yards southwest of Garnett's brigade, at the edge of a cutover woods that adjoined the Wheatfield. There Ronald halted for twenty crucial minutes while he sent a courier to Taliaferro to find out what to do.

Taliaferro, meanwhile, appeared at Garnett's brigade and went out alone in front of Garnett's left-hand detachment, the First Virginia (Irish) Battalion, but he saw no evidence of a Federal attack. However, by the time he got back to the Gate, a courier reported that the Federals were emerging in front of the Irish battalion. Taliaferro hurried the Tenth Virginia Regiment from east of the road to the left rear of Garnett's brigade as support. When Ronald's courier reached Taliaferro, he ordered the Stonewall Brigade to move rapidly to support Garnett.[35]

Jackson returned to the Gate at about 5:15 P.M., as A. P. Hill's division began to arrive. He directed Col. Edward L. Thomas's Georgia brigade to bolster Early's right.[36]

On the Federal side, General Banks, though ignorant of Confederate strength, decided to attack.[37] He formed all but two of his brigades in line of battle. In the center, opposite Taliaferro, Early, and Thomas, he posted two brigades of Brig. Gen. Christopher C. Augur's division, leaving only a tiny 372-man brigade under Col. George S. Greene to guard his left, or eastern, flank. West of the road, in the woods facing the Wheatfield, he drew up the seventeen hundred–man brigade of Brig. Gen. Samuel W. Crawford, leaving George H. Gordon's to the rear as reserve and flank guard.

At about 5:45 P.M. Banks ordered the lines forward. Augur's division drove hard against the three Confederate brigades opposing it but could make little headway against their concentrated rifle fire and artillery, especially the guns on Cedar Mountain, which raked the Union lines with enfilade fire.

The situation was entirely different on the west, where Crawford moved directly against that part of Garnett's brigade facing the Wheatfield. Crawford's right extended well beyond Garnett's left, held by the Irish battalion, while his center and left bore down on the other Rebel regiments: the Forty-second Virginia in the center and part of the Forty-eighth Virginia on the right. The remainder of the Forty-eighth and the Twenty-first Virginia faced east along the Orange-Culpeper road.

To the rear of the Irish battalion the Tenth Virginia was going forward but had not emerged from the woods. Meanwhile, the tardy Stonewall Brigade finally was moving to the western edge of the Wheatfield. There, facing northeast with both of his flanks in the air, it was too far away to save Garnett's brigade but positioned to attack Crawford's extreme right wing.

When Crawford's brigade marched into the open, the veterans of the Forty-second and Forty-eighth Virginia opened fire against the Fifth Connecticut, advancing on them, then settled into terrible volleys that overrode the sound of the artillery. New Englanders dropped, but the survivors marched grimly on. However, the fire of the Irish battalion was ineffective. The men were tense, and when their commander, Maj. John Seddon, ordered the first volley their bullets largely went over the heads of the Twenty-eighth New York and Forty-sixth Pennsylvania moving on them. The specter of the Federals' inexorably marching onward terrified the men and they broke and ran.

This uncovered Garnett's left flank. Most of Crawford's brigade gleefully rolled up the Rebel line from west to east, driving away the remainder of Garnett's brigade, crossing the Orange-Culpeper road, dislodging the Confederate cannons and Taliaferro's brigade, and bearing back part of Early's brigade. The Irish battalion's defection appeared to be bringing on the disintegration of Jackson's army.

However, Early's left-hand regiment, the Thirteenth Virginia, under Col. James A. Walker, made a gallant resistance and slowed the Federal assault, which was already losing impetus. Then Early's Twelfth Georgia, with parts of the Fifty-second and Fifty-eighth Virginia, crashed against the Federals and broke the back of the attack.

Meanwhile, the extreme right of Crawford's line had routed the Tenth Virginia and the Twenty-seventh Virginia, the southernmost regiment of the Stonewall Brigade. Most of the brigade held, however, and wheeled onto the flank of the Third Wisconsin, sending it reeling to the rear. Thereafter the Stonewall Brigade formed an anchor for the extreme Confederate left.

Stonewall Jackson knew that the rest of A. P. Hill's division was coming up. He found Lawrence O'B. Branch's North Carolina brigade already in line of battle west of the road and ordered it forward. He also ordered James J. Archer's Georgia-Tennessee-Alabama brigade to move up on Branch's left and W. Dorsey Pender's North Carolina brigade to swing out north of the Stonewall Brigade to envelop the Federal right flank.

Branch's Tar Heels advanced eagerly, driving back those parts of Crawford's force still west of the road and forcing the main body of Federals who had crossed it to hurry back over the Wheatfield to hide in the woods before they were cut off.

Now, far too late to do any good, General Banks committed Crawford's last regiment, the Tenth Maine. The regiment advanced bravely, alone and unsupported, into the middle of the Wheatfield. Branch's and Archer's brigades unleashed sheets of fire and the Down Easters held their impossible position only a few minutes before rushing back.

Banks, realizing he was about to be beaten, attempted one last, desperate act. He ordered 164 men of the First Pennsylvania Cavalry to charge just as the Tenth Maine was collapsing. The courageous but senseless charge roared down the eastern edge of the Wheatfield next to the road and drew hundreds of Rebel riflemen, who quickly shot down all but seventy-one men.

Jackson now ordered a general advance across the whole line. Branch and Archer drove directly across the Wheatfield against Gordon's brigade, Banks's last intact force on this wing. Against this assault and the pressure of Pender's brigade wrapping around its flank, Gordon's brigade broke in disorder, losing a third of its men. East of the road the Rebels drove Augur's division back, inflicting many casualties and capturing a brigade commander, Henry Prince. During the heat of the action Prince came up to A. P. Hill and began to speak of "the fortunes of war" that "have thrown me in your hands." Hill interrupted: "Damn fortunes of war, general! Get to the rear. You're in danger here."[38]

The Federals retreated rapidly. As darkness fell, the whole Rebel line crossed Cedar Run and swept over a mile north, finally coming to a halt against Ricketts's division, which had rushed forward and lined up in order of battle. Jackson realized that there was no sense attacking at night and withdrew his army.

It had been a complete Confederate victory. Although Jackson had failed to seize Culpeper, he still crushed Pope's advance guard, due to Banks's overconfidence.

The battle had a much broader significance, however: Jackson stopped an army twice the size of his, and Halleck, stunned and uncertain as to the strength of the Confederates, forbade Pope to advance farther than the Rapidan. By this single blow Jackson threw Pope's still-superior army on the strategic defensive and gained more than a week, in which the bulk of Lee's army could come up.

Banks's corps lost 2,381 men out of about 9,000 committed, most killed and wounded. Jackson gained four hundred prisoners, fifty-three hundred stand of arms, and a cannon. Banks's corps had been rendered ineffective and Pope relegated it to guard duties in the campaign about to unfold.[39] Jackson lost 229 men killed and 1,047 wounded, nearly half in Garnett's and Taliaferro's brigades.[40]

NOTES

General sources: Allan, *Army of Northern Virginia,* 151–79; Dabney, 493–508; Cooke, 246–67; Alexander, *Military Memoirs,* 175–82; Henderson, 397–420; Robert K. Krick, *Stonewall Jackson at Cedar Mountain* (Chapel Hill: University of North Carolina Press, 1990); Maurice, 123–33; Freeman, *R. E. Lee,* vol. 2, 256–77; Freeman, *Lee's Lieutenants,* vol. 2, 3–52; Chambers, vol. 2, 89–123; and Vandiver, 323–45.

1. Dabney, 486–87; *Southern Historical Society Papers,* vol. 40, 180–82. John Esten Cooke (Cooke, 247) asserts that Jackson, as he had done when he advocated an attack into the North after First Manassas, raised the example of Scipio Africanus as the proper model for the South. See also Freeman, *R. E. Lee,* vol. 2, 260–61; and Henderson, 397–98. Porter Alexander shared Jackson's view. Lee, he says, could not wait idly at Richmond for the enemy to slowly make up his mind. See Alexander, *Military Memoirs,* 179.

2. Henderson, 397–98.

3. Jackson enunciated this resolve most clearly after the battle of Fredericksburg in December 1862, when he told his staff: "We must do more than defeat their armies; we must destroy them." See Freeman, *Lee's Lieutenants,* vol. 2, 518–19.

4. Lincoln appointed Pope on June 27, 1862, to take command of the forces of Frémont, Banks, and McDowell, totaling fifty thousand men,

plus twelve thousand men garrisoning Washington, as well as Brig. Gen. Jacob D. Cox, with eleven thousand men, coming from West Virginia. See Johnson and Buel, vol. 2, 281 and 451; Allan, *Army of Northern Virginia,* 152; and Henderson, 403. On July 11 Lincoln named Halleck, who had shown some capacity while commanding the western forces, as commander in chief of all Federal armies. Halleck arrived in Washington on July 23. See *Official Records,* vol. 11, pt. 3, 314; Allan, *Army of Northern Virginia,* 154; Henderson, 402; and Alexander, *Military Memoirs,* 177. Lincoln appointed Pope to draw off Confederate troops and relieve pressure on McClellan. He named Halleck to bring about cooperation between McClellan and Pope. Pope's mission, as outlined on June 26, 1862, was to cover Washington, control the Shenandoah, "and at the same time so operate upon the enemy's lines of communication in the direction of Gordonsville and Charlottesville as to draw off, if possible, a considerable force of the enemy from Richmond and thus relieve the operations against that city of the Army of the Potomac." See *Official Records,* vol. 1, pt. 2, 21; Johnson and Buel, vol. 2, 449–50.

5. The losses of the Seven Days had sadly depleted the Confederate forces. Ewell's division had lost 987 men, leaving 4,657; Lawton's brigade, 567, leaving 2,041 (now attached to the Stonewall Division); the Stonewall Division (under Winder), 208, leaving 3,928. This left Jackson with about ten thousand infantry and one thousand artillerymen. In addition he had about one thousand cavalry. By August 9, 1862, Ewell's division had gained about four hundred more men. Losses by other outfits in the Seven Days had been even greater—D. H. Hill's division, 3,767; Whiting's division, 1,192; Longstreet's division, 4,438; A. P. Hill's division, 4,210; Magruder's corps, 2,518; Huger's division, 1,531; Holmes's division, 677. See Alexander, *Military Memoirs,* 174; Allan, *Army of Northern Virginia,* 159; and *Southern Historical Society Papers,* vol. 8, 304.

6. Jackson, not Lee, developed the strategy to defeat Pope before his army could be consolidated and before McClellan's troops could join him. Maj. Gen. Sir Frederick Maurice incorrectly credits Lee with this plan (Maurice, 127). Lee's only purpose in the campaign of Second Manassas was to dislodge Pope from the farms and towns of northern Virginia. It was Jackson, not Lee, who drew Pope into battle. On August 30, 1862, Lee explained his purpose to Davis: "My desire [throughout the campaign] has been to avoid a general engagement, being a weaker force, and by maneuvering to relieve the portion of the country referred to [northern Virginia]" (Lee, *Lee's Dispatches,* 56–58). In addition, Douglas Freeman makes plain that Lee did not intend from early in July 1862 to threaten Washington and thereby force McClellan to withdraw from the James,

the contention of nearly all of Lee's early biographers. Freeman writes that he "has not found one line of evidence to support this claim and a multitude of facts to disprove such a contention" (*R. E. Lee,* vol. 2, 259).

7. Alexander, *Military Memoirs,* 179–80; Freeman, *Lee's Lieutenants,* vol. 2, 1; Henderson, 398; and Allan, *Army of Northern Virginia,* 160.

8. Maurice, 125; Freeman, *R. E. Lee,* vol. 2, 261–62; and *Official Records,* vol. 12, pt. 3, 915–16.

9. *Official Records,* vol. 11, pt. 3, 334; and Henderson, 399.

10. It is possible that Halleck actually did see possibilities for a Federal strike at Petersburg but had no faith that McClellan was capable of executing it and also did not have the courage or position in Washington to relieve McClellan on the spot. Thus he may have ordered McClellan to evacuate the peninsula in order to deprive him of his army indirectly.

11. Alexander, *Military Memoirs,* 178–79. See also *Official Records,* vol. 11, pt. 1, 82 et seq.; Allan, *Army of Northern Virginia,* 155–56; and Freeman, *Lee's Lieutenants,* vol. 2, 18.

12. *Official Records,* vol. 12, pt. 3, 474; Alexander, *Military Memoirs,* 176–77; Henderson, 400; and Allan, *Army of Northern Virginia,* 156.

13. Cooke (252–54), gives graphic examples of how Pope's soldiers exploited the orders to pillage and harass Virginian civilians, stripping smoke-houses of preserved meats, seizing horses and other farm animals, robbing kitchens of cooking utensils, and, at least on one occasion, grabbing the food from a family just seated for dinner. Halleck, on August 15, 1862, issued a War Department general order that "no officer or soldier might, without proper authority, leave his colors or ranks to take private property or to enter a private house for the purpose, under penalty of death."

14. Sears (44–45) cites Roy P. Basler, ed., *The Collected Works of Lincoln* (New Brunswick, N.J.: Rutgers University Press, 1953–55), vol. 5, 336–37; John G. Nicolay and John Hay, *Abraham Lincoln: A History* (New York: Century, 1890), vol. 6, 125–30; and Francis B. Carpenter, *Six Months at the White House With Abraham Lincoln* (Boston: Hurd and Houghton, 1866), 22.

15. Mary Boykin Chesnut, *A Diary From Dixie* (Cambridge, Mass.: Harvard University Press, 1980), 265.

16. Freeman, *R. E. Lee,* vol. 2, 263–64; Henderson, 400–401; and Allan, *Army of Northern Virginia,* 157–58.

17. A. P. Hill's division had suffered 4,210 casualties in the Seven Days and had been reduced to 10,623 men. However, the Louisiana brigade of Brig. Gen. Leroy A. Stafford was attached, raising his force to about twelve thousand men. See Allan, *Army of Northern Virginia,* 165; and Alexander, *Military Memoirs,* 174. Lee advised Jackson subtly that he should confide more in his subordinate commanders, especially A. P. Hill, but Jackson's habit of secrecy was too ingrained and he ignored the good advice. See *Official Records,* vol. 12, pt. 2, 919; Freeman, *Lee's Lieutenants,* vol. 2, 3; and Henderson, 399–400.

18. Henderson, 400.

19. Ibid., 402. Around August 5, cavalryman John S. Mosby, just exchanged after being captured, told Lee that while at Fort Monroe he had learned that Burnside's corps of thirteen thousand men was going not to McClellan, but to Aquia Creek. This virtually confirmed other indications that McClellan was abandoning the peninsula. See Allan, *Army of Northern Virginia,* 159 and 162–63; Freeman, *R. E. Lee,* vol. 2, 269–70; and Cooke, 256. Burnside was ordered to move from Newport News to Aquia Creek on July 30, 1862.

20. Freeman, *R. E. Lee,* vol. 2, 271. Lee left Jackson's movements "to your reflection and good judgment."

21. Henderson, 402.

22. Alexander, *Military Memoirs,* 180; Freeman, *Lee's Lieutenants,* vol. 2, 10–12 and 19–20; Henderson, 403; and *Official Records,* vol. 12, pt. 3, 536. In Jackson's plan to seize Culpeper one can see a silhouette of the kind of strategy he might have followed if Lee and Davis had released enough men to undertake an offensive campaign. Jackson likely would have advanced to a central position between the still-separated parts of Pope's army and tried to destroy each part separately.

23. Allan, *Army of Northern Virginia,* 167; Henderson, 405–6; Freeman, *Lee's Lieutenants,* vol. 2, 12–15; Alexander, *Military Memoirs,* 180–81; and *Official Records,* vol. 12, pt. 2, 180–81 (Jackson's report).

24. Allan, *Army of Northern Virginia,* 170–71; Henderson, 404; and Freeman, *Lee's Lieutenants,* vol. 2, 20–21.

25. *Official Records,* vol. 12, pt. 2, 25; and Allan, *Army of Northern Virginia,* 171.

26. Freeman, *Lee's Lieutenants,* vol. 2, 20; and Allan, *Army of Northern Virginia,* 167, 169. Banks's corps totaled 14,500 infantry and artillerymen and

4,100 cavalry. But he left twenty-five hundred infantry and gunners at Winchester and one thousand at Front Royal, while sickness and heat prevented Banks from bringing more than about eight thousand to eighty-seven hundred men to Cedar Run.

27. Freeman, *Lee's Lieutenants,* vol. 2, 23. William Allan, in *Southern Historical Society Papers* (vol. 8, 178–82), concludes that Jackson got about twenty thousand men into the battle of Cedar Mountain while Banks committed about sixteen thousand, though seven thousand of these were in Ricketts's division, which arrived only in time to stabilize the Federal line. See Krick, 45.

28. The size of this field has been variously reported by witnesses: four hundred to six hundred yards wide by eight hundred yards long by one, three hundred to four hundred wide, seven hundred long by another. See Allan, *Army of Northern Virginia,* 171.

29. Henderson, 408; and Krick, 70–71.

30. Krick, 89.

31. Dabney, 494 and 496.

32. Krick, 111; and *Official Records,* vol. 12, pt. 2, 200.

33. *Official Records,* vol. 12, pt. 2, 188.

34. Ibid., 189. General Taliaferro's successor as commander of the Third Brigade was his uncle, Col. Alexander G. Taliaferro, fifty-three years old.

35. Douglas Freeman complains (in *Lee's Lieutenants,* vol. 2, 45) that Jackson's "instructions to Garnett on his brief call at that officer's post of command seem to have been inadequate." He asks whether Jackson should not "personally have acquainted himself with conditions on a threatened flank and in the air." This is unfair. An army commander cannot go on personal reconnaissances in the midst of a battle. He must rely on reports for information and on the senior commander of the wing for action. Jackson reacted instantly to the report of a possible Federal attack, sending (or possibly ordering Taliaferro to send) forward the Stonewall Brigade. Taliaferro also dispatched the Tenth Virginia. If the Stonewall Brigade had done its job and if the First Virginia Battalion had not run, Jackson's dispositions would have held Crawford's assault. Jackson already was planning for A. P. Hill to envelop the left, the decisive move of the battle. See Krick, 85, 106–7, 110–12, 113–16, 152–53, and 163–64; *Official Records,* vol. 12, pt. 2, 189, 192–93, 195, 197–98, 200, and 230; and Allan, *Army of Northern Virginia,* 173. Freeman (*Lee's Lieuten-*

ants, vol. 2, 26–27) erroneously claims that Jackson assumed that all Federal forces were east of the Orange-Culpeper road and that Taliaferro's brigade was on the left of the road.

36. Krick, 108.

37. Allan, *Army of Northern Virginia,* 172; and Freeman, *Lee's Lieutenants,* vol. 2, 44.

38. *Southern Historical Society Papers,* vol. 19, 182; and Freeman, *Lee's Lieutenants,* vol. 2, 50.

39. *Official Records,* vol. 12, pt. 2, 27; and Allan, *Army of Northern Virginia,* 177.

40. Allan, *Army of Northern Virginia,* 176–77; Alexander, *Military Memoirs,* 182; and Freeman, *Lee's Lieutenants,* vol. 2, 43.

9

THE SWEEP BEHIND POPE

★ ★ ★ Stonewall Jackson saw an opportunity for the Confederacy to destroy Pope's army before it could be reinforced and drew up a plan to bring it about.

The chance came as a result of Halleck's order for McClellan to withdraw from the peninsula. When this happened, the largest and most powerful army of the Union temporarily ceased to exist as a fighting force because, while in transit to Aquia Creek or Alexandria, it could not fight.

Before the Seven Days, Jackson had pleaded with President Davis and Lee to invade the North, predicting such an outcome: McClellan's army would rush to counter Jackson, removing itself from the order of battle for days or weeks. In the interim Jackson could wreak havoc against little opposition. Now Halleck had ordered just this withdrawal—thereby handing to the South gratuitously the very opportunity that Jackson had sought in vain.

Until McClellan's army could disembark, reassemble, and

march overland to join John Pope, the Confederacy had to contend only with Pope's Army of Virginia. In other words, Halleck had, for a time, more than *halved* the opposition that the Army of Northern Virginia faced. And, since McClellan must traverse a roundabout route by water and land, the Confederate army had several crucial days to concentrate at Gordonsville before the Union army could unite against it.

This gave the Army of Northern Virginia a narrow but potentially decisive window of opportunity during which it might isolate Pope's force of perhaps forty-five thousand men and destroy it.

But no time could be wasted. Jackson had to discover a flaw in Pope's dispositions that he could exploit quickly. Federal forces of thirteen thousand would join Pope within a few days, thereby creating a Union army larger than Lee's.

Jackson did find a potentially fatal error. It came about after Halleck, astonished by the completeness of Jackson's victory at Cedar Mountain, directed Pope to remain on the defensive. Pope had lost much of his optimism when he saw how Jackson had rendered Banks's corps unfit for combat. Though Jackson withdrew to Gordonsville on August 11, 1862, hoping to induce Pope to chase behind and again expose part of his army, Pope followed Halleck's orders and concentrated nearly his whole force north of the Rapidan in the vicinity of Cedar Mountain.[1]

In doing this Pope allowed his left, or eastern, flank to remain woefully weak and virtually unguarded. This was the bonanza Jackson had been seeking—it meant that the Confederates could sweep around Pope's left, cut off Federal supplies and any troops coming to help, back Pope's now-isolated force against the Rapidan, and destroy it. Jackson gleefully drew up plans for such an operation.

Meantime, Lee, getting confirmed reports that McClellan was abandoning the peninsula, ordered James Longstreet with ten brigades to move to Gordonsville on August 13.[2] The next day Lee decided to go himself and made arrangements to draw after him most of the remaining Confederate troops still watching Mc-

Clellan. A Confederate force of about fifty-five thousand men rapidly began to assemble at Gordonsville.

On August 15, when Lee met with Jackson and Longstreet to work out a course of action, Jackson presented his proposal to destroy Pope's ill-placed army. Lee accepted Jackson's plan in general but refused to adopt crucial aspects of it.[3]

Jackson wanted the Confederates to cross the Rapidan the next night, August 16, at two fords: Somerville (on present-day U.S. Route 522), eight miles east of Pope, and Raccoon, two miles farther east. But Longstreet insisted on more time to accumulate food supplies. Although Jackson offered Longstreet enough biscuits for the march, Lee delayed the approach to the fords to the seventeenth and the sweep around Pope until the eighteenth.

Jackson knew that if Pope got wind of the movement, he would withdraw before the trap could be sprung. To Jackson, it was imperative to move as quickly as possible. On the morning of August 18, however, Lee postponed the assault another day.

Lee had a number of reasons for his decision, but none was vital: Richard H. Anderson's division, arriving from Richmond, was not in position; the commissary still had not delivered enough hard bread to Longstreet; Lee was not happy with cavalry dispositions on his left; and there was no news from Stuart, whose horsemen were to rush across and burn the bridge at Rappahannock Station (present-day Remington) on the Orange and Alexandria Railroad, Pope's major line of supply.[4]

Stuart was not ready because Fitzhugh Lee, one of his brigade commanders, mistakenly was a day late in getting to the Rapidan. Although Lee did not learn of it at once, a Federal cavalry patrol also had captured Stuart's adjutant, Maj. Norman Fitzhugh, while out hunting for the missing brigade on the night of August 17. The Union horsemen found on Fitzhugh's person a copy of Lee's order outlining the plan of attack.[5]

Lee had put much stock in burning the Rappahannock Station bridge. Therefore, to rest Fitz Lee's horses, he postponed the attack once more—until the morning of the twentieth. Jackson protested and urged that the movement go forward without

Fitz Lee. Jackson asserted that the enemy was quiet and that the Confederates already knew the location of the Union divisions.[6] Jackson had enough cavalry with his force to protect the front and flanks of the whole army. The purpose of the offensive, Jackson emphasized, was to turn Pope's left, move on his rear and annihilate his army, not merely to cut his line of communications. Lee, however, overruled Jackson.[7]

Lee had fixed on breaking Pope's railroad supply line as a means of forcing him into retreat. To Lee, this was more important than attacking quickly. Furthermore, Lee was not seized with the idea of destroying Pope's army. Jackson was. And Jackson knew the value of time. The chance might never come again to fall on Pope while he was so vulnerable and unconscious of danger.

Jackson had wanted to strike immediately, on the evening of August 16. The eighteenth was tardy, the twentieth impossibly late. Speed was more important than biscuits for Longstreet or cavalry to burn a bridge. Speed was surprise, and surprise could bring victory.

Lee's delay proved fatal to Jackson's hopes of destroying Pope. On the morning of August 18 Pope got word of the planned attack from the order found on Major Fitzhugh and from a spy who reported that the Rebel army was assembled just south of the eastern fords. He immediately started his army toward the Rappahannock, twenty to twenty-five miles in his rear. Progress was slow, and the Union army on the morning of August 19 was still some distance from the Rappahannock and not in formation to resist a determined attack. It was not until the afternoon of the nineteenth that Lee discovered the movement from an observation station atop Clark Mountain, just south of the Rapidan.[8]

When the Army of Northern Virginia set out on August 20 in pursuit, therefore, it encountered only rear guards. That day Pope got his army, intact with guns mounted and ably challenging the Confederates, on the north side of the Rappahannock.

Stonewall Jackson, despite ardent efforts, had failed to induce Lee to grasp one of the great opportunities of the Civil War. John

Pope had posted his army in an isolated position. Lee had gotten an army superior in size within striking distance. McClellan's army was still days away. Lee had accepted Jackson's plan to sweep around Pope's eastern flank, thereby interposing the Rebel army between Pope and any reinforcements that might be on the way. The conditions were perfect to eradicate Pope's army before having to deal with Burnside and McClellan. These forces, moreover, were arriving piecemeal and might have been defeated in detail. Lee allowed this to happen because he did not see, or ignored, the opportunity.

From this event or other observations, Stonewall Jackson learned or suspected that forcing Pope out of northern Virginia was *all* that Lee hoped to accomplish. Lee had no plan to shatter Pope's army. Jackson knew such a campaign would achieve no decision and—like the Seven Days—would leave the Confederacy in a worse situation than at the beginning. He knew the South had to gain a commanding victory, and he looked for another opportunity to convince Lee to destroy Pope while he had the chance.

★ ★ ★

For the next four days the two armies skirmished briskly along the Rappahannock, but Pope was alert and offered no opening to turn his line, which stretched fourteen miles, from Rappahannock Station on the south to Waterloo on the north.

On a rainy night, August 22, Stuart raided Catlett Station, eleven miles up the railroad toward Alexandria from Rappahannock Station. The rain prevented his burning the bridge over Cedar Run there, as Lee had hoped for, but he did find Pope's dispatch book and copies of several letters.[9] These showed that Fitz-John Porter's and Samuel P. Heintzelman's corps from McClellan's army, plus Brig. Gen. John F. Reynolds's Pennsylvania division—in all, twenty thousand men—were within two days' juncture with Pope, while Jacob D. Cox, with seven thousand men from West Virginia, Samuel D. Sturgis, with ten thousand from Washington, and the remainder of McClellan's army were not more than five or ten days away. Soon Pope would possess

120,000 men. Lee had called up twenty-one thousand more men from Richmond but these would take days to arrive.[10]

The dispatches showed that Lee had only about seven days to engage Pope's army. Thereafter the odds would become hopeless. The turning point had come.

On the afternoon of August 24, 1862, Lee rode over to Jackson's headquarters at Jeffersonton, about four miles south of Waterloo, and laid out a new plan to cut Pope's railway line and, by this means, eject Pope from the Rappahannock River line and force him northward. Stuart's planned strike at Rappahannock Station had come too late and rain had prevented burning the bridge at Catlett Station. Now Lee audaciously proposed that Jackson undertake an infantry strike to break the line.

Lee would not wait for reinforcements. Jackson would march his twenty-two thousand men far around Pope and plant them at some point on the railroad. This move was sure to compel Pope to give up the line of the Rappahannock and rush back to reopen his supply line. After breaking the railroad, Jackson was to hold Pope at bay until the remainder of Lee's army could reach him. Meanwhile, Longstreet was to demonstrate along the river to divert attention.

Jackson delightedly seized on Lee's idea, seeing in it a chance to bring Pope to battle under conditions favorable to the South. Jackson transformed Lee's modest plan to break the railroad into a strategic campaign of such scope and subtlety as rarely had been seen in history.[11]

Lee's proposal was bold but perilous. He would be committing what was normally a cardinal military error—dividing his army in the presence of the enemy, now already larger than his own. Beyond that, the two halves of his army would be unable to communicate or help each other, a risk Napoleon almost always avoided. Pope might realize what was happening and strike at the now-weakened Confederate force directly in front of him or concentrate against Jackson in his rear. But in the desperate situation in which the Confederacy found itself, any aggressive course involved great risk.[12]

Lee and Jackson did not settle on a precise objective. But the strategic situation dictated a move around Pope's right, or west, against the outriders of the Blue Ridge. Although Jackson could have struck the railroad quicker by a march around Pope's eastern flank, Union cavalry were alert in this sector. Such a move would have left Jackson open to assault by Pope from one side and Porter, coming up from Fredericksburg, on the other.

Jackson called in his chief engineer, Capt. J. Keith Boswell, a native of the region. Determine immediately, he told Boswell, the most covered route around Pope's right with the general objective being Manassas Junction, twenty-five miles in the Federal rear and only eighteen miles from Alexandria! Jackson was not planning merely to break the Orange and Alexandria Railroad at the closest accessible point. He intended to block Pope's retreat to the capital and challenge him to a decisive battle.

Around Jeffersonton, Jackson rapidly assembled his wing of the army—three divisions commanded by A. P. Hill, Richard S. Ewell, and William B. Taliaferro. He ordered his men to cook three days' rations and strip all vehicles from the column except ambulances and ammunition wagons. The haste was so great that some men had no time to prepare rations and had to rely on a herd of cattle being driven with the column and green corn and apples in fields and orchards along the way. For Jackson, there was no waiting until sufficient biscuits could be baked.

Early on the morning of August 25 Jackson's column moved out, marching first to Amissville, six miles northwest, then north across the Rappahannock at Henson's Mill, through Orlean, to Salem (present-day Marshall) on the Manassas Gap Railroad. It was a hard march of twenty-six miles.

The Federals discovered the movement by 8 A.M. and observed it for fifteen miles from a signal station on a mountain near Waterloo. The observers made a fair estimate of its size by counting regimental flags and batteries. Pope and other generals discussed what it meant, but none divined Jackson's aim. No one could imagine that Lee was splitting his army, and Pope supposed that Jackson was on the way to the valley and the rest of Lee's army might be moving upon Front Royal.[13]

Pope reacted most curiously. Though saying he believed Lee had moved west and northwest, he did not reconnoiter toward Jackson to confirm this view. Instead he ordered Franz Sigel at Waterloo and Irvin McDowell at Fauquier White Sulphur Springs, four miles downstream, to attack across the river. Such an attack could not be carried out before the next day, and even then, only McDowell was ready. If Lee was moving toward the valley, then an attack across the Rappahannock was superfluous.[14]

Pope was distracted by Longstreet, who shelled Union positions along the river and made threatening gestures. But this does not explain Pope's bizarre failure to find out what was happening on his right flank.[15]

Jackson's march to Salem went off without incident, except that the journey was long and pressed as hard as Jackson's foot cavalry could go. The standard command in Jackson's army occurred over and over: "Close up! Close up, men!"[16] Near Salem, Jackson climbed on a great stone by the roadside and, taking off his hat, watched his weary soldiers march by. The closest men let out a great cheer, but Jackson, fearing that the enemy might be close, sent a message down the ranks: "No cheering, boys; the General requests it." The soldiers now passed by silently but showed by eloquent waves and gestures their affection and respect for their leader. Jackson turned to his staff, his face beaming, and said: "Who could not conquer with such troops as these?"[17]

Arriving at Salem long after dark, the exhausted men dropped beside their stacked rifles and were quickly asleep, without so much as unrolling their blankets. Their officers stirred them long before dawn and they moved off in the darkness, still only half awake. In usual fashion, no one knew where they were headed. But a great wave of enthusiasm passed through the ranks on the morning of August 26 when the men realized they were marching toward the rising sun, not back into the valley. This meant they were going to fall somewhere on the rear of the enemy!

The march this day was as hard and fast as the day previous. The army passed through White Plains (now The Plains), picking up their first Federals, a dozen straggling horsemen who knew nothing about Jackson's march. The column moved on Thoroughfare Gap in the Bull Run Mountains, the only major obstacle they had to face, eleven miles east of Salem. But the pass was unguarded and Jackson's corps climbed through it and onto the unobstructed plain that spread out below them. Six miles ahead was Gainesville, on the Warrenton-Alexandria turnpike (now U.S. Route 29), and eight miles beyond that village lay Manassas Junction.

Meanwhile, along the Rappahannock, Pope and his major subordinates remained baffled. Since only McDowell's corps was ready, Pope allowed him to decide whether to attack across the river alone and also asked him to find out what had become of Jackson's column. Richard H. Anderson's Confederate division, guarding the river, commenced an artillery duel and McDowell decided against an assault. When McDowell tried to get a cavalry force to move after Jackson, the commanders said their horses and men were broken down and thus they did not get under way until the next morning, August 27. By that time Jackson had made his whereabouts known unmistakably.[18]

McDowell became convinced that the mass of the Rebel army was at or above Waterloo. Pope, agreeing, broke his army away from the Rappahannock in the afternoon. This convinced Lee, watching closely, that he was moving back to counter Jackson.

But Pope actually still had no idea where Jackson was. However, for safety he ordered three of his corps—McDowell's, Sigel's, and Jesse L. Reno's of McClellan's army—to concentrate the next day, August 27, at or near Warrenton, six miles east of Waterloo. He left Banks's still-shaky small corps at Fayetteville (now Opal), seven miles south of Warrenton, and directed Porter's corps of ten thousand men, just arriving, to move toward Warrenton Junction (now Calverton) on the railroad, nine miles southeast of Warrenton, where Heintzelman's corps was located. Pope now had seventy-five thousand men.[19]

When Stonewall Jackson's corps marched into Gainesville at around 4 P.M. on the twenty-sixth, Jeb Stuart and his cavalry arrived as well. They had left Waterloo at 2 A.M. and traveled by back ways through the Bull Run Mountains.[20] Despite Stuart's and Jackson's movements and despite the high columns of dust they raised, the Federal army remained unaware of the presence of a major force in its rear.

Stuart now could screen the march, permitting the infantry to relax and spread out. At Gainesville, Jackson directed the column to move, not on Manassas Junction, but on Bristoe Station, four miles below Manassas. If Jackson could destroy the railroad bridge over Broad Run there, quick repair and reopening of the line would be impossible. Therefore, Pope's supply line would be severed and he would be forced to retreat from the Rappahannock.

The head of the column, a Louisiana brigade under Col. Henry Forno and the Twenty-first North Carolina, reached Bristoe at sunset with Col. T. T. Munford's Second Virginia Cavalry and quickly dispersed the small Federal guard. They failed to stop the first locomotive coming north from Warrenton Junction with a load of empty cars and it rushed on to Manassas Junction to warn the authorities there. But they then cut the telegraph wires and tore up track, which wrecked the second and third trains, though the fourth stopped and retreated south to warn Pope. The Confederates now moved to Broad Run and broke the bridge.[21]

People at Bristoe reported that Pope's main supply base was at Manassas Junction—acres of goods of all kinds lying alongside the tracks and in warehouses. Here was an opportunity not to be missed. Although the army was exhausted, Gen. Isaac R. Trimble volunteered to lead the Twenty-first North Carolina and Twenty-first Georgia, not more than five hundred men all told, up the tracks at once to secure the junction, while Stuart sent the Fourth Virginia Cavalry around to the rear of Manassas. The Rebels overcame feeble Union resistance in minutes, capturing more than three hundred prisoners.

Pope got word of the Bristoe action soon after it happened. He thought it was the work of a handful of cavalry, however, and ordered Heintzelman to send a regiment on a train to repair the wires and protect the railroad. Later Sigel told him that scouts and informers had reported the march of Rebels through Salem, White Plains, and Thoroughfare Gap.

The regiment sent to reopen the railroad at Bristoe returned with the news that the enemy was in force there. Now thoroughly alarmed, Pope, at 7 A.M., August 27, sent Joseph Hooker's division toward Bristoe from Warrenton Junction to do what the regiment could not and at 8:30 A.M. directed most of his army back toward Gainesville.[22] Jackson's thrust had achieved its original purpose: Pope abruptly abandoned the Rappahannock line.

Most of the remainder of Lee's army also was en route to the north. Convinced the afternoon before (August 26) that Pope was withdrawing, Lee had pulled all but Anderson's six thousand men off the river and set out on Jackson's roundabout route. By the morning of the twenty-seventh Lee and Longstreet were well on their way toward a junction with Jackson.[23]

Morning at Manassas on August 27 revealed immense quantities of quartermaster, commissary, and sutler's stores. To the famished and ill-supplied Confederates, it was a wonderland offering every item of clothing and goods they might need and every delicacy they could wish for—from champagne to coffee and canned sardines.[24]

Jackson sent forward the Stonewall Brigade under Col. W. S. H. Baylor, closely followed by the rest of Taliaferro's division and A. P. Hill's division. He left Ewell with three brigades to guard Bristoe Station and Broad Run.

Baylor ran against the Twelfth Pennsylvania Cavalry, sent down from Alexandria, and dispersed it. Soon thereafter the inexperienced First New Jersey Brigade, sent by Halleck, detrained just north of the railroad bridge over Bull Run. The commander, Brig. Gen. George W. Taylor, had been told only to protect the bridge, but, though without artillery or cavalry, he pressed on against what he thought was a small Rebel force.

The brigade ran headlong into a large part of Hill's division. Realizing it was about to be destroyed, Jackson himself rode forward and called on the Federals to surrender. He received a bullet past his ear in reply. The Rebel artillery now opened on the unfortunate brigade and broke it apart. More than 300 Federals surrendered, while 135 were killed or wounded. Taylor himself died. The Confederates destroyed the bridge over Bull Run and the locomotive and cars, and Fitz Lee's cavalry followed the fugitives as far back as Burke's Station, twelve miles from Alexandria.[25]

Jackson knew he could not remain for any length of time in undisputed possession of Bristoe and Manassas Junction. Accordingly, after securing all of the supplies he had space to carry in his few wagons, he threw open the depot to his men. The soldiers exploited this wealth to the fullest. In a wild revel they replaced worn-out clothing, gorged themselves on delicacies, and stuffed their clothes and packs with whatever they deemed most desirable (or tradeable).

All through the afternoon Stuart's patrols sent Jackson report after report of enemy movements—a large force was marching on Bristoe from Warrenton Junction; heavy columns were heading down the turnpike from Warrenton toward Gainesville. A courier, disguised as a countryman, arrived from Lee, informing Jackson that he and Longstreet were following Jackson's own track.[26]

Hooker's division now came up on Ewell below Bristoe Station. In a series of adroit movements, Ewell withdrew his three brigades north of Broad Run with little loss and moved on toward Manassas. Hooker stopped at the watercourse.[27]

General Pope had followed his own advice to leave his lines of supply and retreat "to take care of themselves." Jackson had cut these lines and thereby ousted Pope from the Rappahannock and sent him in full flight.

However, the force Pope was retreating from not only was a third the size of his own but actually had abandoned direct pursuit and was marching out of touch on a circuitous route on the western side of the Bull Run Mountains. Lee had taken an incredible chance in dividing his army. He was taking an even more incredible chance by moving Longstreet's wing through the mountains instead of directly after Pope's army.[28]

Pope now had a stunning opportunity. He did not know exactly where Jackson's main force was, but it had to be somewhere around Manassas. He also knew that Longstreet was west of the Bull Run Mountains. Thus, on the morning of August 27 Pope, at Warrenton, was only ten miles from Thoroughfare Gap and twelve from Gainesville. He easily could beat any Confederate force to either place.

Pope found himself, through no foresight of his own, in the "central position" sought by Napoleon—between the two main enemy forces, with the opportunity to destroy each wing separately. The only feasible exit for Longstreet was Thoroughfare or other gaps nearby. Pope could have blocked these. Even if he merely had concentrated his army at Gainesville he still could have kept Lee's two wings apart, for that point was directly between both.

But Pope did not see this opportunity. With seemingly no conception that Longstreet was hurrying to the side of Jackson, Pope ignored his central position.[29]

NOTES

General sources: Allan, *Army of Northern Virginia,* 151–222; Dabney, 486–522; Cooke, 267–84; Alexander, *Military Memoirs,* 175–97; Alexander, *Fighting for the Confederacy,* 121–31; Douglas, 120–36; Henderson, 396–444; Maurice, 129–40; Freeman, *R. E. Lee,* vol. 2, 256–309; Freeman, *Lee's Lieutenants,* vol. 2, 1–104; Johnson and Buel, vol. 2, 449–67, 501–6, 512–16, and 528–33; Selby, 122–38; Chambers, vol. 2, 124–48; and Vandiver, 345–61.

1. In Jackson's report (in *Official Records,* vol. 12, pt. 2, 185) he says he returned to Gordonsville "in order to avoid being attacked by the vastly superior force in front of me and with the hope that by thus falling back, General Pope would be induced to follow me until I should be rein-

forced." See also Henderson, 420; and Alexander, *Military Memoirs,* 182 and 185. Although Pope was tempted, Halleck restrained him. "Beware of the snare," Halleck warned. "Feigned retreats are 'Secesh' tactics." The day after the battle of Cedar Mountain, Sigel's corps and five thousand more cavalry joined Ricketts's division and Banks's remaining five thousand shaky troops, giving Pope thirty-two thousand troops in place, while Rufus King's division was marching from Fredericksburg and other detachments were coming up. Burnside's corps was arriving at Aquia Creek but had not moved forward to join Pope.

2. *Official Records,* vol. 11, pt. 3, 674–76, and vol. 12, pt. 3, 928; Longstreet, 159; Freeman, *R. E. Lee,* vol. 2, 272–73; and Freeman, *Lee's Lieutenants,* vol. 2, 53.

3. Lee, 56–58; Freeman, *R. E. Lee,* vol. 2, 259 and 282; Henderson, 423–25; Alexander, *Military Memoirs,* 186; Maurice, 127; and *Official Records,* vol. 12, pt. 2, 729, and vol. 12, pt. 3, 940.

4. Freeman, *R. E. Lee,* vol. 2, 284.

5. This same Federal patrol also nearly captured Stuart at Verdiersville, east of Orange. Stuart fled from a house in which he was staying without his new plumed hat, which the Union cavalrymen captured. More important, they also got Stuart's dispatch case, which they took to Pope, with a letter disclosing that Jackson had been strongly reinforced. See Alexander, *Military Memoirs,* 187; Henderson, 424; Freeman, *Lee's Lieutenants,* vol. 2, 57–61; and Freeman, *R. E. Lee,* vol. 2, 284–86.

6. The Federal army was mostly lying placidly in camps scattered in a wide tract of country with the cavalry idle, seemingly unconscious of the proximity of the Confederate army. See Dabney, 511; and Henderson, 424.

7. Dabney, 511; Henderson, 426; Alexander, *Military Memoirs,* 186–89; *Official Records,* vol. 12, pt. 2, 728; and Allan, *Army of Northern Virginia,* 182.

8. Freeman, *R. E. Lee,* vol. 2, 287–88; Henderson, 426–27; and Longstreet, 161–62. A Union officer present during the campaign reported: "It was then most fortunate that Jackson was not in command of the Confederate forces on the night of the 18th of August; for the superior force of the enemy must have overwhelmed us, if we could not have escaped, and escape on that night was impossible" (George H. Gordon, *The Army of Virginia* [Boston: Houghton, Osgood and Company, 1880], 9). See also Henderson, 426. The Reverend Robert Lewis Dabney, writing in 1866,

says: "But the issue [of the attack on Pope's flank on August 20, 1862] showed the importance of that element of strategic combinations, which Jackson so keenly estimated, time. The propitious moment was already forfeited by delay" (Dabney, 511).

9. Stuart also captured some of General Pope's fancy uniforms, stored at his rear headquarters there. The entire Army of Northern Virginia had been vastly entertained by the capture by a Union raiding party of Stuart's new hat and plume at Verdiersville on August 17. The flamboyant Stuart now saw a chance to get even. He wrote the following communication: "Major Genl. John Pope, Commanding, etc. General: You have my hat and plume. I have your best coat. I have the honor to propose a cartel for a fair exchange of the prisoners. Yours respectfully, J. E. B. Stuart, Maj. Genl. C.S.A." The note amused Stonewall Jackson greatly. See Douglas, 133–34.

10. Allan, *Army of Northern Virginia,* 198–99; Alexander, *Military Memoirs,* 189; Freeman, *R. E. Lee,* vol. 2, 297–98; Marshall, 129–30; and Henderson, 430.

11. Although Dr. Hunter McGuire, Jackson's surgeon, believed that Jackson had originated the idea for the movement on Pope's rear (Henderson, 432), it is evident that the proposal had come from Lee. See Freeman, *R. E. Lee,* vol. 2, 300–301; Freeman, *Lee's Lieutenants,* vol. 2, 82–83; *Official Records,* vol. 12, pt. 2, 553–54 and 642–43; and Alexander, *Military Memoirs,* 191–92.

12. Allan, *Army of Northern Virginia,* 200; and Henderson, 490. Lee said after the war, answering complaints on the risks taken, that such criticism was obvious but that the disparity of force rendered risks unavoidable.

13. Alexander, *Military Memoirs,* 192–93; Henderson, 442; *Official Records,* vol. 12, pt. 2, 67, and pt. 3, 654–55; and Allan, *Army of Northern Virginia,* 208–9.

14. Allan, *Army of Northern Virginia,* 208–9; and *Official Records,* vol. 12, pt. 2, 333. Pope, in Johnson and Buel, (vol. 2, 460–61), written some twenty years after the war, attempts to hide the fact that he made no response to Jackson's march on his rear. "Stonewall Jackson's movement on Manassas Junction was plainly seen and promptly reported," Pope writes, "and I notified General Halleck of it." He tries to pass off his responsibility on to unnamed others by saying he had directed some of the forces en route to him to meet this threat but "all of the reinforcements and movements of the troops promised me had altogether failed." However, the editors of *Century* magazine, which published the series, point out in a footnote

that Pope's orders for August 25 disposed his troops on the line of the Rappahannock as for an advance toward the Rapidan.

15. In light of Pope's similar behavior concerning his left flank on August 29 and 30 at Second Manassas and his earlier failure to protect his left flank on the Rapidan, the case can be made that Pope was woefully indifferent to the dangers of envelopment.

16. Johnson and Buel, vol. 2, 533.

17. Dabney, 517. Henderson (434–35) and Cooke (275) give more colorful accounts, but since they cite no sources, Dabney's older, original citation is used.

18. Allan, *Army of Northern Virginia,* 209.

19. Ibid., 211; Johnson and Buel, vol. 2, 461, 463, and 517; *Official Records,* vol. 12, pt. 3, 672, 675, and 684; and Henderson, 442–43. Pope asked that William B. Franklin's ten thousand–man corps of McClellan's army, being directed to Alexandria instead of Aquia Creek, be sent to Gainesville. He also asked that another division, either Jacob D. Cox's from West Virginia or Samuel D. Sturgis's from Washington, be moved to Manassas Junction. None of these forces came forward.

20. Alexander, *Military Memoirs,* 193.

21. Johnson and Buel, vol. 2, 505. Cutting the telegraph line severed Pope's direct connections with Washington from 8:20 P.M., August 26, until the thirtieth. During this period all communications with Pope had to go via Falmouth, just north of Fredericksburg. See Johnson and Buel, 461 n. See also Allan, *Army of Northern Virginia,* 214.

22. *Official Records,* vol. 12, pt. 2, 70–72 and 352; and pt. 3, 672, 675, and 684; Allan, *Army of Northern Virginia,* 216; Johnson and Buel, vol. 2, 464–65; Henderson, 442; and Alexander, *Military Memoirs,* 195. Pope sent McDowell and Sigel's corps, with J. F. Reynolds's division, forty thousand men, directly to Gainesville and Jesse L. Reno's corps and Philip Kearny's division of Heintzelman's corps to Greenwich, four miles southwest of Gainesville. He directed Hooker's division of Heintzelman's corps to oust the Rebels from Bristoe Station, with Porter's corps marching behind to support him. He designated Banks's shattered corps merely to guard the trains in the rear.

23. Maj. Gen. J. F. C. Fuller (Fuller, 165) criticizes Lee for not striking at once for Berryville in the Shenandoah Valley, calling Jackson to join him there by way of Snicker's Gap (on present-day Virginia Route 7), then

advancing his whole army on Harpers Ferry, and from there threatening Washington. This, he says, would have compelled the withdrawal of Union forces to defend the capital and would have avoided a battle. Fuller finds it astonishing that Lee, by moving to join Jackson, abandoned the strategical offensive and assumed the tactical offensive. Since Lee's purpose was to evict Pope from northern Virginia and not engage in a battle, Fuller's assessment of Lee's faulty strategic sense is valid. However, Jackson's purpose in reaching Manassas was quite different from Lee's. His wish was *not* to drive Pope back into Washington, but to defeat and hopefully destroy his army *before* he could unite with McClellan. Lee gave Longstreet a choice of which route to follow—Jackson's roundabout approach or directly behind Pope's army. Longstreet responded: "Along the route to Warrenton were numerous strongly defensive positions where a small force could have detained me an uncertain length of time. I therefore decided to take Jackson's route." See Johnson and Buel, vol. 2, 517; and Freeman, *R. E. Lee,* vol. 2, 306–7.

24. Henderson, 437–38; and Alexander, *Military Memoirs,* 194.

25. Freeman, *Lee's Lieutenants,* vol. 2, 98–99; *Official Records,* vol. 12, pt. 2, 260; Henderson, 439; and Johnson and Buel, vol. 2, 539.

26. Henderson, 440. James Longstreet, in Johnson and Buel, (vol. 2, 517), reports that until late on August 28 "we had received reports from General Jackson, at regular intervals, assuring us of his successful operations and of confidence in his ability to baffle all efforts of the enemy till we should reach him."

27. Henderson, 441; and Freeman, *Lee's Lieutenants,* vol. 2, 102. Jubal A. Early handled the rear guard masterfully.

28. Johnson and Buel, vol. 2, 464; and Freeman, *R. E. Lee,* vol. 2, 307–8. Sigel reported to Pope before midnight on August 26 that the enemy rear guard was at Orlean and the main force at White Plains. See *Official Records,* vol. 12, pt. 2, 70. Actually Longstreet's main force was just north of Orlean and the White Plains reference probably was to Jackson's corps, which already had passed through. Longstreet covered eleven miles on August 26 and had about ten more to reach Salem and twelve to Thoroughfare Gap.

29. Writing two decades later, Pope still had not grasped the fact that he occupied a central position at Gainesville. He wrote at this later time: "I determined [on the morning of August 27, 1862] to throw my whole force in the direction of Gainesville and Manassas Junction, to crush any

force of the enemy that had passed through Thoroughfare Gap [Jackson's corps] and to interpose between Lee's army and Bull Run"—that is, between Lee and Washington, *not* between Lee's army and Jackson. (Johnson and Buel, vol. 2, 464). In fact, Pope did not divide his force between Gainesville and Manassas, as this statement implies, but ordered all of it to concentrate against Manassas.

10

JACKSON DRAWS POPE INTO BATTLE

★ ★ ★ On the night of August 27, 1862, Stonewall Jackson set in motion a strategy so deceptive that Pope abandoned his near-invincible position and allowed Jackson to lure him into a battle backed up against the barrier of Bull Run with only a portion of his potential strength. If Jackson had been in command of the Army of Northern Virginia it is almost certain that he would have destroyed Pope's army.[1]

Jackson skillfully combined two dissimilar strategies, a shield and a trap. To raise his shield, he deliberately had positioned his corps at the doorstep of Washington in order to block Pope if he tried to rush back into the capital's defenses and join the immense reserves McClellan was accumulating there. Pope already had run twice, once from the Rapidan and again from the Rappahannock. Jackson did not intend to allow him to run a third time. If Pope tried, Jackson would fight. However, Jackson put his greatest faith in the trap he had set—he was almost certain that Pope could not resist the temptation to attack his corps. It appeared isolated in the Federal rear, less than a third the size of Pope's army, and Pope would have every reason to believe that he could overwhelm it quickly. Always the student, Jackson had been thinking about the lessons being taught by Civil War battles, and he had come to a startling conclusion as to how they might be won or lost. He intended to test his theory against Pope and was not in the least worried that his force was so small.

On the evening of August 27 Pope arrived at Hooker's division just above Bristoe Station and discovered that no mere cavalry raiding party was occupying Manassas. It was Stonewall Jackson's whole corps. He concluded that Jackson's entire purpose had been a raid and that Jackson had hoped to get back south by moving around Pope's *eastern* flank but Hooker's march to Broad Run had foiled this plan.[2]

He still expected Jackson to attempt to retreat southward, ignoring the fact that Lee was approaching Thoroughfare Gap and that Jackson's logical sally port was *west,* back toward Lee and away from the Federal troop concentrations.

This mistaken conclusion led Pope to believe that he had Jackson blocked at Manassas. Sensing a great opportunity, Pope dispatched a flurry of orders designed to "bag Jackson" the next day—all of his forces were to march on Manassas Junction by dawn on the twenty-eighth, there to attack Jackson from all sides and force his surrender.[3]

Jackson did not know it yet, but Pope had fallen into his trap. The bait was more than Pope could resist. He resolved to retire to the capital, but only *after* defeating Jackson.[4]

The situation on the night of August 27 was as follows: Jackson, with about twenty-two thousand men, was resting at Manassas Junction. Lee and Longstreet, with about twenty-five thousand, were a day's march from Thoroughfare Gap, while Richard Anderson's division of six thousand men was marching north a day's march behind them. Pope had assembled about fifty-five thousand men in the vicinity of Gainesville, midway between Lee and Jackson, while another twenty thousand were moving directly toward Manassas Junction from the south. Portions of McClellan's army and other Federal forces—which would have given Pope a total force of at least 120,000 men—were gathering around Alexandria, some eighteen miles east of Manassas.

Jackson did not know that Pope's plans for the morrow centered on Manassas but he knew he could not remain there. He had to reach a position where he could retreat if disaster struck and where he could reunite quickly with Lee. This meant he had to find a defensible position somewhere westward. However, Jackson could not exclude the possibility that Pope might rush back to Washington.

Jackson solved both problems. Soon after nightfall Jackson sent Taliaferro's division, accompanied by the supply train, northward toward Sudley Springs, some eight miles away. There the division went into bivouac north and east of Groveton above the Warrenton-Alexandria turnpike. The position Jackson selected was splendid. It dominated the pike, which was Pope's best route for getting back to Washington from Gainesville—over the Stone Bridge at Bull Run and through Centreville. It also was close to Lee and Longstreet, and in case of defeat, Jackson could move north through the Aldie Gap of the Bull Run Mountains, a few miles northwest.

Next Jackson directed A. P. Hill to cross Blackburn's Ford on Bull Run to Centreville, nine miles to the north. When Ewell's division arrived from Bristoe later in the evening, Jackson ordered it also to ford Bull Run, move upstream, cross again at the Stone Bridge, and join Taliaferro north of the Warrenton turnpike.

Placing Hill and Ewell beyond Bull Run accomplished two goals. If Pope was retreating toward Washington, Hill and Ewell could block him along Bull Run. If not, sending two divisions toward Washington would confuse him as to Jackson's whereabouts and purpose. The effect was heightened because Fitz Lee's cavalry was raiding Burke's Station and Fairfax Court House, both only about twelve miles from Alexandria.

Jackson's last act at Manassas, at around midnight, was to put the miles of stores to the torch, thereby ensuring that Pope's army would become increasingly hungry and deprived of supplies. As his last soldiers marched away, flames illuminated the horizon.[5]

The next morning, August 28, A. P. Hill, obeying Jackson's orders, remained at Centreville until 10 A.M. Then, seeing no evidence that Pope was moving toward Alexandria, he started down the Warrenton turnpike to join Taliaferro and Ewell, who already had gone ahead. This morning, however, Confederates captured two Union couriers with important orders.

One, seized by cavalrymen with Jackson, directed Sigel at Gainesville to march to Manassas Junction. This was part of Pope's assemblage of forces to encircle Jackson, whom he presumed was still there. Jackson—not believing that Pope could have so deceived himself and perhaps thinking that his position dominating the Warrenton pike had been detected—interpreted the order to mean that Pope was about to retreat by way of Manassas to Alexandria and Washington.[6] He immediately sent a messenger to Hill to block the fords of Bull Run and intercept the enemy.

A. P. Hill, however, had captured another Union courier bearing orders to McDowell to form a line of battle on the Manassas plains. This proved that Pope was trying to "bag Jackson." Hill ignored Jackson's order and marched to join the rest of the corps. Jackson accepted Hill's decision, concluding that the two captured messages indicated that Pope was seeking to destroy his corps and was not retreating to the capital.

Jackson relaxed, awaiting Pope's discovery of his position and preparing for the attack he confidently expected would come. However, during the afternoon Jackson got contradictory indications. Pope arrived at Manassas Junction at around noon and found that Jackson had vanished. Hearing that Hill had been at Centreville and Rebel cavalry had attacked Burke's Station, he assumed that Jackson was near Centreville and ordered all of his forces to concentrate there.[7] This set off a flurry of Union movement, duly reported by Stuart's cavalry, *across* Bull Run. This renewed Jackson's fear that Pope was seeking safety in Washington, when in fact he was seeking Jackson![8]

One such Federal movement reinforced Jackson's fear. Col. Bradley T. Johnson, commanding a brigade at an advanced position on Jackson's right flank closest to Gainesville, discovered a column advancing, he thought, on him. Actually, it was John F. Reynolds's Pennsylvania division, which had not yet received countermanding orders to march on Centreville and was still trying to reach Manassas. Johnson opened fire and Reynolds brought his superior artillery into action. Johnson, overawed, promptly withdrew. Reynolds occupied Johnson's position but, finding no enemy, concluded that the force had been only a reconnoitering party and continued on toward Manassas. To Jackson, however, Reynolds's action appeared to be designed to clear the turnpike for the main Federal army to march on it to Centreville.[9]

Stonewall determined to stop this movement. He marched Taliaferro's and Ewell's divisions to a point only slightly north of the turnpike at Groveton and close to Gainesville.[10]

At around 5 P.M., in response to Pope's orders, Rufus King's division of ten thousand men in McDowell's corps, which had been marching toward Manassas and had reversed course, now started down the Warrenton turnpike in column formation for Centreville. Near sunset the division came opposite Jackson's position.

To Jackson this was confirmation of his fears and he wasted no time. He ordered the infantry to attack and brought twenty pieces of artillery forward, though the ground was so difficult that only two small batteries got into action. King's division, spread out far along the pike, was caught by surprise but rallied quickly. Even so, the battle of Groveton, as it was called, turned into an extremely bloody, stand-up, ill-directed fight because McDowell had gone off to see Pope, King was sick in Gainesville, and both Confederate division commanders were wounded early, Ewell losing a leg.

The contest was fought largely by brigadiers and they brought less than half of either side's force into the engagement. Jackson sent Ewell's second line of Early and Forno in an attempt to turn the Union right flank, but rough terrain and darkness intervened. The main battle was fought on the Union side by North Carolina–reared John Gibbon, commanding a brigade of one Indiana and three Wisconsin regiments,[11] aided by a New York and Pennsylvania regiment from Abner Doubleday's brigade. Against them the major combatants were two brigades, Alexander G. Taliaferro's and the Stonewall Brigade, aided by Alexander Lawton's and Isaac Trimble's brigades. In most places the two sides stood within eighty yards of each other in the open without cover and blasted away, neither side giving way. It was one of the most awful firefights of the Civil War. Only in darkness at about 9 P.M. did King's division slowly fall back. The Confederates suffered more than a thousand casualties while Gibbon's brigade lost a third of its 2,300 men and Doubleday's 350 out of 800 engaged.[12]

While this fight was going on, Longstreet's corps arrived at Thoroughfare Gap. McDowell belatedly, on his own initiative, had sent up James B. Ricketts's division to guard this pass.[13] It arrived just as Longstreet's infantry was occupying it. David R. Jones's division seized the heights commanding the pass, while Cadmus M. Wilcox's force drove through Hopewell Gap, three miles north, and John Bell Hood's division crossed by a trail just north of the pass. Faced with envelopment, Ricketts marched back to Gainesville.[14]

King, resting near Gainesville after the collision with Jackson, talked with John Reynolds, whose division and Sigel's corps had moved up close to the turnpike a short distance east of Gainesville. King indicated that he would remain in position. But when Ricketts arrived and told him that Longstreet was certain to advance through Thoroughfare Gap the next morning, King and Ricketts decided that the better part of valor was to retreat forthwith, King to Manassas Junction, Ricketts all the way to Bristoe Station. They departed at once.[15]

The situation on the night of August 28, thus, was dramatically different from that of the night before. Jackson, having driven off King's division, was resting above the Warrenton turnpike near Groveton. Lee and Longstreet had forced passage of Thoroughfare Gap and were only half a day's march from Jackson. Pope's army was spread out from Centreville to Bristoe Station—King's and Ricketts's divisions were marching away from Gainesville; Sigel's corps was near the junction of the Warrenton pike and the Manassas–Sudley Springs road and Reynolds's division was just to the west and approximately in front of Jackson; Jesse L. Reno's corps and Philip Kearny's division were near Centreville; Joseph Hooker's division was on Bull Run due south of Centreville; Fitz-John Porter's corps was just north of Bristoe and Nathaniel Banks's small corps was with the trains south of Bristoe.[16]

Thus the Northern and Southern armies were nowhere in touch, though in the vicinity of Jackson they were in close proximity.

The clash at Groveton had at last revealed Jackson's location to Pope. However, Pope drew the wrong conclusions. He thought King had foiled an effort by Jackson to retreat to Longstreet, that King and Ricketts were standing fast *west* of Jackson around Gainesville, and that McDowell, in command, could fend off Longstreet while Pope brought up his other forces and destroyed the isolated Jackson.

Pope sent messages to McDowell to hold his ground at Gainesville "at all hazards and prevent the retreat of Jackson to the west." He believed he could crush Jackson before "Longstreet could by any possibility reach the scene of action," and ordered an attack at dawn on August 29 on Jackson by Reynolds and Sigel and the forces he had concentrated at or near Centreville.[17]

Unfortunately, McDowell had gotten lost in the woods and was nowhere to be found, no one was in charge around Gainesville, and the two divisions there had made tracks south.[18]

While the forces around Centreville began moving toward Jackson, the messages never got to McDowell and Gainesville remained wide open. On the morning of August 29 McDowell found his way out of the woods, discovered what had happened to Ricketts and King, and informed Pope that his left wing had evaporated. Pope thereupon ordered McDowell with his two divisions and Porter with his corps to march on Gainesville from

Manassas. However, they were more than eight miles away and could not beat Longstreet to it.

Pope still might have pulled off a victory if he had insisted that Porter and McDowell, with perhaps twenty-two thousand men, hold Longstreet at Gainesville while he evicted Jackson by turning his left, or eastern, flank. Even without Porter and McDowell, Pope had more than twice as many men as Jackson. But Pope possessed no other tactical idea except to crash headlong against Jackson's front. And he gave McDowell and Porter an excuse to back off Longstreet by authorizing them to depart from his orders "if any considerable advantages are to be gained."[19]

Jackson had been preparing carefully for the attack he was certain was coming. More quickly than other senior commanders, Jackson had seen that the Minié ball had made the defense incomparably stronger than in previous wars. The battles of Beaver Dam Creek, Frayser's Farm, and Malvern Hill, especially, had shown that well-positioned infantry armed with the rifle and aided by resolute artillery could fend off even determined attacks by powerful forces.

Jackson had disposed his corps on the ridge at Groveton in a fashion to exploit this now-indisputable superiority of the rifle as a defensive weapon. He added to it a refined system of defense in depth. His first concern was to hold as short a line as possible. At Groveton it was only three thousand yards long, with both flanks safeguarded by Stuart's cavalry. This gave him more than five rifles or muskets a yard. Next he gave each local commander authority to bring up reinforcements at once and on his own authority to any point he saw was threatened. Each brigadier commanded his own reserves in a second line directly behind the first. And, since the enemy might direct a powerful force at any single point in the line, he also gave to each of his three division commanders half of his entire defending force to form a third line, to be thrown forward wherever danger appeared. This gave commanders the means to protect their positions as well as to seize all opportunities for counterstrokes.

In regard to defensive emplacements Jackson was questioning, but had not moved entirely away from, orthodox doctrine, which frowned on troops taking shelter behind field fortifications, on the theory that they would not leave them if called on to attack.

Jackson settled on the next best thing: he drew up his divisions just at the edge of the ridge line mainly along a railroad right of way of cuts and embankments, dug before the war but not completed. This "unfinished railroad" was not a system of trenches and redoubts but it provided significant protection for the soldiers.

By deliberately inviting attack on August 29, Jackson demonstrated that he believed that a smaller force, if determined and well led, could withstand a much larger enemy. If he succeeded his tactics could have war-winning implications.

Jackson emplaced Hill's division on the east, Ewell's (now commanded by Alexander R. Lawton) in the center, and Taliaferro's (now under William E. Starke) on the west. The line began about two-thirds of a mile from the turnpike, near Groveton crossroads, and angled northeast to about a mile and a half from the pike on Jackson's extreme left flank, resting half a mile from the Sudley Springs Ford over Bull Run. Jackson's position was largely screened by woods but faced out on open fields some thirteen hundred yards deep over which the enemy would have to advance, except for woods, four hundred to six hundred yards wide, mostly along Hill's front but also extending into Lawton's. The land rose to the northwest, providing good positions for artillery.[20] This line was the principal scene of the two-day battle about to begin.

A peculiarity about the Federal attacks on August 29 was that they struck almost entirely A. P. Hill's division on the left, although he was farthest from the turnpike. One reason was that Pope—not realizing that Jackson had no intention of going anywhere—was anxious to prevent him from retreating northward toward Leesburg. Another was that the woods in front of Hill permitted Union infantry to approach the railroad cut under cover.

Sigel's corps went into action first, at daybreak, before Kearny and the other forces near Centreville had come up. Sigel contented himself along most of his front with an artillery duel. Only on his extreme east did Carl Schurz's division advance. Some skirmishers got around Hill's left flank and drove away the Confederate trains near Sudley Springs, but Rebel cavalry evicted them. A greater threat appeared in front of Maxcy Gregg's South Carolina brigade, where Schurz's main body advanced through the belt of woods. Gregg did not wait behind the railway cut but rushed into the woods, flanked the "Dutchmen," and attacked so vigorously that his men split two Federal brigades apart and broke the division's center. The bluecoats retreated but rallied, got three fresh regiments to assist, and renewed the assault. Again Gregg's men drove the Federals out of the woods in disorder.[21]

Schurz's division, reinforced by some men from Adolph von Steinwehr's division, jumped off in a third gallant attack against Gregg and Col. Edward L. Thomas's Georgia brigade, lined up just west of Gregg. The battle raged along the railway cut. Some of Schurz's men crossed it but the Rebels threw them back. Now reinforced by L. O'B. Branch's North Carolina brigade, Gregg advanced against Schurz's right and crushed it. Schurz's left, however, pressed over the railway through a small undefended stretch between Gregg's and Thomas's brigades and threatened to isolate Gregg until two Rebel regiments struck either side of the penetration and forced the Federals to retire.

Although Philip Kearny's division formed on Schurz's right at around 10 A.M., his men did not advance because of heavy Rebel artillery fire.[22]

Meanwhile, Lee and Longstreet marched down from Thoroughfare without opposition, arriving at Gainesville at around 11:30 A.M., August 29. Longstreet turned east along the turnpike and drew up on either side of it, facing approximately east and at a near right angle to Jackson's line. Neither Pope nor any of the other Federal commanders facing Jackson was aware of Longstreet's presence.[23]

Pope remained preoccupied with destroying Jackson and permitted Joseph Hooker's division to take the places of Schurz and the separate brigade of Robert H. Milroy.[24] The battle so far had been a disorganized affair of piecemeal, limited Union attacks that had gotten nowhere. Only a small part of the Federal army had been engaged. Reynolds, to the left of Sigel, had only dueled with Rebel artillery.

Meantime, Porter's and McDowell's corps had arrived along Dawkins Branch, over three miles southeast of Gainesville. There they halted, still in column formation, and listened to the sounds of battle on the heights northeast of Groveton while Porter and McDowell debated what to do about Longstreet's forces now emplaced in front of them.

Pope had given Porter and McDowell discretion to change their orders if they saw advantages. Since Longstreet already was emplaced, McDowell saw "advantages" in moving northeast to assist Pope while Porter remained and attacked alone. This made little sense. If two corps found it inexpedient to attack Longstreet, one corps would find it even more so. Nevertheless, McDowell marched his corps up the Sudley Road, arriving late in the afternoon at Reynolds's position near the turnpike and moving King's division (now under Brig. Gen. John P. Hatch) to Reynolds's left. Porter remained at Dawkins Branch but did nothing.

The attacks continued piecemeal against Jackson. The New York–New Jersey–Pennsylvania brigade of Joseph B. Carr in Hooker's division attacked Thomas's Georgians and Charles W. Field's Virginia brigade, reaching the railroad cut but being driven back when W. Dorsey Pender's North Carolina brigade came to Thomas's assistance.

After this, Cuvier Grover's New Hampshire–Massachusetts–Pennsylvania brigade went against Thomas's and Gregg's now-exhausted men. Grover's men marched right up to the railway cut, delivered a single volley, and charged at the point of the bayonet, driving the stunned Rebels beyond the railway. But Confederate artillery staggered the brigade and Rebel reserves swept down and broke the gallant force. Over a fourth of

Grover's two thousand men were killed, wounded, or captured.[25]

Finally, after 5 P.M., Kearny was at last ready to attack on the extreme east. At the same time, Isaac I. Stevens's division of Reno's corps lined up on Kearny's left. Their intention was to storm the position that Gregg had held so stubbornly all day. A. P. Hill saw the two fresh Federal divisions about to assault. A third of Gregg's command was dead or wounded. Hill sent an urgent inquiry: could Gregg hold? The reply instantly passed into Confederate legend. Gregg responded that he thought he could hold; though his ammunition was about exhausted, he still had the bayonet.[26]

Hill was gratified by Gregg's bravery but he looked around for help, finding Jubal A. Early's brigade plus the Thirteenth Georgia and the Eighth Louisiana. The Federal storm burst against Gregg's desperately resisting line, driving it back to a last-ditch stand on a hill. Gregg, carrying a Revolutionary War scimitar, strode from one end of the line to the other, saying, "Let us die here, my men, let us die here!"[27] At precisely the right moment, as the Federal wave had crested and was spent, Early led his band through Gregg's brigade and struck the enemy center with a single, powerful blow. The Union soldiers broke and ran back at great speed, Early's men on their heels, driving them over the railroad cut and beyond.[28]

A. P. Hill sent a message to Jackson: "General Hill presents his compliments and says the attack of the enemy was repulsed." Jackson's face broke into one of its rare smiles and he answered: "Tell him I knew he would do it."[29]

Meanwhile, Longstreet was still being ignored by the Federals, but he did not take advantage of his splendid position and made no move against the undefended enemy left flank. The reason he gave Lee was that Federal forces at Dawkins Branch to his south might attack—although they were no threat and remained in column formation on the road.[30]

Lee asked Longstreet three times whether he was ready to attack, but he accepted Longstreet's decision each time to postpone an assault until the day was so far advanced that nothing was left to do but order a small reconnaissance in force to sound out Federal positions. Despite his questioning of Longstreet, Lee supported Longstreet tacitly. He did not want to bring on a general engagement. Had Jackson not drawn Pope into an engagement, Lee would have made no effort to challenge him to a battle.[31]

As a consequence, the bulk of the Confederate army, with Lee's acquiescence or approval, stood idle within easy striking distance of Pope all afternoon on August 29, 1862, while Jackson sustained assault after assault and almost wholly absorbed the attention of the Federal army, nearly three times the size of his own force. If Lee had attacked Pope's flank, it is extremely likely the Confederate army could have rolled up the entire Federal army south of Bull Run and destroyed it.[32]

Jackson had brought on this great opportunity by drawing Pope into battle with only a part of the total Federal army, which was backed up against Bull Run with only the Stone Bridge and a few fords as a means of retreat. Pope was positioned to be annihilated.

Just as had happened on the Rapidan, Lee approached within striking distance of the enemy but delayed launching the assault until it was too late.

Pope, apparently still unaware that Longstreet was on the field, ordered Reynolds and Schenck, facing Jackson's right, to attack in the late afternoon. They made an effort, but artillery and rifle fire forced them back.[33]

At 4:30 P.M., just as the final assault against Jackson by Kearny and Stevens was being mounted, Pope sent a peremptory order for Porter to attack on the Confederate right or rear. This order did not reach Porter until after 6:30 P.M. and he decided not to launch it. If he had advanced with his ten thousand men against Longstreet's twenty-five thousand he would have been defeated.[34]

Pope, however, thinking that Porter would soon be driving northward, ordered Hatch to attack on the western flank of Jackson's line along the turnpike. This strike went in at about sunset and encountered John B. Hood's division, which Lee at last had ordered forward to reconnoiter. Hood sent Hatch's march-exhausted men reeling. However, Hood stopped with darkness, felt out the Federal positions, and concluded that they were strong. He withdrew to his original position at 1 A.M., August 30.[35]

The first day of Second Manassas, or Second Bull Run, ended. Pope had successfully ignored Longstreet's corps, due to Longstreet's reticence and Lee's acceptance. Though Pope had seventy-five thousand men to Jackson's twenty-one thousand, he had not assembled them all and had thrown individual brigades and divisions separately against Jackson's unyielding line. Because of his defense in depth, Jackson always concentrated more men than Pope at every critical point. Although Jackson sustained heavy casualties, they were only about a third of the eight thousand recorded by Pope.[36] Jackson was never in any danger. His tactics had proved themselves, although Pope's failure to mount a general attack had aided him materially.

NOTES

General sources: Allan, *Army of Northern Virginia,* 225–61; Dabney, 523–32; Cooke, 284–94; Alexander, *Military Memoirs,* 197–210; Alexander, *Fighting for the Confederacy,* 131–33; Douglas, 136–38; Selby, 137–41; Henderson, 444–65; Freeman, *Lee's Lieutenants,* vol. 2, 104–20; Maurice, 140–44; Freeman, *R. E. Lee,* vol. 2, 310–28; Johnson and Buel, vol. 2, 468–85, 495–96, 505–11, 517–20, and 527–28; Chambers, vol. 2, 149–66; and Vandiver, 361–67.

1. The genesis and implementation of this concept were Jackson's. Lee, throughout the Second Manassas campaign, sought to avoid a general engagement and to rely on maneuver to force Pope from northern Virginia. On the morning of August 30, 1862 (the last day of the battle), he wrote this specifically to President Davis. See Freeman, *R. E. Lee,* vol. 2, 259 and 328; and Lee, 56–58. Because of the movements Jackson made on August 27 to place his corps in a position to block Pope and on the twenty-eighth to draw Pope into a fight, there can be no doubt that

Jackson deliberately had planned a general engagement. Jackson likely made these movements knowing that Lee was averse to a battle. He already had witnessed Lee's slowness in attacking on the Rapidan.

2. Allan, *Army of Northern Virginia,* 221. Pope's belief that Jackson had planned only a raid is understandable; that is what Lee had proposed.

3. Henderson, 441–42; Allan, *Army of Northern Virginia,* 222; *Official Records,* vol. 12, pt. 2, 35–36 and 71–72; and Alexander, *Military Memoirs,* 196. Pope ordered Fitz-John Porter's corps forward from Warrenton Junction to Bristoe to help Hooker counter a movement by Jackson around his eastern flank. Pope's ordering all of his forces at Gainesville to march on Manassas proves that he had no idea he was occupying a central position at Gainesville and that he was disregarding the danger of Longstreet's corps approaching Thoroughfare.

4. Allan, *Army of Northern Virginia,* 231; and Henderson, 443–44.

5. Freeman, *Lee's Lieutenants,* vol. 2, 103–4; *Official Records,* vol. 12, pt. 2, 644, 670, and 710; Freeman, *R. E. Lee,* vol. 2, 320; Alexander, *Military Memoirs,* 197; and Henderson, 445–46.

6. Allan, *Army of Northern Virginia,* 225; and *Official Records,* vol. 12, pt. 2, 735.

7. Allan, *Army of Northern Virginia,* 229; Henderson, 443; and *Official Records,* vol. 12, pt. 2, 337 and 360–61.

8. Allan, *Army of Northern Virginia,* 231–32; Freeman, *Lee's Lieutenants,* vol. 1, 105–6; and Alexander, *Military Memoirs,* 197–98. In *Official Records* (vol. 12, pt. 2, 644) Jackson reports: "Dispositions were promptly made to attack the enemy, based upon the idea that he would continue to press forward upon the turnpike towards Alexandria."

9. *Official Records,* vol. 12, pt. 2, 336; Allan, *Army of Northern Virginia,* 227 and 231–32; Alexander, *Military Memoirs,* 198; and Henderson, 446–47.

10. In *Official Reports* (vol. 12, pt. 2, 644–45) Jackson writes: "As he [the enemy] did not appear to advance in force and there was reason to believe the main body was leaving the road and inclining toward Manassas Junction, my command was advanced through the woods, leaving Groveton on the left, until it reached a commanding position near Browner's house [three-quarters of a mile west-northwest of Groveton crossroads]."

11. Gibbon remained with the old army but he had three brothers in the Confederate army and he was best man at the marriage of D. H. Hill.

Gibbon's brigade gained notoriety because he outfitted the men with nonregulation black slouch hats. See Johnson and Buel, vol. 2, 580; and Alexander, *Fighting for the Confederacy,* 563, n. 34.

12. Alexander, *Military Memoirs,* 198–201; Allan, *Army of Northern Virginia,* 232–35; Henderson, 447–52; Freeman, *Lee's Lieutenants,* vol. 2, 107–11; *Official Records,* vol. 12, pt. 2, 369, 378, 645, and 657; and Johnson and Buel, vol. 2, 469.

13. *Official Records,* vol. 12, pt. 2, 383–84 and 564; Allan, *Army of Northern Virginia,* 225 and 228; and Alexander, *Military Memoirs,* 202. McDowell had sent the First New Jersey Cavalry to Thoroughfare Gap on the morning of August 28. When it arrived it found some of Longstreet's men already in possession, though not in strength. When McDowell learned this, he sent Ricketts's division to hold Longstreet in check.

14. Johnson and Buel, vol. 2, 517–18.

15. Ibid., 470–71; *Official Records,* vol. 12, pt. 2, 393; Allan, *Army of Northern Virginia,* 241–42.

16. Johnson and Buel, vol. 2, 469; and Henderson, 454.

17. *Official Records,* vol. 12, pt. 2, 37–38 and 75; Johnson and Buel, vol. 2, 470–72 and 495; Allan, *Army of Northern Virginia,* 240; and Freeman, *Lee's Lieutenants,* vol. 2, 110. Pope directed Philip Kearny at Centreville to advance at 1 A.M., August 29, on Jackson's left, or eastern, flank and to attack at dawn, with Joseph Hooker's division and Jesse L. Reno's corps to support him and Sigel and Reynolds to attack Jackson at daylight from their present positions.

18. Pope justifiably complains in Johnson and Buel (vol. 2, 470–71) regarding the absence of McDowell and the failure of leadership and resolve of all of his division and corps commanders in this sector at the time. Pope's orders during the night of August 28 and early morning of August 29 indicate that he sincerely believed that his left, or western, flank was preventing the junction of Lee and Jackson and thus he could concentrate the remainder of his army against Jackson.

19. Johnson and Buel, vol. 2, 473–74; *Official Records,* vol. 12, pt. 2, 518 and 520; Allan, *Army of Northern Virginia,* 257–58 and 265–66; and Alexander, *Military Memoirs,* 204.

20. Freeman, *Lee's Lieutenants,* vol. 2, 111; Allan, *Army of Northern Virginia,* 245–46; and Henderson, 455–56 and 485–86.

21. *Official Records,* vol. 12, pt. 2, 297–98, 680, and 702; Allan, *Army of Northern Virginia,* 247–48; Henderson, 456–57; Freeman, *Lee's Lieutenants,* vol. 2, 115–19; and Alexander, *Military Memoirs,* 204–5.

22. *Official Records,* vol. 12, pt. 2, 421 and 434; and Allan, *Army of Northern Virginia,* 249.

23. Allan, *Army of Northern Virginia,* 253–54.

24. Ibid., 246; and *Official Records,* vol. 12, pt. 2, 319.

25. Henderson, 458–60; Allan, *Army of Northern Virginia,* 249–51; and Alexander, *Military Memoirs,* 205–6.

26. *Official Records,* vol. 12, pt. 3, 681; Allan, *Army of Northern Virginia,* 252–53; and Freeman, *Lee's Lieutenants,* vol. 2, 116. Gregg started the day with not more than fifteen hundred men. His losses were 613 killed and wounded.

27. *Southern Historical Society Papers,* vol. 13, 34; see also 244.

28. Allan, *Army of Northern Virginia,* 253; Freeman, *Lee's Lieutenants,* vol. 2, 117; *Official Records,* vol. 12, pt. 2, 681; and Henderson, 461–62.

29. Douglas, 138.

30. Johnson and Buel, vol. 2, 481.

31. There is an enigmatic letter written by Longstreet to Fitz-John Porter in regard to Porter's efforts to get his court-martial overturned (he was court-martialed primarily for failing to attack Longstreet on August 29). In this Longstreet writes, concerning the hours at which his command came up to the west of Jackson: "We all were particularly anxious to bring on the battle after twelve M. [presumably *meridies,* or noon], General Lee more so than the rest." See Allan, *Army of Northern Virginia,* 260, referring to a statement of Porter in New York in 1878. This letter seems to be a post-event effort by Longstreet to color over his reluctance to bring on a general engagement on August 29 and possibly to protect Lee.

32. Longstreet, in Johnson and Buel, (vol. 2, 519–20 and 522–23), argues that if he had attacked August 29, Porter's artillery could have caught him in enfilade fire. However, Porter's guns along Dawkins Branch were two miles from Longstreet's main troop concentration along the turnpike, well beyond the effective range of shrapnel (which was about a thousand yards), the only shot capable of much damage against infantry

at long ranges. Also, Confederate guns with D. R. Jones's division facing Porter could have reduced the effectiveness of Porter's cannons with counterbattery fire. Douglas Freeman, in *R. E. Lee* (vol. 2, 322–25), chronicles the discussion between Longstreet and Lee on August 29. He also criticizes Lee (347) for not ordering the attack, even over Longstreet's objections, and mentions that Confederate pursuit on August 31 was greatly hindered on account of mud, whereas the pursuit would have been far more successful if conducted before the huge rainstorm in the evening on August 30. Freeman argues in seeming defense of Lee's decision that Longstreet believed that the recipe for victory was to maneuver the army into a position where the enemy would have to attack at a disadvantage. This meant that an army would move to an offensive only after successfully defending from an attack. (See Maurice, 143.) Yet Jackson *had* been successfully defending against such an attack all day, and Pope's left flank was bare! The moment to launch a flank attack was *while* Pope was engrossed with Jackson. Afterward Lee tacitly acknowledged that he had failed to seize the opportunity Jackson had given him on the twenty-ninth. In a letter to Porter in 1870 Lee wrote that if Porter had attacked before 5 P.M. on August 29, Longstreet would have repulsed him and "the effect would have been an attack on General Pope's left and rear by Longstreet and Stuart, which, if successful, would have resulted in the relief of Jackson and have probably rendered unnecessary the battle of the next day." See Allan, *Army of Northern Virginia,* 260–61; Johnson and Buel, vol. 2, 519, 523, and 539–40; Longstreet, 181–82; *Official Records,* vol. 12, pt. 2, 556 and 565; Henderson, 463; Freeman, *Lee's Lieutenants,* vol. 2, 120–21; Alexander, *Military Memoirs,* 209–10; and Freeman, *R. E. Lee,* vol. 2, 327–28.

33. *Official Records,* vol. 12, pt. 2, 280–81 and 394; and Allan, *Army of Northern Virginia,* 254.

34. *Official Records,* vol. 12, pt. 2, 525; Johnson and Buel, vol. 2, 475; Allan, *Army of Northern Virginia,* 256–57; and Alexander, *Military Memoirs,* 207–8. Pope, in Johnson and Buel (vol. 2, 449–94), criticizes Porter but does not address the fact that he could have used Reynolds and Sigel to interpose between Jackson and Longstreet on the morning of August 29, 1862, since they were nearby, and could have marched Porter and McDowell against Jackson. Pope court-martialed Porter after the battle, largely for not attacking Longstreet east and south of Gainesville; the court cashiered him and it was not until 1882, after a board had largely vindicated Porter, that President Chester Arthur remitted Porter's sentence.

35. *Official Records,* vol. 12, pt. 2, 307, 339, 367, and 605; Allan, *Army of Northern Virginia,* 604–5; Henderson, 463–64; Freeman, *R. E. Lee,* vol. 2, 327–28; and Alexander, *Military Memoirs,* 209–10.

36. *Official Records,* vol. 12, pt. 3, 741; Allan, *Army of Northern Virginia,* 260; and Alexander, *Military Memoirs,* 219. Confederate losses are not separated for the twenty-ninth. However, as Alexander records Jackson's total losses for the entire Second Manassas campaign as 4,387, it is unlikely that his casualties on August 29 could have been more than a third those of Pope, since the battle consisted entirely of desperate charges by Pope's troops and uniform repulses by Jackson's. However, it is likely that Pope's estimate of eight thousand Federal casualties for this day is high and that the losses may have been closer to six thousand to seven thousand Union and fifteen hundred to two thousand Confederate.

11

INCOMPLETE VICTORY AT SECOND MANASSAS

★ ★ ★ August 29 and 30, 1862, were days of missed opportunities. On August 29 John Pope assembled sixty-thousand men and directed them entirely against a corps of twenty-one thousand men under Stonewall Jackson. Pope failed to shake this much-inferior force. In part his attacks miscarried because Jackson was unveiling a defense that combined the power of the rifle, sophisticated use of artillery, a railway line that served partially as field fortifications, and defenders organized in waves or echelons so that reserves could overwhelm any enemy penetration.

Although Jackson's new-model defensive system performed in a spectacular fashion, some of the credit had to be laid at the feet of John Pope. Instead of using his entire force, the Federal commander assembled only fragments and launched one disconnected assault after another. Jackson was able to concentrate against each attack and achieved superiority at every critical point.

Pope's piecemeal attacks were wrong but scarcely unusual,

since commanders on both sides frequently practiced similar tactics. The remarkable, almost unbelievable blunder of Pope lay elsewhere: he ignored a Confederate corps of twenty-five thousand men under James Longstreet arrayed directly against his left flank that could have rolled up his entire line, forcing him against Bull Run, where he had only a single bridge and a few inadequate fords over which to retreat.

As astonishing as Pope's mistake was, the response of Longstreet and Robert E. Lee was even more incomprehensible. They disregarded the opportunity Pope had given them and did nothing, remaining in place the entire afternoon while Pope was absorbed in launching repeated attacks against Jackson's desperately resisting line. Longstreet excused his failure by pointing to a ten thousand–man corps under Fitz-John Porter to his south that at no time posed a threat.

Stonewall Jackson had lured Pope into attacking with inadequate avenues of retreat, knowing that Longstreet was arriving on his flank. Jackson could not have anticipated that Pope would disregard Longstreet; but he also could not have anticipated that Lee would have missed this second opportunity within two weeks to destroy Pope's army.

On August 30 the Confederate army was deployed in the configuration of the day before: Jackson along an unfinished railway line stretching three thousand yards northeast from just above Groveton, Longstreet in a line running south-southwest from Jackson's right. There were two differences in the Federal dispositions: Pope concentrated the main army northeast of Groveton crossroads against Jackson and ordered Porter to join it.

With Porter gone from his south, Lee faced no danger whatsoever to an attack on Pope's still-exposed left flank. The prospects for destroying Pope's army remained as bright as ever.

However, General Lee—inexplicably still not seeing the spectacular chance Jackson had given him—had decided *not* to attack. He held to his original aim of avoiding a general engagement and relying on maneuver to force Pope from northern Virginia. He wrote this to President Davis during the morning. Lee resolved to remain in his position and await events.[1]

General Pope, meanwhile, had convinced himself that he had won the battle on August 29 and that Stonewall Jackson was retreating toward Thoroughfare Gap. He continued to deny that Lee and Longstreet had been on the field since midday.[2] From these inexcusable errors Pope concocted a plan to concentrate against Jackson's supposedly fleeing soldiers on the thirtieth while again largely ignoring his western flank.[3]

At 5 A.M. on August 30 Pope wired General Halleck that "we fought a terrific battle here yesterday. . . . The enemy was driven from the field. . . . The news just reaches me from the front that the enemy is retreating toward the mountains. I go forward at once to see."[4]

Later in the morning Pope became more and more elated as he received reports indicating that Jackson was retreating, coming from Federal officers captured the day before and paroled by the Rebels. Generals McDowell and Heintzelman also made personal reconnaissances of Jackson's position and reached the same hasty conclusion. In fact, Jackson had merely pulled his men into the woods northwest of the unfinished railroad, to rest them and to mystify the Federals.[5]

The plan that Pope and McDowell finally agreed on was flawed so profoundly that it ranks as one of the preeminent examples of how *not* to fight a tactical battle.

Not only did Pope continue largely to disregard Longstreet's corps on his left flank, but he decided to repeat the same tactics against Jackson that had failed so signally the day before: direct assaults straight into Jackson's massed rifles and cannons. The only change was to shift the attack from the left flank toward the center and right of Jackson's line.

This made the plan *worse* than that of the day before and illustrated Napoleon's dictum that the general ignorant of his enemy's strength and dispositions is ignorant of his trade. Since Jackson's and Longstreet's corps together formed a flat crescent, any attack made against Jackson's center or right would send Pope's troops into a cul-de-sac, with both entry and exit blanketed by fire from two directions.

This danger was greatly heightened because two battalions of

Confederate artillery were mounted on an eminence just north of the turnpike at the juncture of Jackson's and Longstreet's lines.

Jackson's artillery chief, Col. Stapleton Crutchfield, had fired eighteen cannons from this quarter-mile-long ridge on August 29. On the morning of August 30 Col. Stephen D. Lee of Longstreet's command put another eighteen guns to the right of Crutchfield's pieces.

These thirty-six cannons faced generally *east* over a wide area of open fields in front of the center and right wing of Jackson's line. The only barrier they encountered was the belt of trees about thirteen hundred yards away in front of Jackson's left wing. These were the woods that had sheltered the Federal attacks on the twenty-ninth. Below these woods the guns could direct devastating enfilade fire against any Federal assault striking the center and right of Jackson's line.

Confederate artilleryman Porter Alexander writes that "a battery established where it can enfilade others need not trouble itself about aim. It has only to fire in the right direction and the shot finds something to hurt wherever it falls. No troops, infantry or artillery, can long submit to enfilade fire."[6]

On the morning of the thirtieth Federal batteries got into a duel with the guns on the hill, while around noon Union skirmishers advanced against them but were forced back.[7] Pope and McDowell, in charge of tactical operations, should have known of the guns and how they were sited.

Since Pope had convinced himself that Jackson was retreating, he ordered Ricketts's division to move around Jackson's extreme left flank and wanted Porter to push along the Warrenton pike around Jackson's right flank. Longstreet, of course, was standing in the way of Porter, and Ricketts abandoned his intended sweep as soon as he discovered Jackson still emplaced along the unfinished railroad. Porter never attempted a flank move, telling McDowell that no pursuit was possible until Jackson had been defeated along his front.[8]

Porter proposed instead an attack of two divisions directly at the center and right wing of Jackson's corps "to develop the strength of the enemy." Pope and McDowell, finally realizing that Jackson was still in position, could think of nothing better. All three generals ignored the thirty-six Confederate cannons emplaced on their left flank.[9]

The Federal generals thus ordered actions that the experience of history has shown should be avoided in war. They advanced on the line of greatest expectation and the line of maximum resistance by the Confederates. They provided for no alternative course in case of failure. And they renewed the attack along the same line after it had failed the day before—a dangerous mistake, since the repulse had strengthened Jackson's men morale and weakened Pope's.[10]

Pope made only one gesture toward protection of this left flank: at around noon or after, he sent Reynolds's division along the south side of the Warrenton turnpike to block any Rebel move in that direction.[11] Just southwest of Groveton, Reynolds ran into a hornet's nest of Rebels and sent back pleas for help. Instead McDowell ordered two brigades of Ricketts's division to Henry House Hill, a mile and a half east of Groveton, while Pope sent Nathaniel C. McLean's brigade of Schenck's division to Bald Hill, a mile east of Groveton. Neither constituted direct help.[12]

Porter, meanwhile, lined up almost twenty thousand men, facing west, north of Groveton and behind the belt of woods that had sheltered the Federal attacks the day before. John P. Hatch's division was on the right and the First and Third brigades of George W. Morell's on the left. Morell's division was commanded by Brig. Gen. Daniel Butterfield because General Morell had mistakenly gone to Centreville with his Second Brigade.[13]

To Butterfield's left rear along the turnpike was George Sykes's division, while Sigel's corps was ordered forward as reserve, though it did not come up until Porter's assault had ended.[14] The two assault divisions gave Porter only a 30-percent superiority of force against Jackson, not sufficient to overwhelm him, yet half of Pope's army remained behind in column formation to watch.

In front of Hatch the protective woods extended to the railroad. In front of Butterfield they were only about a quarter of a mile wide. Beyond stretched about a half mile of largely open fields. Since Jackson's line along the railroad extended northeast-southwest and Porter's assault was directly toward the west, it struck Jackson at an acute angle, Hatch being much closer to Jackson's line than Butterfield.[15]

It was 3 P.M. before Porter's lines finally moved forward. Jackson had altered his arrangements from the day before, having drawn up his corps into two lines of battle, one that moved to the railroad cut as the attack dawned, the other waiting as a reserve in a wooded ridge two hundred yards in the rear.

As soon as he saw Jackson's first line rush out of the woods and reoccupy the railroad line just prior to Porter's attack, Pope directed Reynolds to *abandon* his position on the left flank and move north of the pike to the rear of Porter![16] Pope remained to the last oblivious to the danger on his flank.

Hatch's division struck mainly Ewell's left sector, held by the brigades of Lawton, commanded by Col. Marcellus Douglass, and Jubal A. Early. Here the fighting was severe, but the Rebels repulsed the Federals, though the whole of Ewell's division (commanded by Lawton) and Archer's and Thomas's brigades of A. P. Hill's division on the left became involved. Even then the Union onset was so fierce that Lawton and Hill restored the line only by sending Dorsey Pender's brigade charging into the melee.[17]

The first of Butterfield's three lines of battle emerged from the woods and received severe fire but moved rapidly across the open fields to the unfinished railroad, where Ewell's men and Taliaferro's division (under Starke) were waiting. Here the fighting became wild and sanguinary. Starke's brigade, commanded by Col. Leroy A. Stafford, and Bradley Johnson's brigade held their positions tenaciously. To the right the Federals pushed back the first line of the Stonewall Brigade, but Colonel Baylor led the second line forward and drove Butterfield's men back, though Baylor died at the head of his men. Along Ewell's front to the left Alexander G. Taliaferro's brigade held firmly.[18]

The battle raged in unbelievable fury for twenty to thirty minutes. There was no thought of retreat by either side. The Federals made assault after assault against the railway line but the Rebels stopped them every time. Some of the Confederates ran out of ammunition and grabbed cartridges from dead bodies or snatched up rocks and threw them at the enemy. General Johnson reported: "I saw a Federal flag hold its position for half an hour within ten yards of a flag of one of the regiments in the cut and go down six or eight times, and after the fight one hundred dead were lying twenty yards from the cut, some of them within two feet of it."[19]

Confederate artillery on the elevation on the flank had been unable to direct heavy fire quickly enough to riddle Butterfield's first line as it moved across the open space. Hatch's lines were even harder to interdict because they advanced through the woods. Once engaged in close conflict the Confederate artillery could not fire for fear of striking friends.

As the battle raged along the railway cut, however, the Rebel guns concentrated on the woods from which succeeding Federal lines had to come and on the fields over which they had to pass to reach Jackson's center and right. Butterfield's division, penned in the open between Longstreet's line and the grove of woods, was riddled by Jackson's rifle fire in front and a hail of canister, grapeshot, and shells from the thirty-six guns emplaced on the hill. The deadly barrage reached all the way across to Hatch's lines. As Porter described it: "The enfilading artillery, combined with the direct infantry fire, almost annihilated line after line, as each was about to crown the embankment."[20]

Before this terrible execution had commenced, Jackson had requested reinforcements from Lee. Longstreet had ridden to the front near the turnpike and could see that the artillery was destroying Pope's attack. Instead of sending troops he ordered up two more batteries to the hill. The additional guns added all that was needed to turn the assault into a hurried retreat.[21]

As soon as General Lee witnessed the devastation, he recognized the opportunity and, casting aside his resolve to stand on the defensive, ordered a general attack. Longstreet had anticipated the order and already had summoned his troops to charge. As fast as the word could be delivered, each unit of the Army of Northern Virginia sprang forward in a magnificent advance along a front of four miles, its crimson banners to the fore and the men screaming the Rebel yell.[22]

With Reynolds ordered away, the Federal army had no shield behind which it might have rallied on the flank. Only small forces were in place to contest Longstreet south of the turnpike. The Federals' greatest asset now was time—the Confederates had only a few hours of daylight to seize Henry House Hill on the Federal rear and block the Federal retreat over the Stone Bridge.

Hood's division, composed of his brigade and Col. E. M. Law's, led off the Confederate flank march. Just south of the pike was a guard for Porter: the battery of Capt. Charles E. Hazlett, shielded by the one thousand–man brigade of Col. Gouverneur K. Warren of Sykes's division. Hood's brigade rolled at and around this forlorn force and swept it from the field, killing or wounding 431 Federals. Hazlett had just enough time to pull back his battery.

Hood now ran headlong into Reynolds's Third Brigade under Lt. Col. Robert Anderson. It had been trying to get north of the pike, but Hood's advance overtook it and bowled it over, wiping out the second Federal brigade from the order of battle in a matter of minutes.

Meanwhile, Law's brigade was driving straight down the Warrenton pike and struck Julius Stahel's brigade of Schenck's division near Groveton crossroads. The Federals, realizing that their left rear was collapsing, did not fight long, for Sigel pulled Stahel and the remainder of his corps back to Buck Hill, just north of the pike and west of the Stone Bridge.

The Texans, Georgians, and South Carolinians in Hood's brigade were getting tired, but they kept going. The next objective was Bald Hill, a mile east of Groveton, defended by McLean's brigade and the two brigades of Ricketts's division, under Brig. Gen. Zealous B. Tower, that had rushed over from Henry House Hill. Hood charged, but his exhausted men were unable to carry

Bald Hill on the first assault and the Confederate drive received its first check. The supporting South Carolina brigade of P. F. Stevens also attacked, only to be stopped as well.

Hood's rush had carried him ahead of the rest of the Confederate line and he had to wait until James L. Kemper's division came up on his right, while Richard Anderson's division arrived behind Stevens and Law's brigade attacked on his left. The Rebels struck Bald Hill from three sides and drove McLean's and Tower's lines onto Henry House Hill.[23]

Now the only barrier to the destruction of Pope's army was Henry House Hill, of First Manassas fame, directly east of Bald Hill and just southwest of the Stone Bridge. If the Federals were to hold the Stone Bridge, the only adequate way to get across Bull Run, they had to hold Henry House. As the Confederate lines rushed forward, McDowell had just enough time to hurry a few units to Henry House.

Sigel, meanwhile, sent three regiments and Wladimir Krzyzanowski's brigade to recapture Bald Hill, but David R. Jones's division arrived and drove them off.

McDowell found the Second Brigade of George Sykes's Regular Army division under William Chapman and sent it just in time to fend off Rebels advancing on Henry House. Reynolds—having been on a long, fruitless odyssey around the rear of the Federal army—arrived with his two brigades and reinforced Chapman's and parts of Robert H. Milroy's brigades lining the sunken Sudley Road just west of Henry House.[24]

The Confederates, elated but exhausted, now struck, led by Jones's and parts of Anderson's divisions, evicting Milroy and driving back Chapman and Reynolds and being prevented from carrying the hill only by Sykes's First Brigade, under Robert C. Buchanan, just arrived and drawn up as the second line. Col. George T. (Tige) Anderson, commanding the Georgia brigade in Jones's division, reported that after Buchanan came up, "the fight resumed with all its intensity but the [Federal] men and officers stood to their posts under the most murderous fire I ever witnessed, with the resolve to fall rather than yield. . . . Fresh troops coming up soon after, the enemy were again and finally driven from the field."[25]

Nevertheless, Buchanan's resistance had slowed and weakened Jones and Anderson, and as they climbed toward the crest of Henry House in the gathering darkness they found Jesse L. Reno's division, which had arrived during the engagement, presenting a solid front toward them. The fighting stopped. Soon heavy rain began and continued through the night.

In other parts of the field the Federals had withdrawn rapidly in the face of the Confederate advance, giving up thousands of prisoners. With Henry House Hill holding like a sheet anchor, however, there was nowhere an opportunity to cut off a significant fraction of Pope's army, which streamed away in increasing panic, mostly over the Stone Bridge but in smaller numbers over Sudley Springs and other fords. Pope's survivors drew up a shaky defensive line on the far side of Bull Run around a part of William B. Franklin's corps, which had arrived in the late afternoon.[26]

If, instead of waiting to see what the Federals would do, Lee had ordered Longstreet to attack in the morning before Reynolds moved to the left flank, it is almost certain that the Confederates could have seized Henry House Hill and delivered Pope's army to disaster. Darkness alone prevented complete victory. Once in possession of this eminence the Rebels could have swept the turnpike and the approaches to the Stone Bridge. The vast majority of Pope's men would have had to surrender or be killed or wounded.

The whole campaign cost the North about 10,200 men killed and wounded, while those captured reached about 7,000. Confederate losses were almost ninety-one hundred killed and wounded but only eighty-one missing or prisoners. Thus, total real Southern losses were only marginally lower than Federal. In leaders the loss was brutal—two division commanders, Ewell and Taliaferro, and four brigadier generals wounded, and numerous regimental commanders killed or wounded—in Hill's division five colonels killed, four wounded; in Taliaferro's division (under Starke) regiments were commanded by captains and lieutenants.

Lee had missed one chance to destroy the Northern army the day before. A like victory this day had been foiled because he refused to attack until too late. Now, having merely driven Pope back and not changed the strategic picture, the Confederacy had to hope for a decision at some other place.[27]

The next day, Sunday, August 31, rainy and chilly, Jackson crossed Sudley Springs Ford and marched to the Little River turnpike (now U.S. Route 50) to the northwest in an attempt to turn the Federal right and oust Pope from Centreville.

On September 1 Jackson ran up against the Federal flank guard at Ox Hill, or Chantilly, and fought a hard battle in a driving rain. This convinced Pope to give up Centreville and he withdrew into the Washington defenses.[28]

That was the end of John Pope as commander of an army. President Lincoln relieved him and sent him out to the northwest to fight Indians. Lincoln had no other general to take his place, so he reinstated George B. McClellan.

NOTES

General sources: Johnson and Buel, vol. 2, 485–94, 497–500, 520–26, and 539–41; Henderson, 466–90; Alexander, *Military Memoirs,* 210–19; Allan, *Army of Northern Virginia,* 262–321; Dabney, 532–41; Cooke, 295–307; Selby, 141–44; Maurice, 145–46; Freeman, *R. E. Lee,* vol. 2, 328–49; Freeman, *Lee's Lieutenants,* vol. 2, 120–43; Chambers, vol. 2, 167–77; and Vandiver, 367–71.

1. Lee, 56–58; and Freeman, *R. E. Lee,* vol. 2, 328–29.
2. Allan, *Army of Northern Virginia,* 269; and Henderson, 469.
3. *Official Records,* vol. 12, pt. 2, 18; Johnson and Buel, vol. 2, 486; and Allan, *Army of Northern Virginia,* 267.
4. *Official Records,* vol. 12, pt. 3, 741; Allan, *Army of Northern Virginia,* 267; and Freeman, *R. E. Lee,* vol. 2, 329. Pope tried to hide the fact, in his reports after the battle, that he had actively sought to attack, claiming that he had been trying to "hold my position" and delay any "farther advance" of the Rebels "toward the capital," and that his plans had not involved a general assault on what he termed "superior forces" of the enemy. See Johnson and Buel, vol. 2, 486; and *Official Records,* vol. 12,

pt. 2, 41. As William Allan (*Army of Northern Virginia,* 266) writes: "To lead an inferior and exhausted army in hopeless struggle against a well-posted adversary in order to gain time was not the real part played by General Pope on that memorable day, however fully he may afterwards have persuaded himself that such was the case."

5. *Official Records,* vol. 12, pt. 2, 41, 340, and 413; Allan, *Army of Northern Virginia,* 268–69; Freeman, *R. E. Lee,* vol. 2, 330; Alexander, *Military Memoirs,* 212; and Henderson, 469–70. McDowell and Heintzelman apparently decided that Jackson was departing because Jackson's lines were quiet and there were no Rebel cavalry north of Bull Run, as had been the case on the twenty-ninth. But the cavalry was there because Fitz Lee that day returned from raids on Burke's Station and Fairfax Court House by way of Centreville and Sudley.

6. Alexander, *Fighting for the Confederacy,* 251.

7. Allan, *Army of Northern Virginia,* 262–63 and 274; Henderson, 468; Freeman, *R. E. Lee,* vol. 2, 329; *Official Records,* vol. 12, pt. 2, 577; and Alexander, *Military Memoirs,* 212.

8. *Official Records,* vol. 12, pt. 2, 361; and Allan, *Army of Northern Virginia,* 279–80. Porter's statement reveals a remarkable lack of understanding of a turning movement. Its primary purpose is to avoid having to break an enemy's front by direct attack. A turning movement, whether intended as pursuit or to dislodge an enemy, does not require defeating an enemy along his front as a preliminary.

9. *Official Records,* vol. 12, pt. 2, 361, 384, and 413; and Allan, *Army of Northern Virginia,* 270 and 276.

10. B. H. Liddell Hart, *Strategy* (New York: Frederick A. Praeger, 1954), 347–50.

11. After Hood's reconnaissance along the turnpike at nightfall on August 29, Longstreet reported (Johnson and Buel, vol. 2, 520) that Federal positions did not favor an attack and he withdrew Hood to his original position. It is not clear what these Federal positions were, since most Federal forces moved well east of Groveton crossroads as a result of Hood's advance. In any event, there were no Federal emplacements on Pope's left flank on the morning of August 30 (see map, ibid., 482). Longstreet knew this because he says that he and Lee believed that Pope was trying to withdraw (ibid., 520). Pope does not specify when he sent Reynolds to the left but says that between noon and 2 P.M. on August 30 he ordered Porter to attack west along the Warrenton pike, to be sup-

ported by Sigel and Reynolds, implying that Reynolds did not move until this time (see ibid., 486). This indicates that Pope's left flank was entirely bare until early afternoon on the thirtieth.

12. Allan, *Army of Northern Virginia,* 277–78; and Henderson, 470.

13. Johnson and Buel, vol. 2, 486; Allan, *Army of Northern Virginia,* 280; Alexander, *Military Memoirs,* 211; and Henderson, 470–71.

14. Allan, *Army of Northern Virginia,* 288; and Henderson, 472.

15. *Official Records,* vol. 12, pt. 2, 480, 557, and 647; and Allan, *Army of Northern Virginia,* 280.

16. *Official Records,* vol. 12, pt. 2, 394; Allan, *Army of Northern Virginia,* 286; Henderson, 471–72; and Alexander, *Military Memoirs,* 213–14.

17. *Official Records,* vol. 12, pt. 2, 671; and Allan, *Army of Northern Virginia,* 282.

18. Alexander, *Military Memoirs,* 472–73; and Allan, *Army of Northern Virginia,* 280–82.

19. *Official Records,* vol. 12, pt. 2, 666–67; Allan, *Army of Northern Virginia,* 282; Henderson, 473; Freeman, *R. E. Lee,* vol. 2, 331; and Alexander, *Military Memoirs,* 213.

20. Henderson, 474; Alexander, *Military Memoirs,* 213; and Allan, *Army of Northern Virginia,* 283.

21. *Official Records,* vol. 12, pt. 2, 565; Allan, *Army of Northern Virginia,* 284; Freeman, *Lee's Lieutenants,* vol. 2, 125–26; Douglas, 140; Freeman, *R. E. Lee,* vol. 2, 331–32; and Henderson, 474.

22. Allan, *Army of Northern Virginia,* 285; Freeman, *Lee's Lieutenants,* vol. 2, 127; Henderson, 474–76; and Freeman, *R. E. Lee,* vol. 2, 332–34.

23. Allan, *Army of Northern Virginia,* 287–90.

24. Henderson, 477–79; Allan, *Army of Northern Virginia,* 291–94; and Alexander, *Military Memoirs,* 214–16.

25. *Official Records,* vol. 12, pt. 2, 595; see also 322 and 488; and Allan, *Army of Northern Virginia,* 292–93.

26. Alexander, *Military Memoirs,* 215–16; Allan, *Army of Northern Virginia,* 295–96; Freeman, *R. E. Lee,* vol. 2, 335–36; Henderson, 479; and Johnson and Buel, vol. 2, 540.

27. Allan, *Army of Northern Virginia,* 306–8; Alexander, *Military Memoirs,* 219; and Freeman, *Lee's Lieutenants,* vol. 2, 141–43. Allan's estimated losses for the Federals are higher but Alexander's figures of killed and wounded appear to be more likely and are used. However, his figure of 4,263 Federals missing or captured seems low. Allan reports seven thousand Federals captured by Confederates plus two thousand wounded Federals left on the field, quoting Lee in *Official Records* (vol. 12, pt. 2, 558). Some students have doubted the prisoner figure but, since the Confederates picked up twenty thousand stand of arms on the battlefield, this appears more reasonable than Alexander's.

28. *Official Records,* vol. 12, pt. 2, 557–58; Allan, *Army of Northern Virginia,* 309–10; Henderson, 480–90; Freeman, *Lee's Lieutenants,* vol. 2, 128–34; and Alexander, *Military Memoirs,* 216–18. This battle gave rise to a story that probably is apocryphal but indicates the respect Jackson had gained in the army. The story goes that the rain was so hard that a brigade commander sent Jackson a message that his cartridges were wet from the heavy rain and he requested permission to retreat because he could not maintain his position. "Tell him," Jackson replied, "to hold his ground; if his guns will not go off, neither will the enemy's." See Henderson, 481; and Freeman, *Lee's Lieutenants,* vol. 2, 134–35.

12

A LOST ORDER CHANGES EVERYTHING

★ ★ ★ As the Union army withdrew back into the defenses of Washington and the meticulous, slow-moving McClellan once more gained control, General Lee decided at long last to strike into the North.

Conditions had changed greatly since Stonewall Jackson had proposed invasion in early July. No longer was the bulk of the Federal army bottled up on the peninsula. Now it was united with the remains of Pope's army in Washington, able to march out immediately in pursuit. The hope that Jackson had held of descending upon an almost undefended North could not be realized. Nevertheless, the strategic opportunity, though diminished, still existed.

However, Lee had an entirely different idea about an invasion than the decisive *military* campaign that Stonewall Jackson had envisioned. Lee hoped to exert *political* force to bring peace. Lee proposed to President Davis, once his army had become established on Northern soil, that the Confederate government offer peace based on recognition of Southern independence.

"Such a proposition," Lee wrote, "coming from us at this time, could in no way be regarded as suing for peace; but being made when it is in our power to inflict injury upon our adversary. . . . The rejection of this offer would prove to the country that the responsibility for the continuance of the war does not rest upon us but that the party in power in the United States elect to prosecute it for purposes of their own."[1]

Lee expected the people of the North to be the actors rather than the Confederacy. Stonewall Jackson thought in almost opposite terms. He sought to place the Northern people in such a difficult position that accepting Southern independence would be less painful than enduring further damage. Jackson worked on the application of *certain* force to achieve his ends, not *uncertain* persuasion.

On the other hand, Lee's proposal demonstrated an awareness of the political climate at the time. Despite many Northern victories in 1862—the capture of New Orleans and much of Tennessee and the Mississippi River—the terrible losses suffered at Shiloh and in Virginia had foreshadowed the cost that would be demanded to reunite the nation.

By late summer 1862 many moderate Northerners were wondering whether the Union was worth more thousands of dead and maimed. The prosecution of the war was being seen increasingly as a *party* issue and less a *national* issue. Lee knew that Abraham Lincoln and the Republicans would never accept peace on the basis of a divided country. But he and many politicians also knew that if Lincoln suffered another severe setback and it occurred on Northern soil, a large number of voters would turn against the Republicans in the November congressional elections. This might change the political complexion of the war.[2]

James Longstreet believed that the Confederate army could maintain itself in the North without a military victory, writing that the South "possessed an army which, had it been kept together, the Federals would never have dared attack."[3] It is possible that Lee shared this view before the campaign started. In any event, he did not develop a strategy for a decisive military victory.

Yet the Southern army could not remain in the North without a victory. Abraham Lincoln was intensely aware of the consequences of an election defeat and was certain to demand that the Union army assail the Southern army at the first opportunity.[4] For this reason Lee could secure a political victory *only* if he also achieved a military victory. The danger to the South for failure was even greater than Lee knew, for Lincoln was waiting for a Northern success to transform the war into a crusade—by issuing an emancipation proclamation.

Lee soon realized he had to achieve a military victory and changed his aim accordingly. However, not having developed a plan in advance, he was dependent on chance or circumstance to bring about a triumph. He would reveal after the war that he decided, soon after he invaded, to attack McClellan.[5] Earlier he had planned to avoid a battle, march to Harrisburg, Pennsylvania, and break the long railroad bridge over the Susquehanna River there.[6] He abandoned this plan and events forced him to abandon his alternative plan as well.

Jackson proposed an entirely different strategy. It was based, as were all of his plans now, on destruction of the Union army. He did not want to attack McClellan, he wanted to force McClellan to attack him by threatening to seize one or more Northern cities.

Jackson had first outlined the strategy of threatening Northern targets after First Manassas—a strike to the east or northeast behind Washington to endanger the capital, Baltimore, and Philadelphia.[7]

Jackson knew that Lincoln would require McClellan's army to remain between Washington and the Confederate army. This would leave Philadelphia undefended and, if McClellan moved as slowly as usual, also might uncover Baltimore, where all railways from the north came together. By playing on Lincoln's demonstrated supersensitivity to the protection of the capital, the Confederates could march on Philadelphia and might sever the railways that brought food and supplies to Washington.

To prevent this McClellan would be forced to seek battle on ground of the Confederates' choosing. Jackson had just proved at Second Manassas that a resolute army emplaced in a strong position could *not* be defeated by a greatly superior attacking force. Jackson was confident that the Confederates could withstand any Federal assault and, if the battlefield had open flanks, that it could envelop the defeated Federal army and possibly destroy it.

Seeking to pursue this strategy, Jackson proposed that Lee march east of South Mountain, the extension into Maryland of the Blue Ridge, and there offer battle to McClellan.[8] If McClellan fell into the trap and attacked on a field selected by the Confederates, Jackson was certain that McClellan would be defeated. If he refused and held back to shield Washington, then Philadelphia and possibly Baltimore would be open. Either way McClellan would lose.[9]

Lee, pursuing his own plan for a political solution, rejected Jackson's military strategy. Thus, for a third time in less than a month Stonewall Jackson offered Lee a way to destroy the Union army and Lee refused.

★ ★ ★

Lee resolved first to deceive the Federals by moving east of South Mountain, then to march across the mountain into the Cumberland Valley, the extension into Maryland of Virginia's Shenandoah. He hoped thereby to draw McClellan away from his main supply points.[10]

On the morning of September 3, 1862, Lee abandoned the battlefield of Second Manassas and set the Army of Northern Virginia in motion toward Leesburg, crossing the Potomac at White's Ford, eleven miles south of Frederick, Maryland.[11]

It was not a pretty army. It was exhausted. The horses were lank, the riders tattered, the infantry cadaverous, their uniforms in rags, thousands without shoes, hair uncut, hats battered.[12] In only two matters was the true nature of the Army of Northern

Virginia revealed: the rifles of the infantry were clean, polished, and ready and the cannons that trailed behind the artillery horses were equally clean and deadly.

Almost from the beginning the army dropped stragglers by the thousands, men whose bare feet could no longer stand the strain of rough roads and long miles, men whose constitutions had been undermined by corn on the cob and unripe apples as their main diet for days, and also men who were willing to defend their homes against an alien invasion but were unwilling to invade foreign soil. There had never been straggling like this and it never occurred again in such magnitude. The simple truth was that the Army of Northern Virginia was weary beyond all reckoning. The sick, the sore, and the fainthearted, along with a few highly principled, fell out of ranks as the army moved north.[13]

Nevertheless, the men who stayed were cheerful, enthusiastic, and supremely confident—of themselves and of their leaders. A young Maryland boy saw them march by. "They were the dirtiest men I ever saw, a most ragged, lean and hungry set of wolves," he wrote. "Yet there was a dash about them that the Northern men lacked. They rode like circus riders. Many of them were from the far South and spoke a dialect I could scarcely understand. They were profane beyond belief and talked incessantly."[14]

Thus the Southern soldiers, in high spirits, chattering like magpies, their weapons and horses the only clean things about them, crossed the Potomac on the night of September 5–6 while a few army bands played "Maryland, My Maryland," and marched straight to Frederick, forty-five air miles northwest of Washington and about the same distance west of Baltimore.

McClellan got the news from his new cavalry chief, Brig. Gen. Alfred Pleasonton, and shifted his headquarters to Rockville, Maryland, just northwest of Washington, on September 7. His field army numbered eighty-five thousand men. Another seventy-two thousand men remained in the Washington defenses under Nathaniel P. Banks. Although straggling was rapidly reducing the Confederate army to half the size of the Union field army, Mc-

Clellan continued in his previous ways, more than doubling in his mind the actual Rebel army's size.[15]

Lee halted in Frederick, seeking shoes and other supplies for his army and hoping for an enthusiastic welcome from Marylanders and many recruits (neither of which came). He also hoped to confuse McClellan as to his intentions, and to a large degree he succeeded.

McClellan commenced a slow, hesitating advance on Frederick on a twenty-five-mile arc. One wing, under Maj. Gen. Ambrose E. Burnside, moved along the Baltimore and Ohio Railroad to the north and another, under Maj. Gen. William B. Franklin, marched close to the Potomac, while a third force, under Maj. Gen. Edwin V. Sumner, advanced between them. The aim was to shield both Washington and Baltimore.

McClellan knew he had to be cautious. General Halleck was anxious about Lee's move. It might be a feint, he warned, to draw the Federal army north, exposing Washington to a surprise attack.[16]

Now an unwitting decision by Halleck—plus Lee's reaction to it and the intervention of chance—changed the entire nature of the campaign.

Since General Lee was about to move across South Mountain, some twelve miles west of Frederick, his existing supply line through Culpeper Court House was exposed. He had anticipated opening a new route through the Shenandoah Valley, shielded by the Blue Ridge.

However, General Halleck insisted that Federal garrisons remain at Martinsburg and Harpers Ferry along the Baltimore and Ohio Railroad in Virginia. Lee had assumed that these garrisons would withdraw, as did the one at Winchester, as soon as the Confederate army came between them and Washington. In the face of Halleck's demand, however, the twenty-five hundred Federals from Winchester moved to Martinsburg and the ten thousand–man garrison at Harpers Ferry held on, under Col. Dixon S. Miles. This was the same officer who had been drunk while commanding a division at First Manassas in 1861. He had been reassigned to this backwater post.[17]

Jackson recommended that Lee ignore the Union garrisons at Martinsburg and Harpers Ferry, even though they threatened the supply line. Returning to capture them would be a serious diversion of strength and Lee had no intention of holding them once they were captured. Consequently, there was nothing to prevent their reoccupation after he had proceeded north.

However, Lee apparently felt such contempt for the initiative of McClellan that he believed that his line of communications would remain safe after seizing these two posts. This was not entirely realistic, but Lee's reasoning was characteristic. Lee looked for immediate, achievable goals and found it difficult to see longer-term dangers and implications. The immediate gain from capturing the Harpers Ferry and Martinsburg garrisons outweighed, in Lee's mind, the dangers of splitting his army into fragments.

Lee rejected Jackson's recommendation and Jackson, as always, loyally accepted the decision. Jackson may have reasoned that McClellan was so certain to advance slowly that he could capture both Union posts and get back into Maryland before McClellan could pose a danger.

On September 9 Lee summoned Stonewall Jackson to his tent and announced that he was going to divide his army into four parts, three of which, under Jackson, were to descend upon Martinsburg and Harpers Ferry, and the fourth of which was to remain just west of South Mountain at Boonsboro until seizure of these posts had been completed. Then the entire army would reunite in Maryland and go on with the campaign.

Longstreet, who joined the conference, argued warmly against dividing the army in the face of the enemy. Lee overruled Longstreet and directed the movement to start on September 10. Meanwhile, he prepared orders.[18]

Lee left himself and Longstreet with fewer than twenty thousand men in Maryland while the remainder of the Confederate army, about twenty-five thousand men, moved back in three unsupported, separate columns on the bypassed Federal stations. Lee knew McClellan was advancing with enormously superior forces and could guess that they exceeded eighty thousand men.

Thus if McClellan descended on any of these detached forces, he would outnumber it at least four to one.

However, McClellan's extreme deliberation and Jackson's speed and decision were known factors. The odds were greatly in favor of Jackson's seizing Martinsburg and the Ferry and getting back into Maryland before McClellan could bring himself to fall on any of the exposed Confederate forces.

Instructions (Special Orders no. 191) for the army's movement went out to the commanders on September 9.[19] They called for Jackson with three divisions (perhaps twelve thousand men) to advance the next morning on a long arc to Martinsburg and drive the Federal garrison toward Harpers Ferry.

Meanwhile, Lafayette McLaws, with his own division and that of Richard H. Anderson, totaling about nine thousand men, was to descend on Maryland Heights, the dominating elevation just across the Potomac from Harpers Ferry. The Confederates had to gain these heights to keep the Harpers Ferry garrison from escaping into Maryland on the pontoon bridge over the Potomac there.

At the same time, John G. Walker, with his four thousand–man division, was to cross back into Virginia near the mouth of the Monocacy River, due south of Frederick, march up the south bank of the Potomac, and seize Loudoun Heights, directly east of Harpers Ferry, where the Shenandoah River debouches into the Potomac. With Jackson coming up on Bolivar Heights, the high ground to the west of the ferry, the Federal garrison would be bottled up and unable to escape.

D. H. Hill's division and the remainder of Longstreet's command, two divisions and an independent brigade, were to march west to Boonsboro while Jeb Stuart's cavalry remained to observe east of the Catoctin Mountains, the extension into Maryland of the Bull Run Mountains of Virginia.

Jackson moved with his accustomed speed.[20] He crossed the Potomac at Williamsport on September 11, spread out his divisions to intercept the Union forces at Martinsburg, and forced them to flee straight to Harpers Ferry. Jackson's men occupied

Martinsburg on the morning of September 12 and, held up briefly by the wild enthusiasm of the people, moved on toward Harpers Ferry, arriving there at midday, September 13. His men had marched more than sixty miles in three and a half days.

General Walker's division on September 9 already was on the Potomac, attempting to blow up the aqueduct of the Chesapeake and Ohio Canal over the Monocacy River. He was unable to insert a gunpowder blast into the tightly cemented stones of the aqueduct and, giving up, moved on toward Loudoun Heights on September 10. Although the distance was only about fourteen miles, it took Walker until September 13 to reach his objective, which he found to be unoccupied. The next morning he got five long-range Parrott rifled guns on the heights, ready to help reduce the town.[21]

McLaws, with his two divisions, passed over Brownsville Gap in South Mountain, some ten air miles southwest of Frederick, on September 11 and advanced down the narrow Pleasant Valley between South Mountain and Elk Ridge, whose southern eminence is Maryland Heights. Learning that there was a substantial defending force on the heights, McLaws sent two brigades down the crest of Elk Ridge and, after scattering a green New York regiment on September 13, seized the heights. The next morning McLaws's men cut a road through the woods and dragged up four guns.

With cannons looking down on Harpers Ferry from both Maryland and Loudoun heights and Jackson barring the rear at Bolivar Heights, the Federal garrison was isolated. Its surrender was a matter of time.

Unfortunately, Lee discovered with a shock that he had little time left. On Saturday morning, September 13, most of McClellan's army arrived in Frederick, three days after the Confederates had departed. The Twenty-seventh Indiana bivouacked in a meadow previously occupied by D. H. Hill's division. Corp. Barton W. Mitchell noticed, among other things left behind, a bulky envelope. In it, wrapped around three cigars, was a sheet of paper entitled Army of Northern Virginia, Special Orders no. 191, addressed to General D. H. Hill, ending "By command of Gen. R. E. Lee" and signed "R. H. Chilton, Assist. Adj.-Gen." Mitchell had discovered a copy of the order describing in complete detail the scattering of the Rebel army!

Within minutes it got to Brig. Gen. Alpheus S. Williams, commanding Twelfth Corps. His aide, Col. Samuel E. Pittman, had known Chilton in the old army and verified the signature as authentic. Williams sent the order and a note asserting its veracity to General McClellan, who happened to be receiving a deputation of Frederick citizens. McClellan turned aside to read the message, became visibly elated, and shouted, "Now I know what to do!"

One of the citizens was a Southern sympathizer who recognized that McClellan had received important news relating to Confederate movements. He rode west, found Stuart around South Mountain, and told him the story. Stuart immediately sent word to Lee. Thus Lee knew before daylight on the fourteenth that McClellan probably had Special Order 191, because this was the only directive he had issued that revealed his dispositions.

No one has ever learned how the lost order came to be dropped in the meadow. D. H. Hill got (and kept) a copy from Stonewall Jackson because he was under Jackson's command at the time. But Lee's headquarters mistakenly also sent Hill a copy and somehow never checked to find that it was not delivered.[22]

McClellan now knew almost everything that Lee knew. The only difference was that, because of a rumored advance by a Federal force from the north, Lee had ordered Longstreet from Boonsboro to Hagerstown and had gone along. No Federal force appeared, but he and Longstreet were now thirteen miles away from the only defensible position, the passes of South Mountain east of Boonsboro. Only D. H. Hill's small division of five thousand men was available to halt the advance of the sixty-five thousand Federal soldiers around Frederick. Indeed, Pleasonton's cavalry and part of the Ninth Corps already had advanced toward South Mountain on the thirteenth and were far along by the afternoon.

In addition, Franklin's corps of twenty thousand men was six miles south of Frederick and only twenty miles away from Maryland Heights. McClellan knew Harpers Ferry was still holding out, because signal stations were reporting firing from there. A swift march on the rear of McLaws by Franklin would break the siege and might bag McLaws's two divisions. With Jackson and Walker separated by the Potomac and the Harpers Ferry garrison, there was no way they could come to McLaws's aid.

Now something quite remarkable transpired. The means for the destruction of the Confederate army had been delivered into McClellan's hands, yet it was eighteen hours before he sent the first soldier to exploit his good fortune![23]

This incredible delay saved the Army of Northern Virginia. If McClellan had burst over Stuart's few cavalry outposts on South Mountain on the thirteenth, he would have placed his army in Napoleon's "central position," between McLaws and Longstreet and D. H. Hill. This would have forced McLaws to retreat and permitted the Harpers Ferry garrison to cross the pontoon bridge and join McClellan. Beyond this, McClellan could have overwhelmed at least one of the fragments before it could escape —perhaps both.

But McClellan had nothing Napoleonic about him. It was evening before he completed his plans and sent out orders. None directed his forces to move until the morning of September 14. He ordered his main army to move on Turner's Gap on South Mountain just east of Boonsboro and instructed Franklin to break through Crampton's Gap, six miles south of Turner's, put his corps into Pleasant Valley in the rear of McLaws, destroy his command, and relieve Harpers Ferry. McClellan planned, in his methodical way, to spend the fourteenth getting over South Mountain in preparation for a big fight beyond it on September 15.

But Lee, even before receiving the distressing news about the lost order, already was alarmed by Stuart's reports on the thirteenth of being pushed off the Catoctin mountains and driven west toward Turner's Gap. He ordered D. H. Hill to move back to defend Turner's Gap and told Longstreet to march at daybreak on the fourteenth to the aid of D. H. Hill. He also warned McLaws.

There were two battles on South Mountain on September 14, one at Turner's, the other at Crampton's. They were unrelated.[24]

D. H. Hill started the battle at Turner's against McClellan's main body, while Stuart's cavalry and small infantry forces sent up by McLaws fought at Crampton's. At both gaps the Federal forces were extremely slow in moving forward. At Turner's, Harvey Hill was able to hold on until Longstreet's troops arrived, and together they blocked McClellan until the fighting ended at nightfall. The cost was high to both armies: the Federals lost 1,813, almost all killed and wounded, including Jesse L. Reno, Ninth Corps commander, mortally wounded; the Confederates lost about as many, including one brigade commander, Samuel Garland, Jr., killed, but they also lost several hundred prisoners.

At Crampton's, Franklin halted before only the slenderest defending force. However, some of his own officers got impatient and rushed the pass, threw the Confederates into flight, and, by afternoon, came down into Pleasant Valley. The Federals lost 531 men killed and wounded, the Rebels about the same, except that 400 more Southerners fell prisoner. Franklin had more than twice as many men as McLaws and could have driven down the valley, defeated McLaws, and relieved Harpers Ferry. But he stopped again, balked by a thin battle line that McLaws hastily threw across the valley floor.

The Confederates were holding at Turner's Gap as night fell, but Federals were lapping around Confederate flanks and would burst through in the morning. Lee feared not only for his army but for his campaign. Although Lee did not learn until later in the evening that Franklin had halted in Pleasant Valley, he knew that Franklin could press on in the morning on McLaws's rear.

The lost order had shown McClellan where to move, and though it had not incited him to move fast, McClellan was still on the verge of interposing his army between the Confederate army's three segments: Longstreet and D. H. Hill at Turner's,

McLaws in Pleasant Valley and Maryland Heights, and Jackson and Walker still isolated on the south side of the Potomac. Lee decided the danger was too great. The army must seek friendly soil south of the Potomac. There it could await a new opportunity.

At 8 P.M. Lee sent off a dispatch to McLaws to abandon his positions during the night and get his two divisions behind the Potomac across some ford. He hoped McLaws would find one downstream from the Shepherdstown ford, three miles west of Sharpsburg, for there Lee wanted Hill's and Longstreet's troops to cross back into Virginia.[25]

Meantime, the prospects at Harpers Ferry had improved dramatically. Jackson had a difficult time getting in touch by flag signal with McLaws and Walker but by 3 P.M., September 14, the Rebel guns were firing from three directions into the town. The hail of shells shook the Union garrison, especially as the Federal guns, located far lower than the Rebel pieces, were virtually unable to reply. Jackson made no attempt to storm Bolivar Heights, but by a swift movement he gained commanding ground near them, while Dorsey Pender's brigade advanced to a good assault position along the west bank of the Shenandoah River. Jackson ordered ten cannons to cross the Shenandoah and, along the river under Loudoun Heights, be brought to bear the next morning directly opposite Harpers Ferry.[26]

Jackson sent off a message to Lee at 8:15 P.M. telling of his progress and that he looked "for complete success tomorrow. The advance has been directed to be resumed at dawn tomorrow."[27] This was a strong hint that Jackson expected to carry the town by assault September 15, if it did not surrender first.

When he got Jackson's message, Lee thought he saw a possibility of retrieving his campaign. He reasoned that if Jackson succeeded in taking Harpers Ferry, he, McLaws, and Walker might rendezvous at Sharpsburg with Longstreet and D. H. Hill, retreating from Turner's Gap, only seven miles away. Besides, there was good ground along south-flowing Antietam Creek, just east of the town, to stand on the defensive.

Lee immediately countermanded his order to McLaws to abandon his positions and directed Longstreet and Hill to get their men off Turner's Gap and toward Sharpsburg at once, leaving the dead and seriously wounded behind.[28]

This was the order that lost an enormous battle and perhaps the war for the Confederacy. Lee's mind was so fixed on his campaign in the North that he did not realize that the lost order already had destroyed any possibility of its succeeding.

However ponderously McClellan might move, he held the Confederate army in a strategic vise from which it could extricate itself *only* by withdrawing into Virginia. The Army of Northern Virginia was left with only *one* place in Maryland where it could concentrate: Sharpsburg. And Sharpsburg was a cul-de-sac with both flanks closed by the Potomac River, neutralizing the Southern army's greatest strength—its mobility—and eliminating the possibility of a flank attack, the only way it could win. Besides, with only a single ford behind it, Sharpsburg was a place where the Southern army had to stand or die.

When all of the dispersed elements recombined, Lee would have fewer than forty thousand men and more likely closer to thirty-five thousand—against eighty-five thousand at McClellan's command.[29] No matter how brilliantly the Confederate army fought, it had no possibility of winning. Even a drawn battle would not improve the strategic situation one iota; the Southern army would remain with its back against the Potomac facing a much larger army that could receive mammoth reinforcements. Lee would *still* have to retreat into Virginia to regain maneuvering room.

Jackson had already all but promised a partial victory—the capture of Harpers Ferry with more than eleven thousand Federal troops and much booty. If Lee had allowed this capture to go forward while he withdrew Longstreet's and D. H. Hill's forces across the Potomac, the Confederacy would have achieved a signal success. More important, the North would have failed to achieve a great victory.

Lee should have recognized that the lost order had ended his campaign in Maryland. Despite McClellan's incredibly slow exploitation of its information, he had positioned his army so that the Confederates could achieve nothing more. Even reconcentrating the army at Sharpsburg would require almost unbelievably fast action and exhausting marches—the forces investing Harpers Ferry had to capture it within hours, then march to Sharpsburg before McClellan could give battle. Jackson and Walker were seventeen miles away and McLaws, by way of Harpers Ferry, was even farther, while most of the Army of the Potomac was united and only seven miles distant at Turner's Gap.

Lee's decision to stand at Antietam demonstrated once again his obsession with seeking battle to retrieve a strategic advantage when it had gone awry or he thought it had. He had shown this tendency three times in the Seven Days: at Beaver Dam Creek, at Frayser's Farm, and at Malvern Hill. In none of these cases was it possible to regain his advantage by resorting to the desperate, stand-up, head-on battle he ordered. In all he suffered great losses. Now he was resolved to attempt the same frontal battle again, hoping once more for a miracle. This fixation was Lee's fatal flaw. It and Lee's limited strategic vision cost the Confederacy the war.[30]

Early on September 15, while the Confederate guns began raining shells down on Harpers Ferry, McClellan's forces advanced cautiously into Turner's Gap and discovered that the enemy had slipped away. They set off in pursuit, in high spirits, certain that the Rebels were retreating across the Potomac. At 12:40 P.M., however, a signal observation post reported that the Confederates were forming a line of battle just beyond Antietam Creek.

The bombardment at Harpers Ferry continued in full fury until 8 A.M. Just as Jackson's infantry was preparing to storm the works on Bolivar Hill, a horseman appeared, waving a white flag. Colonel Miles was surrendering. It took a while for the commanders to halt the cannon fire, however, and Miles was mortally wounded by one of the last rounds dropped into the town.

Jackson's orders were to return immediately to Maryland and

he wasted no time on the surrender. He gave generous terms: all of the 11,500 Union prisoners were paroled and allowed to go home until exchanged and the officers could keep their sidearms and baggage. Jackson left A. P. Hill's division to take care of the details and immediately sent Lee news of the capture.

Late in the afternoon Jackson's two remaining divisions marched toward Shepherdstown, halting for the night four miles from Boteler's Ford, east of the village. Even Jackson called the march "severe." Behind him, Walker's division from Loudoun Heights marched, and behind Walker, the two divisions of McLaws, which came down off Maryland Heights, crossed the pontoon bridge into town and took the road to Shepherdstown.[31]

McClellan lost a golden chance to destroy Lee's small force lined up behind Antietam Creek on the fifteenth. It amounted to perhaps sixteen thousand men and, even by McClellan's bloated estimates, was less than a third the force he had. But McClellan could not bring himself to strike fast. Tomorrow, he decided, would be soon enough to deal with this new problem.

The next morning, September 16, Jackson's divisions reached Sharpsburg and dropped down, exhausted. Jackson, covered with dust, reported to General Lee. The intense anxiety that had gripped Lee relaxed.[32] Soon the whole army felt more confident. Around noon one of Longstreet's soldiers came up to Henry Kyd Douglas, Jackson's aide, and asked whether Stonewall had arrived. Douglas nodded and replied: "That's he, talking to your General, 'Old Pete'—the man with the big boots on." "Is it?" the soldier answered. "Well, bless my eyes! Thankee, Captain." Returning to his squad, the soldier exclaimed: "Boys, it's all right!"[33]

In the afternoon Walker's division arrived. McLaws's two divisions were still south of the river. The situation remained critical. McClellan had about seventy thousand men forward, and even with the weary troops brought back by Jackson the Confederate army was well under half his number.

Nevertheless, McClellan allowed this day, too, to pass without more than a skirmish as he moved his troops into position. He and Lee girded for the battle on the morrow.

NOTES

General sources: Allan, *Army of Northern Virginia,* 322–71; Alexander, *Military Memoirs,* 220–45; Cooke, 307–27; Johnson and Buel, vol. 2, 541–695; Sears, 101–74; Freeman, *R. E. Lee,* vol. 2, 350–86; Freeman, *Lee's Lieutenants,* vol. 2, 145–202; Maurice, 146–52; Alexander, *Fighting for the Confederacy,* 138–49; Palfrey, 1–57; Chambers, vol. 2, 178–218; and Vandiver, 372–94.

1. *Official Records,* vol. 19, pt. 2, 600; and Freeman, *R. E. Lee,* vol. 2, 358.
2. The governors of Pennsylvania and Massachusetts were organizing a Northern governors' conference in Altoona, Pennsylvania, in late September, where Lincoln's war leadership was to be challenged. Meanwhile, in Britain, Foreign Secretary Lord Russell asked Prime Minister Palmerston for the cabinet to debate recognition of the Confederacy in October, a proposal designed to lead to a concerted action by European powers. See Sears, 166–67.
3. Johnson and Buel, vol. 2, 663.
4. Few leaders, North or South, had yet absorbed the lesson that Stonewall Jackson had taught at Second Manassas—that attacking an army drawn up in a strong defensive position was extremely dangerous.
5. In an interview with William Allan on February 15, 1868, in Lexington, Virginia, Lee said: "Had McClellan continued his cautious policy for two or three days longer [after part of the Confederate army had gone to capture Harpers Ferry], I would have had all my troops reconcentrated on the Maryland side, stragglers up, men rested and *intended then to attack McClellan* [Lee's emphasis], hoping the best results from state of my troops and those of enemy." See Freeman, *Lee's Lieutenants,* vol. 2, 721.
6. Johnson and Buel, vol. 2, 605. See also Freeman, *R. E. Lee,* vol. 2, 362–63; and *Official Records,* vol. 19, pt. 2, 592 and 603. Lee discussed his plans to break the railroad bridge at Harrisburg with Brig. Gen. John G. Walker. However, this discussion came before he sent Jackson to capture Harpers Ferry, whereas in his 1868 interview with William Allan (see preceding footnote) he indicates that his decision to attack McClellan came after this expedition was under way. Lee's original plan was to cut the Baltimore and Ohio Railroad along the Potomac, then the long bridge of the Pennsylvania Railroad over the Susquehanna. These breaks would sever the two major connections with the western states but not eliminate communications, since other lines ran along the Great Lakes. "After that," Lee said, "I can turn my attention to Philadelphia, Balti-

more or Washington, as may seem best for our interests." This last comment indicates that Lee's thoughts of a strike into Pennsylvania constituted not a strategy of victory but a hope to exploit opportunities as they might arise.

7. This strategy is implicit in Jackson's proposal in October 1861 for the Confederates to cross above the falls of the Potomac, take possession of Maryland, "cut off the communications of Washington, force the Federal government to abandon the capital, beat McClellan's army if it came out against us in the open country," occupy Philadelphia, and destroy parts of Northern industry and commerce. See Henderson, 131–33; and Cooke, 247. Jackson had also proved that he had mastered the concept of threatening alternative objectives by moving along a single line. This is demonstrated in his proposal during the valley campaign to march to Sperryville, east of the Blue Ridge, then advance northward, thereby threatening the valley and Washington simultaneously and preventing defenders of either place to move for fear that he would descend on the undefended target. See *Official Records,* vol. 12, pt. 3, 374; and Allan, *Campaign of Gen. T. J. (Stonewall) Jackson,* 68 n.

8. Dabney, 548–49. Colonel G. F. R. Henderson writes that if Jackson had had his way, "McClellan would have found the whole Confederate army arrayed against him at South Mountain or would have been attacked near Frederick" (Henderson, 707). It is almost certain that Jackson did not plan to attack McClellan, unless the Union commander foolishly exposed his army, as John Pope had done on the Rapidan, so that the Confederates could flank and encircle it. Jackson could not count on McClellan's making such a blunder. Rather, Jackson sought to exploit the strength of the defense that had been demonstrated at Second Manassas, since it would neutralize the North's great advantage in manpower and weapons.

9. Records do not indicate that Jackson enunciated this theory prior to the invasion of Maryland, although it is almost certain that he did. He already had seen at Second Manassas that the plan would work, and two months later he proposed an almost identical strategy: instead of standing at Fredericksburg, to retreat to the South Anna River, induce Burnside to attack, defeat him, and go around his flanks. Also, positioning the Southern army east of South Mountain implied a threat to Philadelphia or Baltimore and was the surest way to force the Union army to attack under conditions favorable to the South. Another astute general faced with the same conditions came to the same conclusion as Jackson. Count Helmuth von Moltke, chief of the Prussian general staff, recognizing the

tremendous defensive power of the rifle at the battle of Sadowa (Königgrätz) on July 3, 1866, in the Austro-Prussian War, resolved that an army should induce the enemy to attack, then gain victory by turning the enemy's flanks. See J. F. C. Fuller, *The Conduct of War, 1789–1961* (New Brunswick, N.J.: Rutgers University Press, 1961), 117–18.

10. *Official Records,* vol. 19, pt. 1, 144–45, and pt. 2, 590–92; Long, 204; Freeman, *R. E. Lee,* vol. 2, 352–53; Allan, *Army of Northern Virginia,* 322–23; and Freeman, *Lee's Lieutenants,* vol. 2, 168.

11. Allan, *Army of Northern Virginia,* 325; Freeman, *R. E. Lee,* vol. 2, 353–54; and *Official Records,* vol. 19, pt. 1, 144.

12. *Official Records,* vol. 19, pt. 2, 590; and vol. 19, pt. 1, 144; Allan, *Army of Northern Virginia,* 322–23; and Freeman, *R. E. Lee,* vol. 2, 352. There was much attempt on the part of the Quartermaster Department to pass the blame for shortages onto unit commanders. The Confederate quartermaster general, Abraham C. Myers, complained that field supply officers failed to notify him of shortages. Instead Lee wrote directly to the secretary of war, George W. Randolph, or President Davis after conditions had become critical. It is evident that neither the department nor unit commanders were blameless. There was less excuse for food shortages, other than difficulties of transportation, since the Confederate Subsistence Department had food stocks for the summer campaign. See Richard D. Goff, *Confederate Supply* (Durham, N.C.: Duke University Press, 1969), 67–68 and 76–78.

13. Freeman, *R. E. Lee,* vol. 2, 411–12; Allan, *Army of Northern Virginia,* 324–25; Freeman, *Lee's Lieutenants,* vol. 2, 149–52; Alexander, *Fighting for the Confederacy,* 141–42; and Henderson, 519.

14. Leighton Parks, *Century,* vol. 70, no. 2, 255 ff.; and Freeman, *R. E. Lee,* vol. 2, 355.

15. Sears, 102–6; *Official Records,* vol. 19, pt. 2, 219; and Allan, *Army of Northern Virginia,* 326–27.

16. *Official Records,* vol. 19, pt. 1, 40–41.

17. Allan, *Army of Northern Virginia,* 330; Freeman, *R. E. Lee,* vol. 2, 359; Sears, 88–89; and *Official Records,* vol. 19, pt. 2, 189.

18. Johnson and Buel, vol. 2, 606 and 662; Freeman, *R. E. Lee,* vol. 2, 359; Freeman, *Lee's Lieutenants,* vol. 2, 160–61; Longstreet, 202–3; and Fuller, 167.

19. *Official Records,* vol. 19, pt. 1, 145, and pt. 2, 603–4; Allan, *Army of Northern Virginia,* 332–33; Long, 264; and Freeman, *R. E. Lee,* vol. 2, 363.

20. On this march Jackson canceled the arrest of the hot-tempered A. P. Hill and restored him to command of his division. On the march north from Manassas on September 4 Hill was slow in getting his men going in the morning and Jackson himself ordered Maxcy Gregg's brigade to start. Hill's division was straggling badly but neither Hill nor any of his staff rode back to check. When the time came for the ten-minute stop per hour that Jackson ordered on all of his marches, Hill continued on and Jackson himself stopped the leading brigade. Hill came storming back to ask why the brigade had halted. Informed that Jackson had ordered it, Hill rode over to Stonewall and, saying something to the effect that if Jackson was to give orders, he had no need for him, Hill unbuckled his sword and handed it to Jackson. Jackson replied: "Consider yourself under arrest for neglect of duty." Hill, after fuming for several days, enlisted Jackson's aide, Henry Kyd Douglas, to intervene to have him restored to his command, at least during the duration of the battle. Douglas presented the request to Jackson, who, without comment, assented, and Hill went back to the head of his division. See Freeman, *Lee's Lieutenants,* vol. 2, 147–48 and 164; and Douglas, 146–47 and 158.

21. Johnson and Buel, vol. 2, 606–9.

22. Sears, 112–13; *Official Records,* vol. 19, pt. 2, 603–4; Allan, *Army of Northern Virginia,* 332 and 343–44; Freeman, *Lee's Lieutenants,* vol. 2, app. 1, 715–23; and Johnson and Buel, vol. 2, 603 and 664.

23. Sears, 115–8.

24. Johnson and Buel, vol. 2, 558–97; *Official Records,* vol. 19, pt. 1, 44–45, 374–76, 817, 826, 908–11, 1019–21, 1032, 1041, and 1049; Allan, *Army of Northern Virginia,* 348–60; Sears, 128–49; Alexander, *Military Memoirs,* 239–40; and Freeman, *Lee's Lieutenants,* vol. 2, 174–82.

25. Freeman, *R. E. Lee,* vol. 2, 373–74; and *Official Records,* vol. 19, pt. 1, 140.

26. Johnson and Buel, vol. 2, 609–10 and 612–18; Freeman, *Lee's Lieutenants,* vol. 2, 194–96; and Henderson, 505–8.

27. *Official Records,* vol. 19, pt. 1, 951. During the night of September 14 over a thousand Union cavalrymen escaped by crossing the pontoon bridge into Maryland and moving northwest, capturing forty-five wagons of Longstreet's ordnance train moving from Hagerstown and fleeing into Pennsylvania. See Sears, 151; and Alexander, *Fighting for the Confederacy,* 144.

28. Freeman, *R. E. Lee,* vol. 2, 375–76; and *Official Records,* vol. 19, pt. 1, 140.

29. Freeman, *R. E. Lee,* vol. 2, 411; and Freeman, *Lee's Lieutenants,* vol. 2, 225. British lieutenant colonel Garnet Wolseley reported that Lee told him in October 1862 that he had no more than thirty-five thousand men at Antietam. See Wolseley's *The American Civil War: An English View,* edited by James A. Rawley (Charlottesville: University Press of Virginia, 1964), 21. In his interview with William Allan at Lexington, Virginia, on February 15, 1868 (Freeman, *Lee's Lieutenants,* vol. 2, 721), Lee said he had about thirty-five thousand men in the battle. See also Cooke, 340–41; Alexander, *Military Memoirs,* 244–45; Palfrey, 63–72; and R. Taylor, 69, 73, and 158.

30. James Longstreet (Johnson and Buel, vol. 2, 666–67) says that Lee should have retired from Sharpsburg the day he learned that Jackson had captured Harpers Ferry. He adds: "The moral effect of our move into Maryland had been lost by our discomfiture at South Mountain and it was then evident we could not hope to concentrate in time to do more than make a respectable retreat, whereas by retiring before the battle we could have claimed a very successful campaign." Porter Alexander (*Fighting for the Confederacy,* 145–46) calls the decision to stand at Antietam "the greatest military blunder that General Lee ever made." His reasons: "In the first place Lee's inferiority of force was too great to hope to do more than fight a sort of drawn battle. Hard and incessent marching and camp diseases aggravated by irregular diet had greatly reduced his ranks and I don't think he mustered much if any over 40,000 men. McClellan had over 87,000 with more and better guns and ammunition and, besides that, fresh troops were coming from Washington and being organized and sent him almost every day. A drawn battle, such as we did actually fight, was the best possible outcome one could hope for. Even that we only accomplished by the Good Lord's putting it into McClellan's heart to keep Fitz John Porter's corps entirely out of the battle and Franklin's nearly all out. . . . Common sense was shouting [to McClellan], 'Your adversary is backed against a river, with no bridge and only one ford. . . . If you whip him now, you destroy him utterly, root and branch and bag and baggage. Not twice in a lifetime does such a chance come to any general.' " See also Alexander's comments against fighting the battle in Alexander, *Military Memoirs,* 242–49. Maj. Gen. Sir Frederick Maurice (Maurice, 152) says: "Of all Lee's actions in the war this seems to me to be the most open to criticism. He was only justified in giving battle if retreat was impossible without fighting or if he had a good prospect, not merely of repulsing attacks, but of beating his enemy soundly. . . . The ground he chose for battle, while admirably suited for defense, left him

no opportunity for such a counterstroke as Longstreet had delivered at the second battle of Manassas. He could at best hope to beat off the Federals. But at the end of such a battle he would be no better off than he was on the morning of the 15th. The Antietam, the most desperately fought struggle of the war, must be numbered among the unnecessary battles." Maj. Gen. J. F. C. Fuller (Fuller, 169) calls Antietam "a totally unnecessary battle," caused, he says, because Lee's "personal pride could not stomach the idea that such an enemy [as McClellan] could drive him out of Maryland." Colonel G. F. R. Henderson takes a different view (Henderson, 515), holding that a retreat across the Potomac would have been viewed as a defeat and consequently increased the morale of the Federals. The South Mountain clashes constituted a Federal victory and, if Lee had retired immediately afterward, the Federals might have claimed that he had been driven out of Maryland. But the South Mountain victory was more than offset by the Confederate capture of Harpers Ferry with its entire garrison. Since Lee had no chance of defeating the Federals at Sharpsburg, his decision to remain meant that the Federals could claim two victories instead of one.

31. Freeman, *Lee's Lieutenants,* vol. 2, 199; and *Official Records,* vol. 19, pt. 1, 951, 955, 967, and 1007.

32. There is evidence that Jackson disapproved of fighting a battle at Sharpsburg. Robert Lewis Dabney, a close associate of Jackson and author of an 1866 book on him (see Dabney in the bibliography), stated this in his first draft. At the direction of Jackson's widow Dabney submitted the draft to Lee. In a letter to Mrs. Jackson on January 25, 1866, Lee disputes a reference in the draft that Jackson doubted the propriety of fighting the battle. Lee writes: "When he [Jackson] came upon the field [of Sharpsburg on September 16, 1862], having preceded his troops, and learned my reasons for offering battle, he emphatically concurred with me. When I determined to withdraw across the Potomac, he also concurred; but said then, in view of all the circumstances, it was better to have fought the battle in Maryland than to have left it without a struggle." See Henderson, 694–95. Dabney eliminated whatever negative comments he attributed to Jackson and in the finished book repeats Lee's language almost verbatim (Dabney, 570). Without further evidence it is impossible to determine whether this exchange hides as much as it reveals. However, Dabney was generally accurate in his reporting of Jackson's thinking and Jackson definitely disapproved of Lee's decision to fight a battle at Fredericksburg three months later in a strategic situation that was in many respects far superior to the situation at Sharpsburg. Jackson's approval may be an example of his loyalty, lauded by Lee's biographer,

Douglas Southall Freeman. Freeman writes (*R. E. Lee,* vol. 2, 561) that Jackson, "after advancing his own proposals, would execute Lee's orders as readily as if they were his own." See also Marshall, 170. When Lee insisted, Jackson loyally suppressed his objections and did everything possible to win. (See chapter 14.)

33. Douglas, 166.

13

THE BLOODIEST DAY

★ ★ ★ The battlefield was defined by two major terrain features: south-flowing Antietam Creek, about a mile east of Sharpsburg, and the Hagerstown pike, which ran along a low ridge directly north from the town. McClellan concentrated his army along the pike and the creek. Lee posted his greatly inferior numbers to defend them.

The position had a glaring weakness from the Confederate point of view: the Potomac River. This large stream described a wide arc around Sharpsburg, creating a tight peninsula with scarcely any room for movement. Both flanks were anchored by the river, making a wide flanking movement impossible and forcing a narrow turning movement directly under the muzzles of Federal cannons. And since there was but a single ford over the Potomac, the Federals had only to get on the Confederate rear to isolate the army.

The position had little of the natural strength that Jackson had sought and found at Second Manassas: a dominating ridge ideal for artillery, woods to shelter troops, an unfinished railway to serve as ready-built entrenchments, a wide-open retreat route, and an open flank for easy envelopment of the Federals.

Jackson had chosen Second Manassas for victory. Lee had chosen Sharpsburg because it was the closest place in Maryland where his army could concentrate.

The Army of Northern Virginia was positioned at Antietam to be destroyed. McClellan's army was more than twice the size of Lee's and he could have cut off and shattered the Southern army by following the tried-and-true method that Napoleon followed in most of his battles. Napoleon assaulted along his front in order to force the enemy to commit all of his reserves to prevent a breakthrough. Once this had happened he launched a flank attack to cut off the enemy's line of retreat.[1]

McClellan might have done the same thing: attacking south down the Hagerstown pike and along Antietam Creek directly east of Sharpsburg and forcing Lee to send in every man to stop him. Then McClellan could have sent a strong force around Lee's southern flank, blocking the road to the ferry and crushing the Army of Northern Virginia from front and rear.[2]

George B. McClellan did none of this and thereby saved the Confederate army. Instead McClellan concocted a plan that was almost the opposite of Napoleon's victory-producing formula.[3] He made no attack along the Antietam directly east of Sharpsburg, although he had planned such an assault and had massed Porter's corps and all forty-two hundred of his cavalrymen along the Boonsboro pike there and was bringing up Franklin's corps to help. But then he launched two separate attacks, on the north and south, but not at the same time. This permitted Lee to move troops from unthreatened points along the Antietam to help block the blow from the north. And because McClellan had kept all of his cavalry on the Boonsboro pike and unable to scout on his flanks, Lee had time to bring up A. P. Hill's division undetected from Harpers Ferry to stop the attack on the south.

McClellan opened the battle with a move down the Hagerstown pike directly toward Sharpsburg with Joseph Hooker's First and Joseph K. F. Mansfield's Twelfth Corps. However, he moved both corps into position *the day before,* thereby signaling where the attack was coming. Stonewall Jackson had ample time to move his corps into blocking position during the night of September 16–17.[4]

At 5 A.M. on September 17 Jackson stood facing Hooker on both sides of the Hagerstown pike with his two divisions, one under John R. Jones, the other under Alexander R. Lawton.[5] Hooker commanded Irvin McDowell's old corps from Second Manassas, but only James B. Ricketts was still leading one of the divisions. Abner Doubleday had taken over from John P. Hatch, wounded at Turner's Gap, and George G. Meade had replaced John F. Reynolds. Hooker's men were around a small forest—the North Wood—mostly east of the Hagerstown pike and two miles north of Sharpsburg. This wood formed a point d'appui, or base, to anchor the Federal position.

Jones's Confederate division rested in and near the West Wood, a block of mature hardwood to the west of the pike and extending northward from the Dunker church, a whitewashed brick building a mile north of Sharpsburg. Lawton's division was in the open to the east of the pike, immediately south of a thirty-acre unharvested cornfield with high stalks of maize that could hide the advance of the enemy. To the east of this field, soon to be known as *the* Cornfield, was another long band of mature hardwood, known as the East Wood.

On the open plateau just east of the Dunker church Stephen D. Lee had banked four batteries with a clear line of fire north and east. A mile to the northwest and close to the Potomac, Jeb Stuart had fourteen cannons on Nicodemus Hill, well posted to hit the Federals in the flank as they advanced. These cannons, protected by Jubal A. Early's brigade, would deliver killing fire all day, but neither Hooker nor any other Federal commander tried to seize Nicodemus Hill.

Hooker planned to strike due south toward the Dunker church with his ten thousand infantry, Doubleday's division along the pike, Ricketts's through the East Wood and Cornfield,

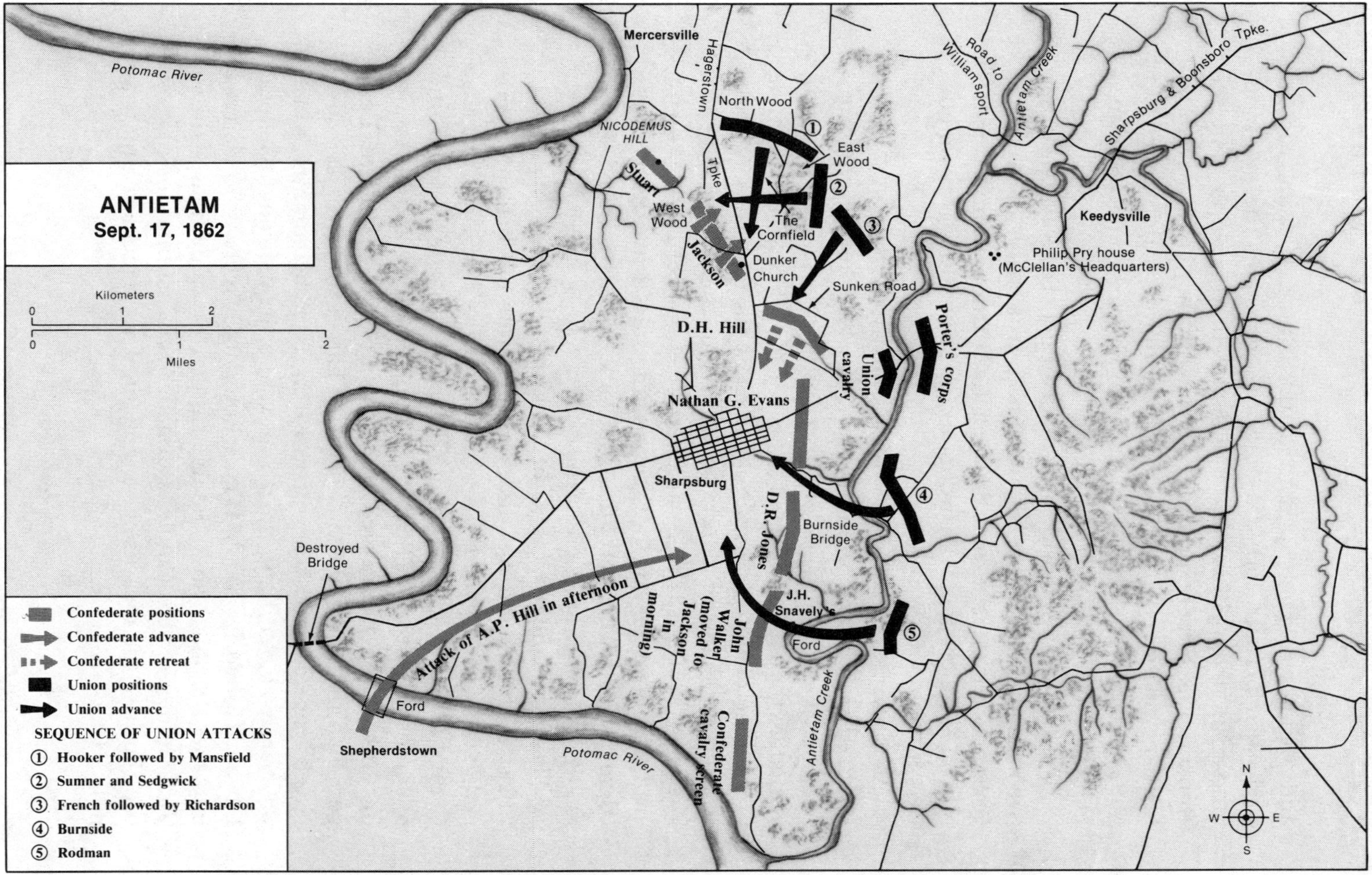
ANTIETAM
Sept. 17, 1862
Kilometers
0
1
2
0
1
2
Miles
Confederate positions
Confederate advance
Confederate retreat
Union positions
Union advance
SEQUENCE OF UNION ATTACKS
① Hooker followed by Mansfield
② Sumner and Sedgwick
③ French followed by Richardson
④ Burnside
⑤ Rodman
Potomac River
Mercersville
Hagerstown
Tpke
NICODEMUS HILL
Stuart
West Wood
North Wood
East Wood
The Cornfield
Dunker Church
Jackson
Sunken Road
D.H. Hill
Nathan G. Evans
Sharpsburg
Union cavalry
Porter's corps
Road to Williamsport
Antietam Creek
Sharpsburg & Boonsboro Tpke.
Keedysville
Philip Pry house
(McClellan's Headquarters)
Burnside Bridge
D.R. Jones
J.H. Snavely's
Ford
John Walker (moved to Jackson in morning)
Confederate cavalry screen
Attack of A.P. Hill in afternoon
Destroyed Bridge
Ford
Shepherdstown
Potomac River
Antietam Creek
N
W
E
S

and Meade's backing up both in the center. Jackson, without Early, had perhaps forty-five hundred men, plus the two thousand–man division of John Bell Hood in reserve around the Dunker church.[6] The odds were heavy but they could have been heavier—no one, from McClellan on down, had planned for Mansfield's corps to coordinate with Hooker's attack. Instead Mansfield rested a mile behind the line.

The battle started with an artillery duel, Federal long-range twenty-pounder Parrott rifles joining from east of Antietam Creek. These guns turned Stephen Lee's cannon emplacements into an "artillery hell," according to Lee, who lost eighty-six gunners to enemy fire.[7]

At 6 A.M. Ricketts's New York Pennsylvania brigade, eleven hundred men under Abram Duryea, attacked through the Cornfield. The Georgia brigade of Marcellus Douglass lay at the southern edge, the men instructed to pick a row of corn as an aiming point. When Duryea's men broke through the corn the Georgians rose up and poured a terrible volley into them. Then the two lines stood 250 yards apart and blazed away until Duryea discovered that no other unit was supporting him, while Rebels were edging into the East Wood to outflank him. He retired, losing nearly a third of his men in thirty minutes.

The commander of one of Ricketts's brigades, William L. Christian, broke and ran under Confederate fire before the brigade was even engaged. The commander of the other brigade, George L. Hartsuff, was wounded and the brigade stood around in confusion until Col. Richard Coulter took over and ordered it forward. When it emerged from the Cornfield, Stephen Lee's guns had the range and met it with a hail of fire. Even so, Coulter's brigade exerted heavy pressure on the Rebel infantry, which was barely able to hang on. To prevent a breakthrough General Lawton rushed in Henry Hays's Louisiana Tigers, who charged into the Cornfield and, though riddled by cannon fire, drove back Coulter's men. Coulter's brigade suffered enormous losses, two-thirds of the men in one regiment. The Tigers lost almost as much, 61 percent.

At last Christian's brigade, now under Col. Peter Lyle, advanced through the East Wood but did not enter the Cornfield, by now cut as close by the bullets as if reaped with a sickle.

Meanwhile, astride the Hagerstown pike, Doubleday's division advanced against Jones, led by John Gibbon's Black Hat Brigade. It met accurate Rebel artillery and skirmisher fire and, once in the Cornfield, sheets of Minié balls from Lawton's men. General Jones was stunned by an artillery air burst and Gen. William E. Starke took over. He led 1,150 men of the two remaining brigades in a desperate charge that stopped Doubleday's attack but left the Rebels in a deadly cross fire. Three bullets struck Starke and he died within an hour. Col. Andrew J. Grigsby took over and ordered the men to pull back. In Lawton's division, Lawton himself and brigade commander James A. Walker were wounded, while Colonel Douglass died, five of his six regimental commanders fell, and nearly half of his brigade's 1,150 men were killed or wounded.

Jackson's line was unbroken but almost had been torn to pieces. Though McClellan got word of Hooker's advance, he ordered no support by Sumner's Second Corps, in reserve just beyond the East Wood, left Mansfield's corps in place behind Hooker, and kept all the rest of his forces along the Antietam inactive.

Lee, seeing no danger from Federals east of the creek, ordered Tige Anderson's Georgia brigade from along Boonsboro pike to Jackson's aid.[8] Meanwhile, a courier from General Lawton reached John Hood and begged for help. Hood ordered up his two brigades, his and Evander Law's. Ignoring the heavy flail of artillery fire, they pushed into the Cornfield, shooting down gunners of a Federal battery that had pushed forward, and in a fierce charge drove Union troops to a rail fence at the northern edge of the field.

This attack forced Hooker to commit his last troops, two Pennsylvania brigades of Meade's division. Three of Law's regiments caught the flank of one of the brigades as it hurried through the

East Wood and inflicted heavy losses. But Meade's brigades held on and shot down many of Law's men.

On the western edge of the Cornfield, Hood's brigade engaged in a murderous battle with Doubleday's division, shooting down gunners who advanced cannons within rifle range. But some of the guns stood their ground and destroyed rows of Confederates with double-shotted canister. There was little left of Hood's division as it retreated below the Cornfield.

It was now 7:30 A.M. In an hour and a half Jackson's and Hooker's commands had virtually destroyed each other as effective forces. Jackson held back only Early's brigade, while Hooker also had only a single brigade guarding his cannons. Jones's division had backed up slightly but the tactical situation had scarcely changed. In Jackson's two divisions a third lay dead or wounded, while Hood's division had suffered nearly 60 percent losses. Hooker had lost about twenty-six hundred men and most of the rest had rushed from the field.[9]

Afterward, soldiers on both sides remembered this morning as the worst they had ever experienced, before or after. Dead and wounded littered the Cornfield, the East Wood, and the ground around Hagerstown pike. Battle lines sometimes had faced each other at fifty or even thirty yards.

McClellan did not come on the field and had made no attempt to reinforce the first limited successes of Hooker's men, though the swift interjection of Mansfield's corps might have broken the Confederate line. Now, after Hooker's corps had been eliminated, he committed Mansfield's corps of eight thousand infantrymen and two divisions, under Alpheus S. Williams and George Sears Greene.

Jackson alone could not have stopped these two fresh forces. But, though Tige Anderson's brigade did not arrive in time, D. H. Hill, who had deployed his division in the natural trench of a sunken road just south and east of the Dunker church, switched over three brigades to block the new threat.

Mansfield's was Nathaniel P. Banks's old corps, shattered at Cedar Mountain and reinforced with "heavy" regiments of newly recruited soldiers. Alpheus Williams's two-brigade division was first on the field. His lead brigade, under Samuel Crawford, had three heavy regiments and they were difficult to form up in the hail of fire.[10] One, the 128th Pennsylvania, lost its colonel and second in command but reformed and charged straight into the Cornfield. Roswell Ripley's brigade of D. H. Hill's division was at the southern edge and mowed down 118 of them. The unnerved regiment fled from the battle.

Meanwhile, a Rebel sharpshooter's bullet struck Mansfield in the chest. He collapsed and died the next day. Williams took command of the corps. After a hurried conference with Hooker, he sent one brigade of Greene's division to shore up Gibbon near the West Wood while George H. Gordon's brigade of his division advanced into the Cornfield. D. H. Hill had got, besides Ripley's, Alfred Colquitt's and Samuel Garland's brigades into position, altogether two thousand fresh troops. Gordon held firm, however, despite severe losses, while Garland's brigade on the right, in a state of shock since the death of its commander on South Mountain, was seized by a sudden panic and ran.

Now Greene's remaining two brigades came onto the field from the East Wood, spearheaded by Hector Tyndale's brigade. It advanced where Garland's brigade had just vacated, came up on the flank of Colquitt, unleashed a murderous volley, and charged into Colquitt's flank. There was a short hand-to-hand fight with bayonets and clubbed muskets before Colquitt's brigade fell back, losing half of its men and all of its field officers.

D. H. Hill saw the danger and frantically extricated his brigades, getting Ripley's away in time, but Colquitt's brigade disintegrated. Greene continued to drive hard, pushing his other brigade (Henry J. Stainrook's) through the East Wood and evicting the remaining Rebels there. Aided by the defection of Garland's brigade and aggressive leadership by its officers, Greene's division drove the Confederates back toward the Dunker church, reaching within two hundred yards of it and forcing Stephen Lee's cannons to displace beyond the West Wood. Meanwhile, the new 125th Pennsylvania from Crawford's brigade, which somehow had missed most of the action, arrived right at the Dunker church and formed nervously in the trees just to the north.[11]

The Confederate line now bowed in dangerously at the church. Stonewall Jackson worked feverishly in the West Wood to reform shattered commands and gather forces for a counterstroke. He already had called for reinforcements and Lee informed him that, in addition to Tige Anderson, he was sending John Walker's division from the right of the line and promised he would order up Lafayette McLaws's division, which, with Richard Anderson's, had arrived.[12]

At McClellan's headquarters on the elevated site of the Philip Pry house, about two miles east of the Dunker church, the fighting raging around the church and Cornfield was visible and McClellan realized that the Federal attacks were running into trouble. At 7:20 A.M. he committed Sumner's corps, though retaining as reserve one of his three divisions, that of Israel B. Richardson.

Thus, the third piecemeal attack of the morning got under way. Sumner crossed a ford due east of the Dunker Church, riding with his lead division, under John Sedgwick, while the second division, under William H. French, followed about twenty minutes behind.

Sumner and Sedgwick's division arrived at the East Wood at about 9 A.M. Meantime, Hooker had ridden his white charger into the pasture south of the Cornfield to direct the battle personally and a Rebel sharpshooter put a bullet in his foot. Hooker lost blood rapidly and had to be carried from the field. He passed Sumner on the way in but was semiconscious and unable to talk. The only commander in Hooker's First Corps Sumner could find was Ricketts, and he gave the impression that the entire corps had been routed. Alpheus Williams of the Twelfth Corps tried to report but Sumner brushed off his efforts.[13]

Sumner concluded that the First and Twelfth corps had been swept away, thus ignoring Greene's penetration into the center of the Rebel line at the Dunker church. If Sumner had fed this success and sent his two divisions directly southwest to Greene, they would have met Jackson's counterattack head-on and might have broken through.

Sumner decided instead to sweep *west* over the Cornfield and through the West Wood north of the church, then pivot and drive south. He hoped to envelop Jackson's force and press down on the remainder of Lee's army and destroy it. He formed Sedgwick's 5,500-man division into three brigade-wide lines, all very close together. Thus Sumner disregarded elementary military precaution by leaving insufficient space for each brigade to face right or left in case its flanks were attacked.

Only Jubal Early's twelve hundred–man brigade and about two hundred men of Jones's division collected by Colonel Grigsby stood in direct line. But Jackson, assembling his reinforcements southwest of the Dunker church, saw that he could strike Sumner on his left flank. Also, Sumner started off before French's division arrived. Thus Sedgwick's division went in unsupported, and when French arrived in the East Wood, Sumner and Sedgwick had disappeared.

Almost from the start, Rebel artillery struck. Maj. John Pelham of Stuart's cavalry had shifted nineteen guns from Nicodemus Hill south to a ridge due west of the Dunker church and his gunners could scarcely miss, arching their shells over the West Wood directly into the tightly massed Federal lines. Despite fearsome losses, Willis A. Gorman's lead brigade pressed forward. The Thirty-fourth New York on the extreme left drifted away to the south when the brigade crossed Hagerstown pike and halted near the 125th Pennsylvania around the church. The rest of the brigade pressed through the West Wood and came out on a pasture beyond. Pelham's guns opened direct fire on it while Grigsby's small force, emplaced in a farmstead, contested the advance.

N. J. T. Dana's brigade came up behind Gorman with four regiments, Dana's fifth, the Seventh Michigan, also having paused at the Dunker church. Oliver O. Howard's brigade brought up the rear.

Sedgwick's division now was halted at the western edge of the West Wood by Grigsby's riflemen and Pelham's cannons. At this moment Stonewall Jackson launched his counterstroke. Jubal Early's brigade moved east while Tige Anderson's brigade and McLaws's division struck from south and west of the church.

First hit was the exposed 125th Pennsylvania. Joseph Kershaw's South Carolinians and William Barksdale's Mississippians from McLaws's division frightened the green Federals with the "jerky, canine cries" of their Rebel yell and the bold flank strike. Soon thereafter Early's and Tige Anderson's men hit the front, dissolving the regiment. Next to catch the flank assault were the two displaced regiments of Sedgwick's division, the Thirty-fourth New York and Seventh Michigan. They collapsed and, with the Pennsylvanians, fled to the East Wood.

While Kershaw's brigade pursued them, only to be halted by cannon fire, Early and Barksdale smashed into the unprotected flank of Howard's brigade, farthest east. To the west McLaws's third brigade, under Paul Semmes, struck Gorman and Dana. For a while Sumner did not react. He was a quarter of a mile away from the terrible fire on the flank. When he finally recognized the disaster he exclaimed: "By God, we must get out of this!"[14]

But Sedgwick's division was disintegrating. Howard's brigade, aligned facing west and unable to turn, collapsed one regiment at a time, from south to north, as Early and Tige Anderson smashed against their flanks. The brigade lost nearly six hundred men in ten minutes and the survivors fled northward.

The left of Dana's brigade collapsed as well, and the Rebels, having passed behind the remaining Federal lines, reached a meadow just east of the West Wood, wheeled west, and struck the remaining Federals still in the wood. Half of Sedgwick's division was dead, wounded, or had bolted and the remainder was being hit from the front, side, and rear, while more Rebel batteries rushed to the eminence where Pelham's guns were firing. Sedgwick himself was struck three times and had to be carried off. Sumner remained fearless, but the only way out of the closing trap was to retreat northward. As the regiments withdrew under intense pressure, some disintegrated, but several retired in good order, stubbornly contesting all the way.

The coup de grace was landed by Paul Semmes's Georgians and Virginians, who moved around on the retreating Federals' flank and threw their lines into disorder. Greatly assisting were Pelham's guns, which leapfrogged northward from position to position, keeping pace with Semmes's men. The remainder of Sedgwick's division fled to the North Wood, pulling with it scattered fragments of Hooker's and Mansfield's corps.[15]

The only bright spot for the Federals was the presence of George Greene's two brigades, which had advanced earlier to the plateau opposite the Dunker church. They remained, by far the most intrusive Federal force, getting a resupply of ammunition and support from a six-gun Rhode Island battery.

Kershaw, arriving back after pursuing retreating Federals, turned part of his brigade against Greene's force, but it drove back Kershaw with heavy losses.

Seeing this, Col. Van H. Manning, commanding John Walker's Second Brigade, advanced out of the West Wood and directly upon Greene's brigades. The Federals, concealed behind the rim of the plateau, let the Rebels approach to within seventy yards and then rose up and delivered a killing volley. The Thirtieth Virginia lost 160 of 236 men; other regiments suffered severely. Manning was badly wounded and the survivors ran back through the West Wood before they could be rallied.

The Federals now stormed into the wood and reached two hundred yards beyond the Dunker church. This was a potentially decisive penetration and Greene, recognizing it, sent back for aid.[16]

Jackson held, but only because Lee had stripped other portions of the front and McClellan had committed his forces one at a time. A determined attack at any point could break Lee's line. He had only Richard Anderson's division as a reserve. A. P. Hill, though marching hard, was still miles away.

At 9:10 A.M. McClellan, learning that Franklin's corps was approaching, finally decided it was safe to order Burnside's four-division Ninth Corps to assault the Confederate right, or southern, flank. He also released Israel Richardson's division and it started toward the East Wood.

It took nearly an hour to deliver the movement order to Burnside and longer for Burnside to go into action. Meantime, as Sedgwick's shattered division retreated northward, William French, left alone and without orders by Sumner, marched his fifty-seven-hundred-man division south from the East Wood, hoping to come out on the left of George Greene's division around the Dunker church.

This movement threw French directly against the twenty-five hundred men still with D. H. Hill's division. They were facing northeast along the zigzagging Sunken Road (the "bloody lane") beginning six hundred yards south and east of the Dunker church.

As French's advance brigade under Max Weber attained a point just under a low ridge in front of the Sunken Road, he ordered his men to fix bayonets and charge. Col. F. M. Parker of the waiting Thirtieth North Carolina warned his men that he would give the order to fire only when the enemy crossed the ridge and the men could see the Federals' belts. Aim at these, he told them. The Tar Heels obeyed precisely. The effect was appalling. Nearly the entire first line of Weber's brigade went down as if cut by a great scythe, 150 men of the Fourth New York falling at virtually the same moment. In five minutes the brigade suffered more than 450 killed and wounded. The survivors fell behind the crest, lay down, and returned fire.

French's Second Brigade, under Dwight Morris, advanced through the shambles. Its men had been in service scarcely a month. Some fired into the backs of Weber's men on the ground. Others broke and ran, while still others joined Weber's men lying under the brow of the ridge.

French now sent in his last brigade, Nathan Kimball's. It advanced at double-quick, bayonets fixed, and met a hail of fire that virtually disintegrated it. Rebels in the rear passed up loaded rifles to men in the front to speed the firing. Federal dead and wounded covered the crest. Although some of French's men remained, the division had been shattered—1,750 men killed and wounded in minutes, most of the survivors streaming to the rear.[17]

Now, after three Federal corps had been virtually destroyed, Richardson's division of four thousand men arrived. It, too, aimed toward the new vortex of the struggle: the Sunken Road. D. H. Hill's men were exhilarated but exhausted, their numbers dwindling. Losses were especially great among officers. One brigade commander, George B. Anderson, suffered a fatal ankle wound and his successor fell as he was taking command. Col. John B. Gordon of the Sixth Alabama was hit six times. Command was falling into disarray.

Longstreet and Jackson desperately fed every man and cannon they could find into the struggle. Lee also committed his last force, Dick Anderson's thirty-four-hundred-man division. As it marched over rising ground south of Hill's position, Federal Parrott guns east of the Antietam found the range and scored a number of casualties, among them Anderson himself, who was severely wounded. The command fell to Brig. Gen. Roger A. Pryor, a former congressman who demonstrated that he could not handle division command. Only Ambrose R. Wright's brigade immediately took up positions in the Sunken Road. The other brigades remained in the rear.

Richardson advanced to the east of the remaining men of French's division, led by the Irish Brigade under Thomas F. Meagher. This brigade had three New York Irish regiments but also the Twenty-ninth Massachusetts of old New England stock. Waiting for it was George B. Anderson's brigade of North Carolinians, now under Col. R. T. Bennett. As the Irish Brigade reached the ridge line it, too, met a lightning blast of rifle fire, which collapsed the charge. The Sixty-third and Sixty-ninth New York lost nearly two-thirds of their men in the first minutes. The brigade could do no more than fall to the ground and return fire.

General Pryor's own brigade and Carnot Posey's brigade of Anderson's division finally reached the Sunken Road and squeezed in among the North Carolinians there. But Anderson's other brigade, under Col. Alfred Cumming, never got to the line.

It was now approaching noon. Richardson's Second Brigade, under John C. Caldwell, swung to the south beyond the Irish Brigade, aiming to outflank the Sunken Road. But it was cautious and slow. Richardson, irritated, searched out Caldwell and found him hiding behind a haystack. Richardson angrily sent the brigade in at double-quick to relieve Meagher. The Rebels watched the advance anxiously. At this moment, Lt. Col. Joseph H. Barnes of the Twenty-ninth Massachusetts ordered a surprise attack from Meagher's position that, though quickly stopped, unnerved the Rebel defenders. Meanwhile, Colonel Posey tried to pull out some of his brigade to relieve crowding in the Sunken Lane. This flurry frightened the men of Dick Anderson's ill-led division and nearly all of them broke for the rear, pulling with them half of George Anderson's brigade of Hill's division, which had held so valiantly.

Almost at the same moment, on the left side of the Sunken Road Lt. Col. J. N. Lightfoot, now commanding the Sixth Alabama, was concerned because of increased enfilade fire against his men, posted at an exposed bend in the Sunken Road. He asked his brigade commander, Robert E. Rodes, for permission to withdraw from the salient. Rodes agreed but Lightfoot misinterpreted his orders, telling the chief of the adjacent regiment that the withdrawal order applied to the whole brigade. This set off disintegration of the entire Sunken Road line and the flight of the men to the rear. Rodes desperately rallied a few but the defection blew a wide hole in the center of the Confederate line.

Richardson's division, with some of French's men coming along, rushed gleefully into this void. Federals quickly swung around and took in devastating enfilade the few North Carolinians still grimly holding parts of the Sunken Road, killing many and forcing the rest to flee.

Richardson's breakthrough was clearly visible from McClellan's headquarters and officers there agreed that now was the time to launch Fitz-John Porter's corps at the center of the Confederate line along the Boonsboro pike.[18] But McClellan was not capable of seizing the opportunity. He held Porter in place and sent no help to Richardson.

Massed Confederate artillery on the hill to the south of the Sunken Road stopped Richardson's advance—twenty guns firing double loads of canister. Though Federal snipers picked off many gunners, the artillery continued to blast away and Hill was not called on to use the tiny line of soldiers he and his officers formed from stragglers. At 1 P.M. Richardson, getting no support, ordered his men to safety behind the ridge line just north of the Sunken Road. While talking to a battery commander, Richardson was wounded when a Confederate shell exploded nearby. He died six weeks later. McClellan replaced Richardson with Winfield Scott Hancock and told him to stay where he was.[19]

Meanwhile, General Greene remained with his salient in the West Wood, reinforced only by the Thirteenth New Jersey and a couple of cannons. Jackson had only a single regiment—the Forty-ninth North Carolina, under Lt. Col. Lee M. McAfee—to deal with this dangerous penetration. Instead of assaulting Greene head-on, as Kershaw and Manning had done, McAfee struck his northern flank, setting off mass confusion and the flight of Greene's whole force of 1,350 men.

A diversionary force drawn together by Longstreet under Col. John R. Cooke of the Twenty-seventh North Carolina joined in the pursuit of Greene but returned to the Dunker church after Federal cannons halted the chase.

Longstreet now ordered Cooke's force to attack. Going with Cooke were 250 Georgians and North Carolinians of McLaws's division under Lt. Col. William MacRae. The assault crossed the plateau east of the church and drove deep into the rear of Richardson's position.

Various Federal officers saw it coming and swung whatever units and cannons were in the vicinity around to meet it. Cooke and MacRae came within two hundred yards of this improvised line and the two sides exchanged volley after volley. But there was no hope of aid and the Rebels withdrew. Greene lost more than half of the 675 men who took part and MacRae brought back only 50 of his 250.

Nevertheless, this abortive counterattack frightened Sumner and McClellan and confirmed in their minds that Lee was planning a major assault on the northern flank.

McClellan already had sent Franklin's corps (William F. Smith's and Henry Slocum's divisions) to bolster the flank in response to Sumner's pleas. In doing so he abandoned his earlier hope to reinforce Porter with Franklin's corps in a planned culminating attack on Lee's center along Boonsboro Road.

William H. Irwin's brigade of Smith's division formed around the Samuel Mumma farmstead, half a mile east of the Dunker church, to deter another Rebel charge. Irwin, apparently intoxicated, ordered three of his regiments to attack toward the church. Cooke's and MacRae's men, resting behind good cover, shot this unsupported charge apart in minutes, killing or wounding 224 Federal soldiers.[20]

With this unnecessary bloodbath most of the action ended on the northern flank. By 1 P.M. the survivors on both sides lay exhausted and stunned. Although drawn back from where they had been at daybreak, the Confederate lines had held.

★ ★ ★

Just as fighting was slowing on the Confederate left, it commenced on the right, demonstrating the uncoordinated nature of McClellan's battle plan. On this flank Burnside exhibited almost no initiative, perhaps because he was angry at McClellan for having withdrawn Hooker's corps from his command.

Burnside had overwhelming superiority, 12,500 infantry versus not more than 2,500 Confederates, under David R. Jones, holding over a mile of the right flank, so nearly stripped of troops it scarcely passed for a line at all.[21] Most Rebels were just outside Sharpsburg, but Robert Toombs had about four hundred men in the Second and Twentieth Georgia under Col. Robert L. Benning on the heights above the Rohrbach Bridge, three-quarters of a mile southeast of town, plus a couple of hundred in an extended skirmish line below the bridge.

Until about 9 A.M. John Walker's division had been emplaced between Jones and T. T. Munford's cavalry screen next to the Potomac. But after Lee moved it to help Jackson, there was nothing to take its place.

The remarkable thing about Burnside's attack is that he concentrated virtually all of his attention on forcing passage of the 125-foot stone Rohrbach Bridge—to go down in history as the Burnside Bridge—directly into the barrels of Benning's riflemen, who were protected by a stone wall and rock quarry, with twelve cannons in close support and two more batteries on the plateau next to Sharpsburg. Yet the Burnside Bridge need not to have been assaulted at all; there was a virtually undefended stretch of creek immediately to the south that could have been forded.

McClellan's battle plan actually called for a force to pin down the Burnside Bridge defenders while a reinforced division under Isaac P. Rodman forced passage at a downstream ford and moved onto the Confederate rear.[22]

Some of McClellan's headquarters engineers studied the creek on the sixteenth and selected a ford two-thirds of a mile below the Burnside Bridge. Neither Burnside, nor Ninth Corps tactical commander Jacob D. Cox, nor Rodman went to see if was suitable. Yet local people had been telling Federal officers since the army arrived that there was an excellent crossing farther downstream, Snavely's Ford.

If a reconnaissance had been carried out, Rodman's division could have been masked behind Snavely's Ford on the sixteenth and he could have crossed as soon as Burnside got the order to advance. With Walker gone he could have cut the Confederate army off from the Potomac and forced its surrender. Nothing like this happened.

When Rodman reached the ford designated by McClellan's engineers he discovered that it was impassable. A high bank rose from the water's edge on the Federal side. Rodman started a slow, methodical search for Snavely's Ford. It took him until around 1 P.M. to reach and cross it, two miles below, against practically no opposition.[23]

The plan was to wait until Rodman crossed behind the Confederate line and dislodged the Rebels guarding Burnside Bridge. The Federals were well aware of the danger of storming this span. The Antietam valley was narrow here and the road on the east side ran close to the creek for 250 yards before turning sharply to cross the bridge.

Yet before Rodman launched his operation, Burnside ordered the Eleventh Connecticut to advance as skirmishers to make way for George Crook's Ohio brigade of the Kanawha Division to rush the bridge. The regiment pressed to the creek and in minutes lost a third of its members killed or wounded and had to withdraw.

Colonel Crook planned to seize the bridge by a coup de main. But he got lost in woods behind the front, missed (or avoided) the treeless hill in front of the bridge, and emerged at the creek about 350 yards *above* the bridge. There Rebel snipers started pecking away and Crook stayed for hours without moving, even though the creek was easily fordable there.

Burnside and Cox gave up on Rodman's flanking attack and decided to storm the bridge. James Nagle's brigade of Samuel D. Sturgis's division drew the assignment. Nagle picked the Second Maryland under Lt. Col. Jacob Duryea to lead, with the Sixth New Hampshire following and the rest of the brigade providing covering fire. Duryea formed a column of fours while every Federal rifle and gun that could bear opened a barrage against Benning's small force.

As the barrage lifted, three hundred Marylanders advanced along the road toward the bridge 250 yards away. As soon as they emerged, the Georgians hit them with a hail of bullets from a hundred yards or less, while the Rebel batteries dropped shell after shell directly on the ranks. Duryea, at the head, looked back and saw the regiment melt before his eyes, the men ducking and running for any cover. Within a few moments the Second Maryland had lost 44 percent of its men.

It was now near noon. McClellan sent his inspector general with orders to press the attack at whatever cost. Sturgis directed his other brigade, under Edward Ferrero, to make the second assault. Ferrero chose his toughest regiments, the Fifty-first New York and the Fifty-first Pennsylvania—670 men. Since any advance along the road would bring disaster, Ferrero charged straight down the hill across three hundred yards of open ground. The Georgians hit them hard before they were halfway down. The men began to falter. The officers, seeing that they could never rush the bridge in a single bound, swung the regiments off to the left and right behind cover just shy of the bridge.

By now Benning's men were almost out of ammunition. One in four had been killed or wounded. The Federal fire was terrific. The Georgians began running, in twos and threes, up the hillside. As the Confederate line disintegrated, Col. Robert B. Potter of the Fifty-first New York saw his chance, pulled the color-bearer along with him and led his men onto the bridge. The Pennsylvanians joined and the two regiments rushed across and seized the western approaches.[24]

It was 1 P.M. Burnside finally had his bridge. It had cost 500 Federal casualties, 120 Confederate.

Soon the remainder of Sturgis's division and the Kanawha Division under Col. Eliakim P. Scammon were across and formed a line of battle on the heights west of the creek. But Sturgis discovered that his men were almost out of ammunition. Moreover, he said, they were exhausted. Cox did not argue and called on Orlando B. Willcox's division in reserve to take Sturgis's place. It took until 3 P.M. for Willcox to come forward. During this time Rodman had crossed Snavely's Ford and linked up with the Federals at the bridge.

Meanwhile, on the northern flank, General Franklin proposed an attack on the West Wood. Sumner was appalled. If Franklin's men were defeated, Sumner said, the Rebels could attack and the entire northern flank could disintegrate. Franklin appealed to McClellan, who, after finally visiting the northern flank, sided with Sumner and ordered the troops to remain in place.[25]

Lee and Jackson *were* seeking to attack on the north. Although Jackson had no more than five thousand men, including cavalry, he examined the enemy front, hoping to swing around the northern flank. He discovered at least four Union brigades and many cannons in the only path he could take, since the Potomac prevented a wide flanking movement. Nevertheless, Jackson alerted his forces.[26]

On the southern flank, Lee knew that Jones's division had no hope of stopping Burnside's attack, but he switched no troops. A. P. Hill rode up at 2:30 P.M., wearing his red battle shirt, and reported that his brigades would be up soon. Literally at the last minute, Lee was getting reinforcements to deal with Burnside.[27]

The Federals, with their cavalry still locked up on the Boonsboro Road, had no idea that A. P. Hill's division was anywhere near, and Burnside took no precautions to protect his southern flank. Shortly after 3 P.M. Cox gave the order for an advance on Sharpsburg, fifty-five hundred men, Rodman on the left, Willcox on the right, facing almost due west, with three thousand men backing them in the Kanawha Division behind, Sturgis in reserve.

Burnside planned to advance to Sharpsburg and the plateau south of it, crack the Confederate right flank, and get astride the road to Boteler's Ford, Lee's only route of retreat. He still had four hours of daylight.

On the left on the hill directly east of Sharpsburg, Jones had posted Richard B. Garnett's Virginia brigade and Micah Jenkins's South Carolina brigade (led by Joseph Walker). In the mostly open fields toward the creek he deployed a mixed South Carolina and Georgia force of skirmishers. Defending the Confederate right were the brigades of Thomas F. Drayton, James L. Kemper, and Robert Toombs. Toombs had relieved the men who had defended Burnside Bridge with his last two regiments, brought up from guarding the army's trains.

Willcox's division advanced on both sides of the road leading up from Burnside Bridge, facing the skirmishers hiding, Indian-fashion, in farmsteads and along fences and delivering deadly rifle fire. Meanwhile, twenty-eight Rebel cannons on the high ground east and south of town rained shells on the advancing Federals, while the gunners endured heavy counterbattery fire from the Federal Parrott guns east of the creek.

Although Colonel Walker brought his brigade down to assist the skirmishers, Willcox's much stronger force threatened the

Rebels with encirclement and Walker withdrew all of his men behind a stone fence on the outskirts of town, closely pursued by Willcox. One more push would carry the Federals into the streets.

Meanwhile, Rodman's two brigades advanced toward the ridge south of Sharpsburg, the men having to charge straight into heavy fire from a dozen Confederate guns on the ridge line half a mile away. Shell and canister killed or wounded many men in Col. Harrison S. Fairchild's New York brigade on the right, which advanced doggedly nevertheless. In the meantime, Col. Edward Harland's Connecticut–Rhode Island brigade on the left flank was slowed because of confusion in orders.

Kemper's Virginians and Drayton's South Carolinians and Georgians—590 men—drew up at a stone wall and rail fence on the crest. Fairchild's brigade emerged abruptly over the sharp ridge scarcely fifty yards away. Both lines stood their ground briefly, swapping volleys, the hail knocking down whole ranks on both sides. Then the New Yorkers charged straight at the fence, winning a short, bitter hand-to-hand battle and forcing the Rebel survivors to run, some into the town. Fairchild's advance was on the verge of cracking the entire Confederate right flank. But the cost had been heavy—half of Fairchild's men were dead or wounded.

Colonel Harland straightened out the disorder in his brigade and advanced toward Fairchild's brigade, General Rodman with it.

Meanwhile, A. P. Hill's division rushed into action, each brigade going in as it arrived. The division was far under its thirty-three-hundred-man strength when it left Harpers Ferry, as uncounted hundreds of exhausted men had fallen by the wayside. Burnside's long delay had given the Confederates just the margin of time they needed. Now Hill was approaching at the last possible moment—and at a deadly angle on Rodman's left flank.

As Harland's brigade advanced, at around 3:30 P.M., someone spotted enemy troops off to the south. Rodman sent an aide to warn Harland, just entering a large unharvested cornfield. He spurred ahead to warn Fairchild. As he galloped in the open, a Confederate sharpshooter struck him with a mortal wound in the chest.

In the meantime, Harland's advance regiment, the Eighth Connecticut, charged one of Hill's batteries under Capt. D. G. McIntosh that had gone ahead and was deployed on the ridge but was unsupported. McIntosh fired double canister but the Eighth Connecticut rushed on, shooting down nearly all of the battery horses. McIntosh ordered his gunners to run and the Federals gleefully seized the cannons. Ahead of the regiment, Toombs's thin force contested the advance while some North Carolinians of Hill's division got to the ridge line and commenced a merciless cross fire. The Connecticut regiment had to retreat, losing half of its 350 men.

Burnside's left flank had now diminished to two regiments of Harland's brigade, the experienced Fourth Rhode Island and the new Sixteenth Connecticut, one thousand men all told. As the force advanced into a depression in the tall corn, Maxcy Gregg's veteran South Carolina brigade of 750 men, emplaced a hundred feet away behind a stone wall at the western edge of the field, unleashed a staggering volley. The green Connecticut regiment milled around in confusion but the Rhode Islanders held their line and replied with desperate volleys. Gregg worked one of his regiments around the enemy flank. This caused the Sixteenth Connecticut to collapse, drawing the Fourth Rhode Island with it. The entire force fled in disorder.

General Cox saw the Federals streaming out of the cornfield and realized that his entire line was in danger. He ordered Fairchild and Willcox to withdraw from the edge of town. Col. Hugh Ewing brought up his Ohio regiments of the Kanawha Division to attempt to mend the break, but A. P. Hill now had three of his five brigades in action—Gregg's, James J. Archer's Tennesseans and Georgians, and L. O'B. Branch's North Carolinians. These brigades outflanked Ewing and he retreated toward the creek. General Branch, riding near the front, was killed instantly by a bullet through the head. This raised the dead and wounded total to nine Confederate and nine Union generals.

Confederate artillery, now forty pieces, outgunned the Union batteries and they began pulling back. The Federal Parrotts to the east of the stream ran out of ammunition. Cox feverishly but successfully constructed a new line covering Burnside Bridge and the heights west of the creek, using Sturgis's division. The nearly fatal assault on the Confederate right had collapsed, a victim of Burnside's delays and the blows of A. P. Hill.

While Cox's divisions were streaming back from Sharpsburg, Jackson attempted the flank movement on the north that he and Lee had been planning. His men had to pass through a corridor less than a mile wide between the Potomac and General Meade's position just above the North Wood. To do so he had to silence Meade's artillery with his twenty-one guns.

But Meade's thirty-four guns ranked hub to hub on high ground silenced Stuart's mostly smaller pieces in about fifteen minutes. Stuart and Jackson sadly concluded that it was impossible to turn McClellan's flank, and men and guns returned to their starting places.[28]

It was now nightfall. The fighting ceased all across the line. It had been the bloodiest day in American history. The Army of the Potomac had suffered 2,108 dead, 9,450 wounded, and 753 missing, many of them dead as well—a total of 12,401, one-quarter of the men who had gone into action. The Army of Northern Virginia had lost about 1,500 dead, 7,800 wounded, and 1,000 missing (most dead)—a total of 10,300, 31 percent of those on the firing lines. The combined American total was over 22,700.[29]

McClellan had committed only fifty thousand men. Over a third of his army did not fire a shot. Even so, his determined and brave soldiers came close to cracking the Confederate line and bringing Lee's army to disaster.

When Lee assembled his commanders after the battle, he rejected immediate retreat across the Potomac. "If McClellan wants to fight in the morning," Lee said, "I will give him battle again."[30]

The Army of Northern Virginia now entered a new and bitter era. It had been grievously, permanently wounded. The aura of inevitable victory no longer enveloped it. It had fought McClellan to a standstill but it had not achieved victory. Soon it would have to retreat. This, to the world, would spell defeat, just as had been unavoidable from the start. Abraham Lincoln was waiting to proclaim emancipation of the slaves and transformation of the war into a crusade. This would guarantee the persistence of the Northern people in the struggle and the drawing back of Britain and France from recognition of the Confederacy.

NOTES

General sources: Allan, *Army of Northern Virginia,* 372–437; Sears, 168–297; Henderson, 522–41; Freeman, *R. E. Lee,* vol. 2, 382–404; Freeman, *Lee's Lieutenants,* vol. 2, 203–25; Johnson and Buel, vol. 2, 596–603, 627–62, 667–72, and 675–85; Douglas, 168–78; Cooke, 327–42; Palfrey, 57–137; Chambers, vol. 2, 218–34; Vandiver, 394–400; and John M. Priest, *Antietam: The Soldiers' Battle* (Shippensburg, Pa.: White Mane, 1989).

1. Once the enemy had stripped forces from a point to defend against the flank movement, Napoleon carried out a decisive third step to ensure victory: he sent a powerful force directly into the weakened enemy point to create a breakthrough. This final coup de grace would not have been necessary for McClellan, since Lee's army was so inferior in size that it could not have withstood a strong turning movement to the south.

2. An alternative plan would have been closer to what McClellan himself proposed but did not carry out: hard attacks on both the north and south, pulling Lee's reserves to these points, then a massive stroke into the center of the Confederate line along Boonsboro pike to split the Southern army in half. This would have resulted in Lee's defeat but might have permitted that part of the army on the south to get across the Potomac.

3. McClellan's original plan, not carried out, was to make the main attack on the Confederate left (north), then to assail the right, and when one or more was successful, to attack the center along the Boonsboro pike. See Johnson and Buel, vol. 2, 633. McClellan disclosed his plan in a preliminary report about a month after the battle. In his later report covering his whole war career (August 4, 1863) he wrote that he planned to use Hooker and Mansfield, supported by Sumner and, if necessary, Franklin, to attack the Confederate left, or north, then, when matters "looked

favorably," to move Burnside on the enemy right, pressing on the ridge to the south and rear of Sharpsburg. Only when either of these movements was successful did he then plan to "advance our center with all the forces then disposable." See Allan, *Army of Northern Virginia,* 380–81; *Official Records,* vol. 19, pt. 1, 55; and Palfrey, 107–8.

4. Although this initial attack was on the northern flank and was described by McClellan as such, tactically it was more nearly a frontal attack against Lee's northern face. This was because Lee had so few troops that he was able to post only Stuart's cavalry and some guns, protected by a single infantry brigade (Early's), on his extreme northern flank. Although this force was a nuisance to the Federals, it was incapable of flanking the Union attack that Jackson saw was coming directly from the north, down the Hagerstown pike. Jackson accordingly aligned his corps to defend against this attack. This had the effect of bending the line in Jackson's sector to front largely north, not east, as did the remainder of the line.

5. This was the last battle in which substantial numbers of Confederates were still firing smoothbore muskets. Only a few Federal troops carried smoothbores. See Alexander, *Military Memoirs,* 245.

6. Figures of forces on both sides are approximate. For an analysis of the figures, see Sears, 181 and 203; Allan, *Army of Northern Virginia,* 379 and 397–98; *Official Records,* vol. 19, pt. 1, 67; and Henderson, 518–19 and 525–26. Johnson and Buel (vol. 2, 603) give total Federal strength as 87,164 and Confederate as "less than 40,000." The Army of the Potomac actually counted ninety-four thousand troops, but this figure included cooks, teamsters, and other detailed men. In addition, a sixty-six-hundred-man division of Porter's corps was at Frederick and marching hard for the battlefield. See Sears, 173.

7. Wise, 289; Sears, 191; and *Official Records,* vol. 19, pt. 1, 845. Porter Alexander (*Military Memoirs,* 235 and 245–47) notes that the Federals had more and better guns than the Confederates, especially twenty-pounder Parrott rifles and twelve-pounder guns, as against the ten-pounder rifles and six-pounder guns of the Confederates. Southern rifled ammunition also was inferior, many shells failing to burst, exploding prematurely or tumbling and thereby losing accuracy. The Federal rifled guns east of the Antietam were placed beyond the effective range of the Confederate guns and fired all day onto Rebel positions, safe from counterbattery fire.

8. *Official Records,* vol. 19, pt. 1, 909–10.

9. Ibid., 224, 243–44, 248–49, 254–55, 937–38, 967–68, and 1008–13.

10. When Mansfield was wounded and Alpheus Williams took over the Twelfth Corps, he relinquished command of his division to Crawford and Col. Joseph F. Knipe assumed command of Crawford's brigade.

11. *Official Records,* vol. 19, pt. 1, 244 and 474–76.

12. Ibid., 865 and 914.

13. Ibid., 476, 485, and 494; and U.S. Senate, *Report of the Committee on the Conduct of the War,* report no. 108 (Washington, D.C.: Government Printing Office, 1863), vol. 1, 368.

14. Sears, 226; and *Official Records,* vol. 19, pt. 1, 874.

15. *Official Records,* vol. 19, pt. 1, 857–60 and 969–71.

16. Ibid., 149, 909–10, 914–21, 938, and 1022–23; and Johnson and Buel, vol. 2, 678.

17. *Official Records,* vol. 19, pt. 1, 323–24, 327, 871–72, 918, 1037, and 1047–48.

18. Johnson and Buel, vol. 2, 684.

19. *Official Records,* vol. 19, pt. 1, 277–78, 294, 299, 323–24, 327, 1023–24, 1037–38, and 1047–48.

20. Ibid., 376–77.

21. Allan, *Army of Northern Virginia,* 377.

22. Sears, 261; and Johnson and Buel, vol. 2, 650–51.

23. Johnson and Buel, vol. 2, 651.

24. *Official Records,* vol. 19, pt. 1, 890–91.

25. Ibid., 62; and Johnson and Buel, vol. 2, 597.

26. Sears, 275; Henderson, 536; Johnson and Buel, vol. 2, 679; and *Official Records,* vol. 19, pt. 1, 151 and 956.

27. *Official Records,* vol. 19, pt. 1, 981.

28. Ibid., 151, 956, and 1010; Sears, 290–91; Henderson, 538–39; and Johnson and Buel, vol. 2, 679–80.

29. Alexander, *Military Memoirs,* 273–75; Henderson, 547–48; Johnson and Buel, vol. 2, 600 and 603; Sears, 294–96; and *Official Records,* vol. 19, pt. 1, 189–200 and 810–13.

30. Henderson, 541; and Johnson and Buel, vol. 2, 672.

14

BURNSIDE FALLS INTO HIS OWN TRAP

★ ★ ★ On the morning of September 18, 1862, the Southern and Northern armies faced each other across a narrow no-man's-land along the Antietam. Lee, Jackson, and the other Confederate commanders expected the Federals to attack. But McClellan had no intention of renewing the battle, although he did expect the Rebels to do so.[1]

Lee and Jackson *did* want to attack. About five thousand stragglers had come up during the night and taken their places. Lee ordered another examination of the northern flank to see if it was possible to break through. He rode out with Jackson, but both confirmed what Stonewall had seen the day before: the Potomac left no space for a movement not swept by Federal artillery. The two generals reluctantly gave up the idea of a counterstroke.[2]

The only choice left was to retire across the Potomac. Lee held the army in place throughout the day to permit medical personnel to evacuate all but the critically wounded. After midnight and on into the morning of the nineteenth, covered by Fitz Lee's cavalry, the Army of Northern Virginia crossed the single ford near Shepherdstown and bivouacked below the southern shore. Lee exhibited no anxiety but he stood at the ford as the last division, under Gen. John G. Walker, crossed over. Walker told him there was nothing behind but wagons with wounded and a single battery of guns. "Thank God!" Lee exclaimed.[3]

Lee left his reserve artillery and a small infantry detachment to guard the ford. Union general Porter pushed a small force across, which seized four guns. But due to the prompt response of Stonewall Jackson, A. P. Hill's division attacked on the morning of September 20 and drove the Federals back across the river, inflicting more than three hundred casualties.[4]

This action ended the Maryland campaign. But its consequences reverberated to the end of the war and beyond. On September 22 Abraham Lincoln issued the Emancipation Proclamation, effective January 1, 1863. It was revolutionary, a presidential edict that ignored procedures for amending the Constitution, struck down constitutional provisions protecting slavery, and changed the war at a stroke from a conflict to preserve the Union into a crusade to free the slaves. The edict did *not* eliminate slavery in the border states that had remained in the Union. It freed only bondsmen in the states that might remain in rebellion as of January 1.

Two days later Lincoln overrode by edict another provision of the Constitution, suspending the writ of habeas corpus, designed to prevent illegal detention by government authorities. Lincoln denied habeas corpus to those persons accused of "discouraging volunteer enlistments, resisting militia drafts or guilty of any disloyal practice, affording aid and comfort to Rebels."[5]

Lincoln's actions drew mixed responses, the abolitionists applauding and conservatives fearing abandonment of the Constitution to radical fanaticism. General McClellan opposed the measures, but his advisers, civilian and military, admonished him to avoid a clash with Lincoln because of the American tradition subordinating the military to civilian authority. McClellan, accordingly, issued a weak general order on October 7, 1862, stating that it was the soldier's duty to support the government and that the remedy for "political errors" was the ballot box.

Lincoln had predicted accurately that McClellan would repeat his procrastination and not advance against Lee. After Antietam McClellan remained in place, demanding that his army be refurbished before he could move. This angered Lincoln, but worse was McClellan's known opposition to his revolutionary decrees. Two suspicions arose in Lincoln's mind: that McClellan would become the Democratic, peace candidate in the presidential election two years hence, and that McClellan was deliberately avoiding destruction of the Southern army to prepare for a compromise peace that would save slavery.[6]

Accordingly, Lincoln ordered McClellan on October 6 to "cross the Potomac and give battle to the enemy." Lincoln once more tried to be a strategist, advising McClellan to take the "interior line," keeping between the Rebels and Washington and promising him thirty thousand more men if he did so instead of advancing up the Shenandoah Valley, as McClellan preferred.[7]

Lee, meantime, had led a remarkable recovery in his army. For five weeks the Army of Northern Virginia rested and refitted in excellent dry weather around Winchester. Food was plentiful and Lee's appeals for clothing, shoes, and blankets brought results. Most men still armed with smoothbores exchanged them for Federal rifles picked up on the battlefield or captured at Harpers Ferry. The army also more than doubled in size as stragglers returned and a constant, if small, stream of conscripts arrived. By October 10 the army numbered 64,273; by November 20, 76,472.[8]

Lee also superintended the reorganization of the army formally into corps, one led by Jackson, the other Longstreet, and the promotion of both of these officers to lieutenant general.[9]

Lee had hoped to recross the Potomac and move upon Hagerstown but gave up the idea because the hazard was too great and a reverse would be disastrous.[10] Nevertheless, Lee wanted to learn what McClellan was planning and he wanted to delay him.

On October 10 he sent Stuart north with eighteen hundred horsemen. The target was the railroad bridge over Conococheague Creek at Chambersburg, Pennsylvania, to cut McClellan's rail supply line from Harrisburg to Hagerstown.

Stuart crossed near Williamsport and reached Chambersburg without incident but found he could not destroy the bridge, since it was made of iron. His troopers still tore up rail facilities and rounded up twelve hundred sorely needed horses. With large groups of Federal cavalry and infantry trying to head him off, Stuart judged it safer—and more dramatic—to make an entire circuit of McClellan's army. He returned by way of Emmitsburg and Hyattstown, bluffed half a regiment to retreat from its position guarding White's Ford, four miles north of Leesburg, and returned safely to Virginia on October 12, having completed an eighty-mile circuit, losing one man wounded and two captured.

This second ride around McClellan's army, repeating the one he had made in June on the peninsula, damaged McClellan's reputation even further, especially with Lincoln.

The ride convinced Lee that McClellan was not planning to approach Richmond by another sea expedition through the Chesapeake Bay but anticipated marching against the Virginia Central Railroad, either up the Shenandoah Valley or toward Gordonsville. This simplified Lee's strategic problem.[11]

It was October 26 before McClellan finally began a leisurely crossing of the Potomac at Harpers Ferry and five miles east at Berlin (present-day Brunswick). It took eight days, the leading elements moving east of the Blue Ridge and advancing about twenty miles into Virginia. The next stage was a move on Warrenton, another twenty miles south, where he could exchange his supply line through Harpers Ferry with the safer Orange and Alexandria and Manassas Gap railroads. By November 4 the new rail lines were secured and substantial reinforcements reached McClellan from Washington.

As soon as he was certain that McClellan was marching east of the Blue Ridge, Lee divided his army, leaving Jackson's corps in the lower valley while he, with Longstreet's corps, marched rapidly to Culpeper, ahead of the slow Federal advance, interposing half of the Southern army between it and the Virginia Central Railroad.

Jackson hoped he could sally out of the Blue Ridge on the flank and rear of the Federal army, but he had to guard as well against a possible reverse thrust by McClellan into the valley in an attempt to divide him from Longstreet.[12]

By November 6 McClellan's advance units were in Warrenton. That was as far as he got. Lincoln already had determined to get rid of McClellan. He did not want to cause a political stir prior to the November 4 congressional elections, but once they were past, he moved immediately. Seven states that voted Republican in 1860 went Democratic in 1862 but the Republicans retained control of both houses of Congress. It was fortunate that McClellan had stopped Lee at Antietam. If a Confederate army had been ranging through Pennsylvania and Maryland on election day, the results might have been disastrous to Lincoln.

The effect was equally beneficial to the Union overseas. Interventionists paused when news of Antietam arrived. No politician wanted to back a loser and all decided to wait until the matter became clearer. Meantime, the Emancipation Proclamation cut the ground out from under them. By failing to win at Antietam, Lee had lost any chance of foreign intervention.[13]

On November 7, Lincoln replaced McClellan with Maj. Gen. Ambrose E. Burnside, an officer with little imagination who honestly protested that he was unqualified for high command. He took the job only because Lincoln said he would appoint Joseph Hooker if Burnside declined. Burnside considered Hooker a devious conniver who had conspired to get independent command at Antietam.[14]

Burnside knew that one of the reasons McClellan had been replaced was because he was dilatory. Lincoln expected quick action. Accompanying the order appointing him was a directive to report what he expected to accomplish. On November 9 Burnside recommended that the army move to Fredericksburg, get supplies through Aquia Creek on the Potomac twelve miles away, then push toward Richmond.[15] This way he would guard the Federal capital while he advanced. Burnside's proposal was so obvious, direct, and lacking in imagination that, to have any hope of success, he had to move with extreme speed. Otherwise Lee would beat him to Fredericksburg.

A far better target would have been Lee's army, already divided, its two wings separated by two days' march, whereas most of the Federal army of 119,000 men and 374 guns was within one day's march of either wing. A swift and resolute commander could have descended on one wing before the other could reach it. But this opportunity did not occur to anyone in authority.[16]

General Halleck preferred a repetition of John Pope's plan of moving toward Gordonsville. But Lincoln and he agreed to Burnside's proposal on the condition that he move fast, cross the Rappahannock River upstream from Fredericksburg, march down the south bank, and capture from the flank and rear the heights parallel to the river about a mile directly south of the town. These heights were the key to Fredericksburg and flanking them was far preferable to assaulting them from the front. However, Burnside approached Fredericksburg from directly across the river.[17]

The authorities in Washington promised to send pontoon bridges at once. Meanwhile, Burnside reorganized the Army of the Potomac into three "grand divisions" of two corps each under generals Sumner, Hooker, and Franklin and ordered Sumner to march to Fredericksburg on November 15. Sumner's advance reached Falmouth, just across the river from the town, on November 17. The remainder of the Union army arrived on the nineteenth.

Lee quickly dissected the Federal intentions and moved to counter them. The keys were Burnside's failure to advance south and news from Stuart on November 13 that the enemy was moving away from the Blue Ridge. On the fourteenth Lee was convinced that Fredericksburg was the objective and the next day he sent a small detachment to reinforce the tiny garrison there.

On the eighteenth Lee ordered part of Longstreet's corps to

Fredericksburg and the next day the remainder followed.[18] By this time Sumner had been standing at Falmouth for two days. The Confederates opposing him were weak, yet Burnside would not allow him to force passage over a ford he had found. Wait for the pontoons, Burnside said. But they were on a slow march from Berlin, Maryland, and did not arrive until November 25.[19]

Meanwhile, Longstreet's corps took up positions on the heights south of the town, at last awakening Burnside to the difficulties of assaulting them. Alarmed, he reconnoitered for a flank movement. Above the town the country was hilly and wooded and the river narrow with several fords. Here a surprise crossing would have been easy. Instead Burnside looked downstream, where the river was tidal and broad, and began preparations to cross at Skinker's Neck, twelve miles below the town. He also investigated crossing at Port Royal, eighteen miles below Fredericksburg, where the river was a thousand feet wide.

On November 21 Sumner demanded surrender of Fredericksburg, failing which he would bombard it. Longstreet replied through the town mayor that the Confederates would not occupy Fredericksburg but would deny Federal possession of it. Sumner did not carry through his threat but Lee advised the people to evacuate while they had the chance. Though the weather was unseasonably cold and snowy, most of the approximately five thousand population abandoned their homes and sought shelter in farmhouses and churches or encamped in woods to the south.

Stonewall Jackson, seeing that Lee was girding to defend Fredericksburg, proposed an entirely different strategy.

Although Jackson had now fully developed his theory that the Confederate army, if stationed in a strong defensive position, could defeat any Union army that attacked, he recognized that Fredericksburg was *not* the place to fight this battle, because the Confederacy could win a victory but not destroy the Union army.

There was no depth to the Fredericksburg position and no way for the Confederate army to swing around the Federal flanks, surround the defeated Union army, and break it up. The river posed a barrier but the great problem was Stafford Heights, directly on the northern bank of the Rappahannock.[20] These heights were far above the river plain on which the town was built, and rifled cannons mounted on them could cover a Federal retreat and prevent any Confederate counterstroke or flank movement.[21]

Jackson told D. H. Hill: "We will whip the enemy but gain no fruits of victory." Jackson urged Lee to adopt delaying tactics, then withdraw to the North Anna River, twenty-five miles south, where there was room for maneuver. There Burnside could be enticed to attack and could be defeated. Thereafter he could be flanked, surrounded, cut off from his supplies, and destroyed.

Three times since mid-August Jackson had proposed a plan to annihilate the Northern army. Lee had delayed implementing his first proposal, to crush John Pope against the Rapidan, until it was too late. At Second Manassas he had drawn Pope into attacking with inadequate routes of retreat and an undefended flank, but Lee again had waited until it was too late. In the Maryland campaign he wanted to place McClellan on the horns of a dilemma: to attack the Confederate army and lose or to give up Philadelphia and possibly Baltimore and still lose. Lee instead followed his own plan, which was to convince the Northern people to accept peace.

Now, for the fourth time, Lee rejected Jackson's strategy to win the war in a swift campaign by eradicating the Northern army. Lee decided to stay at Fredericksburg. His reason was to deny the enemy the territory between the North Anna and Rappahannock. Jackson protested, but to no avail, and resignedly moved his corps to Fredericksburg on November 29.[22]

★ ★ ★

Lee quickly found out Burnside's preparations at Skinker's Neck and his probings at Port Royal. When Jackson arrived he sent his corps to cover both points, moves soon discovered by the Federals.

This suggested an alternative strategy to Burnside. If he could cross at Fredericksburg and drive around Longstreet's right at

Hamilton's Crossing, some five miles southeast of the town, he might interpose between Longstreet's forces in front of Fredericksburg and Jackson's at Skinker's Neck and Port Royal.[23]

Only by prompt and resolute action had the plan any hope of succeeding. Burnside was obliged to strike before Jackson could bring his corps back to Fredericksburg. He had to force passage of the Rappahannock, march along the narrow plain between the river and the heights directly under Longstreet's guns, then sweep around Longstreet's flank and onto his rear.

A brilliant general might have pulled it off. For Burnside, the idea became a trap of his own making. Down the centuries mediocre generals have had occasional flashes of insight and seen how they might strike decisive blows, as Burnside had on this occasion. Yet in all but exceptional cases only masters of war have the boldness and strength of character to suppress doubts, ignore timid counsel, concentrate their forces, and hit at the enemy's weakest point, where a decisive breakthrough can be achieved. The mediocre general may see the chance but he characteristically acts too slowly and irresolutely and does not commit most of his strength. Befuddled when the enemy responds swiftly and the situation changes before his eyes, he usually tries to prevent impending defeat by striking *directly* at the enemy, forgetting that the power of his idea had been to avoid the enemy's strength, dislodge him from his strong positions, and destroy him *indirectly*.

This is precisely how Burnside responded. He intended to outflank Longstreet's position. But he moved far too ponderously, tipped his hand, found his enemy consolidated in front of him, lost his nerve and his sense of purpose, and drove headlong against the most powerful and prominent positions of the enemy, seeking to destroy by brute force what he had been unable to defeat by guile.

Burnside ordered two pontoon bridges to be thrown across the river at the upper end of town, another at the lower end, and two a mile below the town. The pontoon trains, consisting of boats and planking, were to arrive opposite the chosen sites at around 3 A.M. on December 11. The bridges were to be built across the river, 400 to 440 feet wide, in two or three hours and

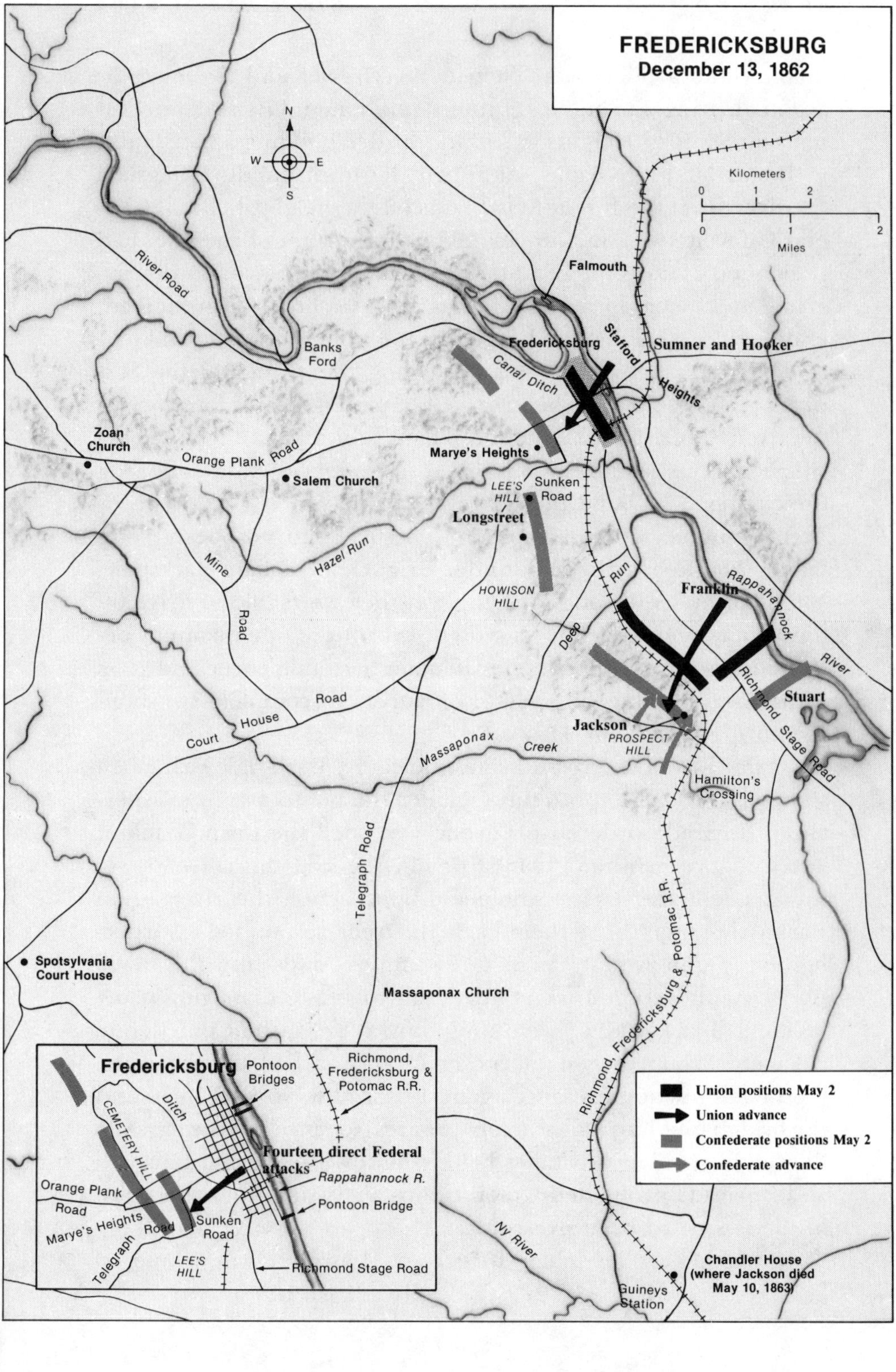

FREDERICKSBURG
December 13, 1862
Kilometers
0
1
2
0
1
2
Miles
N
S
E
W
River Road
Falmouth
Banks Ford
Fredericksburg
Stafford Heights
Sumner and Hooker
Canal Ditch
Zoan Church
Orange Plank Road
Marye's Heights
Salem Church
LEE'S HILL
Sunken Road
Longstreet
Mine Road
Hazel Run
HOWISON HILL
Deep Run
Franklin
Rappahannock River
Richmond Stage Road
Stuart
Court House Road
Jackson
PROSPECT HILL
Massaponax Creek
Hamilton's Crossing
Telegraph Road
Richmond, Fredericksburg & Potomac R.R.
Spotsylvania Court House
Massaponax Church
Ny River
Guineys Station
Chandler House (where Jackson died May 10, 1863)
Union positions May 2
Union advance
Confederate positions May 2
Confederate advance
Fredericksburg
Pontoon Bridges
Richmond, Fredericksburg & Potomac R.R.
CEMETERY HILL
Ditch
Fourteen direct Federal attacks
Rappahannock R.
Orange Plank Road
Pontoon Bridge
Marye's Heights
Sunken Road
Telegraph Road
LEE'S HILL
Richmond Stage Road

infantry and artillery were then to march over and assemble for action. During the night, gunners positioned 179 Federal cannons on Stafford Heights to support bridge building and assaults.

It was far too obvious. Although the town buildings masked the river from the fire of Rebel guns on the heights behind, General Lafayette McLaws, in charge of this portion of the line, had positioned Mississippi and Florida riflemen in pits along the riverside and in the town, with instructions to shoot down the Federal engineers as they tied together the pontoons and planking.

There was heavy morning fog along the river and the best plan by far would have been to send a picked assault force across the river by boat to seize the south bank and drive away the Rebel riflemen. This would have resulted in fewer casualties, allowing the engineers to build their bridges in safety.

This simple solution apparently occurred to no one in command. The Rebel riflemen, under Brig. Gen. William Barksdale, could barely see through the fog, yet they were able to drive off the Union engineers opposite the town. In the open country below the town the Confederate riflemen had little cover and soon withdrew, allowing the Federal engineers to complete two pontoon bridges there by 11 A.M.[24]

At the two town crossing sites, however, Barksdale's riflemen stopped every attempt to put together the pontoons. In exasperation, Burnside ordered his artillery to shell the town. While it lasted, heavy half-hour bombardment silenced the riflemen yet the moment the Union engineers approached the river again Barksdale's men drove them back. Burnside responded by ordering every gun within range to fire fifty rounds into the town. About a hundred guns responded, destroying or damaging many buildings but killing or wounding only a few of the Confederate riflemen. When the engineers again approached the riverside, the Rebels opened fire once again. It was now close to 1 P.M. and the bridge building had scarcely progressed since daybreak. Only the double bridge two miles below the town had been finished, and Burnside prohibited Union troops a crossing until resistance in the town had been overcome.

Burnside's artillery chief, Brig. Gen. Henry J. Hunt, proposed that volunteers fill ten pontoon boats, paddle across, and effect a lodgment on the southern bank. The Confederate riflemen would not be able to cover more than half the width of the stream from their positions back from the bank.

Four regiments volunteered and, though the first boats suffered a few casualties, the Rebels realized that the game was up and began withdrawing. But the Mississippi and Florida riflemen had gained practically an entire day and robbed Burnside of the only merit of his plan: speed.

Burnside now compounded the error. Although he had hoped to catch the Confederate army dispersed, he spent all December 12 in slowly crossing much of his army over the bridges and assembling it on the southern shore.[25] This proved to Lee, Jackson, and Longstreet that the Federal effort was going to be made at and just below Fredericksburg.

By noon Jackson already had moved up the divisions of A. P. Hill and W. B. Taliaferro and hidden them in the woods of Prospect Hill, four air miles southeast of Fredericksburg. This ridge terminated the line of heights behind the town along which Lee's army was posted and formed the extreme right wing of the Confederate position. The hill lay just west of Hamilton's Crossing and Massaponax Creek, which flowed into the Rappahannock two miles east. Jackson also ordered up D. H. Hill's division from Skinker's Neck and Jubal Early's from Port Royal. They arrived on the morning of December 13 after hard marching, forming a reserve on Prospect Hill and thus uniting the entire Confederate army of seventy-eight thousand men.

On the twelfth General Sumner brought over six divisions by the upper bridges, occupied the town, and faced part of Longstreet's corps spread out on and under Marye's Heights, rising 130 feet just behind the town.[26] One of these divisions, under Brig. Gen. W. W. Burns, moved downstream to assist General Franklin, who crossed with six more divisions by the double lower bridge. Franklin faced Jackson's corps, positioned for a little over a mile on the line of Prospect Hill. Two additional Union divisions (Daniel E. Sickles's and David B. Birney's) remained just north of the bridge, ready to cross and support Franklin.

Franklin had nearly sixty thousand men and ample guns available against Jackson's thirty thousand infantry. Although Burnside's plan had been to move around the Confederate right at Hamilton's Crossing, he lost confidence as he was about to put it into operation. It was no longer possible to split Jackson's corps from Longstreet's, but Jackson's right flank was floating in air, with only Stuart's cavalry guarding the open region east of Prospect Hill. If Franklin had attacked here, Jackson could have moved Early's and D. H. Hill's divisions to block him, but he thereby would have lost the splendid defensive position he held on the ridge line.

A now-doubtful Burnside visited Franklin on the evening of the twelfth. Franklin, sensing Burnside's uncertainty, tried to convince him to follow the original plan. Franklin wrote that he "strongly advised General Burnside to make an attack from my [grand] division upon the enemy's right with a column of at least 30,000 men, to be sent in at daylight."[27]

Burnside, apparently agreeing, departed at about 6 P.M., saying he would send along orders soon. However, it was 7:30 A.M. on the thirteenth before Franklin got his instructions, and they were totally different from what he had proposed.

Burnside had come up with a wholly impractical plan with no hope of success. While confusingly ordering Franklin to keep his "whole command" ready for a rapid movement around Jackson's flank, he directed Franklin to send out "a division, at least," to seize Prospect Hill by direct assault and capture a military road the Rebels had cut along the ridge line. The aim was to roll up the Confederate flank from east to west along this road.[28]

After this attack had started and only on Burnside's order was Sumner at Fredericksburg to direct "a division or more" up the Orange Plank Road (now Virginia Route 3) and along the Telegraph Road "with a view to seizing the heights to the rear of the town." The Plank Road met the Telegraph Road near the foot of Marye's Heights, then continued over the heights, while the Telegraph Road circled around the base of Marye's Heights to the east and turned south through the valley of Hazel Run.[29]

The Federal battle was lost before it had begun. Burnside rejected concentrating against the Confederate right, which had at least an outside chance of turning Jackson's line. Instead he substituted two isolated attacks on the left and right, neither of which could be decisive or could support the other. More, he set out to assault the two points on Lee's line that were best prepared to receive him.

Franklin's attack was to be directly against Jackson on the ridge line. There Jackson was protected by woods that prevented accurate enemy artillery fire and along a line so short that he had no space for all his infantry. Jackson deployed only A. P. Hill's division on the front, with his three other divisions as support.[30]

The point of assault that Burnside had directed Sumner to make was equally impregnable. The Telegraph Road skirting the base of Marye's Heights was sunken a couple of feet below the grade and flanked with a stone wall, which formed a perfect defensive parapet impervious to rifle fire. In this Sunken Road of about a quarter of a mile McLaws had posted Brig. Gen. Thomas R. R. Cobb with three Georgia regiments. Extending this line westward another quarter mile to the Plank Road was the Twenty-fourth North Carolina emplaced in an infantry trench. There were about two thousand infantry in the Sunken Road and the trench.

In support on Marye's Heights above were about seven thousand more Rebel infantry of the divisions of McLaws and Robert Ransom, Jr., plus nine cannons of the Washington Artillery in easy canister range of any enemy approaching the Sunken Road. On the heights to the left, or west, of the Plank Road were eight more Confederate cannons, while eight additional guns, including two Parrott rifles, were on Lee's Hill, a 210-foot elevation a mile east. These guns could strike the flank of any advance against Marye's Heights.

When Longstreet suggested to Porter Alexander, commanding his largest artillery battalion, that he needed more guns, Alexander replied that the approach was so well covered that "a chicken could not live on that field when we open on it."[31]

On Jackson's line, fourteen cannons were emplaced on the extreme right, just above Hamilton's Crossing, but there was no other place for artillery except at the left of Jackson's position. There twelve guns had been advanced north of the railroad line that ran at the base of the ridge line, while twenty-one more were emplaced on the hill about two hundred yards behind.

A. P. Hill had deployed his six brigades well except for a single glaring error: between the brigades of James J. Archer and James H. Lane he had left a gap of about five hundred yards because the area consisted of marshy woodland overgrown with underbrush. This was the only part of Jackson's line where the woods extended beyond the railroad line. They offered a covered route by which enemy forces could advance onto the ridge line.

A Prussian officer of Stuart's staff, Heros von Borcke, had suggested cutting down the trees, but A. P. Hill had ignored the advice because he considered the swampy ground impassable. Behind this wooded area Maxcy Gregg's brigade was posted as a second line on the military road along the ridge. Behind Gregg were Early's and D. H. Hill's divisions. Any Federal penetration would not get far but would inflict unnecessary casualties.[32]

In the plain between Jackson's position and the river, Franklin lined up George G. Meade's division on his left, with John Gibbon's division supporting it on the rear right flank. Abner Doubleday's division deployed on the extreme left to defend against Stuart's cavalry. Just as Meade's three brigades started forward, Stuart's artillery chief, Maj. John Pelham, advanced two cannons on the flank of Meade's brigades and opened fire. Although more than a dozen Federal guns tried to silence him, and did disable one gun, "the gallant Pelham," as Lee would describe him, held up Meade's advance for an hour before Jackson ordered him to withdraw.

The Union hosts presented a spectacular sight spread out below the Confederates. Major von Borcke, awed, turned to Stonewall Jackson and expressed doubt whether the Rebels could stop the Yankee assault. Jackson replied: "Major, my men have sometimes failed to take a position but to defend one, never!"[33]

In preparation for Meade's advance, Federal guns opened a furious cannonade on Jackson's entire line. Jackson ordered all of the guns on Prospect Hill to remain silent to preserve the secrecy of their locations and to be ready to destroy Meade's infantry attack that would follow.

At about 11:30 A.M. Franklin, apparently believing that the Rebel cannons had been destroyed, ordered forward Meade's brigades. The broad lines of blue infantry advanced in silence. Not a gun fired on them. But the men serving the fieldpieces on Prospect Hill were waiting. On the flank, eight cannons from the army artillery reserve had joined Pelham. All were loaded, ranges set. When the Federal lines reached within eight hundred yards of the Confederate position, fire erupted from every Rebel cannon and shells tore great gaps in Meade's lines. The Union lines wavered, halted, and recoiled back beyond effective range. The attack failed, but Federal artillery had located the Confederate guns and for the next hour did great damage in counterbattery fire.

Gibbon went to Meade's support, forming a column of brigades on Meade's right flank, while Meade formed up two brigades on his front line with his third behind in close support. Now both divisions advanced against Jackson's line at around 1 P.M. Rebel artillery was weaker now but responded stoutly, and as the Federals came within range, Southern rifle fire staggered them. The twelve advanced Confederate cannons on the left had to pull back but Gibbon's brigades got no farther than the railroad line, losing more than twelve hundred men in a few minutes.

Meade's brigades discovered the wooded marshy area to their front to be mercifully free of Confederate missiles and hidden from view of Rebel soldiers. They pressed into this sector, finding it not too marshy to move, and advanced as a column of three brigades entirely through the woods and fell upon Archer's left flank and Lane's right, capturing about three hundred prisoners, routing two of Archer's regiments, and forcing Lane's brigade back into the woods.

Edward L. Thomas's brigade, on Lane's rear, attacked and quickly halted Meade's westernmost brigade while Archer's men held the easternmost brigade in a hot fight. Meade's center brigade, however, meeting no resistance, advanced unmolested and bore down on Gregg's unsuspecting brigade on the military road. Although Gregg's men quickly grasped their weapons and began firing, General Gregg himself thought that the force was Confederate and rushed forward to stop the firing. Almost instantly he was mortally wounded. One of Gregg's regiments collapsed but the rest held firm.

The Federals were now in deep trouble, far into the center of the Confederate position without support and already in confusion when Jackson ordered Early and Taliaferro to advance and clear the front. E. N. Atkinson's and Robert F. Hoke's brigades from Early's division, already deployed in line of battle, crashed into the Federals, driving Meade's entire division in panic and disorder out of woods, beyond the railroad line, and out into the plain. Gibbon's division likewise fell back in the chaos that ensued.

The Rebels were carried along by passion but they were not organized for a counterstroke, and fresh Union troops desperately rushed forward were able to stop them. The Confederates moved back to the railroad.

Meanwhile, Burnside, impatient that Franklin had not broken through on his left, had ordered Sumner's men to attack Marye's Heights to the west. Here a violent battle was raging. Burnside, seeking support, had sent orders to Franklin at around 1 P.M. to attack with his three-division Sixth Corps on the right of Gibbon. At 2 P.M. Burnside repeated the order, about the time Meade and Gibbons were being driven back. Franklin realized that these two divisions were entirely broken and moved up other forces to shore his left flank. He saw he had no hope of cracking Jackson's line and rationalized that it was too late in the day to make another effort. The failure to attack was to cost him his job.

Stonewall Jackson, seeing the enormous Federal force assembled against him, could not believe that the enemy would stop with an attack of only two divisions and waited for another assault. When it did not come he considered taking the offensive himself. But he called it off when he began a preliminary cannonade and found that the Federal artillery so dominated his front that any attack would be a massacre.

The losses on Jackson's front were about equal on both sides, 3,054 Confederate, 3,120 Federal. Had A. P. Hill not left open a huge door through which Meade could plunge, the Southern casualties would have been far less.

Sumner's attack against Marye Heights began at about noon. There had never been any possibility that his attack could support Franklin's, more than four air miles away. Burnside thus fought two separate battles, neither related to the other. Like Franklin's move against Jackson, Sumner's assault also was on a narrow front led by only a single division, William H. French's.

Despite Confederate artillery fire, the Federals were able to approach the Rebel position, using bridges to cross a large drainage ditch that ran between the town and Marye's Heights. Just south of the ditch was a considerable low, sheltered area where the brigades could form up for the charge. French's division assembled in a column of brigades—Nathan Kimball's in the front, forming a line two men deep, followed by John W. Andrews's, then Oliver H. Palmer's. In close support behind came Winfield S. Hancock's division, also in a column of brigades, with Samuel K. Zook's in the lead, followed by Thomas F. Meagher's and John C. Caldwell's.

The real trouble came as each brigade emerged over the low ridge and onto the largely open plateau between the Sunken Road and the ditch and became exposed to fire for perhaps four hundred yards. Only a few isolated houses, gardens, and fences provided bits of shelter along this entire glacis.

As Kimball's brigade came up over the slope, bayonets fixed, aiming directly at the Sunken Road, the men bent their heads against the hail of artillery and rifle fire that struck them, the Georgians in the Sunken Road resting their rifles on the top of the stone wall and firing with deliberate aim. Kimball's brigade got no closer than a hundred yards to the Sunken Road. The brigade lost 520 men in twenty minutes and disintegrated. Immediately behind came Andrews's brigade, suffering the same deadly fire but breaking sooner and losing 342 men. Palmer, next, lost 291 men before withdrawing.

Confederate general Ransom, seeing preparations for a further attack, reinforced Marye's Heights with John R. Cooke's North Carolina brigade, one regiment going into the Sunken Road and three occupying the crest of the hill.

Scattered remnants of French's division hid in slight depressions in the ground and kept up sporadic fire on the Sunken Road and the heights. Meanwhile, Hancock's division followed at around 12:30 P.M. in a repetition of the pattern and suffered the same results. Zook's brigade got within thirty or so yards of the Sunken Road but no farther, losing 527 men before falling back. Meagher's Irish Brigade lost 545 and Caldwell's 952, being nearly destroyed.

It was an insane waste, the outcome of each brigade assault a foregone conclusion. Yet Burnside obstinately insisted that the direct, head-on attacks continue, the men beating their heads against an impenetrable wall. Oliver O. Howard's division was next. He was preparing to attack to the right of the Plank Road, but Hancock, seeing that his division had been shattered, called for help and Howard followed in the same path as the previous two divisions.

By now the Federal soldiers realized that they were being ordered to their deaths or maiming, and when Howard's First Brigade, Joshua T. Owen's, advanced it did not push so far that it could be broken. Instead the men lay down where they could find a bit of cover. Owen's brigade held its position until nightfall, losing 258 men. Howard's Second Brigade, under Norman J. Hall, went in a little to the right of the ground covered in the preceding charges but got no farther. The brigade broke, rallied, charged again, fell back, and, finding a little shelter, halted and held on until night, losing 515 of its 800 men. Howard's Third Brigade, under Alfred Sully, remained in reserve, although two of its regiments went to reinforce Owen and another to aid Hall. It lost 122 men.

Four hours had passed. One entire Federal corps had been wrecked, over four thousand men lost. Eight separate battles had been fought against a Confederate force not half the corps's size and nothing had been accomplished.

The Federal attacks still were not finished. Sumner ordered up the division of Samuel D. Sturgis, positioned on French's left. Sturgis sent forward a battery and the brigade of Edward Ferrero. Fire from Lee's Hill quickly disabled the battery, killing its commander, while Ferrero's brigade advanced to the left of the ground over which French and Hancock had fought. This force, too, met severe Confederate fire and the men hid in depressions, firing their rifles and waiting out the day. About an hour after Ferrero had been stopped, Sturgis's Second Brigade, under James Nagle, marched in support of Ferrero but, finding some cover in Ferrero's rear, dropped down and spent the day firing at the Rebel lines. Ferrero lost 491 men, Nagle 500.

At about 3 P.M. Ferrero asked for reinforcements. Charles Griffin's division of Hooker's "grand division" had crossed the river and Sumner called on it. Griffin sent the brigade of James Barnes to Ferrero's aid. This brigade made a gallant advance against overwhelming fire and finally took cover with a loss of five hundred men.

Meanwhile, Amiel W. Whipple, commanding a division under Hooker, had occupied the western end of the town. Facing no Rebel forces, he sent one of his brigades, under Samuel S. Carroll, to the aid of Sturgis. When it arrived, Griffin placed one of his brigades, under Jacob B. Sweitzer, alongside it and sent both against the Sunken Road, supported by his last brigade, under T. B. W. Stockton.

This was the eleventh separate charge of the day but the fire from the Sunken Road was swelling, not decreasing. General Cobb had been killed and Cooke severely wounded. Brig. Gen. Joseph B. Kershaw had brought down into the road his South Carolina brigade and General Ransom the remaining three regiments of Cooke's North Carolina brigade. There were now six ranks of riflemen. Each rank fired, then moved back to reload while the next ranks fired in turn. The volleys from the Sunken Road were practically continuous, the bullets killing or wounding anyone who lifted his head.

Facing this incredible curtain of fire, Griffin's charge proceeded only to the point where the men, seeing they had no hope of carrying the road, found some cover and fell to the ground. The three brigades lost 541 men. Now ghastly barricades of dead, dying, and wounded men littered the ground in a broad swath beginning some one hundred yards from the Sunken Road and extending back toward the rise at the ditch.

It was now about 4 P.M. Burnside *still* insisted that the attacks go on, directing Hooker to attack with his whole force. Hooker had intact two divisions, those of George Sykes and Andrew A. Humphreys. Hooker, however, was certain that the Confederate line could not be carried and sent an aide to Burnside advising against another attack. Burnside replied that the attack must be made. Hooker himself crossed the river and tried to talk Burnside out of a hopeless effort. Burnside would not budge.

Hooker, resigned, returned to the front and prepared for another attack. He advanced as many batteries as he could find to the edge of the town and even sent two batteries across the ditch within three hundred yards of the Sunken Road. They suffered heavily from Rebel sharpshooter fire. While this was going on, soldiers in the hollows and dips of the ground reported that the Confederates were withdrawing. This report spread quickly and the Second Corps commander, Darius N. Couch, told General Humphreys: "Hancock reports the enemy is falling back. Now is the time for you to go in."[34]

In fact, the Confederates were not withdrawing. The misconception had arisen because the Washington Artillery on top of Marye's Heights had run out of ammunition, and Porter Alexander and a portion of his artillery battalion hurriedly exchanged places with it.

Humphreys immediately ordered forward the first of his two brigades, Peter H. Allabach's, without waiting for his second, under Erastus B. Tyler. Humphreys and Allabach led the charge. About two hundred yards past the ditch they reached the prone men left over from previous failed charges. Here, despite all of their commanders' efforts, the men also lay down and began to fire from prone positions. Humphreys could see that such fire was practically useless. With much difficulty Humphreys got the brigade on its feet and again pushed it into an advance. The brigade moved forward for only about fifty yards before it broke under the curtain of Confederate fire, some of the men halting where other remnants lay, others rushing back to the ditch.

After some delay Humphreys got Tyler's brigade formed up and ordered the men to charge with fixed bayonets and without firing. He was convinced that the Sunken Road could be carried only by an uninterrupted rush. He believed that the principal reason the previous charges had failed was that the brigades had stopped and fired volleys while charging. These halts had brought shattering Rebel fusillades and led to their disintegration.

Sundown was approaching. Burnside's orders grew urgent. He demanded that Marye's Heights be carried before dark. He called on George W. Getty's two-brigade division on the left, near Hazel Run, to attack but made no effort to have it simultaneous with Tyler's bayonet charge.

As Getty's division moved into position, Tyler's brigade advanced with loud hurrahs toward the men lying on the ground. These men resented a new line passing over them, since it seemed to reflect on their courage, and they did everything in their power to prevent the advance, some actually trying to stop Tyler's men physically. As the brigade passed beyond, the fear arose that the angry men left behind would fire into their backs.

Meanwhile, the cheers had alerted Alexander's gunners on Marye's Heights and they set to work firing full loads of canister at Tyler's advance, while the stone wall became a sheet of flame that enveloped the head and flanks of the column.

Tyler reported: "When we were within a very short distance of the enemy's line a fire was opened on our rear, wounding a few of my most valuable officers and, I regret to say, killing some of our men. Instantaneously the cry ran along our lines that we were being fired into from the rear. The column halted, receiving at the same time a terrible fire from the enemy. Orders for the moment were forgotten and a fire from our whole line was immediately returned. Another cry passed along our line, that we were being fired upon from the rear, when our brave men, after giving the enemy several volleys, fell back."[35]

Humphreys's forty-five-hundred-man division lost more than a thousand men in its two short advances.

These had been the twelfth and thirteenth charges against the Sunken Road. One more was still to follow. Getty's division had farther to advance to reach the field and arrived after Tyler had been defeated. The brigade of Rush C. Hawkins led the assault, directed at the eastern extremity of the Sunken Road, with Edward Harland's brigade to follow.

By now it was practically dark and Getty's charge was even more hopeless than the others. Even so, the darkness permitted Getty's men to get close to the Confederates. Then, some yards away, Hawkins's men opened fire. Their rifle flashes defined the line for the gunners on Marye's Heights, Lee's Hill, and various batteries beyond Hazel Run. A curtain of shells fell upon the hapless brigade. Even so, Hawkins's men got within a few yards of the Sunken Road when the Rebels in it opened a withering fire, while at the same time Federals lying down in their rear also fired into them.

Hawkins's men endured the fire front and rear for a brief time, but the men soon fled back to the ditch. Getty, seeing what had happened, kept Harland's brigade from moving forward.

This horrible day of battle at last ended. Only at two points had the Confederate army been tested. Large portions of the line had stood idle all day. Most of the Confederate officers believed that Burnside would renew the battle the next day. Burnside indeed intended to do so. His proposal for the fourteenth reveals how incompetent he was as a commander. The only plan he could think of was to form the entire three-division Ninth Corps into a column of regiments and lead it in person upon Marye's Heights—thus repeating the maneuver that had failed utterly on the twelfth.

After a long conference, Sumner, Hooker, and Franklin talked him out of the scheme.

The cost of the battle was staggering. The Federals lost 12,647 men, most killed or wounded, the Confederates 5,309. The disparity was greatest at Marye's Heights, with the Federals suffering five times as many losses as the Confederates.[36]

The two armies exchanged some idle fire on the fourteenth but it declined on the fifteenth. On the fifteenth Hooker and Franklin applied to Burnside for a truce to permit removal of the Federal wounded unattended between the lines. Burnside refused and the wounded around Marye's Heights remained. On Franklin's front, however, Jackson honored an informal cease-fire and the Union medical people tended to the surviving wounded and buried the dead. The night of the fifteenth was dark and rainy with a wind from the south. Burnside used it to withdraw his entire army during the night north of the river.

Stonewall Jackson had been right. The Confederates had whipped the Federal army but gained no advantage. The Federals had not been forced into disorder and retreat; they retained the initiative and easily could replace their losses. Jackson's hope for a great and decisive Confederate victory remained as elusive as ever.

NOTES

General sources: Allan, *Army of Northern Virginia,* 445–519; Dabney, 576–630; Cooke, 345–88; Palfrey, 136–90; Alexander, *Military Memoirs,* 276–313; Douglas, 179–207; Johnson and Buel, vol. 3, 70–147; Henderson, 544–96; Freeman, *R. E. Lee,* vol. 2, 415–73; Maurice, 157–73; Sears, 298–344; Freeman, *Lee's Lieutenants,* vol. 2, 226–396; Chambers, vol. 2, 235–308; Vandiver, 401–32; Edward J. Stackpole, *Drama on the Rappahannock: The Fredericksburg Campaign* (Harrisburg, Pa.: Military Publishing Company, 1957); and Vorin E. Whan, Jr., *Fiasco at Fredericksburg* (State College, Pa.: Pennsylvania State University Press, 1961).

1. He so wired Halleck at 8 A.M. on September 18. In his preliminary report on October 15, 1862, McClellan wrote: "A careful and anxious survey of the conditions of my command and my knowledge of the enemy's force and position failed to impress me with any reasonable certainty of success if I renewed the attack without reinforcing columns." See *Official Records,*

vol. 19, pt. 2, 322, and pt. 1, 32; Sears, 298; and Allan, *Army of Northern Virginia,* 442–43.

2. *Official Records,* vol. 19, pt. 1, 151 and 820; Freeman, *R. E. Lee,* vol. 2, 405; Maurice, 154; Douglas, 179; and Henderson, 542–44.
3. *Official Records,* vol. 19, pt. 1, 151 and 841; Johnson and Buel, vol. 2, 682; and Freeman, *R. E. Lee,* vol. 2, 406.
4. *Official Records,* vol. 19, pt. 1, 834, 957, and 982; Dabney, 557–58; Freeman, *R. E. Lee,* vol. 2, 406–7; Sears, 307; and Freeman, *Lee's Lieutenants,* vol. 2, 227–35.
5. Sears, 317–18; Roy P. Basler, *The Collected Works of Abraham Lincoln* (New Brunswick, N.J.: Rutgers University Press, 1953–55), vol. 5, 537; John Hope Franklin, *The Emancipation Proclamation* (Garden City, N.Y.: Doubleday, 1963), 61–62 and 66–67; and Freeman, *R. E. Lee,* vol. 2, 419. The Constitution (Article I, Section 9) permits suspension of the writ of habeas corpus only "in cases of rebellion or invasion" when "the public safety may require it."
6. Sears, 319–25; Alexander, *Military Memoirs,* 276; Maurice, 157–58 and 165; and Basler, vol. 5, 442 and 508. Brig. Gen. Francis Winthrop Palfrey writes: "There was in McClellan a sort of incapacity of doing anything till an ideal completeness of preparation was reached." (Palfrey, 134).
7. Alexander, *Military Memoirs,* 277; Palfrey, 130; Allan, *Army of Northern Virginia,* 450–52; and Sears, 325.
8. Freeman, *R. E. Lee,* vol. 2, 415–17; Alexander, *Military Memoirs,* 278–81; and *Official Records,* vol. 19, pt. 2, 625, 629, 640, 656–57, 660, 674, 679, 713, and 722. On November 20, 1862, the First Corps, under Longstreet, contained 34,916 men and 99 cannons; the Second Corps, under Jackson, counted 31,692 men and 98 cannons. Stuart's cavalry amounted to 9,146 men and 22 guns, and William N. Pendleton's reserve artillery had 36 guns and 718 men. The army also consolidated most of the remaining independent batteries into artillery battalions. Jackson kept his artillery attached to the separate divisions, while Longstreet allowed some artillery to remain with the divisions but formed as corps reserve artillery the nine-gun battalion of the Washington Artillery of New Orleans and the twenty-six-gun battalion of Col. E. Porter Alexander (formerly under S. D. Lee, promoted to brigadier general).
9. *Official Records,* vol. 19, pt. 2, 633–34 and 698–99; Freeman, *R. E. Lee,* vol. 2, 417–18; and Alexander, *Military Memoirs,* 278. Jackson's and Longstreet's promotions were announced on November 6, 1862. The army's cavalry also was reorganized into four brigades, and Lee's son Rooney was promoted to brigadier general and named to command one of the brigades.

10. *Official Records,* vol. 19, pt. 2, 626–27; and Allan, *Army of Northern Virginia,* 451.
11. Allan, *Army of Northern Virginia,* 452–55; Freeman, *R. E. Lee,* vol. 2, 422–23; Maurice, 166; and *Official Records,* vol. 19, pt. 2, 51.
12. Allan, *Army of Northern Virginia,* 455–56; Freeman, *R. E. Lee,* vol. 2, 426–28; Sears, 337–38; and *Official Records,* vol. 19, pt. 1, 88, and pt. 2, 703.
13. Sears, 332–34.
14. Allan, *Army of Northern Virginia,* 456–57; Alexander, *Military Memoirs,* 281–82; Sears, 339–44; and Freeman, *R. E. Lee,* vol. 2, 428. Burnside was an 1847 graduate of West Point, resigned from the army in 1853 to manufacture a new breech-loading rifle of his design, failed, got a railroad job through the efforts of George McClellan, commanded a brigade at First Manassas, captured Roanoke Island and New Bern in North Carolina in early 1862, gained command of the Ninth Corps, but at Antietam showed almost no initiative or imagination.
15. *Official Records,* vol. 19, pt. 2, 546 and 552; and Allan, *Army of Northern Virginia,*, 459.
16. Alexander, *Military Memoirs,* 284.
17. Ibid., 286; and *Official Records,* vol. 21, 46–48 and 84.
18. Alexander, *Military Memoirs,* 285–86; and Freeman, *R. E. Lee,* vol. 2, 430–31.
19. Allan, *Army of Northern Virginia,* 460; and Alexander, *Military Memoirs,* 286.
20. Although the Rappahannock River runs past Fredericksburg in a southeasterly direction, for simplification it is regarded in this account as running eastward and locations given as north or south of the river.
21. By this stage the Union had not only far more artillery than the Confederacy but also a far higher proportion of long-range rifled pieces. In the Army of the Potomac the ratio of rifled to smoothbore cannons was seven to three, in the Army of Northern Virginia two to three. The maximum *effective* range of rifles was about twenty-five hundred yards and of smoothbores fifteen hundred yards, though many could not reach this. Cannons fired solid shot from 350 yards out, shrapnel from 500 to 1,000 yards, canister from 500 yards in. The Federals had far more of the best rifled pieces used by both sides: twenty-pounder Parrott guns with a maximum range of 4,500 yards; ten-pounder Parrotts, range 6,200 yards; and three-inch ordnance guns, range 4,180 yards. The Army of the Potomac also used a twelve-pounder smoothbore with a range of 1,660 yards and both sides used the light twelve-pounder Napoleon gun with a range of 1,300 yards. A large proportion of Confederate smooth-

bores were six-pounder guns, range 1,525 yards, and twelve-pounder howitzers, range 1,070 yards, calibers discarded by the Federals as too light. Confederate ammunition also was defective, Federal largely good. Nearly all cannons on both sides were muzzle loaders. The Federals also had a few 4.5-inch "ordnance" guns and the Confederates a few English Blakely and Whitworth rifles. "Pounder" referred to the weight of the projectile fired, "inch" to the diameter of the bore. See Alexander, *Military Memoirs,* 280; Bigelow, 22–23 and 27–28; Ian V. Hogg, *Illustrated Encyclopedia of Artillery* (Secaucus, N.J.: Chartwell Books, 1988), 92, 194, and 248–49; and the Diagram Group, *Weapons, An International Encyclopedia* (New York: St. Martin's Press, 1990), 171, 174–75, and 179.

22. Dabney, 595–96; Johnson and Buel, vol. 3, 72; Alexander, *Military Memoirs,* 288; Longstreet, 299; Freeman, *R. E. Lee,* vol. 2, 431 and 439; *Official Records,* vol. 21, 1029; and Henderson, 572–73.

23. Alexander, *Military Memoirs,* 288; and Allan, *Army of Northern Virginia,* 470. Lee deliberately avoided building elaborate fortifications and earthworks at Fredericksburg to deceive Burnside. The natural position there was so strong that fortifications might convince Burnside it was impregnable. Instead, by feigning weakness Lee invited attack. See Freeman, *R. E. Lee,* vol. 2, 441–42.

24. *Official Records,* vol. 21, 578; Johnson and Buel, vol. 3, 73 and 86; Freeman, *R. E. Lee,* vol. 2, 443–48; and Alexander, *Military Memoirs,* 291–92.

25. Once in the town, Union officers and men looted the houses and offices systematically.

26. Jubal Early wrote: "Had Burnside moved down the river to the Massaponax after crossing or had thrown other bridges across at or near the mouth of that stream and crossed one of his grand divisions there, he would inevitably have forced us to abandon our line of defense and fight him on other ground." See Jubal A. Early, *Autobiographical Sketch and Narrative of the War Between the States* (Philadelphia: J. B. Lippincott Company, 1912), 183; and Whan, 53.

27. Palfrey, 150–51; Allan, *Army of Northern Virginia,* 475; and testimony of Franklin, December 19, 1862, in U.S. Senate, *Report of the Joint Committee on the Conduct of the War,* report no. 108 (Washington, D.C.: Government Printing Office, 1863), vol. 2 707.

28. Burnside used a large balloon for observation on December 13, 1862. It was hoisted a thousand feet into the air behind his headquarters and operated by T. S. C. Lowe, an aeronaut. The heavy woods limited Lowe's observations of the Confederates but he provided valuable information on Union troop movements. See Whan, 57; and *Official Records,* series III, vol. 3, 294.

29. Palfrey, 152–53 and 160; Alexander, *Military Memoirs,* 294; Freeman, *R. E. Lee,* vol. 2, 457–60; *Official Records,* vol. 21, 70 and 90–91; Whan, 54–55 and 62; and U.S. Senate, 652. Burnside's order to Franklin gave the impression that he still contemplated a sweep around Jackson's flank, since he required Franklin to keep his command ready to march down the old Richmond, or River, Road which ran along the river. This motivated Franklin to assault Prospect Hill with only a small part of his force. According to Burnside's testimony to the Committee on the Conduct of the War, however, he never actually planned a flank attack down the River Road but hoped to crack Jackson's position by a direct assault on Prospect Hill. Around Marye's Heights the Federal commanders made no effort to advance directly up the Plank Road. They also attempted no assault farther west, where the Confederate guns were fewer and less advantageously placed. Instead the assaults on the west went in wholly against the steepest part of the heights and directly against the Telegraph Road.

30. There were few breastworks or emplacements shielding cannons along the Confederate line, except some in Longstreet's sector. The frozen ground and short period of occupation of Prospect Hill had not allowed Jackson's men time to emplace. Officers were now aware of the importance of field fortifications and the battle was to prove their effectiveness. Thereafter the two armies used them regularly. See E. Porter Alexander in *Southern Historical Society Papers,* vol. 10, 384; and Whan, 61.

31. Johnson and Buel, vol. 3, 79.

32. A. P. Hill apparently did not inform Jackson on December 12 about the gap. Otherwise it is almost certain that he would have sealed it. On the morning of December 13 Jackson rode the line and stopped to study the boggy wood that projected toward the Union forces. "The enemy will attack here," he said grimly. But with battle imminent it was hazardous to make major realignments. In his report on the battle Jackson drew attention to Hill's failure to close the gap. See Dabney, 610; Freeman, *Lee's Lieutenants,* vol. 2, 343 and 347; *Official Records,* vol. 21, 631–33; and Allan, *Army of Northern Virginia,* 478–79.

33. Heros von Borcke, *Memoirs of the Confederate War for Independence* (New York: Peter Smith, 1938), vol. 2, 117. This was the first time anyone recorded Jackson as making this statement, which he later repeated and which distilled his theory for destroying the Union army.

34. Alexander, *Military Memoirs,* 306.

35. Ibid., 309.

36. Ibid., 313. Johnson and Buel (vol. 3, 145 and 147) have slightly different figures.

15

HOOKER FLANKS LEE AT CHANCELLORSVILLE

★ ★ ★ As the year 1863 began, the situation for the Confederacy appeared favorable, at least on the surface. The Army of Northern Virginia had thrown back the latest Northern effort at Fredericksburg, in a battle that demonstrated the bankruptcy of Union military leadership. Lee and his soldiers might not be able to force the North to stop the war but they nevertheless appeared to be unbeatable.

Yet the winter of 1863 revealed profound cracks in the Confederate facade. In the west the Federals had wrested control of Kentucky and Tennessee and had seized all but a narrow stretch of the Mississippi River. On January 1 Abraham Lincoln issued his formal Emancipation Proclamation, giving freedom to slaves of masters living in states in rebellion. This had little immediate domestic effect but its impact overseas was decisive—no European state now could side openly with the Confederacy and thereby endorse human bondage.[1] This had been the heritage of Lee's insistence on fighting, and losing, the battle of Antietam.

There was one additional heritage of Lee's leadership that was not so well recognized. At first glance the results had been spectacular since Lee had taken command of the army seven months previously. Lee had sustained 48,171 casualties, while inflicting 70,725.[2] Yet these figures hid a devastating truth: during this period, his army had given up 4,077 prisoners, while it had captured 29,370 Federal soldiers. Since prisoners could be exchanged, this meant that the *actual* Confederate losses, killed and wounded, amounted to 44,094, while the actual Federal losses were 41,345. Lee had suffered *more* real losses than the Federals. With less than one-third the white population of the North, the South could not long endure Lee's method of waging war.

Meanwhile, the Army of the Potomac grew enormously, reaching well over twice the size of the Army of Northern Virginia.[3] Indeed, Lee began to lose troops in early January because of exaggerated fears that the Federals were moving inland from positions they held at New Bern, North Carolina, and Suffolk, Virginia. President Davis and James A. Seddon, who had replaced George W. Randolph as Confederate secretary of war on November 15, 1862, ordered the small division of Robert Ransom, Jr., to North Carolina on January 3 and soon after sent native son D. H. Hill to command the North Carolina department.[4]

General Burnside recognized that his handling of the battle of Fredericksburg had damaged his reputation deeply. He had to advance quickly or President Lincoln would remove him. Burnside knew he could not repeat a frontal attack on Fredericksburg, while crossing the broad Rappahannock east of the town would be extremely difficult. At last he undertook a move on January 19 that had been obvious all along—crossing the river over the narrower fords to the west. But violent rain fell on the twentieth and continued for days and the Federal advance stalled in deep mud.[5]

The "mud march" was the last straw. Lincoln removed Burnside on January 25 and replaced him with "Fighting Joe" Hooker, forty-nine years old, a West Pointer of such complete political ineptitude that not only had he criticized Burnside so openly that Burnside wanted him dismissed from the army, but he had denounced Lincoln as incompetent and suggested that the Union needed a dictator.[6]

Neither Lincoln nor anyone in his cabinet was impressed with Hooker's military abilities. His selection had come almost wholly because he was free from political aspirations and was not a possible rival to Lincoln for the presidency in 1864. Lincoln wrote him on January 26 that "only generals who gain successes can set up dictators. What I now ask of you is military success and I will risk the dictatorship."[7]

But, though Hooker immediately began building supplies and reorganizing his army, abandoning Burnside's cumbersome "grand divisions" and forming seven corps, he could not seek military success immediately. Hard cold set in and both Union and Confederate armies moved into winter quarters and waited for the spring.[8] In February, however, Burnside's Ninth Corps moved by sea to the Union post at Fort Monroe on the peninsula, raising alarm in Richmond that the Federals were planning to march up the James River valley toward the capital or were planning adventures in North Carolina or against the port of Charleston, South Carolina.

Lee quickly sent George Pickett's division and soon after dispatched John Bell Hood's division, both of Longstreet's First Corps. On February 17 he directed General Longstreet to go south and take command. This left Lee with about 60,000 men and 170 guns to meet Hooker's 133,000 men and 428 guns.[9]

Now ensued a diversion of Confederate strength and attention that was to have enormous effects. The assignment south aroused the ambitions of James Longstreet. Although the Federal Ninth Corps soon departed Fort Monroe for Kentucky and Washington sent no substantial reinforcements either to Tidewater, Virginia, or to New Bern, Longstreet became excited by the suggestion of Secretary Seddon to attack Suffolk, a few miles west of Norfolk.

This was an unpardonable blunder. The Federals were garrisoning Suffolk with only twenty thousand troops. Although they restricted the freedom of Confederate commissary officers in requisitioning hams and bacon in the rich hog-growing country west of Suffolk, they presented no strategic danger. Longstreet, Seddon, and President Davis ignored the fact that the principal Federal objective was the Army of Northern Virginia or that, even if Longstreet seized Suffolk, 120 miles from the Rappahannock, it would have no effect on Hooker.

Longstreet pursued an investment of Suffolk that failed to capture the town yet held more than twenty thousand Confederate troops out of the titanic confrontation about to take place between Lee and Hooker. If present, these troops might have made a profound difference in what the Confederates could have accomplished.

Longstreet demonstrated his willingness to sacrifice strategic considerations to his own ambition, but Lee also exhibited a severe weakness of will by not demanding from Davis and Seddon concentration on the main danger to the Confederacy—the Army of the Potomac. Lee took the position that if President Davis thought the need was greater to the south, he would dispatch troops from his army immediately. He always bowed to the civilian leadership of the Confederacy, although this leadership was often militarily inept and succumbed to pressure from politicians who did not want their territories occupied by Federals irrespective of the Confederacy's strategic needs.[10]

★ ★ ★

The first clash in the 1863 campaign was a cavalry engagement on March 17 at Kelly's Ford, twenty-three air miles upstream from Fredericksburg. The Federal cavalry, much improved from the year previous, came off well against Stuart's veterans, and the gallant horse-artilleryman, John Pelham, died from a shell burst. Even so, the Federal cavalry withdrew back across the Rappahannock and the only consequence was to show Lee and Jackson that Hooker was looking westward to make at least part of his general advance.

Upstream the river was narrower, the roads firmer, and the fords more accessible. Lee decided that the turning movement would be in this direction and it would be centered on United States Ford, nine air miles northwest of Fredericksburg. Lee picked this ford because it gave access to Chancellorsville, three miles south, a crossroads where four roads came together, including the Orange Plank Road and Orange Turnpike. If Hooker got on the Plank Road and turnpike (present-day Virginia Route 3) he might press on Lee's flank and drive him out of Fredericksburg.[11]

However, this was not Hooker's original proposal, which had two parts. The first was to send the bulk of his army over the Rappahannock east of Fredericksburg, while crossing or pretending to cross with minor forces at and near U.S. Ford. He hoped to cut the Richmond, Fredericksburg and Potomac Railroad (RF&P), Lee's major supply line, and prevent Lee from attacking his supply base at Aquia Creek, a dozen miles northeast of Fredericksburg. Hooker believed Rebel counterespionage, which spread the false word that Lee had a large pontoon bridge and planned to cross the river.

The second part of Hooker's plan was to send most of his cavalry southwest to seize Gordonsville and other points on the Virginia Central Railroad, then turn east and block the retreat of Lee's army while cutting the RF&P near Ashland, just north of Richmond.

Hooker believed that these movements would force Lee to evacuate Fredericksburg and retreat toward Richmond or Gordonsville, primarily because the Confederate supply system had difficulty keeping more than a few days' rations with the army and Lee would have to fall back on his depots to feed his men.[12] Hooker thus theorized that he could destroy Lee's retreating army by attacking it from the north while Union cavalry blocked its movement southward.

Even if Union cavalry was successful in cutting the railway lines to the south, it was unrealistic to expect Lee's army to turn tail and run the moment its food supply was threatened. Much of this army had subsisted on green corn and apples for days the previous summer and could pull in its belt again, if need be. It also was senseless strategically, because the war already had proved that cavalry could not stand up to infantry fire. The Confederates could have reopened the railroads by sending infantry to drive Union cavalry away. Finally, Lee and Jackson had little history of running; quite the opposite. If they did not run, the cavalry strike would be a blow in the air. In the meantime, much of the Federal cavalry would be unavailable to serve as Hooker's eyes and ears.[13]

Nevertheless, the cavalry strike went forward on April 14, 1863, with about 10,300 cavalrymen under Maj. Gen. George Stoneman beginning to cross the river northwest of Rappahannock Station (present-day Remington). Heavy rain set in early on the fifteenth and continued with short intervals for two weeks. The subsequent rise of the river led Hooker to abandon his first plan.

Now he came up with a new plan that was remarkable in its originality and surprise. According to Porter Alexander, it was "decidedly the best strategy conceived in any of the campaigns ever set on foot against us."[14] It took full advantage of the fact that the Federal army outnumbered the Confederate two to one.

The plan called for two Union corps under Maj. Gen. John Sedgwick to cross the river below Fredericksburg and hold the main Confederate army in its positions on the heights behind the town. Meanwhile, three additional Union corps would march upstream—not to the obvious crossing of U.S. Ford, where Confederate outposts were on alert—but all the way to Kelly's Ford.

There it would cross, turn back down the south bank, and seize from the *south* both U.S. Ford and Banks Ford, five miles west of Fredericksburg.[15] Seizing these fords would put the two wings of the Union army back into contact while unhinging the elaborate Confederate defensive line at Fredericksburg, where Lee's troops had been entrenching since beating Burnside in December.

The brilliance of this plan was that Kelly's Ford was twelve miles above the junction of the Rappahannock and Rapidan rivers. Any movement that far upstream would imply that the Federals were heading toward the Shenandoah Valley, *not* that they intended to cross the river and turn back east. Another factor reinforced this perception: moving down the south bank required a second difficult river crossing, over the Rapidan. Lee would not expect Hooker to go to such extremes to deceive him. Consequently, Hooker was likely to get on Lee's flank almost without opposition.

The Federal campaign started early on April 27, with the Fifth, Eleventh, and Twelfth corps, forty-two thousand men, marching in great secrecy toward Kelly's Ford.

The next day Maj. Gen. Darius N. Couch's seventeen thousand–man Second Corps, except John Gibbon's division, which remained at Falmouth to deceive the Confederates, marched to the north sides of the U.S. and Banks fords. Couch's purpose was to make the Confederates believe that the Federals were preparing to force crossings at these points. Stoneman's cavalry also was supposed to undertake its raid on the railways, but the men found the fords difficult and were slow getting under way.

Meanwhile, General Sedgwick prepared the First and Sixth corps, forty thousand men, to cross the Rappahannock early on the twenty-ninth at two points about three miles below Fredericksburg, opposite the right wing of the Confederate army under Stonewall Jackson. The remaining Union corps, the 18,700-man Third, under Maj. Gen. Daniel E. Sickles, stayed at Stafford Heights ready to reinforce either wing as required.[16]

Lee did not get early word of the magnitude of the march on his left flank. Outposts reported the movement on the twenty-eighth, but Lee believed that the force was moving toward the Shenandoah.[17] By 10 P.M., April 28, Federal soldiers were crossing Kelly's Ford on pontoon bridges and by the morning of the twenty-ninth all three corps were across.

Jeb Stuart guessed the Federal force at about a third its actual size and, now believing that it was headed toward Gordonsville, blocked movement in that direction. The Federals turned southeast, scattered, or captured Rebel pickets and waded Germanna and Ely's fords on the Rapidan, putting their ammunition and haversacks on the tips of their bayonets to keep them out of the chest-high water.

Meanwhile, shielded by fog, Sedgwick crossed the Rappahannock on hastily built pontoon bridges in front of Jackson's corps on the morning of April 29 and began entrenching along the river bank. Jackson proposed an attack. Lee demurred and after Jackson studied the situation he agreed, since Federal cannons on Stafford Heights still dominated the plain over which the Confederates would have to assault.

By the afternoon of the twenty-ninth couriers had informed Lee of the passage of Germanna and Ely's fords. Lee now realized that Stuart's earlier belief in a march toward Gordonsville was wrong and that the Federal force was descending on his left flank. Lee saw that the Chancellorsville crossroads were the immediate Federal objective and dispatched Richard H. Anderson's division to Chancellorsville at once.

By the morning of the thirtieth Stuart had captured prisoners from the three Union corps on the left and Lee now learned the size of the force—two-thirds as large as his entire army. He instructed Anderson to select and entrench a strong position. Anderson moved back about four miles east of Chancellorsville to Zoan Church and began digging in.[18]

Soon afterward Hooker's forces arrived at Chancellorsville and occupied U.S. Ford, where engineers promptly threw up pontoon bridges. The instructions of Henry W. Slocum, commanding the Twelfth Corps and in tactical charge of the whole move, had been to advance straight to seize Banks Ford. But during the morning Hooker ordered his entire right wing to halt at Chancellorsville and await an enemy attack.[19]

During the day the three Union corps closed in on the crossroads, having marched forty-six miles in three days and achieved much. Hooker had maneuvered Lee out of position without a battle. The Confederate line had been flanked and lay exposed directly in front of him. Heavy reinforcements were coming up—two divisions of the Second Corps and all of the Third Corps.

Soon Hooker would have well over 70,000 men and 208 guns on Lee's flank.

However, Hooker had *not* achieved his single most important objective: Banks Ford, about five air miles farther east, which would open a direct connection between both wings of his army. Hooker knew from his intelligence reports that Lee's main army was still at Fredericksburg. Anderson's division was the only force in front of him and it had no entrenchments. One of Hooker's greatest failures was his refusal to press on April 30 to seize the great prize of Banks Ford.[20]

During most of April 30 Lee remained undecided about where Hooker was aiming his principal blow. As the day wore on, however, he became convinced that it was coming from his left flank, not Sedgwick. One reason was that Sedgwick did practically nothing. Hooker had ordered him to demonstrate at 1 P.M. against the Confederate right flank at Hamilton's Crossing, but if he was certain that Jackson was still in force, he was to call it off. Sedgwick found Jackson's line fully occupied and so canceled the demonstration.

This failure to require Sedgwick to attack was a fatal error. The principal reason for most moves against an enemy's flank is to strike at a weakly defended point. One of the surest ways of achieving this is to hold the enemy in place along his front by a powerful attack and thereby prevent him from transferring troops to meet the new threat.

By failing to hold the Confederates at Fredericksburg, Hooker allowed Lee to move his main force to his left flank. This Lee now commenced, ordering Lafayette McLaws to march his division as soon as possible to aid Anderson at Zoan Church, leaving only William Barksdale's Mississippi brigade to defend Marye's Heights. He also ordered Stonewall Jackson to march his corps at daylight the next day to Zoan Church and there take charge and "repulse the enemy." Jackson was to leave only Jubal Early's division, along with William Nelson Pendleton's army reserve artillery, at Fredericksburg.[21]

Thus, by nightfall on August 30—having been restrained in no way by Sedgwick—Lee began concentrating about 48,000 men and 144 guns on the west to confront Hooker. The remainder of his army, about ten thousand men plus Pendleton's artillery, he left on the Fredericksburg heights under Early.

Hooker summed up his expectations with an order of the day: "Our enemy must either ingloriously fly or come out from behind his defenses and give us battle on our own ground, where certain destruction awaits him."[22] Hooker was confident that Lee would "ingloriously fly," as John Pope had done under similar circumstances the summer previous. In the unlikely event that this did not happen, Hooker did *not* plan to attack Lee. Rather, he intended to stand on the defensive.

Burnside's humiliating defeat at Fredericksburg in December had impressed itself deeply upon Hooker. Like Jackson, he had become aware that the Minié ball plus entrenchments had so strengthened the defense that attacks, no matter how strongly made, were likely to fail.

Thus, despite the tremendous strategic advantage he had gained by getting on Lee's flank, Hooker shrank from carrying his advance to its logical conclusion: evicting Lee from his entrenchments, falling on the disordered Confederate army, and shattering it.

Hooker believed that Lee—as soon as he learned of Hooker's presence on his flank—would evacuate Fredericksburg and flee south or southwestward. Hooker did not anticipate that Lee was moving the bulk of his army to him and expected only token resistance on May 1 for the small advance he *did* plan: marching eastward to seize Banks Ford and get out of the singular dark forest known as the Wilderness. In the open country he planned to build field fortifications, deploy his artillery, and stand on the defensive.

The eastern edge of the Wilderness lay about a mile down the road toward Fredericksburg. The original forest, stretching fourteen miles along the Rappahannock and eight to ten miles to the south, had been cleared over the previous half century to make charcoal for iron furnaces in the area. A dense second growth of briars, underbrush, pine, cedar, and low-branched hardwood coppices had created a strange region where visibility extended only a few feet, walking was difficult, and deployment of Hooker's greatest strength, his artillery, was possible only along the few roads and in the few open spaces.[23]

As important militarily to Hooker as reaching the open fields to the east of Chancellorsville was gaining possession of Banks Ford. Without this crossing he would have to fight on two fronts, with Lee in Napoleon's central position between them, able to turn to whichever front was more endangered.

Sure that Lee would retreat, Hooker saw no danger in sending off all of his cavalry with Stoneman except about thirteen hundred horsemen under Alfred Pleasonton. He relied instead on technology to provide the information he needed as to Lee's movements, laying a special telegraph line between his two wings, sending up three captive balloons, and establishing observation posts on heights. But wagons, caissons, and other objects kept breaking his telegraph wires and night marching and river mists hid Confederate columns from observers.

Hooker did not worry about Stuart's cavalry because he was confident that Stoneman's strike against the railways would draw off all of Stuart's forty-four hundred horsemen. This was Hooker's single greatest error, for Stuart detached only about a thousand troopers under W. H. F. (Rooney) Lee to watch Stoneman's ten thousand and concentrated his now-superior strength at the critical point—the front of *both* armies.

This gave Lee and Jackson quick information about every Federal movement and position and denied Rebel information to the Federals, for Pleasonton could not penetrate Stuart's cavalry shield to reconnoiter. And since Lee ignored the cuts to his railway lines, Stoneman's move degenerated into a long but pointless raid.

★ ★ ★

While Hooker wasted precious hours on the morning of May 1 waiting for the last of his reinforcements, the Third Corps, to come up, Stonewall Jackson was marching swiftly to meet him. Jackson had got his corps under way at 3 A.M. and at 8 A.M. he arrived at Zoan Church and took command.

Hooker's plans were to push two divisions of George G. Meade's Fifth Corps along the River Road to uncover Banks Ford, George Sykes's division of the Fifth Corps along the Orange Turnpike toward Zoan Church, and General Slocum's Twelfth Corps along the Orange Plank Road, which arched south from Chancellorsville and then back onto the turnpike near Zoan Church.

Hooker expected Rebel forces in front to retreat hastily in the face of such Federal power. He assumed that Meade would have Banks Ford in his possession shortly and that the main Federal army would be around Zoan Church—out of the Wilderness and with plenty of open space to deploy his infantry and his vastly superior artillery.[24]

Jackson's orders from Lee were only to repulse the enemy. However, Jackson knew the nature of the Wilderness and the extremely constricting effect it could have on military operations. He immediately made a dramatic decision, ordering his forces to advance, abandoning the defensive position that Lee's engineers had laid out for Anderson and McLaws to entrench.

Jackson saw—if he could push Hooker back *into* the Wilderness—that he could severely cripple Federal artillery. He knew, of course, that the Wilderness offered excellent opportunities for defending troops to throw up abatis of logs and brush and make attacks extremely difficult. But both sides could build abatis and entrenchments, whereas bottling up Hooker's guns would equalize the odds between Federals and Confederates.

This was one of Jackson's most masterful decisions. In a stroke Jackson turned a desperate situation that threatened a decisive Confederate defeat into an opportunity for a spectacular victory. By ordering his troops to advance down the pike and Plank Road, he blocked Hooker from deploying in open country, where, with seventy thousand men and over two hundred guns, he would have been practically unbeatable.

In the event Jackson's move had even greater effect. For his advance stunned Hooker, who realized that Lee's army was not withdrawing in panic but had turned on him like a lion and had upset his plan of operation. Instead of making the best of the situation and using his immensely greater power to drive Jackson back so as to reach Banks Ford and the open country to the east, Hooker *withdrew* to Chancellorsville.

Hooker's distraction can be shown in a strange wire he sent at 2 P.M. to his chief of staff, Maj. Gen. Daniel Butterfield, at Falmouth: "From character of information have suspended attack. The enemy may attack me—I will try it. Tell Sedgwick to keep a sharp lookout and attack if he can succeed."[25]

The "information" Hooker had received consisted of two reports: that fifteen thousand or more men had moved from Fredericksburg toward Chancellorsville (this was Jackson's force), while he believed, due to his inadequate cavalry and poor balloon and from observation post reports—that troops at Fredericksburg had not been reduced. Hooker therefore jumped to the erroneous conclusion that Lee had been powerfully reinforced.[26]

Even so, Hooker knew he still possessed far greater strength than Lee. The "information" only provided an excuse to cover the shattering of his confidence that Jackson's advance had produced.

The events of May 1 demonstrate how the action of one commander can work on the mind of another commander to impair his capacity to respond in a rational manner. They show that in the end, battles—and wars—are *not* won by soldiers and weapons but by one commander's mastering the mind of another.[27]

NOTES

General sources: Dabney, 660–71; Cooke, 388–464; Doubleday, 1–19; Johnson and Buel, vol. 3, 152–243; Henderson, 598–662; Alexander, *Military Memoirs,* 317–28; Alexander, *Fighting for the Confederacy,* 194–203; Bigelow, 3–257; Freeman, *Lee's Lieutenants,* vol. 2, 397–538; Freeman, *R. E. Lee,* vol. 2,

476–519; Chambers, vol. 2, 309–79; Vandiver, 433–62; Jedediah Hotchkiss and William Allan, *Chancellorsville* (New York: D. Van Nostrand, 1867), 5–41; and Theodore A. Dodge, *The Campaign of Chancellorsville* (Boston: James R. Osgood and Company, 1881), 1–61.

1. Lincoln exempted from provisions of the proclamation the slave states that did not secede (Delaware, Maryland, Kentucky, and Missouri) and all areas of the Confederacy occupied by Federal troops on January 1, 1863. These included large parts of Louisiana, West Virginia, parts of eastern Virginia, and Tennessee. See *Harvard Classics,* vol. 43, *American Historical Documents* (New York: P. F. Collier and Son, 1910), 344–46.

2. Freeman, *R. E. Lee,* vol. 2, 477.

3. Bigelow, 19; Henderson, 639–40; Freeman, *R. E. Lee,* vol. 2, 506; and *Official Records,* vol. 25, pt. 2, 320 and 696.

4. Freeman, *R. E. Lee,* vol. 2, 478–79; Freeman, *Lee's Lieutenants,* vol. 2, 421–27; and Henderson, 644–45.

5. Freeman, *Lee's Lieutenants,* vol 2, 429; *Official Records,* vol. 21, 68–69, 753–54, and 1101; and Freeman, *R. E. Lee,* vol. 2, 479–80.

6. He said in the battle of Fredericksburg in December 1862 that he went in and fought his troops "until he thought he had lost as many men as he was ordered [by Burnside] to lose." See Dodge, 13.

7. Bigelow, 8–10; Johnson and Buel, vol. 3, 217 and 239; Alexander, *Military Memoirs,* 373; Freeman, *Lee's Lieutenants,* vol. 2, 429; and Freeman, *R. E. Lee,* vol. 2, 484.

8. The Army of Northern Virginia suffered severely from inadequacies of the Confederate commissary system during this winter. Only the efforts of the soldiers' families, who sent food from home, prevented severe repercussions. See Henderson, 629; *Official Records,* vol. 25, pt. 2, 686–88 and 730; Alexander, *Military Memoirs,* 318–19; Freeman, *Lee's Lieutenants,* vol. 2, 477–78; and Freeman, *R. E. Lee,* vol. 2, 491–96.

9. Freeman, *R. E. Lee,* vol. 2, 483; Bigelow, 53–54 and 132–38; and Henderson, 650.

10. Henderson, 645–47; Freeman, *R. E. Lee,* vol. 2, 478–79 and 499–501; Bigelow, 114–19; and *Official Records,* vol. 21, 1096–97. Freeman, (*Lee's Lieutenants,* vol. 2, 467–94) discusses Longstreet's operations in detail.

11. The Orange Plank Road and Orange Turnpike ran together out of Fredericksburg for about five miles to a point just east of Zoan Church, about

four and a half miles east of Chancellorsville. There the Plank Road arched southward but rejoined the turnpike at Chancellorsville. The two roads ran together for about two miles to Dowdall's Tavern (also known as Wilderness Church), where the Plank Road diverged south and pursued a more southerly course to Orange Court House. Present-day Virginia Route 3 pursues the course of the old turnpike past Dowdall's Tavern, while Virginia Route 610 traces the easterly arc of the Plank Road and Virginia Route 621 that part diverging at Dowdall's.

12. Doubleday, 4–5.

13. Henderson, 647–49; and Bigelow, 112 and 139–40.

14. Alexander, *Fighting for the Confederacy,* 195.

15. Bigelow, 165–67.

16. Henderson, 647–48 and 650; and Bigelow, 173–86 and 188.

17. *Official Records,* vol. 25, pt. 1, 796; and Bigelow, 193.

18. Accounts also listed this church as Zion and Zoar. The church was on the turnpike about a mile and a quarter west of the junction of the turnpike and the Orange Plank Road and was immediately west of the entrenchments Anderson and McLaws began constructing on the morning of May 1, 1863. This position also was known as Tabernacle Church, named for the house of worship on the Mine Road three-quarters of a mile southwest of the turnpike–Plank Road junction. The Mine Road cut across the Plank Road and joined the turnpike a third of a mile east of Zoan Church. The intersections of all three of these roads collectively were known as Zoan Church or Tabernacle Church. They are carried here as Zoan Church.

19. Bigelow, 213–16. Why he thought he might be attacked is unclear, since only Anderson's division was nearby and was no match for him.

20. Doubleday, 10.

21. Freeman, *R. E. Lee,* vol. 2, 516; Lee, 86; Bigelow, 232–35; and Freeman, *Lee's Lieutenants,* vol. 2, 527–28.

22. Henderson, 654; and Bigelow, 223.

23. Alexander, *Fighting for the Confederacy,* 197; Henderson, 656; Alexander, *Military Memoirs,* 325; and Dabney, 668.

24. Henderson, 659; *Official Records,* vol. 25, pt. 2, 324; Freeman, *Lee's Lieutenants,* vol. 2, 531–37; and Bigelow, 238–55.

25. Alexander, *Military Memoirs,* 327; Bigelow, 250–51; Freeman, *Lee's Lieutenants,* vol. 2, 647; and *Official Records,* vol. 25, pt. 2, 326 and 328.

26. Henderson (660–61) says that in retiring, "Hooker did what most ordinary generals would have done." This was because before moving out of Chancellorsville he had entrenched his position there. Thus, by returning to prepared positions he felt that his defensive position would be strengthened. However, Henderson points out that defensive works are useless if their flanks are not protected from being turned.

27. Porter Alexander (*Fighting for the Confederacy,* 216) writes: "The most striking feature for me of the military history of the battle is the perfect collapse of the moral courage of Hooker, as commander in chief, as soon as he found himself in the actual presence of Lee and Jackson." General Couch, Second Corps commander, reported to Hooker on the evening of May 1, 1863. "I have got Lee just where I want him," Hooker said. "He must fight me on my own ground." Later Couch wrote: "To hear from his own lips that the advantages gained by the successful marches of his lieutenants were to culminate in fighting a defensive battle in that nest of thickets was too much and I retired from his presence with the belief that my commanding general was a whipped man." See Johnson and Buel, vol. 3, 161; and Bigelow, 259. Hooker's decision to retreat mystified and angered many other of his commanders. See Dodge, 49–55. Douglas Freeman (*Lee's Lieutenants,* vol. 2, 647) points out that "all the advantages that had been won by a surprise crossing of the Rappahannock were thrown away in that single decision [to withdraw to Chancellorsville]. From that hour, the initiative in the Wilderness was with Lee."

16

"LET US PASS OVER THE RIVER"

★ ★ ★ On Friday evening, May 1, 1863, the leading elements of Jackson's force were less than a mile from Chancellorsville, around which Joseph Hooker's army was drawn in an arc to the east and south with additional forces spread out to the Rappahannock to shield U.S. Ford. Around the large two-story brick Chancellor house with a porch framed by pillars—all there was to Chancellorsville—were several hundred acres of open ground.[1] Before they had left in the morning, Hooker's men had begun to build entrenchments, which they extended when they returned that evening.

During the late afternoon Lee had reconnoitered Hooker's left in hopes of finding a place to turn the line and thereby cut Hooker off from U.S. Ford. However, there were too many Federals and not enough space to swing around the northern flank. When he met Jackson to discuss strategy, at around 7:30 P.M., Lee and his subordinate officer knew there were only two possible routes of attack: frontally against Chancellorsville, or a flank movement to the south.

Although Lee believed that Hooker would remain to fight, Jackson thought he would retire across the river before morning. By withdrawing back into the Wilderness at Chancellorsville Hooker had forfeited the advantage he had gained when he unhinged the Confederate line. Now, because he could *not* achieve a decision, Jackson saw little reason for Hooker to remain. Jackson did not realize the degree to which his unexpected advance had distracted the Federal commander, leaving him unable to think of any course except to stand in the Wilderness and fend off the Confederates.

Lee and Jackson sent aides to examine the Federal front. They confirmed what both already had suspected—a frontal assault would be deadly and should not be attempted.

This left only a flanking movement to the south. When they agreed that only one course of action was possible, Jeb Stuart rode up opportunely with the welcome news that Fitzhugh Lee had discovered that the Federal right, on the Plank Road west of Chancellorsville, was floating "in the air," meaning that it rested on no defensive position, either natural or man-made.[2] This revealed that Hooker's position could be turned and that, depending on how far his right extended, his army might be attacked from the rear.

A flank attack required dividing the Confederate army once more. The segment facing Hooker amounted to only about forty-eight thousand men, including cavalry, whereas the Federals had more than seventy thousand. To split this Rebel force again would leave neither segment capable of sustained battle if Hooker discovered the division and attacked either separately. The Wilderness, with its few roads and difficult terrain, would extend the period of vulnerability, because a flanking force would have to undertake a long, exhausting, and dangerous march.

Nevertheless, a flank movement offered the only means of forcing Hooker to retreat back across the Rappahannock. Some time before midnight Lee approved the operation and appointed

Jackson to carry it out, with Stuart to cover the march with his cavalry. Jackson rose, smiling, touched his cap, and said: "My troops will move at 4 o'clock."[3]

Nonetheless, neither the route of the march, the exact objective, nor the number of troops to be used had been decided on. Lee had approved a flank move with the limited objective of forcing Hooker to retreat. But as soon as Jackson realized that Hooker's flank was unguarded he had begun devising a far more ambitious strategy with implications for destruction of Hooker's army.[4]

Early in the morning on May 2, 1863, after a short sleep, Jackson talked about a route with his chaplain, Tucker Lacy, whose family owned land in the region. Lacy traced a possible course but Jackson said it was too close to the enemy. Lacy remembered that Charles C. Wellford, proprietor of Catharine Furnace, lived near the furnace a couple of miles southwest. Jackson sent Lacy with Jedediah Hotchkiss, one of his engineers, to query Wellford. They woke Wellford, who pointed out a covered route and appointed his adolescent son Charles as guide.[5]

Hotchkiss returned to where Lee and Jackson had resumed their discussion and traced the route. There was a moment of silence. Then Lee said: "General Jackson, what do you propose to do?" Jackson: "Go around here." He pointed to the line Hotchkiss had shown. Lee: "What do you propose to make this movement with?" Jackson, without hesitation: "With my whole corps." Lee: "What will you leave me?" Jackson: "The divisions of Anderson and McLaws."

This was a stunning proposal. Jackson was not suggesting the modest turning movement Lee envisioned to force Hooker's retreat, but rather a full-scale descent with the vast bulk of Confederate strength, thirty-one thousand men, to cut off Hooker from the river.

Four times previously Lee had rejected Jackson's proposals to annihilate a Federal army. Now Jackson saw a fifth opportunity, and this time he pressed hard for it.

Jackson's boldness and audacity astonished Lee. But he saw

what Jackson saw—that Hooker had placed himself in a perilous position, with only a single river crossing and the possibility, if Jackson got on his rear, of being forced away from the Rappahannock. If this plan succeeded, Hooker would have nowhere to retreat and could be annihilated between Jackson on the west side and Lee on the east.

Though Lee had rejected past opportunities, this time, knowing that his army was in desperate straits and recognizing that Jackson had seen a chance to transform the situation, Lee answered calmly: "Well, go on."[6]

Thus commenced the war's only occasion in which Lee accepted a Jacksonian plan aimed at destruction of the enemy army.

Jackson's corps began to move forward at about 7 A.M. As the head of the column swung southwest toward Catharine Furnace, Stonewall Jackson rode a short distance behind with his staff. Lee stood by the road to say good-bye. Jackson drew rein and they talked briefly. Jackson pointed ahead, Lee nodded, and Jackson rode on. One of the most spectacular marches in the history of warfare had begun.

★ ★ ★

For most of Jackson's soldiers, the actual march around Hooker was uneventful, merely a long, hard pull of about twelve miles along narrow dirt roads cut through the forest but dustless because of recent rains. Stuart's horsemen shielded them from any disturbance by Federal patrols to the north. The men were enthusiastic and expectant. They knew they were embarked on another of Stonewall's mysterious movements and they reveled in their role. Meanwhile, the forces left with Lee began demonstrations to make the Federals think an attack was coming from the east.

The Federals, despite all of Jackson's efforts at deception, discovered the march soon after it started. Brig. Gen. David B. Birney, commanding a division in Daniel Sickles's Third Corps, had forces on a cleared elevation known as Hazel Grove, a little over a mile southwest of Chancellorsville. At about 8 A.M. some of his scouts reported passage of a long column moving southwest on the Furnace Road running past Hazel Grove. One spot on this road was bare of trees and afforded the view.

Birney reported the news, but Hooker excitedly jumped to the conclusion that the Confederates were, after all, retreating—the direction indicating that Gordonsville was the objective. Although he sent a warning to Henry W. Slocum commanding the Twelfth Corps and Oliver O. Howard commanding the Eleventh Corps about a possible attack on their flanks, he did not regard the threat as great and neither general gave it much attention, although Howard received a number of reports of Rebel movements throughout the day.[7]

Hooker ordered Federal guns to harass the column and at about 11 A.M. a battery at Hazel Grove opened on troops along the exposed part of the Furnace Road. This caused the diversion of Jackson's wagons to another, more protected road, farther east and south. Around noon Hooker authorized Sickles to advance on Catharine Furnace to attack Lee's "trains."

Birney's division moved forward, soon followed by Amiel W. Whipple's. But Carnot Posey's Mississippi brigade of Anderson's division, posted just to the east of the furnace, opposed the advance vigorously along with the Twenty-third Georgia, detached from Jackson's column and defending the furnace. Meantime, Jackson's men and wagons passed far beyond reach of the Federal probes.

After marching to the end of the Furnace Road, Jackson's column moved briefly south down the Brock Road, then turned back north on a lesser-traveled woods road to the west, coming back into the Brock Road (present-day Virginia Route 613) about a mile south of its junction with the Plank Road (now Virginia Route 621).

At about 1 P.M. some Second Virginia Cavalry troopers turned east a short distance up the Plank Road and discovered that they could see the right of the Federal line, being held by General Howard's thirteen thousand–man Eleventh Corps, somewhat

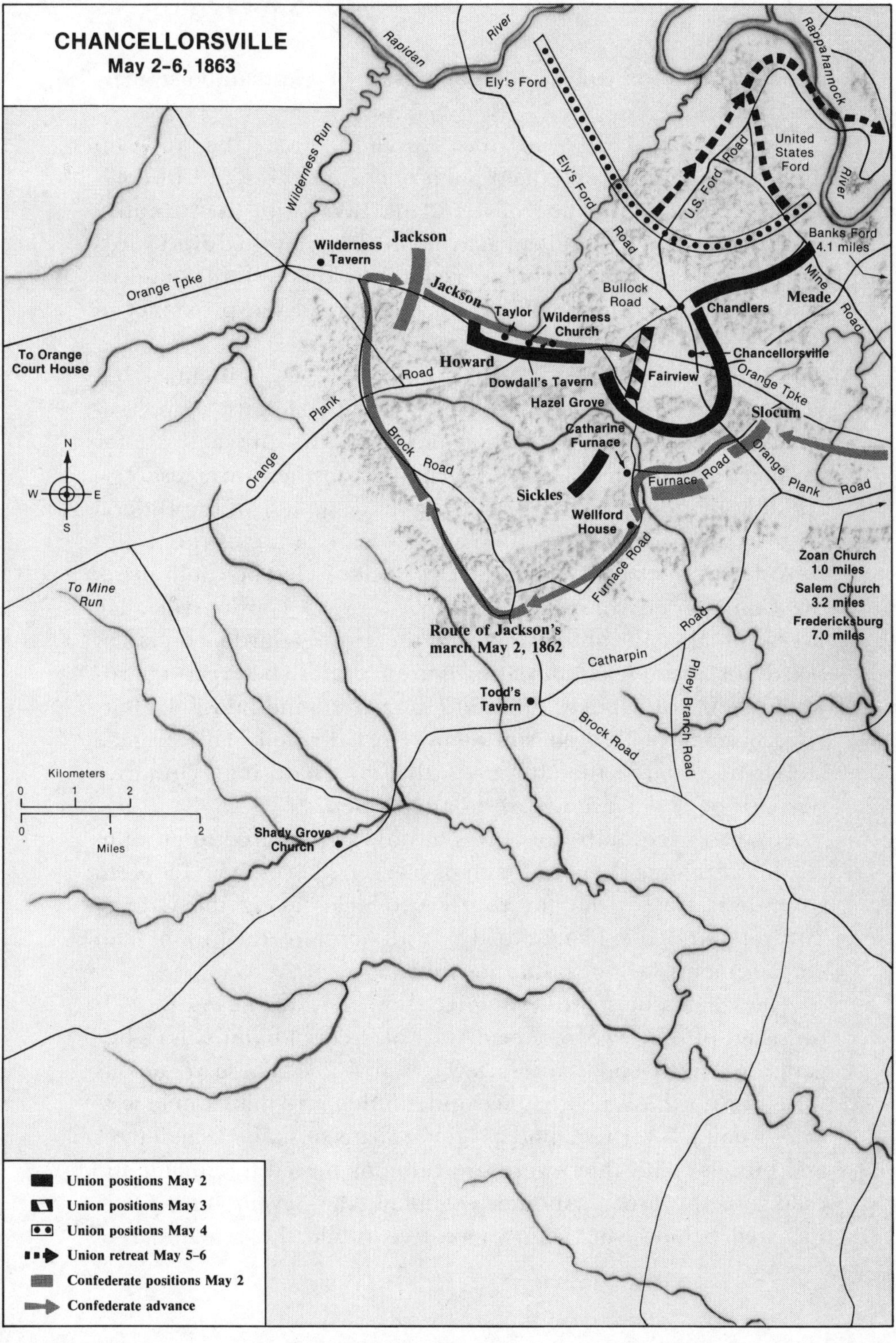

CHANCELLORSVILLE
May 2–6, 1863
Rapidan
River
Ely's Ford
Rappahannock
River
Wilderness Run
Ely's Ford Road
U.S. Ford Road
United States Ford
Banks Ford 4.1 miles
Wilderness Tavern
Jackson
Orange Tpke
Jackson
Taylor
Wilderness Church
Bullock Road
Chandlers
Meade
Mine Road
To Orange Court House
Howard
Chancellorsville
Road
Fairview
Orange Tpke
Dowdall's Tavern
Hazel Grove
Plank
Slocum
Catharine Furnace
Brock Road
Orange
Furnace Road
Orange Plank Road
Sickles
Wellford House
Zoan Church 1.0 miles
Salem Church 3.2 miles
Fredericksburg 7.0 miles
To Mine Run
Furnace Road
Route of Jackson's march May 2, 1862
Road
Catharpin
Todd's Tavern
Brock Road
Piney Branch Road
Kilometers
0 1 2
0 1 2
Miles
Shady Grove Church
Union positions May 2
Union positions May 3
Union positions May 4
Union retreat May 5–6
Confederate positions May 2
Confederate advance

less than half of which was composed of German-born mercenaries.[8]

Fitz Lee quickly informed Jackson and together they rode up the Plank Road to an elevated point only a mile west of Dowdall's Tavern, near the junction of the Plank Road with the turnpike. Jackson saw that Federal entrenchments lay a few hundred yards away, facing *south*, and that Federal soldiers were standing around chatting and smoking, unconscious of the proximity of the Confederate corps.

Jackson had planned to turn up the Plank Road to attack but saw that this would lead him directly against Howard's emplacements. He decided to continue north on the Brock Road for another mile and a half to the turnpike and then turn east, certain that by doing so he would be beyond the *rear* of the Federal position and that none of the Federals were aware of the fact![9]

A short time later General Sickles decided that he could break the Confederate column "retreating" toward Gordonsville. He overwhelmed and captured most of the Twenty-third Georgia but asked for assistance, since he figured that Rebel rear guards would be fierce. Hooker directed Howard to send him F. C. Barlow's brigade of Adolph von Steinwehr's division. This brigade marched toward the furnace, thereby reducing Howard's strength by about twenty-five hundred men.

Howard's Eleventh Corps was in no way prepared to encounter the thirty-one thousand men of Jackson's corps. The Eleventh Corps was spread out for nearly two miles along the Orange Turnpike and the Plank Road,[10] with most of the troops and emplacements facing south, not west.

The corps's most westerly force, however, *was* facing west. It consisted of only two regiments of Col. Leopold von Gilsa's brigade of Brig. Gen. Charles Devens's division. These regiments were just north of the turnpike and a little more than a mile west of Dowdall's Tavern, behind a skimpy abatis of slashed small trees and bushes. With them were two cannons posted to enfilade the road, not the forest. Another regiment, the Seventy-fifth Ohio, was well behind von Gilsa in reserve, while the remainder of

Devens's division was facing south along the pike, its four guns also trained on the road.

Some two-thirds of a mile east of von Gilsa on high, cleared ground about the Taylor house was Carl Schurz's two-brigade division.[11] Most of it also faced south along the turnpike, but two regiments of Alexander Schimmelpfennig's brigade faced west, shielded, like von Gilsa's force, by a slight abatis. The Eighty-second Ohio was to the rear and also facing west. Schurz's battery, like Devens's, covered the turnpike, not the woods.

The remaining brigade of von Steinwehr's division at Dowdall's Tavern was commanded by Col. Adolphus Buschbeck. It faced south, but a shallow shelter trench, several hundred yards long and unoccupied, faced west just north of the highway with several cannons behind. This line, like the other two, was feeble, but Buschbeck, if warned, might be able to occupy it.

Between Howard's Eleventh Corps and Slocum's Twelfth intervened a mile of ground, unoccupied upon the departure of Barlow's brigade, while Slocum's corps faced south and east in an arc around Chancellorsville.

Around Hazel Grove and below Catharine Furnace, well south of the main Federal positions, stood two divisions of Sickles's corps with Barlow's brigade and most of Pleasonton's cavalry, perhaps sixteen thousand men, engaged in the "pursuit" of Lee's supposedly retreating army.

Hooker's tactical situation, therefore, was precarious. Two extremely weak lines of Howard's Eleventh Corps faced west but most of his men and guns looked south.[12] Sickles's corps, with attachments, was so far south that it was out of the fight and could be cut off from the main army if Jackson's advance pushed far enough. The remainder of Hooker's army largely faced south or east, though Hiram G. Berry's division of Sickles's corps was in the vicinity of Chancellorsville and might be called on.

Jackson intended from the outset to bar Hooker's retreat and destroy his army. However, Hooker's line of retreat stretched northward to U.S. Ford. The absence of adequate roads prevented Jackson's moving directly northeast to interpose his corps between the ford and Chancellorsville. Jackson's only feasible route of attack was directly eastward along the turnpike and Plank Road. Although this would roll up the Eleventh Corps and advance into the rear of the corps of Couch, Sickles, and Slocum, Jackson's advance strategically was on Hooker's right flank and *not* athwart his line of retreat.

For this reason Jackson planned to advance to Bullock Road, about a mile west of Chancellorsville, then send some forces along it northeast to seize Chandler's (or White House), the crossroads three-quarters of a mile northwest of Chancellorsville, which controlled both roads to U.S. Ford. This would cut off Hooker's retreat and place the bulk of his army between Jackson and Lee.

★ ★ ★

At about 2:30 P.M. on May 2, 1863, Jackson's lead element, the Fifth Alabama, reached the turnpike and turned east, with the remainder of Jackson's corps coming close behind, save James H. Lane's and J. J. Archer's brigades, at the rear, which had turned back temporarily to block Sickles's advance.[13]

Jackson began to deploy his men, making as little noise as possible. He placed D. H. Hill's division, now commanded by Robert E. Rodes, in the first line. In the second he lined up Isaac R. Trimble's division, now under Raleigh E. Colston, and behind, A. P. Hill's division, partly in column.

The main brunt of the attack was going to be borne by three brigades near the turnpike. These were George Doles's Georgia brigade, lined up just south of the pike, Edward A. O'Neal's Alabama brigade, just north, and Alfred Iverson's North Carolina brigade, to O'Neal's left.

On the far right, in the first line, was Alfred N. Colquitt's Georgia brigade, and directly behind, S. D. Ramseur's North Carolina brigade. A short distance to the south was E. P. Paxton's Stonewall Brigade, poised to march straight up the Plank Road as the assault lines advanced, to clear out any Federal detachments that might be south of the main Union line.

These three brigades, being well south of the pike, were unlikely to face heavy Federal forces. But their advance was vital, for their path would lead them over both Hazel Grove and Fairview, an elevated, open area about two-thirds of a mile southwest of Chancellorsville. As the Confederates were to discover, these two heights were the only places where significant numbers of cannons could be mounted, and their capture in the chaos and panic of Jackson's initial advance would make Hooker's entire position untenable. Also, capture of Hazel Grove would split Sickles's large force from the rest of Hooker's army and probably lead to its destruction.

Jackson gave each commander explicit instructions, as was his style. Each brigade was to push resolutely ahead, allowing nothing to stop it. When any part of the first line needed help, the commander could demand aid from the line to the rear without additional instructions. Under no circumstances was there to be a pause. The Taylor position was to be carried at all hazards because its elevation commanded the second Federal position, Dowdall's Tavern.[14]

Stonewall unleashed his eager and excited soldiers at about 5:15 P.M. Preceded by skirmishers, they rushed forward through the thick forest, their advance completely unexpected by the Federals, who got only an intimation of what was coming when deer, rabbits, foxes and other game stirred up by the Rebel lines rushed in panic through their positions.

Von Gilsa's astonished soldiers were preparing their evening meal when Doles's Georgians descended upon them, one regiment going to the south, another to the north, and two smashing headlong into his position. The Federals stood their ground through three volleys, then disintegrated in panic. Von Gilsa's two cannons, badly placed, fired a few rounds, but the Georgians shot down the horses and the gunners fled. Von Gilsa's regiments facing south sustained withering fire in front, flank, and rear and ran without firing a shot. A few Federals rallied around the Seventy-fifth Ohio, which had marched forward and bravely confronted two Rebel brigades and two of Stuart's guns firing on it with canister from the pike. Incredibly, the Seventy-fifth Ohio held for ten minutes before it, too, disintegrated.

All of Devens's men facing along the turnpike fled pell-mell toward Chancellorsville, only a few rallying around Schurz's division at the Taylor house. The stand there was as brief as at von Gilsa's, the Confederate brigades enveloping Schurz's position and sending the entire division fleeing eastward.

Rodes's three brigades on or near the pike pressed onward toward Dowdall's Tavern, while Colquitt, who had advanced only a few hundred yards, halted, disobeying orders, when he became alarmed about a report of Federals on his flank. This halt also stopped Ramseur and Paxton. Neither Paxton nor Ramseur had seen any Union forces, but Colquitt refused to move until Ramseur, in exasperation, assured him that he would take care of any that might be there. When the advance recommenced, the three brigades, five thousand men, were too far behind Jackson's advance to catch up. Colquitt's disobedience prevented seizure of Hazel Grove and Fairview and the severing of Sickles's large force from Hooker's army. Disgraced, Colquitt was later swapped by Lee with his brigade for a North Carolina force and shipped south.

A little after 6 P.M. about three thousand Federals, the same troops who had come away in formation from the debacles at Devens's position and the Taylor farm, lined up nervously west of Dowdall's Tavern, facing the Confederate juggernaut jubilantly and loudly pressing toward them; the men in the second line were so eager that they were pushing up through the first. The defenders had been thoroughly shaken by the hordes of their fellows stampeding in terror through their positions and down the turnpike to the rear. The Union line held only minutes before it collapsed, and many men threw away their arms and joined the rush to the rear. The Confederates had achieved complete ascendancy.

Colonel Buschbeck's men were fresh and were capable of standing off Jackson's soldiers, though many of the men who joined Buschbeck were on the edge of panic and were spreading their fear to the others. Jackson recognized this as the last organized Federal line and he assailed it along the whole front, while also converging with violent force around both flanks. When the Union soldiers saw that they were about to be surrounded, they threw down their rifles and joined the mighty stream of men and horses fleeing toward Chancellorsville. Thousands did not halt until they reached beyond U.S. Ford.

It was now about 7 P.M., and though there was not much daylight left, Jackson had intended that Rodes continue onward, driving straight through Chancellorsville and making contact with Lee's forces beyond. In this way Hooker's army would be cut into several fragments, opening a clear path to attack Chandler's and thereby cutting off Hooker's line of retreat to U.S. Ford. The combination of these blows, Jackson was certain, would lead to the disintegration and surrender of Hooker's entire force.[15]

Rodes, however, saw that the two lines of his advance, his division and Colston's behind, were getting mixed inextricably together. And though they were continuing onward with ardor and endurance, Rodes feared confusion and disorder. He knew Jackson wanted to continue, but was not gifted with the vision of his commander. Thus his military sense of order prevailed, and at 7:15 P.M. he called a halt, notifying Jackson to send forward A. P. Hill's division to continue the assault while he reformed his and Colston's divisions.[16]

This fateful and unnecessary delay gave the Federals a chance to gather their wits and organize a defense. With darkness falling, every moment of daylight should have been used to press on to prevent Hooker from finding any position from which to block the Confederates.[17]

Hooker did not get the news of the disaster until around 6:30 P.M., when one of his aides, Capt. Harry Russell, hearing violent noise to the west, rushed from the veranda of the Chancellor house to the road and turned his glass down it. "My God, here they come!" he shouted. Russell thought the fleeing Federals were part of Sickles's corps, not Howard's! It was only when Hooker and his aides rushed into the surging mass that they discovered the truth.[18]

Hooker was so thoroughly shaken that he sent word to Sickles around Catharine Furnace to save his command if he could. Hooker thought of retreating and leaving the Third Corps to its fate—sure evidence that if Colquitt had not stopped, contrary to orders, Sickles could have been cut off in the first great rush on Hooker's rear.[19]

Hooker had only an hour to stem the rout. He had two brigades of Hiram Berry's division around Chancellorsville and ordered them to move westward immediately to halt Jackson. It was a stern test of their discipline, but these brigades advanced bravely through the stream of refugees. At around 8 P.M. they began entrenching half a mile west of Chancellorsville and just north of the open elevation of Fairview, where twenty Federal artillery pieces were being unlimbered.[20] Alpheus Williams's division from the Twelfth Corps also arrived soon after to continue Berry's line southward in front of Fairview to protect the guns.

Meantime, Sickles's men rushed northward behind Pleasonton's cavalry, which moved up to occupy Hazel Grove. There Pleasonton took charge of the artillery and organized a defense. His guns discouraged any effort by the few Rebels nearby to seize Hazel Grove, and that defense reconnected Sickles to the main Federal army.

A. P. Hill deployed his division in front of Rodes and Colston, who had withdrawn to reform. Only Brig. Gen. James Lane's North Carolina brigade was immediately available and it was 8:45 P.M. before the brigade was lined up on either side of the Plank Road a mile west of Chancellorsville.

Stonewall Jackson now had come up. He intended to send parts of A. P. Hill's division northeast to seize Chandler's crossroads by way of Bullock Road, which ran directly to it from the advanced Confederate positions. Although the extreme right flank of Berry's division rested near the edge of Bullock Road, the only Federal force in the vicinity of Chandler's was a remnant of William French's division of Couch's Second Corps, while nearby George Sykes's division of the Fifth Corps was spread thinly at several points along the road beyond Chandler's to the northwest. None of these detachments was capable of stopping a determined Confederate advance on Chandler's.[21]

Jackson had not yet established connection with Lee. This he meant to do by pushing Lane's brigade straight on toward Chancellorsville. Thus, when Lane asked Jackson for orders at around 9 P.M., Jackson raised his arm in the direction of the enemy and exclaimed: "Push right ahead, Lane; right ahead."

Shortly thereafter Gen. A. P. Hill arrived and Jackson gave Hill his orders: "Press them; cut them off from the United States Ford, Hill; press them." Hill said he and his staff were unfamiliar with the country and Jackson turned to Capt. J. Keith Boswell, his chief engineer, who was well acquainted with the roads and paths of the Wilderness, and ordered him to report to Hill.[22]

Jackson now went with Hill and his staff in advance of Lane's line to get further knowledge of the terrain in the direction of U.S. Ford.[23] They heard Federal voices and axes cutting trees for breastworks and abatis. Firing erupted in front of them and Jackson and his party hurriedly left the Plank Road and turned onto the little-used Mountain Road a few yards north.

The Eighteenth North Carolina nearby mistook the sounds of the horses for a Federal cavalry attack and the order was given to fire. Jackson's party was not more than twenty paces from the line and the volley was fearfully effective. Captain Boswell and an orderly fell dead. Three bullets struck Jackson—one penetrated his right palm, another went into the wrist of his left hand, and a third splintered the bone of his left arm between the shoulder and elbow, severing an artery. Jackson's horse bolted for the Federal lines but Jackson, despite his pain and being struck by low tree branches, was able to halt the horse and turn it back.

Jackson weakened quickly from loss of blood, though his aides and Hill bandaged his major wound with a handkerchief. Sudden Federal canister fire delayed getting him to the rear, and after he was finally placed on a litter, one of the bearers tripped and Jackson fell heavily on his wounded arm. The aides at last got him to a waiting ambulance and took him to the rear, where his medical officer, Hunter McGuire, and other doctors operated on him, amputating his left arm just below the shoulder.[24]

Shortly after Jackson was hit, Federal artillery wounded A. P. Hill and he relinquished command, first to Rodes and then to Jeb

Stuart, who at the moment was about to conduct an attack at Ely's Ford on W. W. Averell's Union cavalry division, ordered back from Stoneman's raid on the Confederate rear to assist Hooker. Stuart did not arrive at the Chancellorsville front until about midnight. Although A. P. Hill, who remained on the field, doubtless told Stuart of Jackson's plan to block Hooker's retreat by seizing Chandler's, Stuart was intensely aware of the confusion that the loss of both Jackson and Hill had caused and he suspended operations until daylight.[25]

Stuart could not have carried out such a stroke anyway. He was by far the best cut-and-thrust cavalry leader in either army but he was not a good infantry commander, as he was to demonstrate; he had none of the strategic genius of Jackson. Stuart did not see the necessity of an immediate march on Chandler's and concentrated instead on figuring out how to reestablish contact with Lee's forces to the east. Besides, the Confederate window of opportunity was closing by the minute. John Reynolds's First Corps was moving up to assist Hooker, and Reynolds's and George Meade's Fifth Corps were busily building lines to protect U.S. Ford throughout the night of May 2–3. By morning they were more or less in place.

Jackson knew when he launched his assault on the Eleventh Corps in the late afternoon that the opportune time to strike for Hooker's rear was during daylight and then to continue the attack while Hooker's forces were disorganized and panicked. That is why he insisted that his attacking forces stop for nothing, not even reorganization. Though Rodes failed to carry out this order and halted, Jackson saw that he still had a chance to seize Chandler's in the early evening before an effective Federal defense could be organized. That is why he instructed A. P. Hill to block U.S. Ford as soon as possible.

Jackson's incapacitation wrecked the Confederacy's greatest opportunity to destroy much, if not all, of the Army of the Potomac.

It is almost certain that Jackson, had he not been wounded, would have thrust much of his corps between Hooker and U.S.

Ford.[26] If successful, and there is nothing to indicate that it would have been otherwise, it would have resulted in the surrender of all of Hooker's army in the vicinity of Chancellorsville (making up the great bulk of the seventy-six thousand men he had south of the Rappahannock on the evening of May 1).[27] The smaller Federal forces near U.S. Ford, plus the First Corps, which was crossing about this time, would have been in jeopardy of being surrounded and overwhelmed quickly thereafter. Even Sedgwick's corps would have been in danger. With a large part of the Federal cavalry still absent, an alert and experienced Stuart might have slowed Sedgwick's retreat long enough for the Confederate infantry to surround him and force his surrender.

★ ★ ★

Two messengers got to General Lee early on May 3, one with a note about Jackson. Lee, shocked by Jackson's wounding, acquiesced in the naming of Stuart to command, and wrote Stuart: "It is all-important that you still continue pressing to the right [toward Lee], turning, if possible, all the fortified points in order that we can unite both wings of the army."[28] Lee promised to assist by ordering troops on his side to attack toward Stuart.

When Lee authorized Jackson's move early on May 2, he certainly was aware of Jackson's intent to get between Hooker and U.S. Ford. This was the only justification for Jackson to take most of the army with him. However, there is no trace of this concept in Lee's message to Stuart. Perhaps Lee realized that the time for that blow had passed, and, with only a cavalry major general and infantry brigadiers in command of Jackson's troops, the quicker he could bring both wings of the army together, the better.

There was no subtlety in Stuart's tactics. He resolved to strike the enemy lines head-on. He told Porter Alexander, the senior unwounded artillery commander with Jackson's corps, to scout out gun positions for the morning. Alexander found few enough in the heavy woods enveloping the Confederate positions. But he did recognize the importance of Hazel Grove as soon as he saw it, and he convinced Stuart. Alexander realized that this elevation could be used by his guns to enfilade the Federal artillery at Fairview, three-quarters of a mile to the northeast. If the Federals could be forced off Fairview, Hooker's entire position around Chancellorsville would have to be abandoned, for Confederate guns on Fairview could fire into the rear of Federal positions.

Consequently, seizing Hazel Grove, and not the infantry attacks Stuart ordered, was the crucial tactical move of the day, although Hooker so thoroughly missed its importance that he already had ordered the grove's evacuation before the Rebels had mounted their assault. "There has rarely been a more gratuitous gift of a battlefield," Alexander remarked.[29]

The Rebels secured Hazel Grove before 7 A.M. on May 3. Soon after, Alexander crowned the elevation with thirty-one cannons, quickly rising to forty. These, plus twenty more he and other gunners emplaced on the Plank Road, converged their fire on the forty Federal cannons atop Fairview. Although most of the Union pieces were entrenched, the Confederate guns beat them down, the Rebel artillery quickly successful because the Federal guns ran out of ammunition. Inexplicably, Hooker did not order additional shells brought up and the Federal fire diminished.

While this titanic artillery duel was under way, Stuart ordered general infantry assaults against the entire Federal line. The attacks were some of the bloodiest and most violently contested in the Civil War. The Federal troops were behind entrenchments in most cases, some shallow but all better than men standing exposed, while their positions were generally protected by abatis of felled trees and heavy brush. Confederate soldiers had to sustain deadly fire in their advance *and* while they tried to break through the entrenchments and abatis. Rebel determination was so great that defending Federals suffered heavily as well.[30]

There were few instances in the Civil War where the casualties suffered in so brief a period exceeded those on Stuart's front this morning. Stuart lost 30 percent of the men he had engaged, and overall the attacks failed.[31] Several times veteran Confederate soldiers and officers refused to advance into the maelstrom. Even more remarkable was the fact that a number of Federal officers commanding regiments and brigades abandoned their positions and marched their troops off the battlefield without orders. One such commander was court-martialed but there were so many instances that Lincoln, to gloss over the other battlefield defections, revoked the sentence and let the officer retire.[32]

Lee's attacks on the southeast were no better conceived, although they were less intense.

At about 9 A.M. the Federal guns, now mostly out of ammunition, withdrew from Fairview and an hour later Confederate infantry seized the elevation. This, and not Stuart's infantry attacks, set about the withdrawal of Hooker's entire force to positions prepared north of Chancellorsville protecting U.S. Ford.

If Hooker had gotten ammunition to his guns and had protected them more aggressively with infantry, Stuart's and Lee's assaults might have failed. Also, Hooker kept more than thirty thousand of his troops entirely out of the fight.[33] Hooker was painfully injured sometime around 9 A.M. when a Confederate solid shot shattered a pillar at the Chancellor house and flung part of it against his body and head. Hooker did not give up command but his judgment was apparently impaired, and this may have prevented a more effective defense.

Stuart demonstrated that he did not understand the nature of infantry attacks or the use of artillery. Cannons should be employed to beat down other cannons, as Alexander did from Hazel Grove, and to shake enemy infantry to facilitate one's own infantry attack. Stuart should have selected a single point on his southeastern sector, where Alexander's cannons were massed, and battered it with shell fire until it was weakened. And only *then* should he have launched his infantry against it. At other points he should have made feint attacks to hold the enemy in place, to prevent Hooker from reinforcing the point selected for attack. This would have achieved the same results as the costly charges with only a fraction of the casualties.[34] Instead Stuart crashed his infantry against the entire western face of the Federal line, at points where he could bring up little or no artillery support.

★ ★ ★

Before Lee, now reunited with Jackson's corps, could launch another attack, he had to deal with a major threat to his rear. On the night of May 2 Sedgwick, emplaced but essentially idle about three miles below Fredericksburg, got urgent orders to join his corps with John Gibbon's division then crossing from Falmouth to Fredericksburg, so as to defeat Jubal Early's thin force the next morning and attack Lee's rear.[35]

Sedgwick's corps of almost twenty-four thousand men was far superior to Early's half division, about thirty-five hundred men, and could have forced its way through Hamilton's Crossing on Early's right. This would have turned the entire Confederate position and permitted Sedgwick to strike without further resistance straight at Lee's rear. Instead Sedgwick decided to march up the plain in *front* of the Confederate positions to Fredericksburg.

"The result was the singular spectacle of a body of troops practically on the enemy's flank moving to the enemy's front in order to attack him," writes John Bigelow, Jr., chronicler of the Chancellorsville campaign.[36]

Porter Alexander said of Sedgwick: "He seems to me to have wasted great opportunities and come about as near to doing nothing with 30,000 men as it was easily possible to do."[37]

Sedgwick repeated the same assault against the Sunken Road below Marye's Heights behind Fredericksburg that had shattered Ambrose Burnside's offensive in December 1862. This time, however, William Barksdale's Mississippi brigade was all the Confederates had to defend there. Although the first assaults failed, with heavy losses, Col. Thomas M. Griffin, commanding the Eighteenth Mississippi in the Sunken Road, made the irretrievable error of accepting a Federal request for a cease-fire to remove wounded. This permitted the Federals to observe how few Rebels were manning the line. They then attacked again in heavy force and killed, wounded, or captured nearly all of the Rebel defenders.

Thereafter Early withdrew down the Telegraph Road, leading

to Richmond, to protect the Confederate supply line, the RF&P Railroad. However, Cadmus M. Wilcox's Alabama brigade of Anderson's division, which had been guarding Banks Ford, delayed Sedgwick's advance westward on the Orange Plank Road for most of the day.

This gave Lee time to send Lafayette McLaws's division to aid him at Salem Church, six miles east of Chancellorsville. There, at around 5 P.M., the Confederates halted Sedgwick's advance in a sharp engagement. Sedgwick, who still possessed a two-to-one advantage in manpower, allowed this check to stop him completely. He remained immobile all the next day (May 4), while Lee, who had come up himself with Anderson's division, laboriously arranged a converging assault, which finally got under way in the late afternoon and drove Sedgwick across Banks Ford (now held by the Federals).[38]

Almost inconceivably, Sedgwick, who knew that an attack was coming, and Hooker, with an army still twice the Confederates' size, did nothing to thwart Lee's attack.

Hooker had been overmastered psychologically by Jackson and Lee and was incapable of offensive action. Despite the debacle of the Eleventh Corps rout, he had suffered—because of Stuart's unnecessary attacks—only a few more casualties than the Confederates. His army was intact and massed. Though he was still in the Wilderness and could not employ his artillery well, Hooker knew that a large segment of Lee's army had been drawn off to deal with Sedgwick and that a determined assault might break through to bring his two wings together. Part of the reason for Hooker's inaction may have been the blow he received at the Chancellor house, but the principal reason must have been that he feared to attack Lee and Jackson; no opportunity, however alluring, would change his mind.

On May 5 Lee turned back toward Hooker with the intention of attacking the next day. That evening a huge storm broke and Hooker took advantage of it to move his entire force across the Rappahannock, abandoning strong entrenchments and virtually impenetrable abatis. Rarely in military history has a commander been so thoroughly intimidated by opposing commanders. Hooker marched his men back to Falmouth and Lee returned his forces to the heights behind Fredericksburg.

It looked to be a great Confederate victory, but the appearance was deceiving. The Rebels had lost 13,156 men, most of them killed or wounded. The Federals had lost 16,804.[39] Proportionally the Confederates had suffered far more than the Federals. The Union easily could replace its losses; the South could not. Worse, the strategic situation had not improved. The South had missed its opportunity to destroy all or most of the Army of the Potomac and to leave the North powerless to prevent invasion. Stonewall Jackson had been about to achieve just such a victory when he was struck down.

Now the commander who had conceived a second plan of how the South might end the war with the South intact and independent lay dying. Jackson who had been moved back to Guineys Station (now Guinea) on the RF&P to recuperate had contracted pneumonia. He lingered until his death on Sunday, May 10, 1863. In his last hours his mind wandered back to battle and he called out: "Order A. P. Hill to prepare for action! Pass the infantry to the front! Tell Major Hawks—" He became silent for a while, then said quietly and clearly: "Let us pass over the river and rest under the shade of the trees." Stonewall Jackson was dead.[40]

NOTES

General sources: Dabney, 672–735; Doubleday, 20–84; Johnson and Buel, vol. 3, 152–243; Henderson, 662–713; Alexander, *Military Memoirs,* 328–60; Alexander, *Fighting for the Confederacy,* 204–17; Bigelow, 258–439; Freeman, *Lee's Lieutenants,* vol. 2, 538–714; Freeman, *R. E. Lee,* vol. 2, 518–63; Chambers, vol. 2, 379–462; Vandiver, 463–94; Jedediah Hotchkiss and William Allan, *Chancellorsville* (New York: D. Van Nostrand, 1867), 41–152; and Theodore A. Dodge, *The Campaign of Chancellorsville* (Boston: James R. Osgood and Company, 1881), 62–261.

1. Alexander, *Fighting for the Confederacy,* 197.

2. Freeman, *Lee's Lieutenants,* vol. 2, 539; Henderson, 663; and Freeman, *R. E. Lee,* vol. 2, 520.

3. *Southern Historical Society Papers,* vol. 34, 16–17; Freeman, *R. E. Lee,* vol. 2, 521; Henderson, 664 and 694–95; and Freeman, *Lee's Lieutenants,* vol. 2, 541. Maj. Gen. Sir Frederick Maurice, editor of the papers of Col. Charles Marshall, an aide to Lee, maintains that Lee, not Jackson, came up with the idea of the march around Hooker (see Marshall, 163–70). This is a moot point, however, because both generals realized on the evening of May 1, 1863, that an attack on Hooker's right, or southern, flank was the only course of action open to the Confederate army except retreat. Lee had discovered during the afternoon that there was no room and too many Union troops to attack on Hooker's left near the Rappahannock River. Both generals' aides ascertained during the evening that a frontal attack would be disastrous. And Stuart's announcement that Hooker's right flank was floating "in the air" showed that a move in this direction offered the only opportunity for a decision. Consequently, the conference between Lee and Jackson was not about *whether* to attack around Hooker's southern flank but about *how* to carry it out, since both generals realized that a retreat would be disastrous. Lee's original idea was for a simple flanking movement to dislodge Hooker and force him to retreat. Jackson extended this concept to an assault fully on Hooker's rear, with the intention of destroying his army.

4. Dabney, 710.

5. Freeman, *Lee's Lieutenants,* vol. 2, 544–45; and Dabney, 675–76.

6. Henderson, 665 and 694–95 (Henderson's source is a personal letter from Jedediah Hotchkiss); Bigelow, 272; Freeman, *Lee's Lieutenants,* vol. 2, 546–47; and Freeman, *R. E. Lee,* vol. 2, 523–24.

7. For a discussion of the warnings several Federal officers gave concerning Jackson's threat and how they were disregarded, see Doubleday, 22–29; and Bigelow, 279–80 and 287–89.

8. Doubleday, 29.

9. Bigelow, 281–82; and Freeman, *Lee's Lieutenants,* 552–53.

10. The Plank Road and turnpike ran together for a little over two miles from Chancellorsville to Dowdall's Tavern, where the Plank Road turned off southwest and the turnpike continued on in a westerly direction. The part running together was generally known as the Plank Road and is so carried here.

11. This position also is known as the Tally, or Talley, house, located south of the road, whereas the Taylor house was north.

12. Bigelow, 285–87. General Schurz later described the Federal positions: "It was almost impossible to maneuver some of our regiments, hemmed in as they were on the old Turnpike by embankments and rifle pits in front and thick woods in the rear, drawn out in long, deployed lines, giving just enough room for the stacks of arms and a narrow passage." See ibid., 286; and *McClure's,* June 1907, 164.

13. Archer and Thomas turned back without notifying either A. P. Hill or Jackson. See Freeman, *Lee's Lieutenants,* vol. 2, 551; and *Official Records,* vol. 25, pt. 1, 924. At 3 P.M. Jackson sent a message to Lee: "The enemy has made a stand at Chancellors's [Dowdall's Tavern], which is about two miles from Chancellorsville. I hope as soon as practicable to attack. I trust that an ever-kind Providence will bless us with great success. Respectfully, T. J. Jackson, Lt. Gen. P.S. The leading division is up and the next two appear to be well closed. T. J. J." The message implies that Jackson had sent earlier dispatches that represented the Federals as falling back. Dowdall's Tavern was occupied at the time by Melzi Chancellor. See Dabney, 679–80; Johnson and Buel, vol. 3, 206; and Bigelow, 289.

14. Freeman, *Lee's Lieutenants,* vol. 2, 555–56; *Official Records,* vol. 25, pt. 1, 940–41; and Bigelow, 291–93.

15. Henderson (674) points out that the Southerners were only one and a half miles from the Federal center and completely in the rear of the Union entrenchments. "And the White House or Bullock road, only half-a-mile to the front," he writes, "led directly to Hooker's line of retreat by the United States Ford. Until that road was in his possession Jackson was determined to call no halt."

16. *Official Records,* vol. 25, pt. 1, 941; Bigelow, 308 and 315; and Alexander, *Military Memoirs,* 339–40. At some point prior to when Rodes halted the Confederate line, Jackson rode into the mixed ranks of Rodes and Colston and ordered them to press the pursuit irrespective of the disorder. See Henderson, 674. R. L. Dabney is incorrect when he says that Jackson determined to relieve the front line and replace it with A. P. Hill's division (see Dabney, 683).

17. Bigelow (337) writes that Jackson had issued explicit orders that there be no pause in the advance and was disappointed by Rodes's halt. Neither Rodes nor Colston asserted or implied that the troops were exhausted or incapable of further effort. See *Official Records,* vol. 25, pt. 1, 941 and 1004; Colston, in Johnson and Buel, vol. 3, 233; and Henderson, 683.

18. Henderson, 675; and Bigelow, 301.

19. Doubleday, 38–39.

20. Capt. T. W. Osborn, chief of Berry's artillery, wrote afterward: "As we passed General Hooker's headquarters, a scene burst upon us which God grant may never again be seen in the Federal army of the United States. The 11th Corps had been routed and were fleeing to the river like scared sheep. The men and artillery filled the road, its sides and the skirts of the field; and it appeared that no two or one company could be found together. Aghast and terror-stricken, heads bare and panting for breath, they pleaded like infants at the mother's breast that we should let them pass to the rear unhindered." See *Official Records,* vol. 25, pt. 1, 483; and Bigelow, 311.

21. *Official Records,* vol. 25, pt. 1, 507 and 526; Bigelow, 302, map opposite 314, and 315; Cooke, 419; and Alexander, *Military Memoirs,* 339–40. There were other, less direct, roads that could have given access to Chandler's or to positions north and west of it, if necessary. Henderson (689–90) believed that Union forces to the northeast were in superior numbers, but this was not the case until midnight or later. Henderson writes: "Those who think more of numbers than of human nature, of momentum of the mass rather than the mental equilibrium of the general," might think a superior force would stop Jackson. Yet, he says, reports of a victorious enemy of unknown strength pressing forward in the darkness toward the only line of retreat would have so demoralized the Federal commander and soldiers, already shaken, that they would have thought only of securing their safety, not of resistance. Abner Doubleday, a division commander in the Union First Corps, writes concerning the psychological state of the Federal army on the night of May 2, 1863: "An occurrence of this kind always has a tendency to demoralize an army and render it less trustworthy; for the real strength of an armed force is much more in *opinion* than it is in *numbers.* A small body of men, if made to believe the enemy are giving away, will do and dare anything; but when they think the struggle is hopeless, they will not resist even a weak attack, for each thinks he is to be sacrificed to save the rest" (Doubleday, 43).

22. Henderson, 678; and Bigelow, 316.

23. Freeman, *Lee's Lieutenants,* vol. 2, 564–65; and *Southern Historical Society Papers,* vol. 6, 267. Freeman *(Lee's Lieutenants)* cites testimony by David J. Kyle, a courier, who, in response to a question by Jackson, said he knew

the way around Chancellorsville. Kyle pointed out the course of Bullock Road leading to Chandler's. Jackson told Kyle to keep up with him.

24. Dabney, 685–96; Henderson, 378–82; Alexander, *Military Memoirs,* 340–1; Alexander, *Fighting for the Confederacy,* 204–6; *Southern Historical Society Papers,* vol. 6, 230–34 and 266–82; Johnson and Buel, vol. 3, 203–14; Bigelow, 317–19; and Freeman, *Lee's Lieutenants,* vol. 2, 567–83.

25. *Official Records,* vol. 25, pt. 1, 885–87 and 942–43; Dabney, 696–98; Henderson, 681–82; and Bigelow, 339.

26. Hunter McGuire writes: "After the battle, when still well enough to talk, he [Jackson] told me that he had intended, after breaking into Hooker's rear, to take and fortify a suitable position, cutting him off from the river and so hold him until, between himself and General Lee, the great Federal host should be broken to pieces. He had no fear. It was then that I heard him say: 'We sometimes fail to drive them from position, they always fail to drive us.' " See *Southern Historical Society Papers,* vol. 25, 110; and Bigelow, 340 n. Robert Lewis Dabney writes that Jackson, speaking afterward, "said if he had had an hour more of daylight or had not been wounded, he should have occupied outlets toward Ely's and United States Fords, as well as those on the west. . . . If he had been able to do so dispersion or capture of Hooker's army would have been certain" (Dabney, 699–700).

27. Bigelow, 328.

28. Freeman, *R. E. Lee,* vol. 2, 533–35; Bigelow, 342; and *Official Records,* vol. 25, pt. 2, 769.

29. Alexander, *Military Memoirs,* 345. See also Doubleday, 44–47; and Bigelow, 344–45.

30. For a summary of the action on the morning of May 3, 1863, see Bigelow, 342–69; Freeman, *Lee's Lieutenants,* vol. 2, 584–99; Alexander, *Military Memoirs,* 344–49; and Henderson, 683–86.

31. Alexander, *Military Memoirs,* 359; and Dabney, 703.

32. Bigelow, 349–51, 354, 355, and 361; and *Official Records,* vol. 25, pt. 1, 433, 442, 445, 452, 460, 462, 690, and 1006.

33. Doubleday, 53.

34. Bigelow, 355–56 and 373–75. This was not a new idea. One of Napoleon's most successful and characteristic practices was to concentrate artillery at one point to destroy a part of the enemy front to make a gap for

a decisive penetration. Napoleon got the idea from the Comte de Guibert's 1772 *Essai général de tactique* and from Chevalier du Teil's 1779 *L'Usage de l'artillerie nouvelle dans la guerre de campagne.* See B. H. Liddell Hart, *The Ghost of Napoleon* (New Haven, Conn.: Yale University Press, 1933), 77.

35. For an account of activities on the Fredericksburg front on May 1–2, 1863, see Freeman, *Lee's Lieutenants,* vol. 2, 603–12.

36. Bigelow, 338.

37. Alexander, *Fighting for the Confederacy,* 212. See also Henderson, 687.

38. Henderson, 687–88; Alexander, *Military Memoirs,* 352–57; and Freeman, *Lee's Lieutenants,* vol. 2, 613–36.

39. Alexander, *Military Memoirs,* 360–62.

40. Dabney, 723; Henderson, 694; and Bigelow, 439. For a full account of Jackson's death and burial, see Dabney, 707–35.

Epilogue
Could Jackson Have Won?

★ ★ ★ This question has intrigued every generation of Americans since the Civil War.

Stonewall Jackson was mortally wounded precisely at the climax of the most spectacular battle of his life. The audacious campaign of Chancellorsville—the routing of a corps and the defeat of the Union army—was so successful that most students of military history have assumed that these were Jackson's only aims and that he achieved them. Yet when one studies the battle further, one realizes that Jackson's *real* purpose was far greater. His aim was to destroy the Army of the Potomac.

Jackson had concluded that this was the only remaining strategy to achieve Southern independence after Lee and President Davis had repeatedly rejected his proposals to force a peace by striking behind Washington and by threatening destruction of Northern railroads.

Though Lee had refused his new strategic proposals four times previously, Jackson remained fixed in his purpose and at

Chancellorsville he conceived on the spot a fifth plan: to fall on the Federal rear, seal off Hooker's army from its line of retreat, form an entrenched defensive line, and force Hooker—pressed by Lee on his rear—to risk his main force in a fruitless attempt to break through the Southern barrier that blocked the Federals from U.S. Ford. As a follow-up, the scattered Union remnants could have been shattered in swift roundups. With the field army guarding the North eradicated, the South could bring the war to a close.

Jackson was poised, with Lee's approval, ready to end the war when he was struck down. Thus, when one asks whether he still might have pulled off a victory had he lived, one cannot look at the weakness of the Confederacy and conclude that it was impossible; instead one must look at the strength of Stonewall Jackson and wonder what *other* bewildering surprises lay within his mind.

No one, looking at the corner into which the Confederate army had been driven on the evening of May 1, 1863, could have conceived that *half* of this army might be on the threshold of a major victory twenty-four hours later. Even Jackson did not know it. But Jackson, unlike any other Confederate commander—and all but a handful of other great captains in history—knew how to seize the opportunity and to achieve a decisive victory.

Speculative students continue to guess at how the Confederacy would have done if Jackson had been at Gettysburg, fought exactly two months later. The mistakes of Gettysburg were, indeed, legion. Lee allowed Stuart to be absent on another of his "rides" at a crucial time and sentenced the Confederate army to grope forward blindly without proper reconnaissance. Because Richard Ewell did not try to seize Cemetery Hill the first day, the Federals were allowed to anchor their defensive line on the high ground. Lee permitted piecemeal assaults throughout the second day, while James Longstreet delayed attacking until Federal reinforcements were assembled. A. P. Hill failed to support Ambrose R. Wright's Georgia brigade after it broke the Federal line late on the second day. And, finally, the supreme error of all, Lee destroyed the last offensive power of the Confederacy when, despairing, he ordered Pickett's suicidal charge on the third day.

If Jackson had been at Gettysburg, assuming that such a battle would have been necessary, it would have been different.

First, Jackson would have argued that Stuart remain close to the army. The memory of the cavalry's vital role in locating the weak spot of Hooker at Chancellorsville would have been fresh in his mind.[1] He knew it was imperative to have Stuart's horsemen to keep the army informed of where the Union columns were and to discover any weakness in Federal dispositions.

Jackson never missed the importance of critical terrain features and would have done everything possible to capture one as dominant as Cemetery Hill.

Once committed to an attack, he would have pressed for a coordinated general assault, not a succession of separate, fragmented ventures. His policy, if he had to take the offensive, was to strike hard, fast, and in overwhelming strength.

He would have argued vehemently against launching a charge like Pickett's across a mile of open ground covered by artillery and rifle fire and against powerful, heavily manned emplacements. To attack in desperation in the hope, somehow, of pulling off a miracle, the possibility of victory otherwise denied, was not Jackson's way. Jackson attacked only when he was certain of victory; he did not attack to avoid defeat.

Questions as to what Jackson would have done at Gettysburg, however, are largely beside the point. If he had lived, there is little reason to believe that Gettysburg would have been fought. The greatest error at Gettysburg was the selection of that site for battle. Jackson's position as the supreme strategist in the Confederate army had been confirmed at Chancellorsville. Lee would have listened as he had not listened before Chancellorsville. Since Longstreet also was opposed to fighting at Gettysburg, Lee most likely would have avoided the turning-point battle.

Lee went into Pennsylvania with the expressed intention of fighting a *defensive* battle. Since Jackson believed that the South could win by stopping an attack and then sweeping around the

Union army and isolating it, he would have used all of his powers to convince Lee to seek conditions to *force* the Federals to attack, and on ground favorable to the Confederates.

Some decisive move was mandatory because Lee could not *rely* on the Federals attacking. Thus he had to threaten a vital target that the Federal commander, George G. Meade, could not concede to the Confederates. Invasion of the North alone was not enough to bring Meade on to the offensive. Quite the contrary. Meade intended to shield Washington, stand on the defensive, and wait for Lee to attack. Meade and Lee each wished to maneuver the other into such a disadvantageous position that the opponent's only way out necessitated an attack.

The incredible killing power of the Minié ball, together with the effectiveness of field fortifications, had taught commanders by the summer of 1863 that the army that stood on the defensive was likely to win; to attack prepared positions was tantamount to defeat. Jackson had perceived this fact at Second Manassas, expressed it at Fredericksburg, and repeated it after Chancellorsville: "We sometimes fail to drive them from position; they always fail to drive us."[2]

The danger was real that the Union army would stand entirely on the defensive. Meade's original plan was to build a line along Pipe Creek, between Gettysburg and Washington, and await a Confederate assault;[3] And he *did* stand on the defensive at Gettysburg.

The only strategy that could guarantee a Federal attack was to imperil a Union target, like Washington, Baltimore, or Philadelphia, that Meade could not ignore. This is what Jackson had proposed (and Jefferson Davis had rejected) after the battle of First Manassas in 1861 and three other times—twice during the valley campaign and once after the Seven Days.[4]

Although he did not have Stuart's cavalry at hand to scout for him, Lee had attained a splendid strategic position by the time he discovered on June 28, 1863, that Meade was at Frederick, Maryland, standing between him and Washington. Jubal Early already had reached Wrightsville on the Susquehanna River, east of York, and Ewell had reached Carlisle, within striking distance of Harrisburg.

Positioned where he was, Meade shielded Washington and might have guarded Baltimore, but he could *not* protect Philadelphia. No matter how Meade reacted, Ewell could have seized Harrisburg and the important railroad bridge there while A. P. Hill and Longstreet, near Chambersburg at the time, were positioned to join him. Lee could have struck for Philadelphia, using the Susquehanna as a moat to keep Meade away.

Lincoln most certainly would *not* have permitted the barrier between Lee's army and Washington to be removed, for then Lee could have turned directly on the capital. This left the road to Philadelphia undefended. And if Meade had responded slowly, Lee might have been able to beat Meade to Baltimore as well.

Capture of Philadelphia would have created panic, especially if the railroad bridge at Harrisburg had been broken (the one at Wrightsville was burned by Union militia when Early approached). Destroying the Harrisburg bridge and cutting the main East Coast railroad at Philadelphia would have severely curtailed rail links with Washington. If Lee could have reached Baltimore, where all of the rail lines from the North converged, he could have stopped virtually all deliveries of food, ammunition, and reinforcements to Washington, leaving the capital isolated. Seizure of Philadelphia or Baltimore would have forced Meade to attack, permitting Lee to meet him on a field of *his* choice, with open flanks. Just as John Pope did at Second Manassas and Ambrose Burnside did at Fredericksburg, Meade would have had no choice but to wound, gravely, his army by such an attack. If the Confederates, whose ability to move swiftly was among their strongest assets, could have swept around his flanks, Meade's army might even have been surrounded and then destroyed.

Jackson had argued for a similar course of action in Lee's 1862 invasion of Maryland. He would have done so again in 1863. But without him Lee followed an entirely contrary policy. When he learned that Meade was at Frederick, he ordered his army to concentrate at Cashtown, nine miles west of Gettysburg, although he had no indication that Meade was advancing to attack him.

Then Lee fell into a pattern that had seized him in the past. A. P. Hill advanced on Gettysburg, contrary to Lee's orders, and stumbled into a fierce engagement with Federal outriders. Instead of pulling Hill back and maneuvering to find out Meade's intentions while locating a suitable battlefield in case Meade did attack, Lee rashly let Ewell join Hill in attacking at Gettysburg and allowed himself to be drawn into an *offensive* battle. Since his objective was to force the Federals to attack, this was absolutely the wrong strategy.

Furthermore, Gettysburg was an almost inconceivably bad battlefield for the Confederates. Ewell's failure to seize Cemetery Hill forced Lee to take up a concave front five miles long. This made it difficult to move troops or coordinate assaults. Yet the Federals, with an army half again as large, occupied a front a little over three miles long on high ground—it was ideal for defense. Moreover, the Federal front was convex, permitting rapid transfer of troops to any point of danger.

Longstreet perceived the peril and suggested getting on the Union rear between Gettysburg and Washington and forcing the Federals to attack to prevent a Rebel descent on the capital. However, Lee's battle lust had apparently risen as a result of the Southerners' success in driving Union troops south of town on the first day; he told Longstreet: "If he [the enemy] is there tomorrow, I shall attack him." Longstreet responded: "If he is there tomorrow, it will be because he *wants* you to attack him."[5]

Thus Lee demonstrated once again a tendency he had exhibited throughout the war—allowing himself to be drawn into frontal, direct battles. This had happened at Beaver Dam Creek, Frayser's Farm, and Malvern Hill in the Seven Days. It had happened at Antietam. At Chancellorsville, however, Lee had responded to the imagination of Jackson and pursued an ambitious and appropriate battle plan, including an attack on the rear. Significantly, the day after the most splendid indirect tactical move of the Civil War—Jackson's march around Hooker—Lee reverted to head-on, direct attack when he no longer had Jackson in command of the western wing of his army.

Jackson, not Lee, possessed two gifts that are vital for great captains. Jackson understood that victory for a weaker nation could be achieved only if its commanders could "mystify, mislead and surprise" the enemy.[6] And Jackson understood that war's purpose is to force an opponent to agree to one's will. The British military writer Maj. Gen. J. F. C. Fuller puts it as follows: "Jackson possessed the brutality essential in war; Lee did not. He could clasp the hand of a wounded enemy, whilst Jackson ground his teeth and murmured, 'No quarter to the violators of our homes and firesides,' and when someone deplored the necessity of destroying so many brave men, he exclaimed: 'No, shoot them all, I do not wish them to be brave.' "[7]

Jackson possessed a third gift, which he summarized in this way: "To move swiftly, strike vigorously and secure all the fruits of victory is the secret of successful war."[8] Jackson lived by this axiom, even in defensive positions; Lee could not embrace its boldness.

Jackson was strong where Lee was weak and thus the two commanders frequently complemented each other in one of the most successful examples of symbiosis in warfare. Jackson was a secretive, hard, demanding, unbending commander who drew men to him primarily because of his victories.[9] Lee was a warm, supportive, forgiving officer who possessed a magnetism and charisma that led men to identify him as the living symbol of their cause. His lieutenants followed him blindly and with total devotion.

Together Lee and Jackson produced preliminary victories that astonished the world. On May 2, 1863—if Jackson had not been struck down—they might have defeated, even destroyed, the Army of the Potomac. If Jackson had survived, his position as the South's preeminent strategist would have given him greater scope than ever before to exercise his military genius.

Would he have found another grand opportunity for victory? Judged by the manner in which he conceived of triumph in the midst of almost certain defeat at Chancellorsville, the answer can only be guessed at, but it cannot be ruled out. Jackson could have succeeded.

NOTES

1. On May 5, 1863, Jackson said that Hooker never should have sent his cavalry away. "That was his great blunder. It was that which enabled me to turn him without his being aware of it and to take him in the rear. Had he kept his cavalry with him, his plan would have been a very good one" (Henderson, 689).

2. In *Southern Historical Society Papers,* vol. 25, 110, Hunter McGuire quotes Jackson as saying this shortly after his wounding, while his mind was still clear. Jackson made a similar statement at Fredericksburg on December 13, 1862, to the Prussian Heros von Borcke. Alexander *(Military Memoirs,* 365–66) repeats the quote to justify the strategy of the Gettysburg campaign to "force the enemy to attack our army in position." This concept led James Longstreet to write that he "accepted" Lee's proposition "to make a campaign into Pennsylvania, provided it should be offensive in strategy but defensive in tactics, forcing the Federal army to give us battle when we were in strong position and ready to receive them" (Johnson and Buel, vol. 3, 246–47).

3. Johnson and Buel, vol. 3, 274; and Doubleday, 119–20.

4. Henderson, 131–33; and Cooke, 86–88.

5. Alexander, *Military Memoirs,* 386–87. Longstreet, in Johnson and Buel (vol. 3, 339–40), gives somewhat different quotes regarding the interview but the same conclusion as Alexander. See also Fuller (197), referring to Lee's report on Gettysburg, in which he says, "It had not been intended to deliver a general battle so far from our base, unless attacked." Lee defends the decision to attack by saying that the country was unfavorable for collecting supplies. But Porter Alexander notes that the army fought a three-day battle, then foraged for a week afterward north of the Potomac in very restricted territory along the river. Alexander concludes: "It does not seem improbable that we could have faced Meade safely on the 2nd at Gettysburg without assaulting him in his wonderfully strong position" (see Alexander, *Fighting for the Confederacy,* 233–34 and 237).

6. Johnson and Buel, vol. 2, 297. Henderson (640–41) quotes Jackson prior to the Chancellorsville campaign: "We must make this campaign an ex-

ceedingly active one. Only thus can a weaker country cope with a stronger; it must make up in activity what it lacks in strength. A defensive campaign can only be made successful by taking the aggressive at the proper time. Napoleon never waited for his adversary to become fully prepared but struck him the first blow."

7. Fuller, 133. See also Jackson, 310; and Dabney, 397. After the battle of Fredericksburg in December 1862, Jackson's medical officer, Hunter McGuire, spoke of the wickedness of the invading Federals and asked, "What can we do?" Jackson replied: "Do? Why, shoot them." See Freeman, *Lee's Lieutenants,* vol. 2, 518–19.

8. Henderson, 702.

9. For an analysis of Jackson as a commander, see Henderson, 620–29; and Dabney, 519–20. Dabney says that Jackson's only weakness was that he could not abide commanders whom he considered to be "self-indulgent or contumacious." Thus "by his jealousy of intentional inefficiency he diminished the sympathy between himself and the general officers next [to] his person." Henderson writes: "His men loved him, not merely because he was the bravest man they had ever known, the strongest and the most resolute . . . but because he was one of themselves, with no interests apart from their interests."

BIBLIOGRAPHY

Alexander, E. Porter. *Fighting for the Confederacy: The Personal Recollections of General Edward Porter Alexander*. Chapel Hill: University of North Carolina Press, 1989.

———. *Military Memoirs of a Confederate: A Critical Narrative*. New York: Charles Scribner's Sons, 1907.

Allan, William. *The Army of Northern Virginia in 1862*. Boston: Houghton Mifflin and Company, 1892.

———. *History of the Campaign of Gen. T. J. (Stonewall) Jackson in the Shenandoah Valley of Virginia*. Philadelphia: J. B. Lippincott and Company, 1880.

Bigelow, John, Jr. *The Campaign of Chancellorsville*. New Haven, Conn.: Yale University Press, 1910.

Bridges, Hal. *Lee's Maverick General: Daniel Harvey Hill*. New York: McGraw-Hill Book Company, 1961.

Chambers, Lenoir. *Stonewall Jackson*. 2 vols. New York: William Morrow and Company, 1959.

Cooke, John Esten. *Stonewall Jackson: A Military Biography.* New York: D. Appleton and Company, 1876.

Dabney, Robert Lewis. *Life and Campaigns of Lieut.-Gen. Thomas J. (Stonewall) Jackson.* New York: Blelock and Company, 1866.

Davis, William C. *Battle at Bull Run.* Baton Rouge: Louisiana State University Press, 1977.

Doubleday, Abner. *Chancellorsville and Gettysburg.* New York: Charles Scribner's Sons, 1882.

Douglas, Henry Kyd. *I Rode With Stonewall.* Chapel Hill: University of North Carolina Press, 1940 and 1968.

Freeman, Douglas Southall. *Lee's Lieutenants: A Study in Command.* 3 vols. New York: Charles Scribner's Sons, 1942–46.

———. *R. E. Lee, a Biography.* 4 vols. New York and London: Charles Scribner's Sons, 1934–35.

Fuller, Major General J. F. C. *Grant & Lee: A Study in Personality and Generalship.* 1932; Bloomington: Indiana University Press, 1957.

Henderson, Colonel G. F. R. *Stonewall Jackson and the American Civil War.* 2 vols. 1898; reprint 1 vol., New York: Longmans, Green and Company, 1936. (Also reprinted in 1937, 1943, and 1949.)

Jackson, Mary Anna. *Memoirs of Stonewall Jackson.* Louisville, Ky.: Prentice Press, 1895.

Johnson, Robert U., and C. C. Buel, eds. *Battles and Leaders of the Civil War.* 4 vols. New York: Century magazine, 1887–88; reprint, Secaucus, N.J.: Castle, n.d.

Johnston, Joseph E. *Narrative of Military Operations.* Bloomington: Indiana University Press, 1959; New York: Kraus, 1969.

Lee, Robert E. *Lee's Dispatches, Unpublished Letters of General Robert E. Lee, C. S. A., to Jefferson Davis and the War Department of the Confederate States of America 1862–65.* Edited by Douglas Southall Freeman. New York: G. P. Putnam's Sons, 1957 (originally published in a limited edition, 1915).

Long, A. L. *Memoirs of Robert E. Lee.* 1886; Secaucus, N.J.: Blue and Grey Press, 1983.

Longstreet, James. *From Manassas to Appomattox.* Philadelphia: J. B. Lippincott Company, 1903.

Marshall, Charles. *An Aide-de-Camp of Lee*. Ed. Sir Frederick Maurice. Boston: Little, Brown and Company, 1927.

Maurice, Major General Sir Frederick. *Robert E. Lee the Soldier*. New York: Houghton Mifflin Company, 1925; New York: Bonanza Books, n.d.

Official Records. U.S. War Department. *The War of the Rebellion: a Compilation of the Official Records of the Union and Confederate Armies*. 128 parts in 70 vols. and atlas. Washington, D.C.: Government Printing Office, 1880–1901.

Palfrey, Francis Winthrop. *The Antietam and Fredericksburg*. New York: Charles Scribner's Sons, 1882.

Robertson, James I., Jr. *General A. P. Hill, the Story of a Confederate Warrior*. New York: Random House, 1987.

———. *The Stonewall Brigade*. Baton Rouge: Louisiana State University Press, 1963.

Sanger, Donald Bridgman, and Thomas Robson Hay. *James Longstreet*. Baton Rouge: Louisiana State University Press, 1952.

Sears, Stephen W. *Landscape Turned Red: The Battle of Antietam*. New York: Ticknor and Fields, 1983.

Selby, John. *Stonewall Jackson as Military Commander*. London: B. T. Batsford, n.d.; Princeton: D. Van Nostrand Company, 1968.

Southern Historical Society Papers. 50 vols. Richmond, Va.: 1876–1953.

Taylor, Richard. *Destruction and Reconstruction*. Ed. Richard B. Harwell. 1880; reprint, New York: Longman, Green, 1955.

Taylor, Walter H. *Four Years with General Lee*. 1877; reprint, New York: Bonanza Books, 1962.

Vandiver, F. E. *The Mighty Stonewall*. New York: McGraw-Hill Book Company, 1957.

Wise, Jennings Cropper. *The Long Arm of Lee, the History of the Artillery of the Army of Northern Virginia*. Lynchburg, Va.: J. P. Bell Company, 1915; reprint, New York: Oxford University Press, 1959.

INDEX